Corrections in the Community

Corrections in the Community, Seventh Edition, examines the current state of community corrections and proposes an evidence-based approach to making programs more effective. As the U.S. prison and jail systems continue to struggle, options like probation, parole, alternative sentencing, and both residential and non-residential programs in the community continue to grow in importance. This text provides a solid foundation and includes the most salient information available on the broad and dynamic subject of community corrections. Authors Latessa and Lovins organize and evaluate the latest data on the assessment of offender risk/need/responsivity and successful methods that continue to improve community supervision and its effects on different types of clients, from those with mental illness or substance abuse problems to juveniles.

This book provides students with a thorough understanding of the theoretical and practical aspects of community corrections and prepares them to evaluate and strengthen these crucial programs. This seventh edition includes new chapters on pretrial, and graduated responses, as well as updated information on specialty drug and other problem-solving courts. Now found in every state, these specialty courts represent a way to deal with some of the most devastating problems that face our population, be it substance abuse or re-entry to the community from prison. Chapters contain key terms, boxed material, review questions, and recommended readings, and a glossary is provided to clarify important concepts. The instructor's guide is expanded, offering sample syllabi for semester, quarter, and online classes; student exercises; research and information links; and a transcription of the Bill of Rights. A test bank and lecture slides are also available at no cost.

Edward J. Latessa is Professor and Director of the School of Criminal Justice at the University of Cincinnati.

Brian Lovins is a Research Fellow for the University of Cincinnati's School of Criminal Justice as well as the Assistant Director for Harris County Community Supervision and Corrections Department.

Criminal justice students are often taught very little about community corrections, even though 7 out of 10 individuals under correctional supervision in the U.S. are on probation or parole. Latessa and Lovins have written an informative, current text about pretrial, probation, and parole that includes the latest evidence-based approaches. This is a valuable addition to the academic library and will help prepare the next generation of practitioners.

Barbara Broderick,
Chief Maricopa County Adult Probation

With the latest edition of *Corrections in the Community*, Latessa and Lovins have created a comprehensive, highly engaging, and up-to-date book that will easily and effectively guide the reader through America's largest and perhaps most often misunderstood correctional system.

Students will gain a thorough understanding of the history and development of the community correctional system, while also learning about the most recent issues that continue to shape and challenge the profession.

Alexander M. Holsinger, Ph.D.
Criminal Justice Coordinator for Johnson County, Kansas

With the aim of providing a comprehensive review, the authors move beyond the basic concepts of probation and parole to a rich understanding of community corrections. The text stands out for its excellent review of the evidence-based approaches that lead to more effective policies and practices. *Corrections in the Community* is an essential reading for students and professionals alike.

Shelley Johnson Listwan,
University of North Carolina Charlotte

CORRECTIONS IN THE COMMUNITY

Seventh Edition

Edward J. Latessa and Brian Lovins

Routledge
Taylor & Francis Group

NEW YORK AND LONDON

Seventh edition published 2019
by Routledge
52 Vanderbilt Avenue, New York, NY 10017

and by Routledge
2 Park Square, Milton Park, Abingdon, Oxon, OX14 4RN

Routledge is an imprint of the Taylor & Francis Group, an informa business

First edition published by Anderson Publishing 1997
Sixth edition published by Routledge 2015

Library of Congress Cataloging-in-Publication Data
Names: Latessa, Edward J., author. | Lovins, Brian, author.
Title: Corrections in the community / Edward J. Latessa and Brian Lovins.
Description: New York : Routledge, 2019. | Revised edition of Corrections in the community, 2015. | Includes index.
Identifiers: LCCN 2018050230 (print) | LCCN 2018051172 (ebook) |
ISBN 9780429424021 (Ebook) | ISBN 9781138389298 (hardback) |
ISBN 9781138389304 (pbk.) | ISBN 9780429424021 (ebk)
Subjects: LCSH: Corrections--United States.
Classification: LCC HV9469 (ebook) | LCC HV9469 .L27 2019 (print) | DDC 365/.973--dc23
LC record available at https://lccn.loc.gov/2018050230

ISBN: 978-1-138-38929-8 (hbk)
ISBN: 978-1-138-38930-4 (pbk)
ISBN: 978-0-429-42402-1 (ebk)

Typeset in Warnock Pro
by Servis Filmsetting Ltd, Stockport, Cheshire

Printed and bound by CPI Group (UK) Ltd, Croydon, CR0 4YY

Visit the companion website: www.routledge.com/cw/latessa

This book is dedicated to our families:
Sally, Amy, Jennifer, Michael, Allison, and Denise Latessa
Lori, Samuel, Henry, Walter, Charles, and Margie Lovins

Contents in Brief

Contents in Detail

Chapter 6
Offender Assessment

Chapter 7
Roles of Probation and Parole Officers

About the Authors

Edward J. Latessa is Professor and Director of the School of Criminal Justice at the University of Cincinnati. He received his PhD from Ohio State University in 1979 and was a student of Harry E. Allen. Dr. Latessa has published more than 170 works in the area of criminal justice, corrections, and juvenile justice. He is co-author of eight books, including *What Works (and Doesn't) in Reducing Recidivism* (2013), six previous editions of *Corrections in the Community*, and *Corrections in America* (2019, 15th edition). He has directed more than 195 funded research projects, including studies of day-reporting centers, juvenile justice programs, drug courts, prison programs, intensive supervision programs, halfway houses, and drug programs. Latessa and his staff have also assessed more than 1,000 correctional programs throughout the United States, and he has provided assistance and workshops in 48 states. Latessa served as President of the Academy of Criminal Justice Sciences (ACJS) (1989–1990). He has also received several awards including the Ernest Talbert House Award (2018); the Lifetime Achievement Award from Rite of Passage (2018); the William T. Rossiter Award from the Forensic Mental Health Association of California (2017); the Marguerite Q. Warren and Ted B. Palmer Differential Intervention Award presented by the Division of Corrections and Sentencing of the American Society of Criminology (2010); the Outstanding Community Partner Award from the Arizona Department of Juvenile Corrections (2010); the Maud Booth Correctional Services Award in recognition of dedicated service and leadership presented by the Volunteers of America (2010); the Community Hero Award presented by Community Resources for Justice (2010); the Bruce Smith, Sr. Award for outstanding contributions to criminal justice by the ACJS (2010); the George Beto Scholar Award, College of Criminal Justice, Sam Houston State University (2009); the Mark O. Hatfield Scholar Award for contributions in public policy research by the Hatfield School of Government at Portland State University (2008); the Outstanding Achievement Award by the National Juvenile Justice Court Services Association (2007); the August Vollmer Award from the American Society of Criminology (2004); the Simon Dinitz Criminal Justice Research Award from the Ohio Department of Rehabilitation and Correction (2002); the Margaret Mead Award for dedicated service to the causes of social justice and humanitarian advancement by the International Community Corrections Association (2001);

the Peter P. Lejins Research Award from the American Correctional Association (1999); the ACJS Fellow Award (1998); the ACJS Founders Award (1992); and the Dr. Simon Dinitz award by the Ohio Community Corrections Organization (now the Ohio Justice Alliance for Community Corrections). In 2013, Latessa was identified as one of the most innovative people in criminal justice by a national survey conducted by the Center for Court Innovation in partnership with the Bureau of Justice Assistance and the U.S. Department of Justice.

Brian Lovins is a Research Fellow for the University of Cincinnati's Corrections Institute as well as a Principal at Justice Systems Partners. He earned his PhD in Criminal Justice from the University of Cincinnati, School of Criminal Justice. Dr. Lovins has published more than 20 peer-reviewed articles and book chapters in the area of corrections, risk assessment, and juvenile justice. In addition to his work in Harris County, he is currently the Co-Editor for the American Probation and Parole Association's (APPA) *Perspectives* journal. He has contributed to the national discourse with his work in developing a non-proprietary juvenile risk assessment (Ohio Youth Assessment System: OYAS) and an adult risk assessment (Ohio Risk Assessment System: ORAS), as well as redesigning juvenile and adult correctional programs to meet evidence-based standards. Lovins routinely assists community corrections agencies in developing and implementing risk assessment and the delivery of cognitive-behavioral interventions. Lovins has received the Dr. Simon Dinitz Award from the Ohio Justice Alliance for Community Corrections for his work and dedication in helping correctional agencies to adopt evidence-based programs, as well as the Distinguished Alumnus Award from the University of Cincinnati.

Preface

It is hard to believe that it has been more than 20 years since the first edition of *Corrections in the Community* was published. Back in 1997, the field was experiencing unprecedented incarceration rates, and prison construction and populations were expanding at an alarming rate. Much of what was done in community corrections followed the theme of "getting tough" with crime and offenders. Intensive supervision without treatment, boot camps, shock incarceration, and other sanctions were popular, with little success in changing offender behavior. Since that time, much has changed. New prisons are not being built, and the prison population is declining. We have also learned a great deal about how to more effectively improve the programs and services we offer our correctional population. Many of these programs operate in the community and we believe that the field is moving away from risk management toward risk reduction—identifying those most in need of programs and supervision and targeting those criminogenic needs of offenders to actually reduce recidivism rates. Of course, to do that effectively, we need to understand what the research and data tell us about designing and implementing evidence-based practices. A great deal of this edition addresses these important topics—risk assessment, improving supervision practices, using data to measure performance and outcomes, and following some empirically-derived principles that will allow the system to be more effective and humane, and less costly.

Writing a book on a topic as broad and dynamic as community corrections is a very difficult task. It is extremely hard to know when to stop. The field is changing rapidly and, as a result, information and data are quickly outdated. We believe that we have pulled together some of the most recent and salient information available; however, we accept responsibility for any errors or shortcomings. There are several caveats we would like to make concerning this book.

First, as with prior editions, there are a great many charts and tables with data. Memorizing the numbers is not important, as they change daily. What is important are the trends over time. We want students to see patterns of what is happening in community corrections and to use this information to think critically about the issues facing the field.

Second, we recognize that students are not always interested in the historical aspects of a subject, and we have tried to keep that material to a minimum;

however, we also believe that it is important to understand where we came from and some of the reasons why we do things the way we do in corrections. We have also provided key terms, review questions, boxed material, and recommended readings to highlight information that can help the student to navigate the book and to identify more effectively some of the key concepts and ideas. In today's world, we have seen an information explosion, and it is easy to find resources to learn more about virtually every topic in this book. We encourage students to be inquisitive and to seek out additional information that can advance their knowledge and understanding.

Third, we have added quite a bit of new material and chapters. We have a new chapter on pretrial, which has become a hot topic, as communities struggle with jail crowding and the fact that the majority of those held in detention have not yet been convicted of a crime. We also decided to eliminate the chapter on juveniles and to incorporate material on this topic throughout the various chapters. Our reason for doing so was simple; it is much too important a topic to try and squeeze into one chapter. Besides, there are whole classes (and books) devoted to the subject that do a much better job acquainting students with this material than we can. As more and more probation and parole agencies adopt new approaches and interventions designed to help offenders change their behavior, we have moved beyond intermediate sanctions to include a wider range of responses to behavior. The "What Works" chapter has also been eliminated, with the material woven into the book. We also created a separate chapter devoted to women in community corrections. Students will also undoubtedly see that the chapters on probation and parole are longer than other chapters. These two correctional alternatives form the backbone of community corrections, and we felt it important to cover these topics in depth.

Fourth, as with previous editions, you will also recognize our bias. We still believe that we incarcerate too many of our citizens, that this is not good social policy, and that many can be supervised in the community without seriously jeopardizing public safety. Too much public treasure is wasted and human misery increased when we over-incarcerate, and fortunately, many states are now joining efforts to reduce the use of incarceration, and efforts such as the Justice Reinvestment Initiative are helping states to take a close look at their policies and practices. Of course, we recognize that some offenders—those who are violent and would likely cause serious harm to others—belong in prison. We do not believe, however, that all or even a majority of the nearly 2 million or so incarcerated fit that description.

Finally, while probation and parole practices are often slow to change, we are seeing progress on this front. In just a few short years, we have seen more and more agencies and programs move toward evidence-based practices, and if there is one theme to this book, it is that we can indeed use research to improve the field and ultimately the lives of those who come into contact with the correctional system. While there is little doubt that change is slow and that old ideas persist, we also believe that the future of community corrections is bright and filled with promise. It is hoped that the instructors and students who use our book will find the subject of community corrections as interesting and stimulating as we do.

More importantly, we hope we can demonstrate that we do not always have to rely on incarceration, and that many of our solutions to the crime problem can be found in the community, especially when various parts of the system work together to seek solutions.

Edward J. Latessa and Brian Lovins

Acknowledgments

Writing a book requires a great deal of help and support. We realize that it is a cliché to say that it could not have been possible without the following people, but truer words were never spoken.

There are many people who have allowed us to study and learn about community corrections. We have worked with them over the years, and all have contributed immeasurably to our knowledge and experience. In particular, we wish to thank the following friends and colleagues: John Aarons, the late Tim Alley, David Altschuler, Michele Anderson, the late Don Andrews, Sarah Andrews, Dan Aning, Bridget Ansberg, Steve Aos, Brandon Applegate, Troy Armstrong, Jean Atkins, Allen Ault, Cameron Baker, Bob Balboni, Brad Barnes, John Baron, the late Cheryl Barrett, Jenny Bauer, Julie Baxter, Jeff Beard, Tom Beauclair, Alan Bekelman, Renee Bergeron, Tom Berghausen, Simone Bess, Shay Bilchik, Rick Billak, Claudia Black, Julia Blankenship, Mandy Bley, Jim Bonta, Paul Book, Guy Bourgon, Sue Bourke, Bob Borst, James Bralley, Ann Brewster, Barb Broderick, Ski Broman, Doug Brothers, Bob Brown, Kelly Brown, Mike Brown, Victor Brown, Yvonne Saunders-Brown, Bill Bruinsma, Rob Brusconi, Loren Buddress, Ed Camp, Nancy Campbell, Mark Carey, Mimi Carter, Liz Cass, Kelly Castle, Clint Castleberry, Matt Cate, Brian Center, the late Norm Chamberlain, Steve Chapman, Karen Chapple, John Chin, the late John Clancy, Elyse Clawson, Todd Clear, Marshall Clements, Rob Clevenger, Diane Coates, Alvin Cohen, Marcia Cohen, Thomas Cohen, Anne Connell-Freund, Linda Connelly, Ron Corbett, Jim Corfman, Kitty Coriden, Caprice Cosper, Brenda Cronin, Chris Cunningham, Nancy Cunningham, Karen Dalton, Bob Daquilante, David D'Amora, Jim Dare, Patti Davis, Ben de Haan, Linda Delny, Jessica Dennis, LaRon Dennis, Steve Devlin, Monda DeWeese, the late David Dillingham, Dennis Dimatteo, Gayle Dittmer, Frank Domurad, Mike Dooley, Pam Douglas, Bob Dugan, Jim Elder, Joe Ellison, Warren Emmer, Don Evans, Tony Fabelo, Gretchen Faulstich, Dot Faust, Ray Ferns, Mark Ferriera, Joe Fitzpatrick, Nathan Foo, Ralph Fretz, Robert Frommeyer, Tonya Gaby, Chris Galli, Gene Gallo, Judge Garcia, Ryan Geis, Bruce Gibson, Steve Gibson, Rosemary Gido, Barry Glick, Robert Gloeckner, Kathleen Gnall, Michelle Goodman, Ricardo Goodridge, Don Gordon, the late Mark Gornik, John Gramuglia, Richard Gray, Brian Griffiths, Bill Grosshan, Sharon Haines, Ron Hajime, Alicia Handwerk, Patricia Hardyman,

Sharon Harrigfeld, Jennifer Hartman, Joe Hassett, Kirk Hayes, Steve Heimann, Ed Heller, Martha Henderson, Angie Hensley, Domingo Herraiz, Doug Herrmann, Chris Heywood, Tomi Hiers, Rick Hoekstra, Buzz Hoffman, Deborah Holmberg, Dorothy Holmes, Steve Holmes, Alex Holsinger, Deanna Hoskins, Dana Jones Hubbard, Mary Kay Hudson, Bobby Huskey, Mindy Hutcherson, Butch Huyandi, Bernie Iszler, Norma Jaeger, Stephanie James, Linda Janes, Bob Jester, Arthur Jones, Justin Jones, Dan Joyner, Phil Kader, Colleen Kadleck, George Kaiser, Sharon Kennedy, Maureen Kiehm, Bill King, Peter Kinziger, Lea Klingler, Kevin Knight, Melissa Knopp, Debi Koetzle, Ed Kollin, Rosemary Kooy, Igor Koutsenok, Sally Kreamer, Barry Krisberg, Bill Kroman, Don Kuhl, Fred LaFluer, Steve Lamberti, Glen Lammon, Jim Lawrence, Mike Link, Dominic Lisa, Shelley Johnson Listwan, Mary Livers, Stephan LoBuglio, Fransaia LoDico, Dan Lombardo, Kirk Long, Denise Lord, Arthur Lurigio, Jennifer Luther, Alan Mabry, Pam McClain, Cindy McCoy, Denise McDonald, Scott MacDonald, Terri McDonald, Dale McFee, David McGriff, Tom Madeo, Marty Magnusson, Lauren Maio, Joe Marchese, Vicki Markey, Bob Markin, Cheryl Marlow, Carole Martin, Ginger Martin, Betsy Matthews, Tina Mawhorr, Theresa May, Robert Mecum, Harvey Milkman, Michael Minor, Linda Modry, Gary Mohr, Chris Money, Sandy Monfort, Chris Monroe, Melissa Moon, Ernie Moore, Karhlton Moore, Larry Motiuk, Tom Muhleman, Linda Murken, Larry Muse, Geraldyne Nagy, Jim Neal, Steve Nelson, Maria Nemec, Mike Nickols, Wendy Niehaus, Linda Nixon, Michael Noyes, Phil Nunes,Tom O'Connor, Denise O'Donnell, Julie Okamoto, Steve Oldenstadt, Gaylon Oswalt, Sharon Owsley, Beth Oxford, Ted Palmer, Mario Paparozzi, the late Evalyn Parks, George Parks, Brian Parry, Grafton Payne, Marc Pelka, Linda Penner, Geno Natalucci-Persichetti, Dan Peterca, Candi Peters, Colette Peters, Ellyn Peterson, Sharon Pette, Margie Phelps, Hannah Phillips, Merel Pickenpaugh, Barbara Pierce, Dianne Poindexter, Vince Polito, Dan Pompa, Bruce Ponder, Jerry Powers, Rocco Pozzi, John Prevost, John Prinzi, Craig Prysock, Pakkiri "Raj" Rajagopal, Nina Ramsey, Brian Rector, Harvey Reed, Brent Reinke, Ed Rhine, Sue Righthand, Bryan Riley, Debbie Rios, James Rivers, Carole Roberts, Charles Robinson, Denise Robinson, Jim Robinson, Renee Robinson, Casey Rogers, Claudia Rowlands, Kathy Russell, Loretta Ryland, Reece Satin, Bill Sawyer, John Schneider, Pat Schreiner, Dave Schroot, Jane Seigel, Richard Seiter, Alison Shames, Tim Shannon, Lisa Shoaf, Nancy Shomaker, Cliff Simonsen, Jennifer Skeem, Jerry Smith, Linda Smith, Mary Smith, Larry Solomon, Bill Sondervan, Kim Sperber, Mary Spotswood, Barry Stodley, Colleen Stoner, Susan Storm, Evelyn Stratton, Tom Strickrath, Kathleen Strouse, Mary Jo Sullivan, Jodi Sundt, Bob Swisher, Mike Tardy, Scott Taylor, Juliana Taymans, Faye Taxman, Scott Taylor, Mike Thatcher, Yvette Thériault, Morris Thigpen, Cara Thompson, Mike Thompson, John Thurston, Neil Tilow, Patty Tobias, Jim Toner, Julie Truschel, Mike Turner, Scott Vanbenschoten, Cecilia Velasquez, Vicki Verdeyen, Ute Vilfroy, John Vivian, Ray Wahl, Dennis Waite, Myra Wall, Mike Walton, Bernie Warner, Roger Warren, Kathy Waters, Ralph Watson, Beth Weiman, Carey Welebob, Bonita White, the late Jim Wichtman, Reggie Wilkinson, Diane Williams, Larry Williams, Matt Wojack, Marlon Yarbor, Gary Yates, the late George Yefchek, Gary Zajac, Andrew Zalman, Carole Rapp-Zimmerman, and Linda Zogg.

A number of current and former research assistants and graduate students at the University of Cincinnati assisted us with this and previous editions of the book: Kristin Bechtel, Lesli Blair, Lori Brusman-Lovins, Alex Burton, Chris D'Amato, Stephanie Duriez, Angela Estes, Tony Flores, Lia Gormsen, Jessica Halliday, Erin Harbinson, Ryan Labrecque, Rich Lemke, Christopher Lowenkamp, Matthew Makarios, Kelsey Mattick, AJ Myer, Kristin Ostrowski, Jordon Papp, Jennifer Pealer, Damon Petrich, Batya Rubenstein, Ian Silver, Charlene Taylor, and Jessica Warner. A special word of thanks to several University of Cincinnati full-time staff members for all their help and support: Erin Cochran, Jean Gary, Janice Miller, Shelley Paden, and John Schwartz. We also want to thank our colleagues in the University of Cincinnati Corrections Institute (UCCI) for all their inspiration and dedication to advancing evidence-based correctional practices: Jamie Bonecutter, Tammy Dean, Eva Kishimoto, Jenni Lux, Meagan Mueller, Jamie Newsome, Kelly Pitocco, Amanda Pompoco, Maggie Schweitzer, Mindy Schweitzer, Jen Scott, Jodi Sleyo, Stephanie Spiegel, Carrie Sullivan, and Eric Willoughby. They do incredible work and we have learned a great deal from them.

We also wish to thank Dr. Pamela Chester, the Acquisitions Editor at Routledge Publishing, as well as the old Anderson crew, for all their help and support over the years. Much of the copyediting, proofing, and sundry tasks associated with the production of a book were in the very capable hands of Kate Taylor. We also want to especially thank Ellen Boyne, who has been a very good friend and supporter of our book. We would also be remiss not to mention the assistance and support of our good friend Mickey Braswell, and the helpful review of the first edition from John Whitehead at East Tennessee State University. Finally, we would like to thank Helen Lund for her painstakingly thorough copyediting of our book. Her meticulous attention to detail and keen eye helped make it a better book. We are grateful for all her assistance.

To our colleagues and friends, without whose support and expertise this book would never have been possible: Harry Allen, Frank Cullen, Chris Eskridge, Jim Frank, Paul Gendreau, Larry Travis, Patricia Van Voorhis, and Jerry Vito. We also need to thank Paula Smith for her contributions to previous editions.

Finally, we wish to thank Amy, Jennifer, Michael, and Allison, for all their love and support, and Sam, Walter, and Henry who remind Brian every day that delinquency prevention begins at home. And to Sally and Lori for your endless support and care, we love you.

Edward Latessa and Brian Lovins

Chapter 1

The Criminal Justice System

Key Terms

community corrections

corrections

courts

criminal justice system

incarceration

incarceration rates

jail

law enforcement

parole

prison

probation

prosecution

> It is hard to identify the benefits inmates gain from prison, but the harm done there is readily seen. If you want to increase the crime problem, incite men to greater evil, and intensify criminal inclinations and proclivities, then lock violators up in prison for long periods, reduce their outside contacts, stigmatize them and block their lawful employment when released, all the while setting them at tutelage under the direction of more skilled and predatory criminals. I know of no better way to gain your ends than these. —Harry E. Allen

Crime is everywhere, in all nations great and small. It can affect where we live, where we shop, where we send our children to school, how much we pay for automobile insurance and taxes, and how safe we feel when we are in our communities. In the United States, crime is a violation of criminal statutes passed by elected representatives. These statutes are enforced by a variety of social control agencies, including law enforcement, **prosecution**, court, and post-adjudication components (e.g., prisons, probation, and parole). These varied agencies and actions, along with their philosophical bases and objectives, are usually called the "criminal justice system."

No one imposed this specific set of agencies on the nation. We invented them ourselves and, if there is something amiss with an agency or mission, it can be changed. One fact about the American **criminal justice system** is that it is rapidly evolving and changing as a result of the volume of crime, emerging national priorities, available funding, and changing political ideologies. Behaviors deemed particularly heinous in one epoch may become regulated, if not accepted, behavior in another. For example, the "Great Experiment" of prohibition attempted to protect our national character and youth, increase productivity, lessen collateral problems of idleness, and improve the moral fiber of those using alcohol. It was later abandoned as a national crusade; earlier twentieth-century law enforcement efforts instead lapsed into strategies to regulate alcohol as a controlled substance, concerned only in large part with keeping alcohol out of the hands of youthful consumers and collecting taxes. More recently, we have seen a number of states legalize marijuana, when not so long ago one could be imprisoned for its use.

One component of the criminal justice system is **corrections**, defined as "post-adjudication processing of convicted criminal offenders." This definition, if it were ever adequate, probably best fits the correctional scene of the early twentieth century, when the major sentencing options available to sentencing courts were committing the offender to prison or granting probation. In fact, the study of post-adjudication processing of criminal law offenders was, until about 1969, commonly referred to as "penology." As shown in subsequent chapters, post-adjudication has become much more complex in the United States.

The field of corrections, like most of the justice system, has undergone rapid change in the past three decades. Programs have been developed to allow prosecutors to suspend prosecution of alleged criminals, provided they become and remain actively involved in seeking personal development and rehabilitation under a "deferred prosecution" program. Pretrial detention of accused law violators is now used less frequently due to the development of personal recognizance programs that have reduced the importance of bondsmen in the pretrial

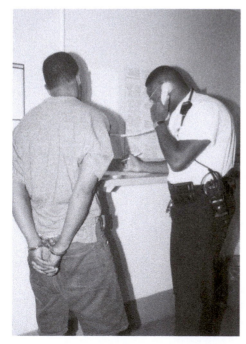

Booking into local jail. *[Photo courtesy of Beth Saunders]*

portion of the system. In addition, the tools of technology have grown greatly in the past three decades, expanding probation supervision into conventional probation, intensive supervised probation, house arrest (with or without electronic monitoring or global position system [GPS] tracking), community service, day-reporting centers, and restitution programs. There are even probation variations that combine serving a sentence in jail before probation begins, and several probation programs that require a period of imprisonment prior to return to the community under probation supervision. These latter programs, incidentally, are part of the "intermediate sanctions" that have emerged in the past 40 years: offender control programs that fall somewhere between probation and imprisonment. All of this and more will be discussed later in this book.

What has corrections become? How can we best define it at the present time? For us, corrections is the social control agency that provides societal protection through **incarceration** and community supervision of and rehabilitation services for persons accused or convicted of behavior that violates criminal law. This definition includes restorative justice and pretrial diversion programs, as well as the more traditional probation and parole services. It also embraces intermediate sanctions and alternative early release programs for inmates in prisons across the nation. In sum, corrections involves social control of persons whose behavior has brought them to the attention of the justice system. The missions, objectives, procedures, and even principles that govern our definition of corrections are continually changing. In this book, we hope to describe the recent developments and emerging dimensions that define community corrections today.

COMPONENTS OF THE CRIMINAL JUSTICE SYSTEM

The traditional components of the criminal justice system include law enforcement, courts, and corrections. Although the focus of this book is on community corrections, the other components of the criminal justice system all play an integral part in how the community correctional system operates. Let's start with law enforcement, since this is often the first contact people have with the criminal justice system.

Law Enforcement

When we think of law enforcement officers, we commonly think of the police, but prosecutors also fall into this category, although their roles are different. The traditional role of the police includes investigating crime and making arrests, but the police also have a great deal of discretion. They can decide not to make an arrest,

Harris County Jail. *[Photo courtesy of Jeff McShan]*

or even divert someone to a community agency instead of jail. In some larger cities, the police work closely with probation and parole officers to identify potentially violent individuals or drug users and steer them into rehabilitation programs. The role of the prosecutor also includes investigation, as well as the responsibility to bring charges when they deem it is appropriate. They too have a great deal of discretion. They have to decide if there is enough evidence to bring charges and whether to recommend pretrial release, and they are involved in sentencing recommendations to the judge or jury. Since the vast majority of defendants plead guilty, plea bargaining plays an important role in whether someone is incarcerated, placed on probation, or given another alternative sentence (such as drug court or community service). As part of this process, conditions are also negotiated, such as the requirement for treatment or jail time prior to probation. It is also common, especially in larger cities, to see prosecutorial mediation and diversion programs. With mediation, disputes can sometimes be handled before a formal process is initiated. With prosecutorial or pretrial diversion programs, the prosecutor agrees to dismiss charges if the defendant agrees to certain conditions, such as completing a drug court program.

Courts

The courts play a pivotal role in corrections, since the sentencing decision is often in the hands of a judge. Although some offenses require mandatory sentences to prison, the vast majority do not. Judges can decide whether to release or detain someone accused of a crime, whether to impose jail or prison time, probation, or some other alternative or combination if they are found guilty, set conditions of supervision, and decide whether to revoke supervision if a violation has occurred. In some states, judges can also grant judicial or early release from incarceration. As we shall learn later, the spread of drug and other problem-solving courts has also dramatically changed the role of many judges from that of impartial official to one closely involved in all aspects of supervision and treatment.

This short review is not meant to downplay the importance of law enforcement and the courts; indeed, they are the drivers of the correctional system, but the focus of this book is on community corrections.

CORRECTIONS IN THE COMMUNITY

This book describes and explains corrections in the community, or "**community corrections**." This term refers to numerous and diverse types of supervision, treatment, reintegration, control, restoration, and supportive programs for criminal law violators. Community corrections programs, as shown later, are designed for offenders at many levels of both the juvenile and criminal justice systems. First, community corrections programs are found in the pre-adjudication level of the justice systems and include diversion and pretrial release programs, as well as treatment programs provided by private sector agencies, particularly for juveniles (Allen et al., 2018). Second, corrections is also involved at every level of government—federal, state, and local.

As correctional clients enter the justice system, community corrections programs have been developed and designed to minimize their further processing and placement into more secure settings. These pre-imprisonment programs include restitution, community services, active probation, intensive supervised probation, house arrest, and residential community facilities, such as halfway houses (please note that all of these programs are described in detail in later chapters). One assumption underlying this effort to minimize offender penetration into the justice system is that community corrections is more effective at reducing future crime and is more cost-efficient. Community corrections is certainly no less effective in reducing recidivism than is prison, and there is strong evidence that community correctional programs, if administered properly, can significantly reduce recidivism.[1]

Another assumption is that community corrections is more humane, although there is some contemporary debate over whether corrections should be humane rather than harsh.

Community corrections continues after incarceration (and in some cases is combined with incarceration),[2] and among the many programs found at this level are split sentences (jail followed by probation), shock incarceration and shock probation, prison furlough programs, work and educational release, shock parole, and parole programs and services.[3]

The various points at which community corrections programs have been developed are suggested in Figure 1.1, which identifies the flow of clients into and through the justice system.

The diagram shown in Figure 1.1 first appeared in President Lyndon Johnson's Crime Commission report, *The Challenge of Crime in a Free Society* (President's Commission on Law Enforcement and Administration of Justice, 1967). It outlined the basic sequence of events in the criminal justice process. Police, courts, and corrections were thus viewed as elements that were interrelated and interdependent. The idea was to demonstrate the manner in which successful crime prevention was the goal of the entire system. Community corrections fits squarely into this goal: Offenders whose criminal behavior is reduced or eliminated through programs in the community will commit fewer, if any, crimes in the future.[4]

Box 1.1
Probation and Parole

Probation is a sentence imposed by the court that does not usually involve confinement and imposes conditions to restrain the offender's actions in the community. The court retains authority to modify the conditions of the sentence or to re-sentence the offender if he or she violates the conditions.

Parole is the release of an offender from confinement prior to expiration of his or her sentence on condition of good behavior and supervision in the community.

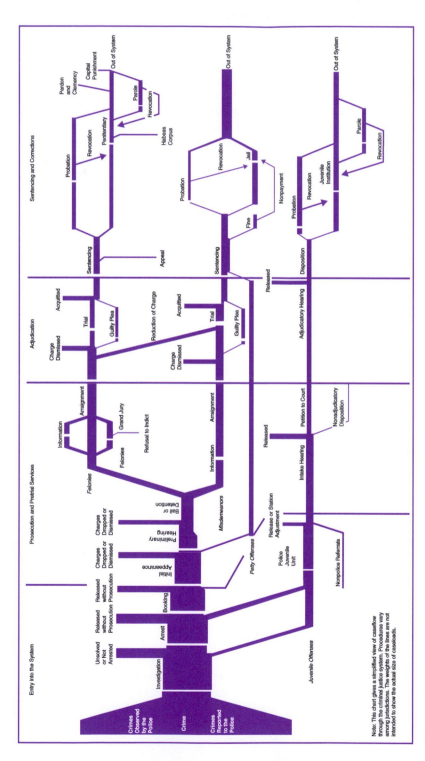

Figure 1.1 Sequence of Events in the Criminal Justice System

Source: Adapted from President's Commission on Law Enforcement and Administration of Justice (1967).

Two major factors should be pointed out as shown in Figure 1.1. First, the major ways out of the system are probation and parole, shown here as system outputs. The second conclusion is that the number of cases flowing through the system decreases as offenders are processed at the various decision points (prosecutor, court, sentencing, and release from prison). The majority of offenders under correctional control are in the community. It is also noteworthy that since 2009 the correctional population has declined. This 9-year trend halts what had been an ever-growing number of Americans in the correctional system.

The percentage of offenders in each major correctional sanction can be found in Figure 1.2. Non-incarceration sentences were imposed for nearly 56 percent of offenders in 2016. Another 13 percent who were sentenced were released from prison onto parole supervision. Together this represents nearly 4.6 million offenders. Even a large percentage of those offenders sentenced to jail may be released onto probation as part of a split sentence. It should be obvious that community corrections handles a large proportion of the offenders in the nation. For example, the Bureau of Justice Statistics (Kaeble & Cowhig, 2018) reported that one in every 38 adult residents of the nation was under correctional control (prison, jail, probation, or parole) at the start of 2017. This is the lowest rate since 1997. It was also estimated that one in every 53 adults was supervised on probation or parole. On the basis of 100,000 adult residents in the nation, 1,810 were on probation or parole, and 860 in prison or in jail (see Table 1.1). These rates have dropped over the past few years. More than two out of three offenders are living in the community on any given day. A list of the **incarceration rates** for each state is shown in Table 1.2. Louisiana leads the nation with a rate of 1,270 per 100,000, and Maine has the lowest with 380 (Kaeble & Cowhig, 2018).

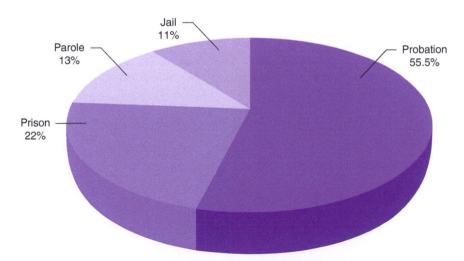

Figure 1.2 Correctional Populations in the United States, 2016

Source: Kaeble, D., Cowhig, M. (2018). *Correctional populations in the United States, 2016.* Washington, DC: U.S. Department of Justice, Bureau of Justice Programs.

Table 1.1 Number of Adults under Correctional Supervision in 2006 and 2016 per 100,000 Residents

	Rate per 100,000	
	2006	**2016**
Probation or Parole	2,320	1,810
Prison or Jail	1,000	860

Source: Kaeble, D., Cowhig, M. (2018). *Correctional populations in the United States, 2016.* Washington, DC: U.S. Department of Justice, Bureau of Justice Programs.

Table 1.2 States by Incarceration Rates, 2016 (Inmates per 100,000, Ages 18 or Older)

State	Rate
Alabama	1,080
Alaska	800
Arizona	1,030
Arkansas	1,050
California	670
Colorado	740
Connecticut	530
Delaware	880
Florida	900
Georgia	1,160
Hawaii	500
Idaho	900
Illinois	620
Indiana	850
Iowa	560
Kansas	780
Kentucky	1,010
Louisiana	1,270
Maine	380
Maryland	610
Massachusetts	360
Michigan	730
Minnesota	380
Mississippi	1,260
Missouri	940
Montana	700
Nebraska	610
Nevada	890
New Hampshire	410
New Jersey	460

Table 1.2 (Continued)

State	Rate
New Mexico	930
New York	480
North Dakota	540
Ohio	790
Oregon	640
Pennsylvania	810
Rhode Island	370
South Carolina	820
South Dakota	880
Tennessee	930
Texas	1,050
Utah	540
Vermont	340
Virginia	880
Washington	530
West Virginia	690
Wisconsin	790
Wyoming	870
U.S. Total:	850

Source: Kaeble, D., Cowhig, M. (2018). *Correctional populations in the United States, 2016.* Washington, DC: U.S. Department of Justice, Bureau of Justice Programs.

Box 1.2
Jail

A jail is a confinement facility, usually administered by a local law enforcement agency, intended for adults but sometimes containing juveniles, that holds persons detained pending adjudication and/or persons committed after adjudication for sentences of generally 1 year or less. Some states do allow longer sentences to be served in jail, although these are the exception. Jails are usually supported by local tax revenues and, as such, are particularly vulnerable to resource reductions.

Additional categories of jail inmates include mentally ill persons for whom there are no other facilities or who are awaiting transfer to mental health authorities, parolees and probationers awaiting hearings, court-detained witnesses and persons charged with contempt of court, federal prisoners awaiting pick-up by marshals, and offenders sentenced to state departments of corrections for whom there is not yet space, but who cannot be released ("holdbacks").

Box 1.3
Prison

A **prison** is a state or federal confinement facility having custodial authority over criminal law-violating adults sentenced to confinement for usually more than 1 year.

Probation in America

The majority of the adults under correctional care or custody are on probation, the largest single segment of the community correctional system. As shown in Tables 1.3 and 1.4, Georgia had the largest number of its citizens on probation, and the highest rate: 5,570 per 100,000 adult residents. Three other states each had a rate of more than 2,500: Idaho, Ohio, and Rhode Island. The lowest state rate was New Hampshire (366 per 100,000).

Even though there was a decline of 1.4 percent between 2015 and 2016, it is clear that a great number of convicted persons are placed on probation. In most cases, probation agencies monitor the offender's compliance with the conditions of probation release (restitution, community service, payment of fines, house arrest, drug/alcohol rehabilitation, etc.). The crucial roles that probation plays in community corrections and the justice system become even more apparent when institutional and parole population figures are examined.

Table 1.3 Probation among the States, 2016*

Ten states with the largest probation populations	Number supervised
Probation	
Georgia*	410,964
Texas	374,285
California	239,735
Ohio	236,754
Florida	214,066
Pennsylvania	180,492
Michigan*	175,189
New Jersey	140,589
Illinois	113,989
Indiana	108,702

*Note: Georgia and Michigan did not report totals for 2016, so these numbers are based on 2015 figures.

Source: Kaeble, D. (2018). *Probation and parole populations in the United States, 2016.* Washington, DC: U.S. Department of Justice, Bureau of Justice Programs.

Table 1.4 Ten States with the Highest and Lowest Rates of Persons Supervised on Probation per 100,000 Adult U.S.

Ten highest

State	Rate
Georgia	5,570
Rhode Island	2,680
Ohio	2,624
Idaho	2,578
Delaware	2,049
Minnesota	2,280
Michigan	2,276
Indiana	2,135
New Jersey	2,018
Colorado	1,870
Ten lowest	
New Hampshire	366
West Virginia	448
Utah	568
Nevada	601
New York	628
Maine	632
Kansas	758
California	791
New Mexico	798
South Carolina	839

Source: Kaeble, D. (2018). *Probation and parole populations in the United States, 2016*. Washington, DC: U.S. Department of Justice, Bureau of Justice Programs.

The U.S. Prison Population

Because the rate of parole in a given state is affected by the size of the prison population, it is necessary to examine the size of the U.S. prison population before considering parole figures. A census of state and federal corrections institutions is conducted at mid-year and year-end by the Bureau of Justice Statistics. At the end of 2016, the number of people incarcerated in prison was 1,505,400, a decline of more than 21,000 from 2015 (Kaeble, 2018). Figures from the Bureau also reveal that 57 percent of all those incarcerated are either black or Hispanics (Carson, 2018). See Figure 1.3 for the number of persons incarcerated in prison in 2006, and in 2016. As we see, the number has declined by more than 63,000 in 10 years.

These figures are important to the parole rates in part because they represent the source of clients for the parole system. In many states, prisoners enter the

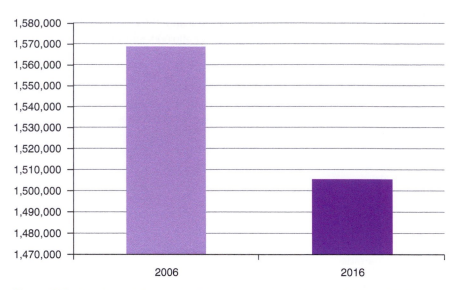

Figure 1.3 Number of Persons in Prison in the United States: 2006 and 2016

Source: Kaeble, D., Cowhig, M. (2018). *Correctional populations in the United States, 2016.* Washington, DC: U.S. Department of Justice, Bureau of Justice Programs.

parole system by a parole board decision or by fulfilling the condition of mandatory release. Typically, at some time between their minimum and maximum sentences, inmates are released from prison and placed on parole. Mandatory releasees enter parole supervision automatically at the expiration of their maximum terms (minus sentence reductions for time credit accumulated for good time, jail time, and other "gain" procedures). Traditionally, this has been the manner in which a parole system operated under the indeterminate sentencing model presently in force in one-half of the states. The "abandon parole" movement began in 1976, and a number of states have changed their statutes to remove the authority of the parole board to release offenders before the expiration of their sentences. This issue is discussed in more detail in the chapters that follow.

Parole in America

Adults on parole at the beginning of 2017 totaled 874,800, up 4,300 from 2015. As seen in Table 1.5, two states, Texas and Pennsylvania, each had over 110,000 on parole, which accounted for more than 25 percent of the nation's total. Table 1.6 shows that the parole rate ranged from a high of 1,097 in Pennsylvania to a low of two in Maine. Maine abolished parole in the late 1970s, which explains the low rate; only those sentenced to parole before 1976 continue to be supervised.

In sum, parole statistics reveal the relationship between the size of the prison population and the number of parolees. These figures indicate that both prison and parole populations increased dramatically from 1995 through to 2008, and only began abating since 2009. Changes in sentencing options and sentence length have also meant that prisoners were actually serving longer sentences than they were in 1995.

Table 1.5 Ten States with the Largest Parole Population

State	Number supervised
Texas	111,287
Pennsylvania	111,087
California	93,598
New York	44,426
Louisiana	30,707
Illinois	29,428
Arkansas	23,792
Georgia	22,386
Wisconsin	20,401
Ohio	19,633

Source: Kaeble, D. (2018). *Probation and parole in the United States, 2016.* Washington, DC: U.S. Department of Justice, Bureau of Justice Statistics.

Table 1.6 Ten States with the Highest and Lowest Rates of Persons Supervised on Parole per 100,000 Adult U.S.

Ten highest	
State	**Rate**
Pennsylvania	1,097
Arkansas	1,038
Louisiana	864
Texas	537
Wisconsin	453
Kentucky	448
South Dakota	410
Idaho	402
Missouri	377
Mississippi	381
Ten lowest	
Maine	2
Virginia	25
Florida	27
Massachusetts	34
Rhode Island	54
Delaware	52

(*Continued*)

Table 1.6 (Continued)

State	Rate
Oklahoma	64
Nebraska	76
Connecticut	119
North Dakota	138

Note: This table excludes the District of Columbia, an urban jurisdiction; Georgia probation counts, which included probation case-based counts for private agencies; and Idaho probation counts in which estimates for misdemeanors were based on admissions.

*Rates are computed using the U.S. adult resident population on January 1, 2017.

Source: Kaeble, D. (2018). *Probation and parole in the United States, 2016.* Washington, DC: U.S. Department of Justice, Bureau of Justice Statistics.

SUMMARY

This brief consideration of statistics from major components of the correctional system (probation, prisons, and parole) demonstrates their crucial linkage within the criminal justice system. Imagine what would happen if probation and parole were abolished completely and all convicted persons were required to serve their full prison terms; if this happened today, the prison population would be more than 7 million! Naturally, the prison system is not equipped to handle such a large number of inmates, nor would it be good social policy to attempt such a foolish venture.

We do not wish to suggest that all offenders could and should be released to community corrections. At least 15–25 percent of the prison population are too dangerous or pose too great a threat to community safety to allow their immediate release, even onto "intensive supervised parole" (Allen et al., 2018).

It is the function of probation and its many variants (the so-called "intermediate sanctions"), as well as parole, to determine how the population of convicted persons can be managed in a fashion consistent with not only the capacity of the prison population, but also the goals of societal protections and offender rehabilitation and reintegration.

In short, the examination of corrections in the community is the theme of this text. We consider key issues, such as: What are the best methods for classifying and supervising offenders? What background, education, and training should various community corrections agents possess? How effective are community corrections programs in terms of public safety? And at what cost? What are the recent innovations in community corrections and intermediate sanctions? How effective are these compared to incarceration? How are juveniles handled in the community? The consideration of these (and other) issues will provide readers with the opportunity to form their own opinions and ideas concerning the proper use of community correctional programs and how to coordinate these in the criminal justice system.

Review Questions

1. What is corrections in the community?
2. If probation and parole were abolished completely, what effect would this have on prison systems?
4. Develop an argument for increased use of community corrections.
5. Why do law enforcement and the courts play a part in corrections?
6. Describe the current distribution of offenders across the main components of the criminal justice system.

Notes

1. An extensive body of research has demonstrated that community correctional programs can have a substantial effect on recidivism provided certain empirically derived principles are met. For a summary of this research, see Latessa and Lowenkamp (2007).
2. For example, in Ohio, the state funds "community-based correctional facilities." These facilities are operated by local community corrections boards, they are designed to provide treatment, and they often utilize local community services. They are, however, secure facilities and after being released, offenders are usually on probation. Texas funds similar facilities.
3. Some would argue that many so-called "community" correctional programs are essentially institutional correctional facilities because they are state-run. However, we believe that state-operated programs can indeed be considered community correctional programs, provided they include some type of supervision in the community. For a different perspective on this issue, see Duffee (1990). See also Burke (1997); and Gendreau et al. (2000).
4. See Lowenkamp et al. (2006); and Wilson et al. (2000).

Recommended Readings

Allen, H.E., Latessa, E.L., Ponder, B. (2018). *Corrections in America: An introduction.* 15th ed. Upper Saddle River, NJ: Pearson/Prentice Hall.
Latessa, E.J., Holsinger, A. (2015). *Correctional contexts: Contemporary and classical readings.* Los Angeles: Roxbury.

References

Allen, H.E., Latessa, E.L., Ponder, B. (2018). *Corrections in America: An introduction.* 15th ed. Upper Saddle River, NJ: Pearson/Prentice Hall.
Burke, P.B. (1997). *Policy-driven responses to probation and parole violations.* Washington, DC: U.S. Department of Justice.

Carson, E.A. (2018). *Prisoners in 2016*. Washington, DC: U.S. Department of Justice, Bureau of Justice Statistics.

Duffee, D.E. (1990). Community characteristics: The presumed characteristics and argument for a new approach. In: D.E. Duffee, E.F. McGarrell (Eds.), *Community corrections: A community field approach*. Cincinnati: Anderson.

Gendreau, P., Goggin, C., Smith, P. (2000). Generating rational correctional policies. *Corrections Management Quarterly* 4(2), 52–60.

Latessa, E.J., Lowenkamp, C. (2007). What works in reducing recidivism. *St. Thomas Law Journal* 3, 521–535.

Lowenkamp, C.T., Latessa, E.J., Holsinger, A. (2006). The risk principle in action: What we have learned from 13,676 offenders and 97 correctional programs. *Crime & Delinquency* 51(1), 1–17.

Kaeble, D. (2018). *Probation and parole in the United States, 2016*. Washington, DC: U.S. Department of Justice, Bureau of Justice Statistics.

Kaeble, D., Cowhig, M. (2018). *Correctional populations in the United States, 2016*. Washington, DC: U.S. Department of Justice, Bureau of Justice Programs.

President's Commission on Law Enforcement and Administration of Justice. (1967). *The challenge of crime in a free society*. Washington, DC: U.S. Government Printing Office.

Wilson, D.B., Gallagher, C., MacKenzie, D. (2000). A meta-analysis of corrections-based education, vocation, and work programs for adult offenders. *Journal of Research in Crime and Delinquency* 37(4), 347–368.

Chapter 2

Pretrial Bond, Bail, and Diversion

Key Terms

actuarial assessment	Manhattan Bail Project
bail	money bonds
bond	post-arrest diversion
bond conditions	post-conviction diversion
commercial bonding agencies	pre-arrest diversion
failure to appear	pretrial diversion

> Deprivation of liberty pending trial is harsh and oppressive,
> subjects defendants to economic and psychological hardship,
> interferes with their ability to defend themselves, and in many
> instances, deprives their families of support. —American Bar
> Association, 2018, 10–1.1.

One of the most prominent decisions in the criminal justice processing of defendants is whether to release a person from jail prior to adjudication (Oleson et al., 2015). In the United States, individuals who are arrested are presumed innocent until proven guilty, so many argue that holding them prior to adjudication goes against the core values of our criminal justice system. The American Bar Association (2018, 10.1–1) identifies that the "deprivation of liberty pending trial is harsh and oppressive, subjects defendants to economic and psychological hardship, interferes with their ability to defend themselves, and in many instances, deprives their families of support." In addition, pretrial detainment has been linked to higher conviction rates, higher incarceration rates, and longer sentences both at the juvenile and adult levels (Bechtel et al., 2017; Frazier & Cochran, 1986; Lowenkamp et al., 2013; McCoy, 2007). For these reasons, holding individuals prior to being convicted has always been controversial (Goldkamp, 1984); hence the need for effective pretrial services.

THE PURPOSE OF PRETRIAL SERVICES

In the United States, individuals who have been arrested are often booked into jail to await their trial. In 2016, there were 10.6 million people arrested and booked into local jails. The average daily population for these jails was 731,300 inmates of which 65.1 percent were being held prior to their trial, otherwise known as pretrial status (Zhen, 2016). The Eighth Amendment to the Constitution of the United States reads that excessive bail shall not be required. The Supreme Court has ruled that courts should take into consideration the person's ability to pay when setting bond and that alternatives to incarceration be explored. Of course, holding people who have not yet been found guilty of a crime in jail must be balanced with the safety of the community and the likelihood that the person returns to court to stand trial. Ultimately, the decision as to whether to hold someone in jail or release them prior to the determination of a case is often based on the likelihood that the defendant will return to court, and that any victims as well as potential witnesses remain safe from retaliation or interference (American Bar Association, 2018). To this end, pretrial services become incredibly important in the release decision.

While the services that pretrial agencies offer vary significantly across jurisdictions, there are generally two key functions that most pretrial agencies perform:

1. They provide information to the court regarding the defendant's current situation. This assessment is often short, yet timely, and focuses on a combination of the defendant's criminal history, previous failures on pretrial, and criminogenic needs (e.g., substance use, employment).
2. They provide supervision for those granted pretrial release. Supervision generally includes monitoring conditions set forth by the court, sending reminders of upcoming court hearings, and reporting back to court regarding the defendant's compliance.

THE HISTORY OF PRETRIAL SERVICES

A version of pretrial release can be tracked as far back as 1,500 years to the Anglo-Saxon judicial system. The laws of the day called for bonds to be posted for individuals accused of financial crimes equal to the ultimate fine so as to ensure that they returned to court (Schnacke et al., 2010). Fast forward 1,000 years, and the money bail concept remains a crucial component of the U.S. criminal justice system. The idea of money bail is that an individual who is arrested puts up a determined amount of money to ensure his or her return to court—and if they do not return to court, they risk forfeiting the money. While historically, the defendant would either put up his or her own money or borrow it from friends or family, by the late nineteenth century, most personal cash bonds yielded to commercial bonds. Commercial bonding agencies posted the full bond amount ordered for a fee to be paid by the defendant. Depending on the amount of the bond, commercial bonding agencies would place a lien on the defendant's personal property as collateral for the full bond amount—only taking a portion of the money as a fee for the services (usually 10 percent of the bond). These bond agencies were then responsible for ensuring that the defendant returned to court or risk losing their money.

There have been several concerns levied against the money bail process, but the most relevant is that release from jail is dependent on an individual's ability to raise enough money to pay the bonding agent (or the underlying bond). While there were several attempts throughout the early twentieth century to mitigate money bail, it was not until 1961 with the implementation of the Manhattan Bail Project that an alternative to money bail was available (McElroy, 2011). With the Vera Institute of Justice's help, Manhattan was the first jurisdiction that explored the opportunity for defendants to be released with just a promise, or on their own recognizance, to return to court.

The results of the Manhattan project were convincing. The project was a study comparing defendants released on their own recognizance (OR) to those released on monetary bail. Major lessons were learned from this project that would change how pretrial services would operate moving forward. Initially, recommendations made to the judge about whether or not to release a defendant were based on the opinion of the pretrial assessor. However, the Vera Institute quickly implemented an objective measure of risk (a pretrial assessment) to support the recommendation of whether to release. In the end, 59 percent of those who were recommended for release were released by the judge, compared to 16 percent of the control group in which judges were making the decision without the support of a pretrial assessment and recommendation. Moreover, the time from arrest to final disposition for defendants on OR was significantly quicker, and they were sentenced to prison significantly less often (16 percent compared to 96 percent of the control group) (Vera Institute of Justice, 2011).

A nationwide movement in corrections was born from the results of the Manhattan project. Over the next 5 years, jurisdictions across the United States began to implement pretrial release programs—by 1965, 44 programs were established. In 1966, the United States Congress passed the Bail Reform Act for the federal system. This Act established presumptive releases for all non-capital federal cases who would likely appear in court. With the authorization to release defendants, federal judges were given a range of options including bail, cash deposit, house arrest, or custody of a third party, to name a few.

Up to this point, the primary concern with pretrial releases was whether the defendant was going to return to court. During the 1970s, which was the beginning of the "tough on crime" era, the concern shifted from a failure to appear in court to the risk of harm to the community. State and federal congresspersons began to modify previous bail reform legislation to include preventative detention. Preventative detention allows for a judge to refuse to release a defendant on pretrial release due to the potential harm to the community. Generally, preventative detention is reserved for individuals who engage in capital murder or other violent offenses for which the defendant is charged. This shift from failure to appear to protecting the community was a significant departure from innocent until proven guilty—demonstrating that community safety (at least under certain circumstances) trumps individual freedom.

Local jails paid a heavy price for the "tough on crime" movement. Jail crowding became a significant concern and the safety of both inmates and staff was the subject of a significant number of lawsuits. These lawsuits resulted in advocacy groups negotiating for jail population caps—ensuring that populations could not exceed a predetermined ceiling based on physical space. During this period, many jurisdictions responded by building more jails and bigger jails, but other options to solve the problem of jail crowding were also explored. To reduce the likelihood of jails hitting the caps, local jurisdictions also began to develop alternatives for jail confinement, including pretrial release options as well as pretrial diversion programs.

PRETRIAL PROCESS

Arrest

In many jurisdictions, the pretrial process begins at arrest. Once a suspect is identified and detained, law enforcement officers are making determinations as to whether the person needs to be arrested, transported to jail, and booked into jail. At any point, law enforcement officers can choose not to place the suspect under arrest, can offer him or her a pre-charge diversion program (if applicable in the jurisdiction), issue a summons to court, or book the person into jail. During the arrest process, some pretrial agencies start collecting information from the officer immediately. For example, in Harris County Texas (Houston), law enforcement officers can call the district attorney's office 24 hours a day to determine if there is probable cause and to discuss what charges should be pressed. Harris County Pretrial Services has pretrial officers embedded in the process so that they can conduct an assessment, and make a recommendation to the magistrate as to whether the defendant is appropriate for release on a personal recognizance (PR) bond (which is similar to the OR bond discussed above).

Jail Booking

In most jurisdictions, law enforcement officers arrest a suspect on suspicion of committing a crime, book them into jail, and then there is a probable cause hearing where the initial charges are filed. For these jurisdictions, pretrial services work pretty similarly. At some point in the booking process (it varies across jurisdictions), pretrial services are notified that a defendant has been booked into the jail. Pretrial services then start the assessment process—usually by gathering the person's criminal record.

Assessment

Prior to 1961, defendants in jail were generally at the mercy of the judge or magistrate who took into account the current offense (and sometimes criminal record) to make a determination as to whether they should receive bond, and if so, in what amount. By 1967, the process had significantly changed due to the **Manhattan Bail Project** of 1961. One outcome of the bail project was the recognition that, with better information, judges and magistrates will make different decisions, and in order to get better decisions, there needed to be a set of staff available to assess defendants at the pretrial stage. Quickly, the Vera Institute realized that assessors felt uncomfortable just giving their opinion of whether someone should be released, so they borrowed from the field of probation the concept of actuarial assessment (see Box 2.1). Interestingly, a byproduct of the Manhattan Bail Project was the first actuarial pretrial release assessment.

Since the inception of pretrial agencies, pretrial assessments have become an integral part of the release decision. Remember, pretrial release decisions should be based on whether a defendant is likely to appear for subsequent court hearings or get arrested for a new offense during the pretrial process. Pretrial risk assessments provide an objective means to assess both of these factors. Generally, pretrial assessments are short screening instruments that can be done rather quickly, with or without a face-to-face interview. While there is a range of pretrial assessments available, many of them measure similar factors:

- Criminal history
  - Number of priors
  - Seriousness of priors
- Current offense
  - Number of charges
  - Level of offense
- History of appearance in court
  - Number of prior failures to appear.

While some assessments only include criminal history and offense-related factors, other assessments collect information on a broader range of criminogenic needs (see Figure 2.1):

- Employment
  - Employed at time of arrest
- Housing
  - Stable housing up to the point of arrest
- Stability in the community
  - Friends/family in the local community
- Substance use
  - Problems with substance use.

Box 2.1
Actuarial Assessment

An **actuarial assessment** is an objective way of measuring risk for an event to occur. Actuarial assessments are found in the field of corrections, but are also found specifically in determining insurance rates. Built using statistical modeling, these types of assessments are designed to measure the characteristics of a person and determine the likelihood that the person will engage in a specific event. For pretrial purposes, actuarial assessments usually collect prior history, characteristics of the current offense, and some crime-related variables to determine who is more likely to reoffend.

OHIO RISK ASSESSMENT SYSTEM: PRETRIAL ASSESSMENT TOOL (ORAS-PAT)

Name: _____   Date of Assessment: _____

Case#: _____   Name of Assessor: _____

Pretrial Items		Verified

1.1. Age at First Arrest
    0=33 or older
    1=Under 33
	☐	☐

1.2. Number of Failure-to-Appear Warrants Past 24 Months
    0=None
    1=One Warrant for FTA
    2=Two or more FTA Warrants
	☐	☐

1.3. Three or more Prior Jail Incarcerations
    0=No
    1=Yes
	☐	☐

1.4. Employed at the Time of Arrest
    0= Yes Full-time
    1= Yes, Part-time
    2= Not employed
	☐	☐

1.5. Residential Stability
    0=Lived at current residence past six months
    1=Not lived at same residence
	☐	☐

1.6. Illegal Drug Use during Past Six Month
    0=No
    1=Yes
	☐	☐

1.7. Severe Drug Use Problem
    0=No
    1=Yes
	☐	☐

	Total Score: ☐	

Scores	Rating	% of Failures	% of Failure to Appear	% of New Arrest
0-2	Low	5%	5%	0%
3-5	Moderate	18%	12%	7%
6+	High	29%	15%	17%

Figure 2.1 Ohio Risk Assessment System: Pretrial Tool

Source: University of Cincinnati, Corrections Institute.

Recently, the Arnold Foundation developed the Public Safety Assessment (PSA) that was designed to assess three different outcomes: failure to appear, new arrest, and new arrest for a violent offense. Traditionally, pretrial assessments have been conducted through a face-to-face interview, which, while informative, is incredibly labor-intensive. The Arnold Foundation approached the development of the PSA from this perspective—what would happen if only criminal history was used to score the assessment. In addition to eliminating the need for a face-to-face interview, the PSA also uses the defendant's prior history of violence to predict the likelihood that the defendant will engage in a violent offense while on pretrial status.

Regardless of whether pretrial agencies use all these factors or just some of them, the importance of using an actuarial pretrial assessment has been clearly established (see Cadigan & Lowenkamp, 2011). The use of a structured risk assessment maximizes the number of people that can be released while minimizing the likelihood of defendants failing to appear for subsequent hearings (Toborg et al., 1984). In fact, jurisdictions that use a risk assessment tool based on a mix of quantitative and qualitative factors are significantly more likely to release more defendants, have fewer failures to appear, and those released are less likely to be arrested compared to when either no assessment is conducted or one that takes into account assessor opinion only (Levin, 2006).

Pretrial risk assessment is not without its limitations. Although there have been a number of studies conducted on pretrial release over the past 50 plus years, there are several methodological and practical issues, some of which are unique to pretrial release, which can affect the results of this research. These include:

1. The quality and availability of data.
2. The inability to have random assignment. As a result, the samples used in most studies are skewed since many high-risk/serious defendants are not granted pretrial release and are therefore under-represented in the samples.
3. Since we are primarily concerned about outcomes during the pretrial release period, the result is a relatively short follow-up period and low base rates of failure. This makes prediction more difficult, especially when trying to hone in on the prediction of violence.
4. The defendant has a right to remain silent. Therefore, the legal status of the defendant often limits the type of information that can be gathered.
5. Time constraints for assessment also limit the amount and verification of the information gathered.
6. There are generally two outcomes of concern: the likelihood of failure to appear and the possibility of new criminal activity. Having two distinct outcomes is somewhat of a challenge since some of the indicators of each are not always similar. For example, some studies of pretrial release have found length of residence to be a predictor of failure to appear, but not a predictor of future criminal behavior.

TYPES OF RELEASE

As soon as a suspect is arrested and booked into jail, the pretrial release process is started. While the timing and order of procedures are different across jurisdictions, there are generally two ways in which defendants can be released pretrial: 1) personal recognizance (PR) or on their own recognizance (OR); or 2) surety bond or some form of money bail.

Personal Recognizance Bonds

Personal recognizance bonds (or own recognizance bonds) are granted most often by either a magistrate or judge. In some jurisdictions, sheriffs also have the ability to grant a type of PR bond. A PR bond is considered an unsecured bond, rather like a promissory note, in which the defendant agrees to appear at his or her court hearings and in return is released from jail. While PR bonds can have no conditions attached, many jurisdictions require individuals released on a PR bond to be supervised by pretrial services.

Money Bail

There are two forms of money bail: cash bail and commercial bonds. At the time of a pretrial arraignment hearing (or in some jurisdictions based on a bail schedule alone), a defendant is granted a bail release if a specific sum of money can be submitted to the court to ensure the return of the defendant. This bail amount is often predetermined by the seriousness of the offense and some measure of failure to appear. If the defendant has the ability to raise the amount ordered, they can post the money (bail) to the court and be released (Box 2.2). Unfortunately, many defendants are not able to raise the amount of cash needed to be released. In a study of the Philadelphia bail system, 40 percent of the defendants who were ordered to pay $500 were not able to secure release (Stevenson, 2017).

In most states, commercial bonds dominate the means by which defendants are released from jail. Commercial bonds are issued by private, for-profit bonding agencies which "put up" the court-determined amount and promise that the defendant will return to court for the subsequent hearings. In exchange, the defendant pays a non-refundable fee, generally 10 percent of the total bond, for the bonding agency's services. This allows the defendant to raise a smaller amount of cash initially to secure their release, but this comes at a cost (see Box 2.2). If the defendant does not show up for court, the bonding agent has the legal right to find them and bring them

---

Box 2.2
An Example of Case Bail versus Commercial Bond

A defendant is arrested and charged with Theft of a Motor Vehicle. At the bond hearing the judge sets the bond amount at $10,000.

	Cash Bail	Commercial Bond
Bond ordered	$10,000	$10,000
Defendant pays	$10,000	$1,000 + Collateral
Collateral	Can be used instead of cash in some jurisdictions	Must be used for most commercial bonds in addition to fee
Successful completion of case	Cash/collateral property returned	Fee forfeited and collateral property returned

to justice. Sometimes the bonding agent will employ bounty hunters (through either direct employment or contract) to find the missing defendant. An example of this can be found on the popular television show from the 2000s entitled *Dog the Bounty Hunter*. While made into a reality television show, the show did capture the essence of what happens when someone skips bail and chooses not to show up for court.

In order to avoid the issues associated with commercial bonds, several states have moved to eliminate commercial bonds. By the fall of 2016, four states had eliminated commercial bonds: Wisconsin, Illinois, Oregon, and Kentucky. In place of commercial bonding agents, each of these states have devised ways in which defendants can be released safely to the community without payment of money. For example, Kentucky has a system that is based on presumptive release—meaning that if someone is arrested, the standard decision is to release the person from jail, except for extenuating circumstances. Where most systems are designed to presumptively hold defendants and the defendant (or sometimes their council if allowed) must argue why they should be released, Kentucky's shift to presumptive release puts the burden on the state to argue that a defendant who is a flight risk or dangerous needs to be held. Furthermore, Kentucky has set a bail credit for those who are held pretrial (excluding a few types of offense). The bail credit is a dollar amount that is earned for every day in jail. Once the defendant earns enough money to either bail him or herself out of jail or bring the total amount down sufficiently to make a 10 percent cash bond, the defendant is released. If the defendant does put up some cash bail to the court, it is returned to him or her as long as there are no failure-to-appear charges associated with the case (KY Rev Stat, 2011).

Box 2.3
Commercial Bond Agencies

Commercial bonds have been coming under fire recently. Once the only mechanism to ensure pretrial released, commercial bonding is becoming less and less favored compared to other types of release. **Commercial bonding agencies** have become the target of many advocacy groups as the idea of the money bond is being challenged as a tax on the poor. Unlike cash bail in which the defendant's money is returned to the defendant upon successful completion of the court procedures, commercial bonding agencies keep the 10 percent "fee" as a payment for their services. So even if the person is found not guilty or the charges are dropped, the commercially-bonded defendant is not entitled to a refund from the bonding agent.

PRETRIAL SUPERVISION

Initially, pretrial agencies were solely charged with assessing defendants and providing the results to the court for the release decision. As jails became more crowded, the courts were forced to let a broader array of offenders out on pretrial release. With the expansion of the type of defendants, judges were reluctant to let defendants out without any supervision, so they began to order the defendant to undergo conditions of release. Naturally, the supervision of these defendants fell to the pretrial agencies.

Now, if a defendant gets released prior to his or her trial, they are often supervised by a pretrial officer, a bondsman, or sometimes both. Pretrial supervision is intended to mitigate the risk of a defendant either failing to appear or engaging in new criminal behavior (Clarke, 1988). To this end, pretrial officers are tasked with monitoring a set of conditions that are established by the judge or magistrate who granted the release. While the Supreme Court has ruled that conditions must be individualized and specific to the nature of the offense, there are some standard conditions that are placed on defendants regularly. They must:

- commit no crimes or have no contact with the police for a new criminal offense;
- maintain their current residence or provide updates to the court if their address changes;
- avoid contact with the victim or witnesses.

Beyond the standard set of conditions, there are other conditions that judges will order in an effort to provide a comprehensive "net" around the defendant to ensure his or her return to court and reduce the likelihood of him or her committing a crime while on pretrial release. These conditions can vary across judges, and defense lawyers can get rather creative when trying to get their defendant released. While there is no definitive list, some of the conditions can include:

- attending a substance abuse treatment center;
- submitting to regular drug testing;
- obtaining/maintaining employment;
- attending supervision meetings;
- electronic monitoring;
- house arrest.

If conditions are ordered, it is generally the pretrial supervision agency that is charged with monitoring the defendant's compliance. Similar to probation, pretrial services are often called on to see defendants on a regular basis, administer drug tests, and monitor external devices (electronic monitoring, GPS, interlock). Although this is somewhat controversial since the defendant has not been found guilty of an offense, some judges will order the defendant into treatment as a condition of bond. It is the role of pretrial services to monitor the compliance with treatment as well.

CURRENT STATE OF PRETRIAL SERVICES

In an article published in 2015 by Bechtel et al. (p. 23), the authors state that, "Pretrial research is still in its infancy, and this area of criminal justice research does not compare with the extensive research conducted in the post-dispositional field." In a later article, Bechtel and colleagues state that "multiple pretrial studies have not yet been subjected to rigorous blind peer review and replication" (Bechtel et al., 2017, p. 460). Several additional findings can be summarized from this study. First, despite finding a total of 811 manuscripts for review, only 163 were actually quantitative while most were simply legal or theoretical discussions. After applying criteria to gauge the rigor of the studies included, only 16 studies remained, representing just over 391,000 defendants. The authors concluded that, "Overall, the quality of the research that could be included in the current analysis was not very good, with some noted exceptions" (Bechtel et al., 2017, p. 460). Those exceptions included one study that utilized a randomized controlled trial. The authors drew several conclusions. While noting that the results should be viewed with caution because of lack of demographic and criminal history information, they concluded that more restrictive bond types resulted in lower **failure-to-appear** (FTA) rates. They did find that court notifications also had a positive effect on FTA rates.

Pretrial Diversion Programs

The use of pretrial diversion programs is on the rise. Pretrial programs can range from law enforcement diversion to formal programs operated by pretrial services, probation, or even the district attorney's office. Diversion programs are different from pretrial release. As discussed earlier, pretrial services are designed to be an alternative to detention while the defendant is awaiting trial. Pretrial diversion programs are considered alternatives to adjudication or conviction.

While there are no nationwide standards for what should be included in a pretrial diversion program, there are some common characteristics across most diversion programs (National Association of Pretrial Services Agencies [NAPSA], 2009). First, diversion programs are, by nature, in lieu of a conviction. Participants are offered the pretrial intervention in place of a formal charge or conviction and, in turn, the criminal justice system can reduce its burden of a trial and incarceration. While there are some critics of pretrial diversion programs, mainly from the point of view that there is no formal finding of guilt and that innocent people could be caught up in the process, most people find the use of pretrial diversion programs as positive—ultimately providing first-time offenders with a way to avoid a conviction.

Second, if the person completes the diversion program, the charges are usually dropped. In some situations, the diversion program reduces the final disposition from a felony to a misdemeanor, but in most cases, the result of the pretrial diversion program is for the final charges to be dropped. The benefit to the defendant is that he or she can now apply for jobs, housing, and loans without the burden of having to report the arrest or conviction.

Third, most diversion programs target lower-level offenses, first-time offenders, or specialized populations (e.g., those with mental health issues). Generally, the elected officials who implement these programs can justify allowing lower-level offenders pretrial diversion while still facing their constituents. In all, the goal of pretrial diversion programs is to offer interventions that aim to address the underlying cause of the criminal behavior (e.g., substance abuse) while avoiding the collateral consequences of a conviction (NAPSA, 2010).

Pretrial diversion programs are generally found at three different stages of the criminal justice system. These include pre-arrest, post-arrest, and post-conviction programs. Each of these types of program has benefits (and drawbacks).

1. **Pre-arrest diversion** programs: Probably the most beneficial of the diversion programs, pre-arrest diversion programs also come with some of the greatest risks. A pre-arrest diversion program is generally implemented by law enforcement agents who come into contact with an individual whom they believe meets criteria for a pre-arrest diversion program. Once the person is so identified, the officer chooses to divert them completely out of the criminal justice system, thus avoiding an arrest, and refer them to an alternative intervention. Generally, these programs are offered to people with serious mental health issues, substance abuse issues, or other behaviors which suggest that the individual is not engaging in the criminal behavior through his or her own choice (e.g., trafficked into prostitution) (Mire et al., 2007). In the end, pre-arrest programs offer individuals with significant non-legal issues a way to stay out of jail and avoid criminal charges.

2. **Post-arrest diversion** programs: Probably the most common version of pretrial diversion, the post-arrest diversion programs are usually implemented somewhere between being booked into jail and a trial (Cowell et al., 2004). Post-arrest diversion programs can be offered by law enforcement, but are generally found within the courts. Defendants are usually determined eligible by the district attorney's staff or court personnel through a screening/assessment process. Once the defendant is so identified, the post-arrest diversion program includes some intervention designed to address the underlying issue—assuming that if this is resolved, the defendant will discontinue their criminal behavior.

3. **Post-conviction diversion** programs: Similar to post-arrest diversion programs, post-conviction diversion programs are designed to identify individuals who would benefit from specific treatment interventions while ultimately avoiding a permanent conviction. Post-conviction diversion programs start with a conviction and then work backwards. In exchange for completing a formal treatment program (e.g., specialty court), the final conviction is vacated and the individual's record is sealed. Post-conviction diversion programs are generally offered to individuals with substance abuse issues.

While all three of these diversion programs have their unique differences, ultimately, they are all working for the same common principle: Those with underlying drivers of criminal behavior (mental health issues, substance abuse, coercion) should be given opportunities to undergo an alternative intervention in lieu of a conviction. There are now several studies that suggest being placed deeper into the criminal justice system brings with it a series of collateral consequences that have lifelong implications, including barring access to housing, federal grants, and employment (Olivares et al., 1996; Pinard, 2010).

SUMMARY

As a person enters the criminal justice system, each stage is designed to filter out those who do not need to move further into the system. Pretrial release is an important component in that filtering system. With significant ramifications for those held pretrial (higher conviction rates, higher prison rates, and longer sentences), the pretrial release decision is one that cannot be taken lightly. For a long time in the United States, being released from jail was tied to the ability for an individual to pay. Recently, initiatives have emerged to help change this. Jurisdictions have begun implementing alternative ways for defendants to be released including blocking the use of commercial bonds.

Along with less reliance on money bonds, pretrial diversion programs have expanded significantly through the 2010s. A resurgence of pre-arrest and post-arrest programs have been developed to offset the collateral consequences of a conviction. Ultimately, the criminal justice system has begun to right itself, providing more opportunities for individuals to avoid a criminal record but still receive treatment services.

While pretrial detention is a hotly contested issue throughout the United States, the empirical research that has been conducted to date is inconsistent, often contradictory, and overall lacks academic and methodological rigor. While validated risk assessment tools can help courts to make decisions about pretrial release, they are not foolproof. These tools often place defendants into risk categories, commonly "low," "moderate," or "high" for likelihood to fail to appear or continued criminal behavior; however, the seriousness of the current charge is a commonly used factor that courts take into consideration when making pretrial decisions. In essence, seriousness often trumps risk. Finally, until additional well-designed studies are conducted, conclusions about the effects of pretrial detention are speculative at best.

Review Questions

1. What are the ways in which a person can be released from jail during the pretrial stage?
2. When did the United States implement an alternative to money bail?
3. What is the impact of being held in jail pretrial?
4. What is a pretrial diversion?
5. Who offers a pretrial diversion program?
6. Who is eligible for a pretrial diversion program?
7. What components are generally found in a pretrial diversion program?

Recommended Readings

American Bar Association. (2018). *ABA criminal justice standards: Pretrial release.* Chicago: ABA.

Bechtel, K., Holsinger, A., Lowenkamp, C., Warren, M. (2017). A meta-analytic review of pretrial research: Risk assessment, bond type, and interventions. *American Journal of Criminal Justice* 42(2), 443–467.

Stevenson, M.T. (2017, January 12). Distortion of justice: How the inability to pay bail affects case outcomes. George Mason Legal Studies Research Paper No. LS 18–30. Available at: https://ssrn.com/abstract=2777615

References

American Bar Association. (2018). *ABA criminal justice standards: Pretrial release.* Chicago: ABA.

Bechtel, K., Flores, A., Holsinger, A., Lowenkamp, C. (2015). Trademarks, press releases, and policy: Will rigorous research get in the way? *Federal Probation* 80(1), 22–29.

Bechtel, K., Holsinger, A., Lowenkamp, C., Warren, M. (2017). A meta-analytic review of pretrial research: Risk assessment, bond type, and interventions. *American Journal of Criminal Justice* 42(2), 443–467.

Cadigan, T., Lowenkamp, C. (2011). Implementing risk assessment in the Federal Pretrial Services system. *Federal Probation* 75(2), 48–55.

Clarke, S. (1988). Pretrial release: Concepts, issues and strategies for improvement. *Research in Corrections* 1(3), 1–40.

Cowell, A.J., Broner, N., Dupont, R. (2004). The cost-effectiveness of criminal justice diversion programs for people with serious mental health illnesses co-occurring with substance abuse: Four case studies. *Journal of Contemporary Criminal Justice* 20, 292.

Frazier, C., Cochran, J. (1986). Detention of juveniles: Its effects on subsequent juvenile court processing decisions. *Youth and Society* 17(3), 286–305.

Goldkamp, J. (1984). The development and implementation of bail guidelines: Highlights and issues. Washington, DC: National Institute of Justice, U.S. Department of Justice.

KY Rev Stat § 431.066 (1996 through Reg Sess). (2011).

Levin, D. (2006). *Examining the efficacy of pretrial release conditions, sanctions and screening with the state court processing statistics dataseries.* Washington, DC: Pretrial Justice Institute.

Lowenkamp, C., VanNostrand, M., Holsinger, A. (2013). The hidden costs of pretrial detention. The Laura and John Arnold Foundation. Retrieved from: www.arnold foundation.org/wp-content/uploads/2014/02/LJAF_Report_hidden-costs_FNL.pdf

McCoy, C. (2007). Caleb was right: Pretrial decisions determine mostly everything. *Berkeley Journal of Criminal Law* 12(2), 135–150.

McElroy, J. (2011). Introduction to the Manhattan Bail Project. *Federal Sentencing Reporter* 24(1), 8–9.

Mire, S., Forsyth, C.J., Hanser, R. (2007). Jail diversion: Addressing the needs of offenders with mental illness and co-occurring disorders. *Journal of Offender Rehabilitation* 45, 19–31.

National Association of Pretrial Services Agencies (NAPSA). (2009). Pretrial diversion in the 21st century: A national survey of pretrial diversion programs and practices. *The NAPSA Monograph*.

National Association of Pretrial Services Agencies (NAPSA). (2010). Promising practices in pretrial diversion. *The NAPSA Monograph*.

Oleson, J.C., Lowenkamp, C.T., Wooldredge, J., VanNostrand, M., Cadigan, T. (2015). The sentencing consequences of federal pretrial detention. *Crime and Delinquency*. doi: 10.1177/0011128714551406. First published on September 26, 2014.

Olivares, K.M., Burton, V., Cullen, F.T. (1996). The collateral consequences of felony conviction: National study of state legal codes 10 years later. *Federal Probation* 60(3), 10–17.

Pinard, M. (2010). Collateral consequences of criminal convictions: Confronting issues of race and dignity. *New York University Law Review* 85(2), 457–534.

Schnacke, T., Jones, M., Brooker, C., (2010). Glossary of terms and phrases relating to bail and the pretrial release or detention. Washington, DC: Pretrial Justice Institute.

Stevenson, M.T. (2017, January 12). Distortion of justice: How the inability to pay bail affects case outcomes. George Mason Legal Studies Research Paper No. LS 18–30. Available at: https://ssrn.com/abstract=2777615

Toborg, M., Yezer, A., Tseng, P., Carpenter, B. (1984). *Pretrial release assessment of danger and flight*. McLean, VA: Lazer Management Group.

Vera Institute of Justice. (2011). Fair treatment for the indigent: The Manhattan Bail Project. *Federal Sentencing Reporter* 24(1), 10–12.

Zhen, Z. (2016). *Jail inmates in 2016*. Washington, DC: United States Department of Justice, Bureau of Justice Statistics.

Chapter 3

SENTENCING AND COMMUNITY CORRECTIONS

Key Terms

community service
concurrent sentences
consecutive sentences
determinate sentence
deterrence
discretionary parole release
felony
indeterminate sentencing
jail
mandatory minimum sentence
mandatory release
misdemeanor

parole
parole boards
plea bargaining
prison
restitution
retribution
selective incapacitation
sentencing disparity
split sentence
"three-strikes" sentencing laws
tourniquet sentencing
work release

> Justice is itself the great standing policy of civil society; and any eminent departure from it, under any circumstances, lies under the suspicion of being no policy at all. —Edmund Burke

CONTEMPORARY SENTENCING PRACTICES

Historically, the American criminal justice system was an adversarial combat between the state and the accused defendant in a criminal trial. The accused denied committing the alleged offense, and the trial jury was charged with determining the fact of innocence or guilt. If the accused was found guilty, the presiding judge, using all available information and guided by the pre-sentence investigation report ordered previously from the court's investigators, would then impose sentence on the guilty in the interest of justice and to achieve some recognizable correctional objective. Such objectives could include punishment, rehabilitation, reintegration, retribution, reparation, or deterrence.

Box 3.1
Deterrence

Deterrence is the prevention of criminal behavior through the threat of detection, apprehension, and punishment.

As a policy, deterrence programs can be directed against individuals or the general society. Individual or specific deterrence is designed to prevent a person from committing a crime and can take such forms as punishment, persuasion, deprivation of liberty, or even death. "Scared Straight" programs that fleetingly mix hardened convicts with impressionable juveniles are believed by some to be a specific deterrent.

A societal deterrence program reminds potential offenders of what may happen to them if they violate the law. Driving automobiles while intoxicated, for example, is believed to be prevented or discouraged by a well-planned and coordinated television advertisement, linked to staunch enforcement by local policing agencies and mandatory loss of driving privileges or short periods of incarceration in jail. The death penalty is frequently cited as a deterrent, both general with the belief that it will deter others; and specific— at least those executed will not commit another crime.

Perhaps this model typified the justice system a half-century ago, but it is atypical of sentencing practices in the 2000s and 2010s. Determination of guilt, however, is seldom decided by a jury. Instead, most of those convicted (95 percent) plead guilty for considerations, and the judge usually complies with the negotiated plea struck by the prosecutor and defense counsel. Only about 5 percent of the total convicted cases are found guilty through trial, and 60 percent of those are convicted by the judge in a bench trial (Durose & Langan, 2007). A definition of plea bargaining is found in Box 3.2.

Regardless of the avenue of conviction, 69 percent of those convicted felony offenders were sentenced to incarceration (either prison or jail). The remaining 31 percent were sentenced to probation. Of course, probation is the umbrella and the workhorse of corrections, under which many other community-based alternatives reside. Before we look at sentencing options, it is important to examine the purpose of correctional sanctions and overall sentencing approaches.

Harris County Courthouse. *[Photo courtesy of Jeff McShan]*

> **Box 3.2**
> **Plea Bargaining**
>
> **Plea bargaining** is exchange of prosecutorial and/or judicial concessions, commonly a lesser charge, the dismissal of other pending charges, a recommendation by the prosecutor for a reduced sentence, or a combination thereof, in return for a plea of guilty.

THE PURPOSE OF CRIMINAL SANCTIONS

While maintaining public safety and serving "justice" are paramount considerations of the sentencing process, there are multiple purposes of criminal sanctions. These include:

- **Retribution:** The offender is punished because someone has broken the law and needs to be held accountable for their actions. Enforcing the law without consequences could lead to a breakdown of society and would render laws meaningless.
- **Deterrence:** There are two types of deterrence, general and specific. With general deterrence, the belief is that the sanction deters potential offenders by inflicting punishment or suffering on actual offenders. In other words, when we see or hear of someone being sentenced to prison, we might think twice before committing a similar act. Specific deterrence is less concerned with the effect on potential offenders and is more concerned with the actual ones. If someone is punished, the premise of specific deterrence is that the individual receiving the sanction will not commit a crime in the future so that they can avoid further punishment.
- **Incapacitation:** We most commonly see incapacitation in the form of incarceration; when we incarcerate someone, we limit their ability to commit another crime. It is fair to say that incapacitation has been the underlying purpose of our correctional system since the 1980s, and is just now abating. The idea, of course, is that if we lock up all the criminals, we will reduce crime since they will not be free to steal, sell drugs, or hurt others.
- **Restoration:** Some believe that true crime control lies with the community and that victims and the community should be central to the process of restoration. This approach is commonly seen in community corrections through community service orders, restitution payments to the victim, mediation of disputes, sentencing circles (where the community participates in the decision), and other processes designed to "make the community whole" again by requiring the offender to make amends.
- **Rehabilitation:** This approach focuses on changing the behavior of the offender through treatment and services. With this approach, the offender chooses to refrain from new crimes rather than being unable to commit them.

Box 3.3
Retribution

Philosophically, this term generally means "getting even" with the perpetrator. *Social revenge* suggests that individuals cannot exact punishment, but that the state will do so in their name.

   Retribution assumes that offenders wilfully choose to commit the evil acts, are responsible for their own behavior, and should receive the punishment they deserve. The "just deserts" movement in sentencing reflects the retribution philosophy. For many, it provides a justifiable rationale for the death penalty.

As we will see, these multiple purposes are not independent from each other. Some offenders are placed on community supervision to punish them and to deter them, it is hoped, from future crime by holding a **prison** sentence over their heads. Sanctions such as electronic monitoring may be used to try to "incapacitate" them by restricting where and when they can go out. The probationer may also be required to perform **community service** or make some **restitution** to the victim. Finally, the court may require the offender to attend programs and services designed to help them change their behavior and learn new skills to avoid future risky situations. As you learn more about community corrections, you will see all of these purposes play out as part of the sanctions that are imposed.

SENTENCING OPTIONS

In the plea-bargaining process, the defense counsel may negotiate the sentence outcome to avoid incarceration of the accused. Thus, the decision to incarcerate may, in part, depend on the outcome of negotiated justice. The two major incarceration outcomes are imprisonment in a penal facility or in a jail. The major alternative to incarceration is probation and other intermediate punishments such as weekend confinement, house arrest, residential treatment (such as a halfway house or community correctional center), electronic monitoring, fines, restitution or work centers, intensive supervised probation, and other alternatives.

   If the decision is made to place the person on probation or other intermediate punishment, usually as a condition of probation, the offender is typically supervised by an officer of the local or state probation department. Conditional freedom under probation requires the probationer to meet certain conditions of behavior (see Chapter 4). If the probationer is in danger of substantively violating these conditions or is determined to be in need of additional service or more intensive supervision, the supervising officer may request that the judge increase the conditions of supervision to include additional restrictions or program participation. The intent of this practice, often called tourniquet sentencing, is to lessen the risk of failure and recidivism and assist the probationer in deciding to conform to court

> **Box 3.4**
> **Tourniquet Sentencing**
>
> **Tourniquet sentencing** is tightening or increasing the conditions of probation to encourage the client to conform to legal and supervisory expectations. A probation officer requests the court to order additional restrictions or to mandate participation in identified programs. The correctional objective is reintegration or avoidance of criminal activity. One example of tourniquet sentencing is the probationer convicted of indecent exposure who continues to consume alcohol. The court may order participation in substance abuse treatment, as well as house arrest with electronic monitoring, or decree that the probationer takes Antabuse (disulfiram), a medication that generally sickens the person who imbibes alcohol.
>
> Source: The term "tourniquet sentencing" is attributed to Judge Albert Kramer, District Judge, Quincy, MA. Klein, A. (1980). *Earn it: the story so far.* Waltham, MA: Brandeis University.

expectations. The implicit alternative to non-conforming behavior is incarceration, frequently in the local jail, for a period of time to be imposed by the judge. To understand tourniquet sentencing, it is necessary to examine the jail and its role as a hub of community corrections.

Remember, a judge may have a number of options available to them at sentencing, or can modify or change the conditions as the situation changes. While judges can make requirements more stringent, they can also lessen them if the offender is abiding by the rules. This can range from reducing reporting requirements to outright release from supervision. Let's now take a look at sentencing models and how they have changed over the years.

THE DEVELOPMENT OF THE INDETERMINATE SENTENCE

A basic tenet underlying sentencing in the nineteenth century was a belief in the perfectibility of humans. The American Revolution engendered a great deal of interest and enthusiasm for reform. The emerging nation threw off the dread yoke of British imperialism, including the harsh and widely hated British laws in place throughout the colonies that relied so heavily on the death penalty. In their place, a more rational system of "corrections" arose—the ideal of certain but humane punishment believed to most certainly deter offenders from criminal careers. America

> **Box 3.5**
> **Sentencing: Concurrent or Consecutive?**
>
> If the offender is to be sentenced for more than one crime and receives a **concurrent sentence**, the offender would start serving time for all his or her crimes beginning on the day of arrival in prison. If a **consecutive sentence** is imposed, the offender must generally serve the minimum sentence for the first crime before beginning to serve time for the second offense. Offenders obviously prefer the concurrent over the consecutive sentence option because they would be eligible for release from prison much earlier.

entered the "Progressive Era" in which "rational men" would be able to pursue their best interests and maximize gain and reward while avoiding penalties or pain. This famous principle ("hedonistic calculus") was accepted wholeheartedly as a guiding objective in the question being asked by concerned citizens, lawmakers, and public officials: "Who are offenders and what shall we do with them?" Under British codes, they were seen as inherently evil and thus to be punished, killed, or disabled. Under the Progressive Era, the answer that emerged was quite different: They are people out of touch with God and, given a chance to change by thinking about their crime and relationship with God and fellow humans, they will opt to repent and change. Prison was the answer to the policy question of what to do with offenders, and America embraced prisons with its general zeal for humanitarianism and enthusiasm, building huge "fortress" prisons that emphasized reform and repentance. The American **penitentiary** ("place to do penance") was a contribution to corrections throughout the world.

Yet in the emerging penitentiary and later reformatory movements there remained the philosophical quandary: what should be done with the reformed offender who continued to be held in prison years after actual reformation. During this period sentencing codes were determinate or "flat" and inmates were expected to serve their sentences to the day, although reductions in sentences could be granted for good behavior, or if the prison system was overcrowded. In this philosophical environment, correctional administrators began to innovate, and we see the first significant changes in our sentencing philosophy, which is impossible to discuss without seeing how it developed through the creation of parole.

In the British outpost of Australia, offenders who had been sentenced to exile by transportation to Australia occasionally continued their violent criminal behavior. Transported felons were failures because they had committed crimes in England; when they continued their miscreant behavior in Australia, they were shipped to Norfolk Island, onto a bleak and inhospitable shore some 1,000 miles to the east. These "double failures" of Australia who were subsequently sentenced to death thanked God, but those sentenced to Norfolk Island sank into the deepest depression and sadness. Such was the place that Captain Alexander Maconochie inherited when he was posted as managing officer in 1842.

Maconochie quickly determined that the violence, treachery, and staff–inmate confrontations had to stop and seized upon what is now known as the "mark" system (also known now as a form of token economy). Assembling the inmates, he promised that there was hope of freedom if any inmate could amass 100 marks (credits). Each inmate was to be billed for food, clothing, and tools; marks were to be assigned for quantity and quality of work. Through hard work and frugal living, inmates could save marks; when an inmate amassed 100 marks, he was free from correctional control, free to marry and live on the island, and conduct himself with proper behavior. Assault and violence immediately declined with this innovative and constructive management approach, but the Royal Marines assigned to prison officer duty thought Maconochie was too lenient and that he mollycoddled offenders. Maconochie was quickly removed, and Norfolk Island slid rapidly back into the slough of despair it was before Maconochie's innovative management.

Fortunately, Maconochie's ideas spread: Imprisonment could be used to prepare an offender for a productive life and eventual return to the community under what could be seen as an "indeterminate sentence." The implications of this demonstration were that sentence length should not be arbitrary or "flat," but should be related to the reform and rehabilitation of the inmate. Sir Walter Crofton in Ireland used Maconochie's concepts when he developed what became known as the "Irish" system.

Crofton reasoned that if penitentiaries were places where offenders reflect on their crimes and decide to stop their criminal activities ("repent"), then there should be some mechanism or scheme to detect when the reform had occurred, as well as for releasing the offender when this had happened. Crofton established a three-stage system, each of which would bring the convict closer to freedom within the community. The first phase consisted of solitary confinement and tedious work, such as picking oakum (separating coconut fibers for the purpose of making rope). After 6 months, the convict could be assigned to public works on a team, each member of which was responsible for the behavior of every other team member (an early use of "peer pressure"). Anyone who misbehaved would cause all team members to be returned to Phase One. The last phase was assignment to a transitional prison permitting unsupervised day work outside the prison. If the inmate's behavior was good and he could find employment in the community, he was given a "ticket of leave," in effect extending the limits of confinement to include placement in the county on "conditional pardon." While the ex-inmate could not leave the county and was required to produce his "ticket" upon demand by law enforcement agents, he was nonetheless free of correctional control for the duration of his sentence. Of course, if his conduct was bad, the ticket could be revoked and the offender returned to prison (Phase One). In effect, Crofton established conditional liberty in the community, what would now be called **parole**, which will be discussed further in Chapter 5.

By 1870, prison crowding in the United States had become so massive and the related management problems so complex that a conference was deemed necessary. Prison administrators, wardens, religious leaders, concerned leaders, and innovators met in Cincinnati, Ohio, in 1870 in the first meeting of what would become the American Correctional Association. Spurred on by Crofton and empowered by eloquent oratory from Zebulon Reed Brockway, the assembly adopted standards and principles that addressed new types of buildings to be constructed, as well as

---

Box 3.6
Indeterminate Sentencing

Under the **indeterminate sentencing** system, the sentencing judge pronounces a minimum and maximum period of incarceration, such as from 3 to 5 or 5 to 10, or 1 to 20 years, and so on. Correctional personnel are expected to assist the offenders in changing their behavior and preparing for eventual return to the community, and the parole board is to monitor offender behavior and change. The actual decision on parole readiness and release is detailed to a parole board, charged with protecting society and releasing offenders onto community correctional supervision. The actual conditions of parole are set by the parole board, which retains authority to return non-adjusting offenders to the prison for further treatment and punishment. In essence, the sentencing judge shares sentence length determination with the executive branch in which parole boards are located.

an early release system. In 1876, Brockway initiated parole in the nation by the ticket of leave system. New York quickly passed enabling legislation and parole became a reality.

Other states responded by changing their sentencing structures as well as by authorizing parole as a mechanism for releasing reformed offenders. The resultant sentencing system was the indeterminate sentence, the dominant sentencing structure in the United States until the mid-1970s. As we will see, while the indeterminate sentence was the primary structure for about a century, there have been many changes in the past 40 or so years.

RAPID CHANGES IN SENTENCING

By 1930, most states and federal courts were operating under the indeterminate sentencing structure. The wide range of sentence lengths reflected the dominant rehabilitation goal of the correctional system and the belief that once the offender had been rehabilitated, the parole board would detect the change and then order parole release.[1] Using their authority of discretionary release, parole boards actually determined the length of the sentence served.

Following a very long period of relative inactivity (1930–1974), American sentencing laws and practices began to undergo rapid change, a fundamental restructuring of the sentencing process. The causes that have been identified are as follows:[2]

1. Prison uprisings (such as at Attica in New York and others in California, Florida, New Mexico, and Oklahoma) indicated that inmates were particularly discontented with the rhetoric of rehabilitation and the reality of the prison environment.
2. The abuse of discretion caused concerns about individual rights, as prosecutors, judges, and parole boards were immune from review and some practiced arbitrary uses of discretion.
3. Court orders and decisions led to a movement that demanded accountability in official decision making and outcomes.

Box 3.7
Parole Board

A **parole board** is any correctional person, authority, or board that has the authority to release on parole those adults (or juveniles) committed to confinement facilities, to set conditions for behavior, to revoke from parole, and to discharge from parole. Parole boards also recommend executive clemency through pardon or sentence commutation (shortening), as well as setting policies for supervision of parolees.

---

4. The rehabilitation ideal was challenged, both empirically and ideologically, which undermined the rationale of the indeterminate sentence's "parole after rehabilitation" corollary.

5. Experimental and statistical studies of judicial sentencing found substantial disparity and both racial and class discrimination. Such inconsistencies and disparities fostered the conclusion that sentencing practices were unfair. (Sentencing disparity occurs when offenders committing the same crimes under the same circumstances are given different sentences by the same judge.)

6. Crime control and corrections became a political football, useful for those seeking election to public office. Such political opportunists led the general public to believe that lenient judges and parole boards were releasing dangerous offenders back into the community, with little concern for public safety.

MOVE TO A MORE PUNITIVE APPROACH

Although corrections in the 1970s generally reflected the utilitarian goal of rehabilitation, other discussions from the reform movement brought additional correctional goals to the forefront in the 1980s, such as the incapacitation of persons likely to commit future crimes and its variant of selective incapacitation, in which the highest-risk most serious offenders would receive much longer sentences in order to prevent any more criminal activity. The specific deterrence of sentenced offenders—and the general deterrence of those contemplating committing a crime—was legitimized as a social policy goal. One emerging example of this

---

Box 3.8
Selective Incapacitation

This doctrine of isolating the offender, or causing "social disablement," proposes "adopting a policy of incarcerating those whose criminal behavior is so damaging or probable that nothing short of isolation will prevent recidivism." This "nothing-else-works" approach would require correctly identifying those offenders who should receive long-term imprisonment and diverting others into community corrections. Thus, we would be able to make maximum use of prison cells, a scarce resource, to protect society from the depredations of such dangerous and repetitive offenders. The "three strikes and you're out" approach is a continuation of this theme.

Current correctional technology does not permit us to correctly identify those who require incapacitation. Rather, the evidence is that we would probably incarcerate numerous non-eligibles (a "false positive" problem) and release to lesser control many of those eligible (a "false negative" problem). Whatever benefits might accrue to this sentencing doctrine have thus far eluded corrections.

new goal was the "three-strikes" policy that many states adopted, particularly in California,[3] mandating long-term incarceration (at least 25 years) for those persons convicted of a serious or violent third felony. In addition, retribution as a goal became attractive, inasmuch as it would impose deserved punishment. (Such a "just deserts" strategy looks back to the offender's personal culpability, focuses on the nature of the act, and considers the harm done.)

SENTENCING FAIRNESS

As a result of the sentencing reform movement, sentencing practices were also changed in the belief that such practices would limit disparity and discretion and establish more detailed criteria for sentencing or new sentencing institutions. These contradictory options included:

1. abolishing plea bargaining;
2. establishing plea-bargaining rules and guidelines;
3. setting mandatory minimum sentences;
4. establishing statutory determinate sentencing;
5. setting voluntary or descriptive sentencing guidelines or presumptive or prescriptive sentencing guidelines;
6. creating sentencing councils;
7. requiring judges to provide reasons for their sentences;
8. setting parole guidelines to limit parole board discretion;
9. abolishing parole;
10. adopting or modifying good-time procedures; and
11. routinizing appellate review of sentences (Allen et al., 2018, pp. 91–92).

> **Box 3.9**
> **Sentencing Disparity**
>
> **Sentencing disparity** is the divergence in the types and lengths of sentences imposed for the same crimes, with no evident reason for the differences. It is also known as unequal treatment of similarly situated offenders.

Those options represent only the principal steps designed to limit unbridled discretion under the guise of making sentencing fairer, enhancing justice, and lessening discrimination.

REFORM EFFORTS

Over the past four decades, dramatic changes in sentencing structures and practices thus became evident. Discretionary release by a parole board was abolished in at least 18 states, and parole sentencing guidelines had been established in one-half of the others. This is discussed further in Chapter 5.

In 1987, the U.S. Federal Sentencing Guidelines were promulgated, and today fewer federal offenders are paroled by the U.S. Parole Commission. With traditional parole, most inmates were released through a discretionary process by which a parole board determined if someone should be released. As more and more states moved to a determinate sentencing structure, the number of inmates released on discretionary parole has been considerably smaller than it had been in the past.

<table>
<tr><td>

Box 3.10
Parole Release

Discretionary parole release means that the parole board opted to release an offender before the maximum sentence was met. **Mandatory release** means that the offender had to be released because the maximum sentence (or its equivalent) had been attained. It should be noted that both can imply parole supervision in the community.

</td></tr>
</table>

Today, about 47 percent of inmates are granted discretionary release (Kaeble, 2018), and the method of release varies dramatically from state to state.

Determinate Sentencing

Critics have identified several unwarranted and unwanted problems with indeterminate sentencing, as well as parole board decision making. Reformers, neoclassical theorists, politicians, and organized political action groups with punitive agendas coalesced to attack rehabilitation and parole. The primary substitute for the indeterminate sentence is the determinate sentence, a throwback to the tradition of "flat time" in our earlier history. A determinate sentence is a fixed period of incarceration imposed on the offender by the sentencing court. The ideology underlying determinate sentencing is retribution, just deserts, incapacitation, and selective incapacitation.[4]

Travis and Petersilia (2001) found that 18 states have created sentencing commissions whose guidelines have restricted judicial sentencing discretion, that legislation creating mandatory minimum sentences has been enacted in all 50 states, and that 39 states now have sentencing laws requiring inmates to serve

Table 3.1 Truth-in-Sentencing Requirements by State

Meet Federal 85% requirement	50% of minimum requirement	100% of minimum requirement	Other requirements
Arizona	Missouri	Idaho	Alaska
California	New Jersey	Indiana	Arkansas
Connecticut	New York	Kentucky	Colorado
Delaware	North Carolina	Maryland	
Dist. of Col.	North Dakota	Massachusetts	
Florida	Oklahoma	Nevada	
Georgia	Oregon	New Hampshire	
Illinois	Pennsylvania	Nebraska	
Iowa	South Carolina	Texas	
Kansas	Tennessee		
Louisiana	Utah		
Maine	Virginia		
Michigan	Washington		
Minnesota	Wisconsin		
Mississippi			
Ohio			

Source: Ditton, P., Wilson, D. (1999). *Truth in sentencing in state prisons.* Washington, DC: U.S. Bureau of Justice Statistics.

at least 50 percent of their sentences in prison. Of those 50 states, 25 (including the District of Columbia) have statutes requiring offenders to serve at least 85 percent of their sentence in prison. See Table 3.1 for a list of truth-in-sentencing requirements by state.

Sentencing Guidelines

Some states have decided to structure sentencing by creating sentencing guidelines. Sentencing guidelines for structuring the penalty decisions of judges work by providing decision makers with criteria and weights on which the sanction decision should be based (Hoffman & DeGostin, 1975). By explicitly stating factors deemed relevant to the sentence decision and by providing guidance to the judge or other sentencing authority, these guidelines ensure a greater degree of uniformity in criminal penalties. Explicit sentencing guidelines then work to limit the effect of extralegal factors on the sentencing decision.

> **Box 3.11**
> **Presumptive Sentences**
>
> **Presumptive sentences** are similar to guidelines with minimum, average, and maximum terms: i.e., Aggravating 7 years, Average 5 years, Mitigating 3 years. With this sentencing option, judges can select a term based on the characteristics of the offender as well as mitigating or aggravating factors related to the case.

Such a sentencing structure limits judicial control over sentencing, as the legislature heavily influences the sentence length. Whether there are unforeseen problems in presumptive sentencing remains to be proved, but the Federal Bureau of Prison's population problems may well be due to a corollary of presumptive sentencing: abolition of the parole board early release authority that has been used to control prison overcrowding in the past (the Federal Bureau of Prisons is now the largest single prison system in the world).

Mandatory prison-term statutes now exist in all states. Those statutes apply for certain crimes of violence and for habitual criminals, and the court's discretion in such cases (regarding, for example, probation, fines, and suspended sentences) has been eliminated by statute. In some states, imposition of a prison term is constrained by sentencing guidelines, such as those shown in Figure 3.1. Guidelines are usually set by a governor's commission, including a cross-section of the state population. As noted by a major study (Coleman & Guthrie, 1988):

> A sentencing commission in each state monitors the use of the guidelines and departures from the recommended sentences by the judiciary. Written explanations are required from judges who depart from guideline ranges. The Minnesota Sentencing Guidelines Commission states that "while the sentencing guidelines are advisory to the sentencing judge, departures from the presumptive sentences established in the guidelines should be made only when substantial and compelling circumstances exist." Pennsylvania sentencing guidelines stipulate that court failure to explain sentences deviating from the recommendations "shall be grounds for vacating the sentence and resentencing the defendant." Furthermore, if the court does not consider the guidelines or inaccurately or inappropriately applies them, an imposed sentence may be

> vacated upon appeal to a higher court by either the defense or the prosecution.
>
> (Coleman & Guthrie, 1988, p. 142)

Box 3.12
Mandatory Minimum Sentences

A **mandatory minimum sentence** means that a person convicted of a crime must be imprisoned for a minimum term, as opposed to leaving the length of the punishment up to a judge.

The range and particular format for sentencing guidelines can include such things as specifically worded statutes and grids with a range of judicial options. Similarly, parole guidelines are sometimes closely prescribed, and sometimes wide discretion is afforded to the parole board. The amount of flexibility in such decisions can directly enhance or detract from the efforts to relieve crowded prison conditions. Because most parole decisions are not based on time, but on perceived "risk to the community," tighter and tighter criteria make it difficult to manage prison population size by such decisions.

Three-Strike Laws

No discussion of sentencing changes would be complete without exploring **"three-strikes" sentencing laws**. Although sentence enhancement statutes exist in most states (such as habitual or repeat offender laws), legislation that specifically identified a group of repeat offenders for lengthy incapacitation began to bloom in 1993 when Washington became the second state to enact three-strike legislation.[5] Currently, 27 states and the federal government have enacted so-called three-strikes laws, all designed to remove offenders convicted of repeated serious offenses

Offender: ______________________ Docket number: __________

Judge: ______________________ Date: __________

Offense(s) convicted of: ______________________

____

Crime score:

A. Injury
 0 = No injury
 1 = Injury
 2 = Death ________ +

B. Weapon
 0 = No weapon
 1 = Weapon
 2 = Weapon present and used ________ +

C. Drugs
 0 = No sale of drugs
 1 = Sale of drugs ________ = [ ]

Crime score

Figure 3.1 Sentencing Guidelines *(continued)*

Offender score:
  A. Current legal status
      0 = Not on probation/parole, escape
      1 = On probation/parole, escape   _____   +
  B. Prior adult misdemeanor convictions
      0 = No convictions
      1 = One conviction
      2 = Two or more convictions   _____   +
  C. Prior adult felony convictions
      0 = No convictions
      2 = One conviction
      4 = Two or more convictions   _____   +
  D. Prior adult probation parole revocations
      0 = None
      1 = One or more revocations   _____   +
  E. Prior adult incarcerations (over 60 days)
      0 = None
      1 = One incarceration
      2 = Two or more incarcerations   _____   =

                                                                      Offender
                                                                      score

Guideline sentence: _____

Actual sentence: _____

Reasons (if actual sentence does not fall within guideline range): _____

_____

Crime score

4–5	4–6 years	5–7 years	6–8 years	8–10 years
3	3–5 years	4–6 years	6–8 years	6–8 years
2	2–4 years	3–5 years	3–5 years	4–6 years
1	Probation	Probation	2–4 years	3–5 years
0	Probation	Probation	Probation	2–4 years
	0–1	2–4	5–7	8–10

Offender score

The sentencing judge first determines the crime score, typically concerned
with the actual crime, injury, weapon used, and drug sale. Points are assigned
as above under "Crime score." Second, the judge scores the offender's prior
behavior, using those items identified under "Offender score." Determining the
guideline sentence entails finding the grid cell that corresponded to the crime
and offender score, and then imposing a sentence that falls within the suggested
range.

Figure 3.1 Continued

Source: Kress, J., Calpin, J.C., Gelman, A.M., Bellows, J.B., Dorworth, B.E., Spaid, O.A. (1978).
Developing sentencing guidelines: Trainers handbook. Washington, DC: National Institute of
Criminal Justice.

from society for a long period of time, if not for life. In California, for example, the minimum sentence under three-strikes legislation was 25 years, with no "good-time" credit. Time served was no less than 25 years. As might be expected, some unusual cases have arisen in California. For example, one defendant was given a 25-years-to-life sentence for shoplifting golf clubs (with previous convictions for burglary and robbery with a knife). In one particular notorious case, Kevin Weber was sentenced to 26-years-to-life for stealing four chocolate chip cookies after two previous convictions (Ellingwood, 1995). California also enacted a two-strikes law that doubled the presumptive sentence. In 2000, however, California voters supported an amendment to provide drug treatment instead of life imprisonment for most offenders convicted of possessing drugs; and in 2012, voters passed an amendment that required the third felony to be either "violent" or "serious" in order for a 25-years-to-life sentence to be passed. See Table 3.2 for a list of states that enacted some sort of three-strikes sentencing law.

Table 3.2 States That Have Some Sort of a Three-Strikes Sentencing Law

State	Year adopted
Arizona	2006
Arkansas	1995
California	1994
Colorado	1994
Connecticut	1994
Florida	1995
Georgia	1994
Indiana	1994
Kansas	1994
Louisiana	1994
Maryland	1994
Massachusetts	2012
Montana	1995
Nevada	1995
New Jersey	1995
New Mexico	1994
North Carolina	1994
North Dakota	1995
Pennsylvania	1995
South Carolina	1995
Tennessee	1994
Texas	1974
Utah	1995
Vermont	1995
Virginia	1994
Washington	1993
Wisconsin	1994

There are many critics of three-strikes legislation and there is little evidence that three-strikes laws contributed significantly to reductions in crime rates. In 2015, the Supreme Court in *Johnson v. United States* curtailed the use of three-strike laws and a number of states have subsequently narrowed the criteria upon which these laws are based.[6]

A NEW ERA HAS BEGUN

This review of the changes in sentencing practices and their consequences clearly shows the shifts that have taken place. Although discretion in determining sentence length has been somewhat removed from the sentencing judge and parole board, it was reduced by legislatures through their enactment of new sentencing structures. In turn, in many jurisdictions, the prosecutor's discretion was increased.[7] Recently, a number of states have sought to reduce their prison populations and have enacted legislation designed to lessen the punishment for certain types of offenses. Table 3.3 presents a brief description of what several states have recently done to change their sentencing laws. Many of these changes would have been unthinkable just a couple of years ago, but as more and more states grapple with the ever-increasing costs of incarceration, they have sought sentencing changes to reduce the number of offenders in prison and, in some cases, have reduced sentence lengths.

While we often think of probation or prison when we think about sentencing options, jails also play an important role, and when it comes to sentencing, are widely used in conjunction with community corrections.

Table 3.3 Examples of What Some States Are Doing to Change Sentencing Laws

California: Expanded parole and alternatives to prison for eligible incarcerated person

Connecticut: Reclassified felony drug possession as a misdemeanor

Maine: Reclassified certain drug possession offenses from felonies to misdemeanors

Maryland: Scaled back certain mandatory minimums for drug offenses

Montana: Created Sentencing Commission

Nebraska: Abolished the death penalty and authorized prison population reduction measures

North Dakota: Authorized judicial departures for certain drug mandatory minimums and reclassified certain felony penalties to misdemeanors

Oklahoma: Expanded judicial discretion for certain offenses, modified sentence reduction policy and scaled back life without parole for certain offenses

Texas: Reformed felony property thresholds

Source: Porter, N. D. (2016). *The state of sentencing 2015: Developments in policy and practice.* Washington, DC: The Sentencing Project.

Box 3.13
California Public Safety Realignment

On May 23, 2011, the U.S. Supreme Court upheld the ruling by a lower three-judge court that the State of California must reduce its prison population to 137.5 percent of design capacity (approximately 110,000 prisoners) within 2 years to alleviate overcrowding. In response, the California State Legislature and governor enacted two laws—AB 109 and AB 117—to reduce the number of inmates housed in state prisons starting October 1, 2011.

The Public Safety Realignment (PSR) policy is designed to reduce the prison population through normal attrition of the existing population while placing new non-violent, non-serious, non-sex offenders under county jurisdiction for incarceration in local jail facilities. Inmates released from local jails will be placed under a county-directed post-release community supervision program instead of the state's parole system. The state is giving additional funding to the 58 counties in California to deal with the increased correctional population and responsibility; however, each county must develop a plan for custody and post-custody that best serves its needs.

THE JAIL

The local detention facility, usually administered by a county law enforcement agency, is generally known as the "jail." There are nearly 3,400 jails across the nation, housing more than 740,000 persons in 2016 (Zeng, 2018). Jails incarcerate a wide variety of people. Jails receive individuals pending arraignment and hold them awaiting trial, conviction, and sentencing. They also readmit probation, parole, and bail-bond violators, and absconders, as well as temporarily detaining juveniles pending transfer to juvenile authorities. Further, they hold mentally ill persons pending their movement to appropriate health facilities, as well as individuals for the military, for protective custody and contempt, and for the court as witnesses.[8] In addition, jails release convicted inmates to the community upon completion of their sentence and transfer inmates to state, federal, and other local authorities. They temporarily incarcerate convicted felons sentenced to prisons but for whom there are no bed spaces (Minton & Golinelli, 2014), and relinquish custody of temporary detainees to juvenile and medical authorities (Beck & Karberg, 2001). Finally, they sometimes operate community-based programs such as **work release** programs and other alternatives to incarceration and hold inmates sentenced to short terms (generally under 1 year) (see Table 3.4). It is small wonder that local jails admitted 10.6 million persons in a 12-month period ending in 2016 (Zeng, 2018).

Table 3.4 Persons under Jail Supervision, 2016

Confinement status and type of program	Number
Total	758,700,700
Held in jail	704,500
Supervised outside of a jail facility[a]	52,200

Note: [a]Excludes persons supervised by a probation or parole agency.

Source: Zeng, Z. (2018). *Jail inmates 2016.* Washington, DC: U.S. Department of Justice, Bureau of Justice Statistics.

Split Sentences

While jail is a common sanction for those sentenced on a misdemeanor, frequently, sentencing judges impose a short term of incarceration in the local jail to be followed by a term of probation. For example, the **split sentence** (jail plus probation) is the most frequently imposed sentence for felony convictions in California (Lundgren, 2001).

A variation on "jail plus" is weekend confinement. To lessen the negative impacts of short-term incarceration and allow offenders to retain current employment, as well as keep their dependants off welfare rolls, some jurisdictions permit sentences to be served during non-working weekends. Such weekend confinement allows offenders to check into the jail facility on Friday after work and to leave on Sunday morning, sometimes early enough to attend religious services. A "weekender" serving his or her sentence over a number of months would generally be credited with 3 days of confinement per weekend. Some jurisdictions have so many "weekenders" that specific buildings are set aside for their short-term detention. In larger jurisdictions, in which sufficient numbers of offenders work on weekends, but not every day during the ordinary working week, those buildings operate all week but at reduced staffing levels.

> **Box 3.14**
> **Jail**
>
> A **jail** is a confinement facility, usually administered by a local law enforcement agency, intended for adults, that holds persons detained pending adjudication and/or persons committed after adjudication for sentences usually of 1 year or less.

> **Box 3.15**
> **Felony versus Misdemeanor**
>
> A **felony** is a more serious offense, and for those incarcerated, usually involves a sentence of 1 year or more. A **misdemeanor** is a less serious charge and usually involves a sentence of less than 1 year, usually in a local jail facility. Some states, like Texas, sentence some lower-level felons to a jail facility.

SUMMARY

The primary mission of the correctional system is protection of the public. Programs must be designed with that objective in mind or they will be doomed to early failure and public rejection. What seems to be needed is a system that offers as many alternatives to incarceration as are possible for the individuals who appear to have some hope of benefitting from them and who will present little, if any, danger to the community. The residual population may be required to remain in more secure institutions until new interventions can be found for them. The prison, in a modified form, has a valuable place in a correctional system for the estimated 15 to 20 percent of the convicted offenders who require this level of control. For most convicted offenders, however, the use of either partial or total alternatives to imprisonment is a more reasonable and less costly response than is incarceration.

Prisons should be the "last choice" of sentencing judges faced with the difficult decision of how to manage the offenders before them and how best to attain the correctional objective being sought. Judges are increasingly turning to "tourniquet sentencing" as a promising strategy for determining those sanctions.

Whatever good prisons do is difficult to measure, but the damage done is detected easily. If our objective is the protection of society from criminal recidivism, long-term strategies must be developed. If we are determined to control offenders and lower the costs of over-incarceration, it will become necessary to develop a system of community corrections that includes extensive program alternatives and increasing levels of control over the offender in the arms of the law. Developing an effective community corrections program will require formulating social policy that requires handling local problems in the community, setting priorities for control of crime, and making resources available to develop and maintain the proposed system. Probation is one of the major elements in such a system.

Review Questions

1. Compare past sentencing practices to more contemporary ones.
2. What is the difference between a determinate and an indeterminate sentence?
3. What alternatives to incarceration can help alleviate jail crowding?
4. What are sentencing guidelines?
5. How is the jail the center of community corrections?
6. What are the main purposes of imprisonment?
7. What are alternatives to "bricks and mortar" as a solution to prison overcrowding?
8. How do prisons eventually contribute to the workloads of community corrections?
9. Does your state use determinate or indeterminate sentencing?
10. What is a split sentence?
11. What are some of the causes given for rapid changes in the U.S. sentencing laws?

Notes

1   Some historians argue that the noble ideals of rehabilitation were never really implemented and that the "convenience" of punishment won out over the "conscience" of rehabilitation. See Rothman, D. (1980), *Conscience and convenience: The asylum and its alternatives in progressive America* (Boston, MA: Little, Brown). See also Irwin, J., Schiraldi, V., Ziedenberg, J. (2000), "America's one million non-violent prisoners," *Social Justice* 27(2), 135–147.

2   See the following: Kopel, D. (1994), *Prison blues: How America's foolish sentencing policies endanger public safety* (Washington, DC: Cato Institute; Tonry, M. (1999), "Parochialism in United States sentencing policy," *Crime and Delinquency* 45(1), 48–65; The Sentencing Project (2011), "The Sentencing Project submits letter to the U.S. Sentencing Commission recommending future priorities," at https://www.sentencingproject.org/issues/felony-disenfranchisement/; James, N. (1995), *Disparities in processing felony arrests in New York State* (Albany:

New York State Division of Criminal Justice). See also Chung, J. (2013), "Felony disenfranchisement," at www.sentencingproject.org/publications/felony-disen franchisement-a-primer/; *The Economist* (2013), "Prison reform: An unlikely alliance of left and right," at https://www.economist.com/united-states/2013/08/17/ an-unlikely-alliance-of-left-and-right; Gest, T. (2001), *Crime and politics* (Oxford: Oxford University Press); Mayeux, S. (2015), "The unconstitutional horrors of prison crowding," *Newsweek*, at www.newsweek.com/unconstitutional- horrors-prison-overcrowding-315640

3   California recently revised its law to impose life sentences only when the new felony conviction is "serious or violent."

4   Roche, D. (1999), "Mandatory sentencing: Trends and issues," *Australian Institute of Criminology* 138(1), 1–6.

5   Texas is credited with being the first state to enact such a law in 1974 with a mandatory life sentence.

6   King, R., Mauer, M. (2002), *State sentencing and corrections policy in an era of fiscal restraint* (Washington, DC: The Sentencing Project).

7   Austin, J., Clark, J., Hardyman, P. (1999), "The impact of 'Three strikes and you're out'," *Punishment and Society* 1(2), 131–162; Burt, G., Wong, S., Vander Veen, S. (2000), "Three strikes and you're out," *Federal Probation* 64(2), 3–6.

8   The "material" witness detained in jail to ensure his or her presence at trial is a seldom-studied actor in the justice system; hence, little is known about this category of jail inmate.

Recommended Readings

Clear, T. (1994). *Harm in American penology: Offenders, victims, and their communities*. Albany: State University of New York Press.

Irwin, J., Austin, J. (1997). *It's about time: America's imprisonment binge*. Belmont, CA: Wadsworth.

Petersilia, J. (2003). *When prisoners come home: Parole and prisoner reentry*. New York: Oxford University Press.

Rothman, D. (1980). *Conscience and convenience: The asylum and its alternatives in progressive America*. Boston, MA: Little, Brown.

Travis, J. (2000). *But they all come back: Rethinking prisoner reentry*. Washington, DC: National Institute of Corrections.

References

Allen, H.E., Latessa, E.L., Ponder, B. (2018). *Corrections in America: An introduction*. Upper Saddle River, NJ: Pearson Prentice Hall.

Beck, A., Karberg, J. (2001). *Prison and jail inmates at midyear 2000*. Washington, DC: U.S. Bureau of Justice Statistics.

Coleman, S., Guthrie, K. (1988). *Sentencing effectiveness in preventing crime*. St. Paul, MN: Criminal Justice Statistical Analysis Center.

Ditton, P., Wilson, D. (1999). *Truth in sentencing in state prisons*. Washington, DC: U.S. Bureau of Justice Statistics.

Durose, M.R., Langan, P. A. (2007). *Felony sentences in State Courts, 2004* (NCJ 215646). Washington, DC: U.S. Department of Justice.

Ellingwood, K. (1995, October 28). Three-time loser gets life in cookie theft. *Los Angeles Times*, pp. 1–28.

Hoffman, P., DeGostin, L. (1975). An argument for self-imposed explicit judicial sentencing standards. *Journal of Criminal Justice* 3, 195–206.

Johnson v. United States, 135 S. Ct. 2551 (2015).

Kaeble, D. (2018). *Correctional populations in the United States, 2016*. Washington, DC: U.S. Department of Justice, Bureau of Justice Programs.

Kress, J., Calpin, J.C., Gelman, A.M., Bellows, J.B., Dorworth, B.E., Spaid, O.A. (1978). *Developing sentencing guidelines: Trainers handbook*. Washington, DC: National Institute of Criminal Justice.

Lundgren, D. (2001). *Crime and delinquency in California, 2000: Advance release*. Sacramento, CA: Department of Justice.

Minton, T.D., Golinelli, D. (2014). *Jail inmates at midyear 2013*. Washington, DC: U.S. Department of Justice, Bureau of Justice Statistics.

Porter, N.D. (2016). The state of sentencing 2015: Developments in policy and practice. Washington, DC: The Sentencing Project.

Travis, J., Petersilia, J. (2001). Re-entry reconsidered: A new look at an old question. *Crime & Delinquency* 47(3), 291–313.

Zeng, Z. (2018). *Jail inmates 2016*. Washington, DC: U.S. Department of Justice, Bureau of Justice Statistics.

Chapter 4

Probation in America

Key Terms

Cesare Beccaria
community work orders
conditions of probation
community service
individualized justice
intermittent incarceration
John Augustus
Killits decision
pre-sentence investigation report

probation
probationer fees
restitution
revocation
selective incapacitation
sentencing hearings
shock probation
split sentences
victim impact statement

I can forgive, but I cannot forget, is only another way of saying, I will not forgive. Forgiveness ought to be like a canceled note—torn in two, and burned up, so that it never can be shown against one. —Henry Ward Beecher

Probation. *[Photo courtesy of Jeff McShan]*

In many respects, probation is a way of giving an offender another chance. Probation represents one of the unique developments within the criminal justice system; it provides a mechanism to divert offenders from deeper penetration into the correctional system while still maintaining some oversight over the offender. To really understand the role that probation plays in community corrections today (and tomorrow), it is important to understand why probation started and how it has evolved from its early years. This chapter is split into three sections. The first will examine how probation, both for adults and for juveniles, was formed, why it was formed, and the initial purpose of probation. The second section of this chapter focuses on the current role of probation, and how probation functions currently. The third section describes the state of the evidence in regard to the effectiveness of probation.

Probation is a conditional sentence that diverts the offender from jail or prison and allows him or her to remain in the community in exchange for following a set of conditions. While on probation, the offender is neither incarcerated nor without supervision. Supervision by a probation officer is almost always a condition of release. Probation's staff, known generally as probation officers, monitor a set of rules, called conditions, and report back to the court when the offender has either completed their term of probation or, in some cases, when the offender violates the conditions of probation.

As indicated by the National Advisory Commission on Criminal Justice Standards and Goals (1973), the term probation can refer to a type of sentence, but also refers to the services provided to those individuals once placed on probation. As a type of sentence, it relates to the status of an offender; an offender is on probation. Those individuals who are on probation are neither in jail nor prison. They are considered under the control of the court through a term of community supervision. The term probation also refers to the agency or organization that administers the probation supervision. As part of probation supervision, agencies perform a myriad of tasks, including but not limited to, completing assessments, submitting reports for the court, supervising probationers, and providing services for those serving probation. These activities are undertaken by the probation officer as a part of his or her regular duty.

Box 4.1
Definition of Probation: Adults

Probation is a sentence in which an offender is ordered to follow a set of rules or conditions in exchange for remaining in the community. Ultimately, the sentencing court maintains authority to modify the conditions of probation or to impose sanctions, which could include revoking probation and ordering the offender to either jail or prison for the remaining time of the original sentence.

While the functions and services that probation agencies offer have remained relatively consistent throughout the years, the population they serve has shifted significantly over the past 100 years. Initially, as Reed (1997) notes, probation was designed to serve safe risks to the community: lower-risk offenders who are good "bets," meaning individuals, who when given a second chance, will self-correct and refrain from future criminal behavior. This rationale for the use of probation has been clearly stated by Dressler:

> the assumption that certain offenders are reasonably safe risks in society by the time they appear in court; it would not facilitate their adjustment to remove them to institutions, and the move might well have the opposite effect. Meantime, the community would have to provide for their dependents. And the effect of such incarceration upon the prisoner's family would be incalculable. If, then, the community would not be jeopardized by a defendant's presence, and if he gave evidence of ability to change to a law-abiding life, it served both society and the individual to give him the chance, conditionally, under supervision and guidance.
>
> (Dressler, 1962, p. 26)

As the criminal justice system's reach widened during the late 1980s/early 1990s with "get tough" policies like mandatory minimums and three-strikes laws, the type and number of offenders under supervision changed significantly. Between 1990 and 2005, the probation population rose 55.9 percent with the largest jump between 1995 and 2000. In 2005, the probation population ultimately topped 4 million— nearly 1 in 53 adults were under some level of community supervision (Table 4.1). Since 2005, the probation population has begun to decrease slowly. Once focused on lower-risk offenders, the system has begun to refocus its efforts to serve higher-risk individuals in an effort to reduce incarcerated populations. To best understand where probation is headed, we must first explore how it got here.

Table 4.1 Probation Population 1990 to 2016

Year	Probation Population	% Change
1990	2,670,234	–
1995	3,044,531	14.0
2000	3,839,400	26.1
2005	4,162,300	8.4
2010	4,055,900	−2.6
2015	3,789,800	−6.6

Source: Adapted from Kaeble, D. (2018). *Probation and parole in the United States, 2016.* Washington, DC: U.S. Department of Justice, Bureau of Justice Statistics.

FOUNDERS OF PROBATION

While probation was not an official sentence until 1878, there were many early examples of supervision in lieu of incarceration. Dressler (1962, pp. 12–13) cites the 1841 activities of Matthew Davenport Hill of Birmingham, England, as one of the earliest documented examples of probation. In Warwickshire, Hill observed that, in the case of youthful offenders, magistrates often imposed token sentences of 1 day with the special condition that the defendant remain under the supervision of a guardian. The purpose of this was to divert young offenders, who otherwise would have gone to prison, out of the system and place them under the supervision of a guardian. Once Hill became a magistrate, he modified this procedure suspending the sentence of young offenders and placed the offender on supervision. Hill's program has some of the same elements as Augustus's method (discussed later in this section): hand pick "low-risk" cases, hand out suspended sentences, and offer diversion from prison. While this opportunity was afforded to a select set of offenders, Hill was also ready to take action against any repeat offenders he considered a risk to the community and revoke the diversion opportunity. In fact, Hill often requested that the superintendent of police investigate the conduct of persons placed under a guardian's supervision.

In the United States, one of the earliest proponents of "probation" in lieu of incarceration was Judge Peter Oxenbridge Thacher of Boston. The first documented example of probation in the United States, Judge Thacher allowed defendants to defer sentence and remain in the community as long as they reported to court upon summons. In these situations, a defendant remained in limbo until the defense or prosecution decided to bring the charges back to court, inevitably making the original court supervision period indefinite. In 1878, based partly on Judge Thacher's ruling in the *Commonwealth v. Jerusha Chase*, Massachusetts passed legislation to allow for a sentence of probation to be ordered as long as local law enforcement provided a probation officer to supervise the offenders.

Although probation was not officially recognized by Massachusetts until 1878, it was a court volunteer, **John Augustus**, who is most often given credit for the establishment of probation in the United States. Augustus first appeared in police court in Boston when he stood bail for a man charged with drunkenness and then helped the offender to find a job. The court ordered the defendant to return in 3 weeks, at which time he demonstrated great improvement. Instead of incarcerating this individual, the judge imposed a 1-cent fine and ordered the defendant to pay costs.

From this modest beginning, Augustus proceeded to bail out numerous offenders, supervising them and offering guidance until they were sentenced. Over an 18-year period (from 1841 until his death in 1859), Augustus "bailed on probation" 1,152 men and 794 women (Barnes & Teeters, 1959, p. 554). He was motivated by his belief that "the object of the law is to reform criminals and to prevent crime and not to punish maliciously or from a spirit of revenge" (Dressler, 1962, p. 17). Augustus obviously selected his candidates carefully, offering assistance to first-time offenders and those who were deemed rehabilitable.

He also considered the

> previous character of the person, his age and influences by which he would in the future be likely to be surrounded and, although these points were not rigidly adhered to, still they were the circumstances which usually determined my action.
>
> (United Nations, 1976, p. 90)

In addition, Augustus provided his charges with aid in obtaining employment, an education, or a place to live, and also made an impartial report to the court. The task was not without its frustrations, as Augustus noted:

> While it saves the country and state hundreds and I might say thousands of dollars, it drains my pockets instead of enriching me. To attempt to make money by bailing poor people would prove an impossibility. The first two years of my labor I received nothing from anyone except what I earned by my daily labor.
>
> (quoted in Barnes & Teeters, 1959, p. 554)

His records on the first 1,100 individuals whom he bailed out revealed that only one forfeited bond (Dressler, 1962). It is also important to note that virtually every basic practice associated with probation was initiated by Augustus, including the idea of a pre-sentence investigation, supervision conditions, case work, reports to the court, and revocation of probation supervision (Petersilia, 1997). When Augustus died in 1859, he was destitute—a most unfitting end for a humanitarian visionary.

PHILOSOPHICAL BASES OF PROBATION

The purpose of the criminal justice system often mirrors the current socio-political climate. Based loosely on English law, the United States' criminal justice system was designed to punish offenders for their crimes and to deter others from doing the same. As public support waned for harsh punishment and public shaming, the criminal justice system began to restructure penalties to balance the level of the offense with the offender's criminal history. It was a development influenced by contemporary European thought. In a larger sense, probation is an extension of these newer Western European philosophical arguments about the functions of criminal law and how offenders should be handled and punished. The older, harsher punishment philosophy was born out of the practices of kings, emperors, and other rulers of Europe who focused on the crime and attempted to treat all crimes equally. They viewed the purposes of criminal law as a way to punish, to deter others, and to seek revenge and vengeance for violations of the "king's peace." Widespread use of the death penalty, torture, banishment, public humiliations, and Probation resulted from "disturbing the king's peace."

In the eighteenth century, French philosophers created a controversy by focusing on liberty, equality, and justice. Famous French philosophers and lawyers attempted to redefine the purpose of criminal law in an effort to find some way to make the criminal justice system of their age more attuned to the humanitarian ethos of the Age of Enlightenment. A major figure of the time was **Cesare Beccaria**, a mildly disturbed Italian genius who only left his country once, when invited to visit Paris to debate with the French philosophers.

When Beccaria (1764/1963) published his classic work, *Essay on Crimes and Punishments*, he established the "Classical School" of criminology, which attempted to reorient the law toward more humanistic goals. This would include not torturing the accused in order to extract confessions, no secret indictments and trials, the right to defense at a trial, improvement of the conditions of imprisonment, and so on. His work focused on the offense and not on the offender. He believed that punishment should fit the crime. His work was widely read throughout Europe and even attracted the attention of Catherine the Great, the Russian empress, who invited Beccaria to revise Russian criminal law. Unfortunately, he never took her up on her offer.

The philosophical ferment of the period quickly spread to England and, from there, to the colonies. When the United States emerged from the Revolutionary War (1775–1783), the remaining vestiges of the harsher English penal codes were resoundingly abandoned. What emerged was a constitutional system that incorporated the major components of the humanitarian philosophy, along with a populace imbued with a belief in the inherent goodness of humankind and the ability of all persons to rise to their optimal level of perfectibility.

The difference between the earlier approach to handling offenders (public displays of corporal punishment, harsh penalties, and frequently used capital punishments) and the emerging reformation emphasis of the last decade of the eighteenth century lay primarily in (1) the way offenders were viewed, and (2) the focus and intent of the criminal law. Prior to the Revolutionary War, offenders were seen as inherently evil, deserving punishment so that they might "get right with God." In the period after the Civil War (1861–1865), Americans had generally accepted that humankind was inherently good and that crime was a manifestation of societal ills, not individual evils. The Civil War further added to the movement toward democracy, the rise of the reformation movement, and the further individualization of treatment and punishment. Eventually the following question arose: Do all offenders need to be imprisoned in order for them to repent and stop their criminal behavior? It was in this philosophical environment that Massachusetts began to answer the question, specifically in regard to juvenile offenders.

THE GROWTH OF PROBATION

Influenced by Augustus's example, Massachusetts quickly moved into the forefront in regard to juvenile probation. An experiment in providing services for children (resembling probation) was inaugurated in 1869, under the auspices of the Massachusetts State Board of Health, Lunacy, and Charity (Johnson, 1928). A statute enacted in that year provided that when complaints were made in court against a juvenile under 17 years of age, a written notice must be furnished to the state. The state agent was then given an opportunity to investigate, to attend the trial, and to safeguard the interest of the child (equivalent to the modern-day Guardian ad Litem).

Box 4.2
Definition: Guardian ad Litem

Guardian ad Litem (GAL) is an individual, usually not associated with the justice system, who acts in the best interest of the child. Often GALs are the voice of the youth—ensuring that his or her interest is heard and taken into consideration.

Despite the early work of Augustus and others with adult offenders, probation was supported more readily for juveniles. It was not until 1901 that New York passed the first statute authorizing probation for adult offenders, more than 20 years after Massachusetts passed a law for juvenile probation (Lindner & Savarese, 1984). Although the development of probation for adults lagged behind that of juveniles, by 1923, most states had a law authorizing probation for adults (Table 4.2), and by 1956, all states had adopted adult and juvenile probation laws.

DEVELOPMENT OF PROBATION AT THE FEDERAL LEVEL

Although probation quickly became universal in the state-run justice systems, no early specific provision for probation was made for federal offenders, either juvenile or adult. As a substitute, federal courts suspended sentence in instances in which imprisonment imposed special hardships. However, this practice was quickly called into question by legal scholars.

The primary question was: Did federal judges have the constitutional authority to suspend a sentence indefinitely or did this practice represent an encroachment upon the executive prerogative of pardon and reprieve, and was it, as such, an infringement upon the doctrine of separation of powers? This issue was resolved by the U.S. Supreme Court in the *Killits* **decision** (*Ex parte United States* 242 U.S. 27, 1916). In a case from the northern district of Ohio, John M. Killits suspended the 5-year sentence of a man who was convicted of embezzling $4,700 from a Toledo bank. The defendant was a first-time offender with an otherwise good background and reputation who made full restitution for his offense. The bank officers did not wish to prosecute. The government contended that such action was beyond the powers of the court. A unanimous opinion held that federal courts did not have the power to suspend a defendant's sentence indefinitely and it was not appropriate

> to continue a practice which is inconsistent with the Constitution, as its exercise in the very nature of things amounts to a refusal by the judicial power to perform a duty resting upon it and, as a consequence thereof, to an interference with both the legislative and executive authority as fixed by the Constitution.
>
> (*Ex parte United States* 242 U.S. 27, Chief Justice Opinion)

Table 4.2 The Year States Enacted Juvenile and Adult Probation Laws

	Year enacted	
State	**Juvenile**	**Adult**
Alabama	1907	1915
Arizona	1907	1913
Arkansas	1911	1923
California	1903	1903
Colorado	1899	1909
Connecticut	1903	1903
Delaware	1911	1911
Georgia	1904	1907
Idaho	1905	1915
Illinois	1899	1911
Indiana	1903	1907
Kansas	1901	1909
Maine	1905	1905
Maryland	1902	1904
Massachusetts	1878	1878
Michigan	1903	1903
Minnesota	1899	1909
Missouri	1901	1897
Montana	1907	1913
Nebraska	1905	1909
New Jersey	1903	1900
New York	1903	1901
North Carolina	1915	1919
North Dakota	1911	1911
Ohio	1902	1908
Oklahoma	1909	1915
Oregon	1909	1915
Pennsylvania	1903	1909
Rhode Island	1899	1899
Tennessee	1905	1915
Utah	1903	1923
Vermont	1900	1900
Virginia	1910	1910
Washington	1905	1915
Wisconsin	1901	1909

Source: Adapted from Johnson, F. (1928). *Probation for juveniles and adults* (pp. 12–13). New York: Century Co.

However, instead of abolishing this probationary practice, the *Killits* decision actually sponsored its further development. Interested parties interpreted the reversal of the "doctrine of inherent power to suspend sentences indefinitely" to mean that enabling legislation should be passed that specifically granted this power to the judiciary.

At the federal level, the National Probation Association (then headed by Charles Lionel Chute) spearheaded a national campaign to support the legislative creation of probation (Chute & Bell, 1956). While there was general support, the prohibitionists were concerned that the addition of probation would minimize the punishment offered in the Volstead Act.[1]

> What we need in this court is not a movement such as you advocate, to create new officials with resulting expense, but a movement to make enforcement of our criminal laws more certain and swift. . . . In this county, due to the efforts of people like yourselves, the murderer has a cell bedecked with flowers and is surrounded with a lot of silly people. The criminal should understand when he violates the law that he is going to a penal institution and is going to stay there. Just such efforts as your organization is making are largely responsible for the crime wave that is passing over the country today and threatening to engulf our institutions.
>
> (Symes, 1923, as cited in Evjen, 1975)

Objections also arose from the Justice Department. Staff in Attorney General Daugherty's office lamented that the addition of probation would reduce the benefit of prison and would allow for offenders to remain in society freely. Furthermore, the Justice Department's stance on probation was that it would afford criminals rights that they did not deserve and that it would lead to a devaluation of prison.

Approximately 34 bills to establish a federal probation system were introduced in Congress between 1909 and 1925. Despite such opposition, a bill passed on its sixth introduction to the house. The bill was sent to President Coolidge who, as a former governor of Massachusetts, was familiar with the functioning of probation. He signed the bill into law on March 4, 1925. This action was followed by an appropriation to defray the salaries and expenses of a limited number of probation officers (Burdress, 1997; Lindner & Savarese, 1984; Meeker, 1975). Table 4.3 highlights some of the significant events in the development of probation.

Table 4.3 Development of Probation Timeline

Date	Event
Middle Ages	*Parens patriae* established to protect the welfare of the child in England
1841	John Augustus becomes the "Father of Probation"
1869	Massachusetts develops the visiting probation agent system
1875	Society for the Prevention of Cruelty to Children established in New York, paving the way for the juvenile court

(Continued)

Table 4.3 (Continued)

Date	Event
1899	The first juvenile court in America was established in Cook County (Chicago) Illinois
1901	New York passes the first statute authorizing probation for adults
1925	Congress authorizes probation at the federal level
1927	All states but Wyoming have juvenile probation laws
1943	Federal Probation System formalizes the pre-sentence investigation report
1954	Last state enacts juvenile probation law
1956	Mississippi becomes the last state to pass authorizing legislation to establish adult probation
1965	Ohio is the first state to create "shock probation," which combines prison with probation
1967	*In re Gault* decided by the U.S. Supreme Court
1969	Jerome Miller is appointed Youth Commissioner in the State of Massachusetts and begins to de-incarcerate state institutions
1971	Minnesota passes the first Community Corrections Act
1973	National Advisory Commission on Criminal Justice Standards and Goals endorses more extensive use of probation
1974	Congress passes the Juvenile Justice and Delinquency Prevention Act establishing the Federal Office of Juvenile Justice and Delinquency Prevention
	Restorative justice and victim/offender mediation programs begin in Ontario, Canada
1975	The state of Wisconsin receives funding from the Law Enforcement Assistance Administration to develop a case classification system. Four years later, the Risk/Needs Assessment instruments are designed and implemented
1980	American Bar Association issues restrictive guidelines to limit use of pre-adjudication detention
1982	"War on Drugs" begins
1983	Electronic monitoring of offenders begins. Georgia establishes the new generation of Intensive Supervised Probation programs
1984	Congress passes Sentence Reform Act to achieve longer sentences, "just deserts," and equity in sentencing
1989	President Bush displays clear plastic bag of crack on primetime television
1994	American Bar Association issues proposals to counteract the impact of domestic violence on children
1998	National Institute of Corrections begins national correctional training on implementing community restorative justice programs
2000	American Probation and Parole Association issues monograph: *Transforming Probation through Leadership: The Broken Windows Model*

Table 4.3 (Continued)

Date	Event
2001	Evaluation of sex-offender notification on probation in Wisconsin finds high cost to corrections in terms of personnel, time, and budgetary resources
2003	Evaluation of strategies to enforce drug court treatment by aggressive probation officer involvement results in significant drop in drug use in Maryland
2008	Evaluation of strategies to more fully integrate the principles of effective intervention into face-to-face interactions between probation and parole officers and offenders
2009	Probation populations begin to decline for the first time in three decades
2011	Probation populations continue to decline, dropping below four million for the first time in 8 years
2015	Probation departments begin to embrace technology to assist in delivering evidence-based interventions
2017	Harvard's Kennedy School issues "Toward an approach to community corrections for the 21st century," calling for a mass overhaul of community corrections

Source: Compiled by authors.

PROBATION TODAY

Today's probation looks very different from where it started in the nineteenth century. Initially reserved for the "best of the best," probation now serves a significant range of offenders and offers an array of services to address the offender's needs and ensure the community's safety. Table 4.4 illustrates the most serious offense for offenders on probation in 2016. As might be expected, probation tends to be

Table 4.4 Adults on Probation in 2016: Most Serious Offense

Offense	Percent
Sex offense	4
Domestic violence	4
Other violent offense	13
Property offense	26
Drug law violations	24
Driving under the influence	14
Other traffic offenses	2
Other	13

Source: Kaeble, D. (2018). *Probation and parole in the United States, 2016.*
Washington, DC: U.S. Department of Justice, Bureau of Justice Statistics.

granted more prevalently for non-violent offenders, predominantly for property, drug, and DUI crimes. So, what is probation, why is it used so frequently, and what is the process by which so large a proportion of offenders are placed on probation?

OBJECTIVES AND ADVANTAGES OF PROBATION

Probation is an alternative to incarceration that is used most often for non-violent offenders. It provides jurisdictions with front-end alternatives to manage incarcerated populations as well as minimize the potential collateral consequences of prison and jail (Kirk & Wakefield, 2018). While probation is seen as a viable option for offenders, both state and federal jurisdictions have enacted statues that limit the type of offenders who are eligible for probation. While varying widely across jurisdictions, offenders who are not generally eligible for probation include individuals who committed crimes of violence, crimes with a possibility of a life sentence, armed robbery, rape, use of a firearm in a crime, or habitual offenders.

However, despite the existence of legislatively defined exclusions, granting probation is a highly individualized process that usually focuses on the criminal rather than on the crime—opening the door for even violent offenders to have an opportunity to be supervised in the community. The following are the general objectives of probation:

1. reduce reoffending;
2. protect the community from further criminal behavior;
3. provide probation conditions (and services) necessary to change offenders and to achieve the aforementioned objectives.

While probation granting is individualized, judges and corrections personnel generally recognize the advantages of probation:

1. provides the least restrictive intervention to affect change in the offender;
2. fiscal savings over imprisonment;
3. avoidance of imprisonment, which tends to exacerbate the underlying causes of criminal behavior;
4. keeping offenders' families intact;
5. improved outcomes over prison or jail;
6. a sentencing option that can permit "selective incapacitation."

Probation, the most frequent disposition for offenders and widely recognized for its advantages (Dawson, 1990), has also received strong endorsement from numerous groups and commissions, including the prestigious National Advisory Commission on Criminal Justice Standards and Goals (1973), the General Accounting Office (1982), and the American Bar Association (ABA) (1970). The National Advisory Commission recommended that probation be used more extensively, and the ABA endorsed probation as the presumed sentence of choice for almost all non-violent felons. Others have argued (Finn, 1984) that universal use

Post-Conviction	Daily	Monthly	Annually
BOP Facility	$79.16	$2,412.33	$28,948.00
Residential Reentry Centers	$73.78	$2,244.17	$26,930.00
Supervision Probation Officers	$9.17	$220.29	$2,643.50

Figure 4.1 Average Daily Cost per Federal Probationer

Source: Administrative Office of the U.S. Courts (2013). Supervision costs significantly less than incarceration in Federal system. Retrieved from: www.uscourts.gov/news/2013/07/18/supervision-costs-significantly-less-incarceration-federal-system

of probation would reduce prison populations. It is important to remember that prison space is a limited and, some would say, a scarce resource. The economics of corrections are such that probation is essential if the system is going to manage its finite resources effectively (Clear et al., 1989). While costs range considerably, it is clear that the cost per offender for probation supervision is significantly lower than the cost of prison. Even in the federal system, the cost per day for probation officers is $9.17 compared to incarceration at $79.16 a day (see Figure 4.1).

GRANTING PROBATION

While many believe that sentencing is the role of a judge, the actual disposition of the case (sentence) is often determined by the prosecutor and defense attorney. This is because, prior to the determination of guilt, the prosecuting attorney and defense counsel have engaged in a conversation that results in a plea bargain. During this interaction, any (or even all) of the following outcomes may have been negotiated:

1. the defendant's pleading guilty to a lesser crime, but one that was present in the illegal behavior for which the penalty is considerably more lenient;
2. the frequency of the crime ("number of counts") to which the defendant will plead guilty;
3. the number of charges that will be dropped;
4. whether the prosecutor will recommend that the defendant receives probation or be sentenced to incarceration in jail or prison;
5. the recommended length of time (months or years) of incarceration;
6. whether the sentence will be consecutive or concurrent.

It appears that the judiciary tends to accept and acquiesce to the negotiation outcomes (Dixon, 1995; Glaser, 1985). However, in many cases, judges still decide the sentence, of which one alternative may be probation. The process of granting probation begins after the offender either pleads guilty (frequently for favorable personal considerations) or is judged guilty following a trial. For those offenders whose crime falls within the list of probation-eligible offenses, or in those states where it is mandated by law, a pre-sentence investigation will be ordered. One of

> **Box 4.3**
> **Selective Incapacitation**
>
> **Selective incapacitation** refers to a crime control policy of identifying high-risk offenders for incarceration on the premise that, while imprisoned, such offenders would be incapable of committing further criminal acts and may be deterred from illegal behavior when released.

the major functions of a pre-sentence investigation report is to assist the court in determining the most appropriate sentence.

Based on observations of the defendant at trial—including demeanor, body language, evidence of remorse, harm to the victim, and behavior—as well as the recommendation in the pre-sentence reports and the prosecutor's recommendation for sentence, judges determine the appropriate sentence for a particular individual. Judges are aware that **individualized justice** demands that the sentence fit not only the crime but also the criminal.[2] Many of these factors are brought forth in a document called the **pre-sentence investigation report** (PSI).

Perhaps the most important component of the PSI is the recommendation of the probation officer. The role of the pre-sentence report recommendation is a major factor, for the extent of concurrence between the probation officer's recommendations and the judge's sentencing decision is quite strong. Liebermann et al. (1971) found that, when probation was recommended, judges followed that recommendation in 83 percent of cases; Carter (1966) found an even stronger agreement—96 percent of the cases. Liebermann and colleagues (1971) also found that when the recommendation was for imprisonment, the judge agreed in 87 percent of the cases. Macallair (1994) found that defense-based disposition reports for juveniles that recommended probation alternatives consistently lowered commitments to state correctional facilities. So, what is the PSI?

THE PRE-SENTENCE INVESTIGATION REPORT

One of the responsibilities of probation agencies is to assess an offender and provide a report to the court. This includes gathering information about the current offense, victim statement(s), previous probation and technical violations, employment history, information on family and friends, in order to complete the PSI for use in **sentencing hearings**.

The concept of the PSI was developed as the option for probation became more prevalent.[3] Judges originally used probation officers to gather background and personal information on offenders to "individualize" punishment.[4] In 1943, the Federal Probation System formalized the PSI as a required function of the federal probation process. The PSI can have a great deal of significance in the sentencing process. In 2017, 97.2 percent of all federal trials resulted in a guilty plea (United States Sentencing Commission, 2018). Unlike the prosecutor and the defense attorney

New client orientation. *[Photo courtesy of Jeff McShan]*

who have regular contact with the victim(s) and defendant, the judge's knowledge of the defendant is usually limited to the information contained in the pre-sentence report. As Walsh (1985, p. 363) concludes, "judges lean heavily on the professional advice of probation."

In a study of the acceptance of the PSI recommendation, Latessa (1993) examined 285 cases in Cuyahoga County, Ohio (which includes the city of Cleveland). He found that judges accepted the recommendation of the probation department in 85 percent of the cases when probation was recommended and in 66 percent when prison was the recommendation.

As mandatory minimum sentences have become more popular, some jurisdictions report that fewer PSIs are being prepared. However, for others, the PSI remains an important function of probation. For example, in terms of the agency workload, almost one-half (45 percent) of agencies that conduct pre-sentence investigations reported that more than 25 percent of their workloads were devoted to these reports.

Functions and Objectives

The primary purpose of the PSI is to provide the court with succinct and precise information upon which to base sentencing decisions. The PSI is usually ordered when there is a disagreement between the prosecutor and defense attorney on the appropriate sentence (non-agreed recommendation). The disagreement is generally for one of two reasons: Either there is a disagreement between the defense attorney and the prosecutor as to whether probation is appropriate (non-agreed recommendation); or there is a disagreement about the length of sentence. At sentencing, judges usually have a number of options available to them: impose a fine, require restitution, incarcerate, impose community supervision, and so on. The PSI is designed to aid the judge in making the appropriate decision, taking into consideration the needs of the offender as well as the safety of the community.

Over the years, many additional uses have been found for the pre-sentence report. Basically, these functions include the following:

1. aiding the court in determining sentence;
2. determining the length of sentence;
3. assisting correctional authorities in classification and treatment in release planning;
4. giving the parole board useful information pertinent to consideration of parole;
5. aiding the probation officer in rehabilitation efforts during probation.

A PSI includes more than the simple facts about the offense. Effective PSI reports include all objective historical and factual information significant to the decision-making process, an assessment of the character and needs of the defendant and the community, and a sound recommendation with supporting rationale that follows logically from the evaluation (Bush, 1990). A reliable and accurate report is essential, and the officer completing the report should make every effort to ensure that information contained in the PSI is reliable and valid. Generally, information that has not been validated should be indicated.

Content

Like the criminal justice system itself, PSI reports vary significantly across jurisdictions, but there seem to be some common areas that are included. These generally comprise:

1. Offense
   Official version
   Defendant's version
   Co-defendant information
   Statement of witnesses, complainants, and victims
2. Prior record
   Juvenile adjudications
   Adult record
3. Personal and family data
   Defendant
   Parents and siblings
   Marital status
   Employment
   Education
   Health (physical, mental, and emotional)

          Military service
          Financial condition
          Assets
          Liabilities
4. Evaluation
          Alternative plans
          Sentencing data
5. Recommendations.

Basically, these areas of the PSI should be succinct and summarize the data in a useful manner. Carter (1976, p. 9) suggests that "in spite of the tradition of 'larger' rather than 'shorter,' there is little evidence that more is better." This permits flexibility by allowing for expansion of a subject area and increased detail of circumstances as warranted. However, a subsection may be summarized in a single narrative statement.

Carter suggests that it is not necessary to know everything about an offender. Indeed, there is some evidence that in human decision making, the capacity of individuals to use information effectively is limited to five or six items of information. Quite apart from questions of reliability, validity, or even the relevance of the information are the time and workload burdens of collecting and sorting masses of data for decision making. The end result may be information overload and impairment of efficiency.

A sample outline of a PSI from the Harris County Community Supervision and Corrections Department (Houston, TX) is shown in Figure 4.2. During development of the PSI, special attention is also given to seeking innovative alternatives to traditional sentencing dispositions (jail, fines, prison, or probation). In addition to the defendant's information, there has been increased attention given to the victim (Roy, 1994; Umbreit, 1994). Many probation departments now include a section pertaining to the victim as part of their PSI report. An example of a **victim impact statement** from the Harris County Community Supervision and Corrections Department is presented in Figure 4.3. This section includes an assessment of the harm done to the victim, a review of the monetary/resource costs of the crime, and often includes the victim's comments concerning the offense and offender.

Evaluation and Recommendation

As stated previously, two of the most important sections of the PSI are the evaluation and the recommendation. Although the research evidence is mixed, there appears to be a correlation between the probation officer's recommendation and the judge's decision (Hagan, 1975; Walsh, 1985). There is also some evidence that the recommendation section is the section most read by judges.

The evaluation should contain the probation officer's professional assessment of the objective material contained in the body of the report. Having gathered all the facts, the probation officer must now consider the protection of the community

HARRIS COUNTY CSCD PRESENTENCE INVESTIGATION
Evaluation Conducted By: [first name, last name], Community
Supervision Officer

Route to Court _____ Assistant DA _____ Defense Attorney _____ Probation/TDCJ _____

Client Name: **SPN Number:**   **SID Number:**

Date of Birth: **Date of Evaluation:**   **Date of Report:**

Case Number: **Judge:**   **Court:**

Reason for Referral

Disclosures
Procedures, Tests, and Collateral Information

CRIMINAL JUSTICE INVOLVEMENT

Current Offense
[Mr./Ms. Last Name] is currently charged with (INSERT CURRENT CHARGES). The following provides relevant details of the current offense:
- (INSERT SUMMARIZED DETAILS FROM POLICE REPORT)
- (INSERT THE CLIENT'S BRIEF ACCOUNT OF THE ARREST)

Supervision History

Criminal History
The following criminal history was obtained via the NCIC/TCIC criminal history records. Except where noted, the following charges were filed in the jurisdiction of Harris County, Texas.

Date (Most Recent First)	Offense	Outcome

Age of Onset Age _____
Misconduct while incarcerated   Yes/No
Supervision revoked   Yes/No

TRAS Criminal History Domain   **Low/Mod/High**

Education
Highest Education Level
General behavior in school

Figure 4.2 The Harris County Community Supervision and Corrections Department Presentence Report

Source: The Harris County Community Supervision and Corrections Department.

Employment
Current employment
Employment at arrest
Structured time
Stable financial situation

Education, Employment, and Financial Situation Domain Low/Mod/High

Family and Social Support
Parents' engagement in criminal activity
Support received
Level of satisfaction with family
Residential stability

Family and Social Support Domain Low/Mod/High

Neighborhood/Social Setting
General criminal behavior surrounding living environment
Drug availability around surrounding living environment

Neighborhood/Social Setting Domain Low/Mod/High

Substance Abuse
Age of onset
Drug use
Drug use caused general problems in functioning
Drug use caused problems with employment
Drug use impacted social support

Substance	Age First Use	Age/Date Last Use	Pattern of Use Amount/Frequency:		+ UA/ Breathalyzer last 12 months
			Recent	Heaviest	

Substance Abuse Domain Low/Mod/High

Peer Association
Percentage of prosocial/antisocial peers
Plan to avoid contact with past criminal associates
Gang involvement
Criminal activities

Peer Associations Domain Low/Mod/High

Criminal Attitudes and Behavioral Patterns
Criminal beliefs
Concern for others
Maladaptive coping

Figure 4.2 Continued

Self-regulation
Risk seeking
Aggressive personality
Egocentric

Criminal Attitudes and Behavior Patterns Domain Low/Mod/High

Responsivity and Protective Factors
- [BULLETTED LIST OF RESPONSIVITY AND STENGTHS/PROTECTIVE FACTORS]

Recommendations

Respectfully Submitted,

_____   (Date of report)
[first name, last name]   Date

Figure 4.2 Continued

Harris County Community Supervision and Corrections Department

Victim Impact Statement

Name of Defendant: _____   Judge: _____
Case Number: _____   Disposition Date: _____

A. Victim's Statement Regarding Offense
B. Economic Loss Due to Offense
C. Physical Injuries
D. Psychological Impact
E. Desired Outcome in Sentencing

Figure 4.3 Victim Impact Statement

Source: The Harris County Community Supervision and Corrections Department.

and the need of the defendant. First, the probation officer should consider the offense. Was it situational in nature or indicative of persistent behavior? Was violence used? Was a weapon involved? Was it a property offense or a personal offense? Was there a motive?

Second, the community must be taken into consideration. For example, does the defendant pose a direct threat to the safety and welfare of others? Would a disposition other than prison deprecate the seriousness of the crime? Is probation a sufficient deterrent? What community resources are available?

Finally, the probation officer has to consider the defendant and his or her special problems and needs, if any. What developmental factors were significant in contributing to the defendant's current behavior? Was there a history of antisocial behavior? Does the defendant acknowledge responsibility or show remorse? Is the defendant motivated to change? What strengths and weaknesses does the defendant possess?

Is the defendant employable or supporting any immediate family? The probation officer should also provide a statement of sentencing alternatives available to the court. This does not constitute a recommendation, but rather informs the court which services are available should the defendant be granted probation.

A sound recommendation is the responsibility of the probation officer. Some alternatives may include the following:

Anger management programs	Restitution
Cognitive behavioral groups	Fine
Probation	Mandatory drug treatment
Work release	House arrest/electronic monitoring
Incarceration	Community service
Split sentence	Psychiatric treatment
Shock probation	Day fines
Halfway house	Victim mediation
Family counseling	Shock incarceration
Day reporting	No recommendation

If incarceration was recommended, the probation officer would indicate any problems that may need special attention on the part of the institutional staff. In addition, if the defendant were considered a security risk, the investigator would include escape potential, as well as any threats made to or received from the community or other defendants. Regardless of the recommendation, the probation officer has the responsibility to provide a supporting rationale that will assist the court in achieving its sentencing goals.

Factors Related to Sentencing Decisions

As mentioned previously, the PSI involves a great deal of a probation department's time and resources. The pre-sentence report is the primary comprehensive source of information about the defendant available to the sentencing judge. Although most judges agree that the PSI is a valuable aid in formulating sentencing decisions, there appear to be some differences of opinion about the value of the recommendations section of the report.[5]

Several studies have attempted to identify those factors that appear to be of primary importance to sentencing judges. Carter's 1976 survey found that the two most significant factors were the defendant's prior criminal record and the current offense. An earlier study by Carter and Wilkins (1967) found that the most important factors for judges in making a decision to grant probation included the defendant's educational level, average monthly salary, occupational level, residence, stability, participation in church activities, and military record. But, again, when factors were ranked according to their importance in the sentencing decision, the current offense and the defendant's prior record, number of arrests, and number of commitments were ranked most important. Welch and Spohn (1986) also concluded that prior record clearly predicts the decision to incarcerate; however, their research suggests that a wide range of indicators have been used to determine "prior record," but that the safest choice to use is prior incarceration.

In another study, Rosecrance (1988, p. 251) suggests that the PSI report serves to maintain the myth that criminal courts dispense individualized justice. His conclusions are "that present offense and prior criminal record are the factors that determine the probation officer's final sentencing recommendation." Rosecrance (1985) also believes that probation recommendations are designed to endorse prearraigned judicial agreements and that probation officers structure their recommendations in the "ball park" in order to gain judicial acceptance. Rogers (1990) argues, however, that the pre-sentence investigation individualizes juvenile justice.

In another study, Latessa (1993) examined both the factors that influenced the probation officer's recommendation, as well as the actual judicial decision. He found that offenders were more likely to be recommended for prison if they were repeat offenders, had committed more serious offenses, there was a victim involved, and if the offender had a prior juvenile record. Factors that influenced the actual sentencing decision included the recommendation, drug history, mental health history, seriousness of offense, and having been incarcerated previously in a state prison. Latessa concluded that in this jurisdiction, sentencing factors were based mainly on offense, prior record, and the presence of a victim. It is important to note that demographic factors, such as race, sex, and age, did not play a factor in either the recommendations or the decisions of the judges.

CONDITIONS OF PROBATION

When probation is granted, the court may impose certain reasonable conditions on the offender, which the probation officer is expected to monitor during the supervision period. The **conditions of probation** must not be capricious and may be both general (required of all probationers) and specific (required of an individual probationer). General conditions include obeying laws, submitting to searches, reporting regularly to the supervising officer, notifying the officer of any change in job or residence, and not being in possession of a firearm, or associating with known criminals, refraining from excessive use of alcohol, and not leaving the court's jurisdiction for long periods of time without prior authorization.

Specific conditions are generally tailored to the needs of the offender or philosophy of the court. For reintegration or other such purposes, the court may impose conditions of medical or psychiatric treatment; residence in a halfway house or residential center; intensive probation supervision, electronic surveillance, house arrest, community service, or active participation in a drug abuse program; restitution or victim compensation; no use of illegal drugs (such as cocaine or marijuana); observing a reasonable curfew; staying out of bars; group counseling; vocational training; or other court-ordered requirements. Such required conditions are specifically designed to assist the probationer in the successful completion of probation. An example of standard conditions of probation from a district court is presented in Figure 4.4.

Conditions of Probation

HARRIS COUNTY COMMUNITY SUPERVISION AND CORRECTION DEPARTMENT

Standard Felony Conditions of Probation

On this the __ day of _____, the defendant being granted __ community supervision for the felony offense of _____ in accordance with section 5 of Article 42.12 of the Texas Code of Criminal Procedure is hereby ordered to abide by all of the following conditions and terms of community supervision during the period of supervision. Specifically, you shall:

1. Commit no offense against the laws of this or any other State or of the United States. You are to report any arrests within 24 hours upon release.
2. Not use, possess, or consume any illegal drug or prescription drug not currently prescribed to you by a medical professional. You shall bring all current prescription bottles to your Community Supervision Officer to have them documented. If new medication is prescribed, you must bring the new prescription bottle by your next scheduled report date.
3. Report to the Community Supervision Officer as directed for the remainder of the supervision term unless so ordered differently by the Court.
4. Abide by the rules and regulations of the Harris County Community Supervision and Corrections Department (hereinafter referred to as HCCSCD).
5. Permit a Community Supervision Officer to visit you at your home, place of employment or elsewhere.
6. Work at suitable employment and/or attend school full-time. Present either verification of employment or provide a log of all attempts to secure employment to your Community Supervision Officer as directed. You must notify HCCSCD of any change in your employment status by your next scheduled reporting date.
7. Remain within Harris County or any counties directly touching Harris County. You may not travel outside these locations unless you receive prior written permission from the Court through your Community Supervision Officer.
8. Notify HCCSCD by your next report of any change in residence.
9. Submit a non-diluted, valid, unaltered sample upon request for the purpose of alcohol/drug monitoring at the request of the HCCSCD.
10. Participate in the HCCSCD Community Service Restitution Program (CSRP). You shall perform __ hours as directed by HCCSCD CSRP policy. Hours must be completed 60 days prior to termination.

Figure 4.4 Conditions of Probation and Supervised Release, Harris County.

Source: Harris County Community Supervision and Correction Department.

(Continued)

11. Submit to a screening and/or assessment through HCCSCD Assessment Unit by _____ and participate in any program recommended based upon the assessment until successfully completed or until further order of the court.

12. Submit to an evaluation of your educational skill level by _____. If it is determined that you have not attained the average skill of students who have completed the sixth grade in public schools in this State, you shall participate in a program that teaches functionally illiterate persons to read. If you are non-English speaking, you will participate in English as a Second Language (ESL) program, if it is determined there is a need in order for you to meet the state mandate beginning upon referral until successfully discharged or released by further order of the Court.

13. Support your dependents as required by law. Provide your Community Supervision Officer with a certified copy of all court orders requiring payment of child support.

14. Not ship, transport, possess, receive, or purchase a firearm, altered firearm, or ammunition, or attempt to ship, transport, possess, receive, or purchase a firearm, altered firearm, or ammunition.

15. Report in person to HCCSCD to provide a DNA sample to the Department of Public Safety at the direction of and through HCCSCD for the purpose of creating a DNA Record by _____ unless a sample has already been submitted under other state law.

16. Pay the following fees through HCCSCD. All payments MUST be in the form of a Money Order, Cashier's Check or credit card. Credit card can be used to submit online payments at http://www.go2gov.net/go/hccscd. A $2.00 transaction fee will be charged by HCCSCD to process each payment.

17. Pay a Supervision Fee at the rate of (xx) per month for the duration of your community supervision beginning _____to HCCSCD.

18. Pay a fine of_____ and court costs of _____ at the rate of _____ per month beginning_____ to Harris County through HCCSCD.

19. Pay a donation of _____ to (drop down of options) by_____ through HCCSCD.

Figure 4.4 Continued

Probation Fees

As part of the conditions of probation, many jurisdictions have included **probation fees** as both a means of accountability as well as a way to fund services. Fees are levied for a variety of services, including the preparation of pre-sentence reports, electronic monitoring, ignition interlock devices, work-release programs, drug counseling and testing, and regular probation supervision (Lansing, 1999; Ring, 1988). Fees range anywhere from $10 to $120 per month, with the average estimated to be about $32 per month. The imposition of supervision fees has increased dramatically over the years (Baird et al., 1986; Camp & Camp, 2003; Lansing, 1999). In addition, some states, such as Ohio, now require probation officers to assist in collecting child support payments from parents under probation supervision.

Critics of probation fees argue that it is unfair to assess a fee to those most unable to pay. Others argue that probationer fees will result in a shift from treatment and surveillance to fee collection, which in turn will turn probation officers into bill collectors.

Others, however, believe that probation fees can be a reasonable part of the probation experience (Wheeler, Macan et al., 1989; Wheeler, Rudolph et al., 1989). Harlow and Nelson (1982, p. 65) point out that successful fee programs serve a dual purpose: "both an important revenue source and an effective means of communicating to the offender the need to pay one's own way."[6]

It appears that probation fees are rapidly becoming a fixture in probation. Not only are they a means of raising revenue and offsetting the costs of supervision, treatment, and surveillance, but they can also be used as a form of punishment (or to promote responsible behavior depending on your viewpoint). Where fees have become a necessity to fund probation services, there is a growing concern that probation is only for those who can afford it and that individuals who do not have the financial means are otherwise revoked.

Restitution and Community Service

Two more recent but related trends in conditions the court may impose are restitution and community service orders. **Restitution** requires the offender to make payment (perhaps monetary) to a victim to offset the damages done in the commission of the crime. If the offenders cannot afford to repay at least a part of the loss suffered by the victim, it is possible to restore the victim's losses through personal services. Probation with restitution thus has the potential for being a reparative sentence, and Galaway (1983) argues that it should be the penalty of choice for property offenders. Restitution can lessen the loss of the victim, maximize reconciliation of the offender and community, and marshal community support for the offender, perhaps through enlisting a community sponsor to monitor and encourage the offender's compliance. A good example of this can be seen in California, where in 1982, voters passed a victim's bill of rights. Part of this initiative was a crime victim restitution program that enables the court to order offenders to repay victims and the community through restitution or community service (see van Dijk et al., 1999).

Community service as a condition of probation appears to be used increasingly in conjunction with probation, particularly if there are no direct victim losses or the nature of the crime demands more than supervised release. Examples of community service would include requiring a dentist convicted of driving while intoxicated to provide free dental services to a number of indigents or ordering a physician to provide numerous hours of free medical treatment to jail inmates, perhaps on Saturday mornings. More often, offenders are ordered to work for community agencies that provide social services to the general public, engaging in litter removal, cutting grass, painting public buildings or the homes of elderly people. Both restitution and **community work orders** can serve multiple goals: offender punishment, community reintegration, and reconciliation. The four reasons cited most commonly for using community service are as follows:

1. It is a punishment that can fit many crimes.
2. The costs of imprisonment are high and are getting higher.
3. Our jails and prisons are already full.
4. Community service requires an offender to pay with time and energy.

ALTERNATIVE PROBATION PROCEDURES

In addition to the most frequent procedures described earlier, there are six other variations of granting probation that need to be discussed before we consider the legal process of revoking the probation of those who cannot or will not abide by court-imposed conditions of liberty in the community:

1. prosecutorial diversion;
2. court-monitored pretrial diversion without adjudication;
3. shock probation;
4. intermittent incarceration;
5. split sentences;
6. modification of sentence.

While probation is imposed most frequently by a trial judge after a guilty plea or trial, it may also replace the trial completely, in which case it is called "pretrial intervention." In practice, the process embraces two separate programs: one operated by the prosecutor (a form of deferred prosecution); and the other by the judge in that limited number of jurisdictions in which state legislation permits a bifurcated process (determining guilt, followed by adjudication as a felon). Both result in supervision but are vastly different.

Prosecutorial Pretrial Intervention

Part of the broad power accorded a prosecutor in the United States is the ability to offer the accused deferred prosecution. In those programs in which the prosecutor grants deferred prosecution, the accused will generally be asked to sign a contract accepting moral (but usually not legal) responsibility for the crime and agreeing to make victim restitution, to undergo specific treatment programs (substance abuse, methadone maintenance, anger management, etc.), to report periodically to a designated official (usually a probation officer), and to refrain from other criminal acts during the contract period. If these conditions are satisfied, the prosecutor dismisses (*nolle prosequi*) the charge. If the accused does not participate and cooperate actively in the program, the prosecutor can, at any time during the contract period, carry the case forward to trial.

Probation by Withholding Adjudication

This process refers to a judge's optional authority available in those states (such as Florida) where statutes permit a bifurcated process: First determine guilt and then declare the defendant a convicted felon. By refraining from declaration of a guilty felon, the judge can suspend the legal process and place the defendant on probation for a specific time period, sometimes without supervision being required (a "summary" or non-reporting probation). Thus, the judge gives the offender a chance to demonstrate his or her ability and willingness to adjust and reform. The offenders know that they can still be returned to court for adjudication of guilt and sentencing, and frequently imprisonment.

The advantages of this option fit squarely in the general philosophy of probation and may be of particular use in intimate-partner assaults (Canales-Portalatin, 2000). Not only is treatment in the community emphasized, but the collateral benefits are also considerable:

> [The judge] places him or her on probation without requiring him to register with local law enforcement agencies as a previously convicted felon; without serving notice on prospective employers of a previous conviction; without preventing the offender from holding public office, voting, or serving on a jury; without impeding the offender from obtaining a license that requires "reputable character"; without making it more difficult than others to obtain firearms; in short, without public or even private degradation.
>
> (Allen et al., 1981, pp. 361–362)

Combining Probation and Incarceration

There are a number of alternatives to placing an offender on probation, other than **shock probation**, that include a period of incarceration (Parisi, 1980). Generally, judges will order an individual to serve a short term of jail, up to 6 months, and then place them on probation upon release.

Combinations of probation and incarceration include the following:

- **Split sentences:** where the court specifies a period of incarceration to be followed by a period of probation (Parisi, 1981).
- Modification of sentence: where the original sentencing court may reconsider an offender's prison sentence within a limited time and change it to probation.
- **Intermittent incarceration:** where an offender on probation may spend weekends or nights in jail (Bureau of Justice Statistics, 1997).

PROBATION REVOCATION

The judge usually imposes the conditions that must be observed by the offender while on probation and has absolute discretion and authority to impose, modify, or reject these conditions. Some examples of conditions a judge might impose are routine urine testing to detect drug use and abuse, participation in a substance abuse program if the probationer has an alcohol or other drug problem, driving limits, restitution to victims of the probationer (but probation may not be revoked if the offender cannot make payments because of unemployment [*Bearden v. Georgia*, 1983]),[7] and not leaving the court's jurisdiction without prior approval. Many cases have challenged the conditions that courts might impose, but case law has determined that any condition may be imposed if it is constitutional, reasonable, clear, and related to some definable correctional goal, such as rehabilitation or public safety. These are difficult to challenge and leave the court with broad power and tremendous discretion in imposing conditions. Such discretion has contributed to the volume of civil rights lawsuits (del Carmen, 1985).

Once placed on probation, offenders are supervised and assisted by probation officers who are increasingly using existing community agencies and services to provide individualized treatment based on the offender's needs. Assuming that the offender meets the court-imposed conditions, makes satisfactory progress in resolving underlying problems, and does not engage in further illegal activities, probation agencies may request the court to close the case. This would terminate supervision of the offender and probation. Probation may also be terminated by completion of the period of maximum sentence or by the offender having received "maximum benefit from treatment." Table 4.5 shows the various ways that adult offenders terminated probation in 2016. Fortunately, most offenders completed their term of probation successfully.

In supervising a probationer, officers should enforce the conditions and rules of probation pragmatically. In doing so, they should consider the client's individual needs, the understanding of the probationer, and the potential effects of enforcing rules on a client's future behavior and adjustment (Koontz, 1980). Because many clients have alcohol and other drug problems, they may be tested for substance abuse.

Probationers vary in their ability to comply with imposed conditions, some of which may be unrealistic, particularly those that require extensive victim restitution or employment during an economic period of high unemployment (Smith

Table 4.5 Reasons for Termination from Probation in 2016

Type of Exit	Percent
Completion	50
Incarceration	12
Absconder	3
Other Unsatisfactory	14
Other	5
Unknown or not reported	16

Source: Kaeble, D. (2018). *Probation and parole in the United States, 2016.* Washington, DC: U.S. Bureau of Justice Statistics.

> **Box 4.4**
> **Technical Violation of Probation**
>
> A technical violation refers to an infraction of a court order, often in the form of a probation condition. It is generally not considered a new crime *per se*, but can be used by the probation officer to bring an offender back in front of the judge. An example of a technical violation would be failure of a probationer to meet with his or her probation officer as scheduled. Technical violations can lead to the revocation of probation and the imposition of incarceration or another sanction.

et al., 1989). Some probationers are also indifferent or even hostile, unwilling, or psychologically unable to cooperate with their probation supervisor or the court. Others commit technical violations of court orders that are not new crimes *per se*, but are seen as links to future illegal activity. In these circumstances, probation officers must deal with technical probation violations in a way that brings the probationer back into compliance.

Probation officers, charged with managing such cases, may determine that technical violators need a stern warning or that court-imposed conditions should be tightened (or relaxed, depending on individual circumstances). These determinations may lead to an offender's reappearance before the court for a warning or redefinition of conditions. Judges and probation officers, ideally, collaborate in such cases to protect the community or increase the probability of successful reintegration. Offenders are frequently returned to probation, and supervision and treatment continue.

If the warning and new conditions are not sufficient, if the offender repetitively violates conditions of probation or is arrested for an alleged new crime, a probation revocation hearing may be necessary. If the probationer is not already in jail for the alleged new crime, a warrant may be issued for his or her arrest. It is also clear that technical violations can be a major source of failures in probation and that rates can vary considerably from jurisdiction to jurisdiction.

A probation **revocation** hearing is a serious process, posing potential "grievous loss of liberty" for the offender. Both probation officers and judges vary considerably as to what would constitute grounds for revoking probation and re-sentencing to imprisonment. Punitive probation officers may contend that technical violations are sufficient for revoking probation; judges may believe that the commission of a new crime would be the only reason for revocation.

Revocation and Legal Issues

Probation is a privilege, not a right (del Carmen, 1985). This was decided in *United States v. Birnbaum* (1970).[8] Once probation is granted, however, the probationer has an interest in remaining on probation. The due process rights of probationers at a revocation hearing were generally ignored until 1967, when the U.S. Supreme Court issued an opinion regarding state probationers' rights to counsel at such a hearing (*Mempa v. Rhay,* 1967). This case provided the right to counsel if probation was revoked under a deferred sentencing statute, but this decision did not specify that a court hearing was required. That issue was resolved in *Gagnon v. Scarpelli* (1973), a landmark case in due process procedures in probation. The U.S. Supreme Court ruled that probation cannot be withdrawn (revoked) unless certain basic elements of due process are observed. If a court is considering removing the offender from probation (through a "revocation" hearing), the following rights and procedures must ensue: The probationer must (1) be informed in writing of the charge against him or her, (2) have the written notice in advance of the revocation hearing, and (3) attend the hearing and be able to present evidence on his or her own behalf. The probationer also has a right (4) to challenge those testifying against him or her, (5) to confront witnesses and cross-examine them, and (6) to have legal counsel present if the charges are complicated or the case is so complex that an ordinary person would not be able to comprehend the legal issues.[9]

The probation officer is responsible for seeing that conditions imposed by the court are met and, if not, for calling violations to the attention of the court. As such, the probation officer functions both as a helper and as a supervisor of the probationer. Legal liability is greater for the probation officer than the court; although an agent of the court, the probation officer does not enjoy the absolute immunity from liability that the court enjoys.

Some areas of potential liability for the probation officer include acts taken or protective steps omitted. For example, a probation officer may be liable for failing to disclose a probationer's background to a third party if this results in subsequent

---

Box 4.5
Modifications of Conditions of Sentence

Probation officers supervise clients assigned by sentencing courts and, during the period of community release, may find that certain probationers refuse to abide by the court-imposed rules or that their clients' personal circumstances change so markedly that additional court direction may be needed.

If the client has difficulty accepting the legitimacy of community control, probation officers may recommend additional surveillance or treatment options. These range from imposing house arrest to electronic monitoring or daily surveillance by the officer. Clients may also be required to reside in a residential setting, such as a halfway house, or appear daily at a day-reporting program until their behavior or circumstances change.

Increasing the requirements for conformity to court-ordered liberty is frequently referred to as "tourniquet sentencing." Conditions may be relaxed as behavior improves.

serious injury or death. Case decisions have generally held that the probation officer should disclose the past behavior of the probationer if he or she is able to reasonably foresee a potential danger to a specific third party. This would include an employer hiring a probationer as an accountant in a bank when the instant crime was embezzlement, or hiring a child molester to work in a grade school position. Insurance for certain liabilities can be obtained from the American Correctional Association.[10]

As a counselor to probationers, probation officers are often faced with the problem of encouraging their clients to share their problems and needs. Frequently, during the monthly contact, a probationer will reveal involvement in criminal activities. Under these non-custodial circumstances, probation offers are required to warn the probationer against self-incrimination through *Miranda* warnings[11] or the evidence cannot be used in a court of law. Any discussion with a probationer under detention circumstances must be preceded by *Miranda* warnings. Litigation is so extensive within the probation area that the probation officer must frequently take an active role as a law enforcement officer rather than a helper, a sad development from the original role John Augustus initiated and correctional personnel usually pursue.

PROBATION EFFECTIVENESS

As with other correctional services, the availability of quality research on the effectiveness of probation is limited. Making it difficult to evaluate, (1) probation can be found at local, state, and federal levels; (2) there are municipal and county probation departments; probation (as with parole) often combines other sanctions and programs (such as electronic monitoring, referral to treatment programs, halfway houses, day reporting, etc.); (3) probation serves both misdemeanants and felons; and (4) probation is often combined with other types of interventions (e.g., treatment programs). These make it very difficult to conduct research in probation and to tease out the independent effects. The shortage of research gives us a limited sense of the true picture of the effectiveness of probation as a standalone intervention.

The research on probation effectiveness is divided into five groups: studies that (1) compare the performance of offenders receiving alternative dispositions; (2) simply measure probation outcome without comparison with any other form of sanction; (3) measure probation outcome and then attempt to isolate the characteristics which tend to differentiate between successful and non-successful outcomes; (4) examine the cost-effectiveness of probation; and (5) examine probation combined with therapeutic drug courts.

Probation versus Alternative Dispositions

One means of identifying if probation is effective is to compare those who are sentenced to probation to individuals who were sentenced to an alternative disposition. In this first section, we explore how well probation stacks up against prison.

Early research regarding the effectiveness of probation services suggests that people serving probation had lower recidivism rates than those who were sentenced to prison (see Babst & Mannering, 1965; Vito, 1978). While the previous studies focused on a range of offenders, Mitchell et al. (2017) examined the impact of prison specifically on felony drug offenders. They compared re-incarceration rates for individuals with drug offenses who were sentenced to prison, local jail, or probation. Overall, they found drug offenders who were sentenced to prison had similar re-incarceration rates as those who were sentenced to jail and probation. As they disaggregated the types of offenses that led to the re-incarceration, they found that those who were sentenced to probation committed significantly fewer drug offenses than those who were originally sentenced to prison.

More recently, Caudy et al. (2018) compared the effectiveness of probation to local incarceration (jail) for males and females in a large urban county. They found that men who were sentenced to jail, controlling for criminal history, risk, and demographic factors, reoffended at a rate 2.4 times higher than those who received probation. Similarly, women who were sentenced to jail were 2.17 times more likely to be rearrested than those sentenced to probation. Even more interestingly, they found that low-risk males who served jail time were 2.48 times more likely to be arrested than those who were placed on probation, while high-risk males who served jail time were 3.31 times more likely to be arrested. Ultimately, Caudy et al. (2018) concluded that jail, controlling for criminal risk, had significant criminogenic effects over probation as an alternative sentence for low-risk offenders and provided no deterrent effect for higher-risk offenders.

These studies illustrate that probation, as a disposition, appears to be more effective than incarceration, even for short periods of time, especially for first-time offenders. This may be due, in part, to the fact that probationers immediately return to the community, their jobs, and their families—avoiding the iatrogenic effects of incarceration. While probation is more effective than incarceration, it is important to understand the differences within probation as well.

Probation with Treatment

In a large-scale study of probation and community correctional programs, Lowenkamp et al. (2006) examined community correctional programs, including intensive supervision probation, day-reporting centers, and electronic monitoring programs, and found that programs which targeted higher-risk offenders and provided treatment and services were more effective than those that did not. Specifically, higher-risk offenders who were identified, targeted, and given increased services experienced significant reductions in recidivism compared to those receiving minimal interventions. Table 4.6 and Figure 4.5 illustrate these findings. They also examined the quality of the programming, and found that high-quality supervision programs had the most effect on recidivism. Figure 4.6 shows that poorly designed and implemented probation programs actually

Table 4.6 Type of Community Supervision Program Did Not Matter: Four Factors Were Significantly Related to Outcome

- Proportion of higher-risk offenders in program (at least 75% of offenders in programs were moderate- or high-risk)
- Level of supervision for higher-risk offenders (high-risk offenders averaged longer periods of supervision than low-risk offenders)
- More treatment for higher-risk offenders (at least 50% more time spent in treatment)
- More referrals for services for higher-risk offenders (at least three referrals for every one received by low-risk [offenders])

Source: Lowenkamp, C.T., Pealer, J., Smith, P., Latessa., E.J. (2006). Adhering to the risk and need principles: Does it matter for supervision-based programs? *Federal Probation,* 70(3), 3–8.

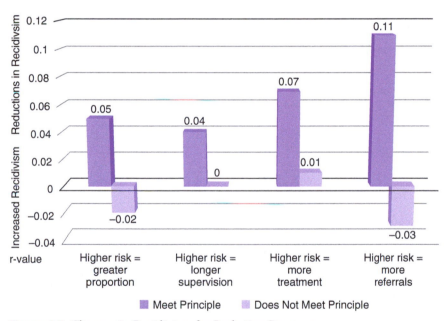

Figure 4.5 Changes in Recidivism for Probation Programs

Source: Lowenkamp, C. T., Pealer J., Smith, P., Latessa, E. J. (2006). Adhering to the risk and need principles: Does it matter for supervision-based programs? *Federal Probation* 70(3), 3–8.

increased recidivism while high-quality, well-implemented programs were the most effective.

Lowenkamp and his colleagues (2010) also examined the effects of the philosophy of the probation department (control-oriented or service-oriented) and found that the most effective probation departments were those that had a rehabilitation orientation. Figure 4.7 shows these results.

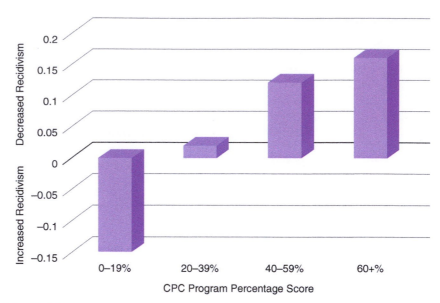

Figure 4.6 Program Integrity—Relationship between Program Integrity Score and Treatment Effect for Community Supervision Programs

Source: Lowenkamp, C.T., Latessa, E.J. (2005). *Evaluation of Ohio's CCA Programs.* Cincinnati, OH: Center for Criminal Justice Research, University of Cincinnati.

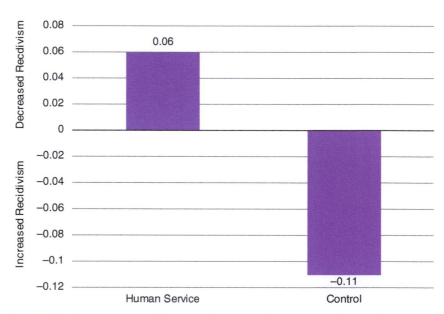

Figure 4.7 Changes in Recidivism by Probation Department Philosophy

Source: Lowenkamp, C., Flores, A., Holsinger, H., Makarios, M., Latessa, E. (2010). Intensive supervision programs: Does program philosophy and the principles of effective intervention matter? *Journal of Criminal Justice* 38, 368–375.

Probation Outcome and Statistics

In addition to measuring the effectiveness of probation, a number of studies have also attempted to isolate characteristics that could be related to offender rehabilitation. Keeping in mind the methodological differences among the studies in terms of definition of failure and specification of follow-up period, it appears that the one characteristic found to be associated most commonly with failure is the probationer's previous criminal history. Other factors frequently cited are the youthfulness of the probationer, marital status other than married, unemployment, and educational level below 11th grade.

Factors such as employment and education are dynamic factors that are correlated with outcome. Because these areas can be addressed during supervision, one can reasonably view these factors positively; we have a clear indication of offender needs, and they can be improved with appropriate intervention. However, a question remains as to whether probation officers are addressing these needs adequately. When probation agencies fail to meet offender needs that are correlated with outcome, the result is often higher failure rates.

COST-EFFECTIVENESS

While the public has demanded tougher sentences, it has become increasingly apparent that the cost associated with more incarceration and prison construction is astronomical. Estimates place the cost of constructing a maximum-security prison at approximately $100,000 per bed, and while the annual cost of maintenance and housing inmates varies from state to state, average costs are more than $31,000 per year per inmate and range from $14,603 in Kentucky to $60,076 in New York (Henrichson & Delaney, 2012). While the construction boom of the 1990s has slowed considerably, 371 new prisons have opened since 1991 (Camp & Camp, 2003), and prison space remains a scarce resource. Many states have re-examined their love affair with incarceration, and many legislators have grown reluctant to vote for new prison construction. Recently, the Bureau of Justice Assistance teamed up with the Pew Research Center and the Council of State Governments (CSG) to fund a Justice Reinvestment initiative. The CSG describes justice reinvestment as a data-driven approach to improve public safety, reduce corrections and related criminal justice spending, and reinvest savings in strategies that can decrease crime and reduce recidivism. There have been 29 states that have gone through justice reinvestment with CSG. Because of the increasingly high cost associated with incarceration, researchers have begun to focus on the cost-effectiveness of alternatives.

In light of these factors, and in addition to research aimed at measuring effectiveness in terms of recidivism, there have been attempts to demonstrate the cost-effectiveness of probation. Typically, with criminal justice agencies, costs are usually divided into three types: processing, program, and client-centered. Processing costs include monies spent in identifying and selecting individuals for a given program. Program costs are expenditures associated with incarceration and include direct costs, such as loss of earnings, and indirect costs, such as the psychological effects of alienation/prisonization, social stigma, and other detrimental effects upon the prisoner's marriage and family (Nelson, 1975).

Similarly, benefits generated by probation could include savings to society through the use of diversion (maintaining people in the community safely), while generating wages and taxes from the participants, and reduced crime or recidivism rates (Vito & Latessa, 1979). In addition, there are the costs associated with failure, such as the monetary loss, cost of new case processing, and grief experienced by the victims.

Studies that provided the most thorough financial comparisons were those that treated the cost–benefit analysis as their primary focus and considered direct and indirect costs and benefits.

In a review of seven cost–benefit analysis studies conducted on correctional alternatives, Welsh and Farrington (2000) found that for each dollar spent on programs, the public received a return of $1.13 to $7.14 in various savings. Likewise, Cohen (1998) determined the monetary value of saving a high-risk youth at between $1.7 million and $2.3 million. In a recent study comparing community placement of juveniles versus residential or institutional placement, Latessa et al. (2014) found that Ohio saved between $13.60 and $40.40 for every $1.00 spent on community programming instead of placing a youth in a residential or state facility. Perhaps the best examples of cost–benefit analyses are conducted by the Washington State Institute of Public Policy. Over the years they have examined a wide range of programs and calculated the cost savings from selected correctional programs based on expected reductions in recidivism rates (see Table 4.7).

Table 4.7 Cost–Benefit of Selected Correctional Interventions

Program	Benefit to cost ratio*
Correctional education in prison	$19.65
Vocational programs in prison	$13.23
Mental health courts	$6.76
Risk, need, responsivity supervision (high/moderate-risk offenders)	$3.73
Sex-offender treatment in the community	$8.18
CBT for high- and moderate-risk offenders	$24.76
TC** in the community	$4.76
Work release	$11.20
Outpatient intensive drug treatment in community	$10.87
Intensive supervision with treatment	$1.57
Intensive supervision (surveillance only)	$0.59
Drug courts	$1.26
Domestic violence treatment	$4.61

Note: *Denotes return for every dollar spent. For example, for every dollar spent on mental health courts, taxpayers received $6.76. Conversely, for every dollar spent on intensive supervision without treatment, taxpayers received only 59 cents.
**Therapeutic Community.

Source: Adapted from Washington State Institute for Public Policy: Adult Criminal Justice. Data available at www.wsipp.wa.gov/BenefitCost.

SUMMARY

This chapter began by tracing historical, philosophical, and legal developments in the field of probation over the past two centuries. While John Augustus is given credit as the "father" of probation, we have seen that many others played an important part in developing and shaping probation. Probation continues to serve the bulk of adult offenders. This chapter also described court options and procedures for placing offenders on probation, as well as some issues in supervising offenders. It should be obvious that probation requires a judge to weigh the "individualization" of treatment as well as the "justice" or "just deserts" associated with the crime that was committed. In addition, this chapter examined the pre-sentence investigation report. Because the PSI is one of the primary responsibilities of probation agencies, its importance is highlighted by the fact that the vast majority of defendants plead guilty and their only contact with the judge is during sentencing.

Finally, the imposition of conditions, and the probation officer's monitoring of offenders' behavior, are important parts of the probation process. Accordingly, revoking probation is not an action that is taken lightly, as it often results in the incarceration of the offender. Granting probation and supervising probation clients are complicated procedures requiring considerable skill and dedication, issues that are also raised in granting parole.

Review Questions

1. How did philosophical precursors of probation contribute to its development?
2. Why was probation established much earlier for juvenile offenders than for adult offenders?
3. Define probation.
4. Should probation be the disposition of choice for most non-violent offenders?
5. What are the general objectives of probation?
6. Describe the advantages of probation.
7. How is justice individualized?
8. What functions does the pre-sentence investigation serve?
9. What is the potential value of a victim impact statement?
10. Identify and define five supervision conditions that might be included in the PSI recommendation.
11. List five conditions of probation generally required of all probationers.
12. What are three grounds for revoking probation and sentencing to incarceration?
13. List five possible sentencing recommendations that can be made.
14. Explain why probation revocation rates might be higher in rural versus urban areas.

Notes

1 The Volstead Act authorized the enforcement of anti-alcohol legislation—the "Great Experiment" of the Thirteenth Amendment to the U.S. Constitution. As Evjen (1975, p. 5) has demonstrated, letters from judges to Chute clearly denounced the practice of probation.

2 Some evidence shows that sentencing is in part influenced by judges' personal goals, such as potential for promotion to a higher court (Cohen, 1992; Macallair, 1994).

3 For a thorough discussion of early development of the PSI, see The Presentence Report (1970).

4 See Sieh (1993).

5 For example, in Cincinnati, Ohio, a single probation department serves both the municipal court and the court of common pleas, yet each court requires a different PSI. The court of common pleas does not permit probation officer recommendations to be included in the report, but the municipal court requires them.

6 For a description of the Texas Program, see Finn and Parent (1992).

7 10 461 U.S. 660 (1983).

8 421 F.2d 993, *cert. denied,* 397 U.S. 1044 (1970).

9 411 U.S. 778, 93 S. Ct. 1756 (1972).

10 The current mailing address for the American Correctional Association is 4380 Forbes Boulevard, Lanham, MD 20706–4322 (www.aca.org).

11 *Miranda* warnings: (1) that the suspect has the right to remain silent; (2) that any statement he does make may be used as evidence against him; (3) that he has a right to the presence of an attorney; and (4) that if he cannot afford an attorney, one will be appointed for him prior to any questioning if he so desires.

Recommended Readings

California Department of Corrections Rehabilitation. (2013). *2011 Public Safety Realignment: The cornerstone of California's solution to reduce prison overcrowding, costs, and recidivism.* Sacramento, CA: California Department of Corrections and Rehabilitation. Retrieved from www.cdcr.ca.gov/About_CDCR/docs/Realignment-Fact-Sheet.pdf [This report provides a good review of the efforts to reduce the prison footprint while resetting the resources available to probation.]

Columbia University Justice Lab. (2018). *Too big to succeed: The impact of the growth of community corrections and what should be done about it.* Available at: http://justicelab.iserp.columbia.edu/img/Too_Big_to_Succeed_Report_FINAL.pdf [Provides a forward examination of the issues associated with probation.]

Dressler, D. (1962). *Practice and theory of probation and parole.* New York: Columbia University Press. [A cogent and well-documented analysis of the historical development of probation.]

Gill, C.E. (2014). Intensive probation and parole. In: G. Bruinsma & D. Weisburd (Eds.), *Encyclopedia of criminology and criminal justice*. New York: Springer. [A good overview of intensive supervision.]

Gowdy, V. (1993). *Intermediate sanctions*. Washington, DC: U.S. Department of Justice. [An excellent overview of the range of intermediate punishments and the issues surroundingthem.]

Jones, M., Johnson, P. (2012). *History of criminal justice*. 5th ed. Waltham, MA: Elsevier (Anderson Publishing). [Now available from Routledge. This book provides a history of criminal justice and probation and examines the philosophy of individualized justice.]

Lindner, C., Savarese, M. (1984). The evolution of probation: Early salaries, qualifications and hiring practices; The evolution of probation: The historical contributions of the volunteer; The evolution of probation: University settlement and the beginning of statutory probation in New York City; The evolution of probation: University settlement and its pioneering role in probation work. *Federal Probation* 48(1–4). [This four-part series examines the early rise of probation in the United States.]

Lowenkamp, C.T., Latessa, E.J. (2005). *Evaluation of Ohio's CCA Programs*. Cincinnati, OH: Center for Criminal Justice Research, University of Cincinnati.

Lucken, K. (2017). *Rethinking punishment*. London: Routledge. [This book provides a good review of punishment and how it applies to the current role of corrections.]

Rothman, D. (1980). *Conscience and convenience: The asylum and its alternatives in progressive America*. Boston, MA: Little, Brown. [Chapter 3 provides a critical assessment of the early use of probation and development of the pre-sentence investigation.]

References

Allen, H., Friday, P., Roebuck, J., Sagarin, E. (1981). *Crime and punishment*. New York: The Free Press.

American Bar Association. (1970). *Project standards for criminal justice: Standards relating to probation*. New York: Institute of Judicial Administration.

Babst, D., Mannering, J. (1965). Probation versus imprisonment for similar types of offenders. *Journal of Research in Crime and Delinquency* 2(2), 60–71.

Baird, C., Holien, D., Bakke, J. (1986). *Fees for probation services*. Washington, DC: National Institute of Corrections.

Barnes, H., Teeters, N. (1959). *New horizons in criminology*. Englewood Cliffs, NJ: Prentice-Hall.

Bearden v. Georgia, 461 U.S. 660 (1983).

Beccaria, C. (1764). *Essay on crimes and punishments*. Indianapolis, IN: Bobbs-Merrill (H. Paulucci, trans., 1963).

Burdress, L. (1997). The federal probation and pretrial services system. *Federal Probation* 61(1), 5–111.

Bush, E.L. (1990). Not ordinarily relevant? Considering the defendant's children at sentencing. *Federal Probation* 5(1), 15–22.

Camp, C., Camp, G. (2003). *Corrections yearbook: Adult corrections 2002*. Middletown, CT: The Criminal Justice Institute.

Canales-Portalatin, D. (2000). Intimate partner assailants. *Journal of Interpersonal Violence* 15(8), 843–854.

Carter, R. (1966). It is respectfully recommended. *Federal Probation* 30(2), 38–40.

Carter, R. (1976). *Prescriptive package on pre-sentence investigations* (unpublished draft). Washington, DC: Law Enforcement Assistance Administration.

Carter, R., Wilkins, L. (1967). Some factors in sentencing policy. *Journal of Criminal Law, Criminology and Police Science* 58(4), 503–514.

Caudy, M., Skubak Tillyer, M., Tillyer, R. (2018). A gender-specific test of differential effectiveness and moderators of sanction effects. *Criminal Justice and Behavior*. https://doi.org/10.1177/0093854818766375

Chute, C., Bell, M. (1956). *Crime, courts, and probation*. New York: Macmillan.

Clear, T.R., Clear, V.B., Burrell, W.D. (1989). *Offender assessment and evaluation: The presentence investigation report*. Cincinnati, OH: Anderson.

Cohen, M. (1992). The motives of judges: Empirical evidence from antitrust sentencing. *International Review of Law and Economics* 12, 13–30.

Cohen, M.A. (1998). The monetary value of saving a high-risk youth. *Journal of Quantitative Criminology* 14, 5–33.

Dawson, J. (1990). *Felons sentenced to probation in state courts*. Washington, DC: U.S. Department of Justice.

del Carmen, R.V. (1985). Legal issues and liabilities in community corrections. In: L.F. Travis (Ed.), *Probation, parole and community corrections* (pp. 47–70). Prospect Heights, IL: Waveland.

Dixon, J. (1995). The organizational context of criminal sentencing. *American Journal of Sociology* 100, 1157–1198.

Dressler, D. (1962). *Practice and theory of probation and parole*. New York: Columbia University Press.

Evjen, V. (1975). The federal probation system: The struggle to achieve it and its first 25 years. *Federal Probation* 39(2), 3–15.

Finn, P. (1984). Prison crowding: The response of probation and parole. *Crime & Delinquency* 30, 141–153.

Finn, P., Parent, D. (1992). *Making the offender foot the bill: A Texas program*. Washington, DC: U.S. Department of Justice.

Gagnon v. Scarpelli, 411 U.S. 778 (1973).

Galaway, B. (1983). Probation as a reparative sentence. *Federal Probation* 46(3), 9–18.

General Accounting Office. (1982). *Federal parole practices*. Washington, DC: GAO.

Glaser, D. (1985). Who gets probation and parole: Case study versus actuarial decision-making. *Crime & Delinquency* 31, 367–378.

Hagan, J. (1975). The social and legal construction of criminal justice: A study of the presentence report. *Social Problems* 22, 620–637.

Harlow, N., Nelson, K. (1982). *Management strategies for probation in an era of limits*. Washington, DC: National Institute of Corrections.

Henrichson, C., Delaney, R. (2012). The price of prison: What incarceration costs taxpayers. New York: Vera Institute of Justice, Center on Sentencing and Corrections.

Johnson, F. (1928). *Probation for juveniles and adults*. New York: Century Co.

Kaeble, D. (2018). *Probation and parole in the United States (2016)*. Washington, DC: U.S. Department of Justice, Bureau of Justice Statistics.

Killits decision, *Ex parte United States* 242 U.S. 27 (1916).

Kirk, D., Wakefield, S. (2018). Collateral consequences of punishment: A critical review and path forward. *Annual Review of Criminology* 1, 171–194.

Koontz, J.B. (1980). Pragmatic conditions of probation. *Corrections Today* 42, 14–44.

Lansing, S. (1999). *Parental responsibility and juvenile delinquency*. Albany: New York State Division of Criminal Justice Services.

Latessa, E. (1993). *An analysis of pre-sentencing investigation recommendations and judicial outcome in Cuyahoga County adult probation department*. Cincinnati, OH: Department of Criminal Justice, University of Cincinnati.

Latessa, E., Lovins, B., Lux, J. (2014). *Evaluation of Ohio's RECLAIM programs*. Cincinnati, OH: University of Cincinnati, Center for Criminal Justice Reform.

Liebermann, E., Schaffer, S., Martin, J. (1971). *The Bronx Sentencing Project: An experiment in the use of short-form presentence report for adult misdemeanants*. New York: Vera Institute of Justice.

Lindner, C., Savarese, M. (1984). The evolution of probation: Early salaries, qualifications and hiring practices. *Federal Probation* 48(1), 3–9.

Lowenkamp, C., Flores, A., Holsinger, H., Makarios, M., Latessa, E. (2010). Intensive supervision programs: Does program philosophy and the principles of effective intervention matter? *Journal of Criminal Justice* 38, 368–375.

Lowenkamp, C.T., Pealer, J., Smith, P., Latessa., E.J. (2006). Adhering to the risk and need principles: Does it matter for supervision-based programs? *Federal Probation* 70(3), 3–8.

Macallair, D. (1994). Disposition case advocacy in San Francisco's juvenile justice system: A new approach to deinstitutionalization. *Crime & Delinquency* 40, 84–95.

Meeker, B. (1975). The federal probation system: The second 25 years. *Federal Probation* 39(2), 16–25.

Mempa v. Rhay, 389 U.S. 128 (1967).

Mitchell, O., Cochran, J., Mears, D., Bales, W. (2017). The effectiveness of prison for reducing drug offender recidivism: A regression discontinuity analysis. *Journal of Experimental Criminology* 13, 1–27.

National Advisory Commission on Criminal Justice Standards and Goals. (1973). *Corrections*. Washington, DC: U.S. Government Printing Office.

Nelson, C. (1975). Cost benefit analysis and alternatives to incarceration. *Federal Probation* 39, 45–50.

Parisi, N. (1980). Combining incarceration and probation. *Federal Probation* 46(2), 3–10.

Parisi, N. (1981). A taste of the bars. *Journal of Criminal Law and Criminology* 72, 1109–1123.

Petersilia, J. (1997). Probation in the United States. In: M. Tonry (Ed.), *Crime and justice: A review of research* (vol. 22; pp. 149–200). Chicago: University of Chicago Press.

Reed, T. (1997). *Apples to apples: Comparing the operational costs of juvenile and adult correctional programs in Texas*. Austin, TX: Texas Criminal Justice Policy Council.

Ring, C. (1988). *Probation supervision fees: Shifting costs to the offender*. Boston: Massachusetts Legislative Research Bureau.

Rogers, J. (1990). The predispositional report: Maintaining the promise of individualized justice. *Federal Probation* 54(1), 43–57.

Rosecrance, J. (1985). The probation officers' search for credibility: Ball park recommendations. *Crime & Delinquency* 31, 539–554.

Rosecrance, J. (1988). Maintaining the myth of individualized justice: Probation presentence reports. *Justice Quarterly* 5, 235–256.

Roy, S. (1994). Victim offender reconciliation program for juveniles in Elkhart County, Indiana: An exploratory study. *Justice Professional* 8(2), 23–35.

Sieh, E. (1993). From Augustus to the progressives: A study of probation's formative years. *Federal Probation* 57(3), 67–72.

Smith, B., Davis, R., Hillenbrand, S. (1989). *Improving enforcement of court-ordered restitution*. Chicago: American Bar Association.

The Presentence Report. (1970). An empirical study of its use in the federal criminal process. *Georgetown Law Journal* 58, 12–27.

Umbreit, M. (1994). *Victim meets offender: The impact of restorative justice and mediation*. Monsey, NY: Criminal Justice Press.

United Nations. (1976). The legal origins of probation. In: R.N. Carter, L.T. Wilkins (Eds.), *Probation, parole and community services* (pp. 81–88). New York: John Wiley and Sons.

United States Sentencing Commission. (2018). *U.S. Sentencing Commission's 2017 sourcebook of federal sentencing statistics*. Available at www.ussc.gov/research/sourcebook-2017.

United States v. Birnbaum, 421 F.2d 997, cert. denied, 397 U.S. 1044 (1970).

van Dijk, J.J.M., van Kaam, R.G.H., Wemmers, J.A.M. (1999). In: J.J.M. van Dijk-Kaam, R.G.H. van Kaam, J.Wemmers (Eds.), *Caring for crime victims* (pp. 1–12). Monsey, NY: Criminal Justice Press.

Vito, G. (1978). *Shock probation in Ohio: A comparison of attributes and outcomes* (Doctoral dissertation). The Ohio State University, Columbus.

Vito, G., Latessa, E. (1979). Cost analysis in probation research: An evaluation synthesis. *Journal of Contemporary Criminal Justice* 1(3), 3–6.

Walsh, A. (1985). The role of the probation officer in the sentencing process. *Criminal Justice and Behavior* 12, 289–303.

Welch, S., Spohn, C. (1986). Evaluating the impact of prior record on judges' sentencing decisions: A seven-city comparison. *Justice Quarterly* 3, 389–407.

Welsh, B.C., Farrington, D.P. (2000). Monetary costs and benefits of crime prevention programs. In Tonry, M. (Ed.), *Crime and justice: A review of research* (Vol. 27, pp. 305–361). Chicago, IL: University of Chicago Press.

Wheeler, G., Macan, T., Hissong, R., Slusher, M. (1989). The effects of probation service fees on case management strategy and sanctions. *Journal of Criminal Justice* 17, 15–24.

Wheeler, G., Rudolph, A., Hissong, R. (1989). Do probationers' characteristics affect fee assessment, payment and outcome? *Perspectives* 3(3), 12–17.

Chapter 5

Parole in America

Key Terms

absconder
American Prison Association
community residential centers
conditional release
deterrence
discretionary release
flopped
good-time credits
incapacitation
indeterminate sentence
mandatory release

mark system
pardon
parole
parole board
parole conditions
parole guidelines
parole revocation
penal colony
sentencing disparity
shock probationers
transportation

The most vivid disagreements over the matter of rights were caused by the ticket-of-leave system. There were only three ways in which the law might release a man from bondage. The first, though the rarest, was an absolute pardon from the governor, which restored him all rights including that of returning to England. The second was a conditional pardon, which gave the transported person citizenship within the colony but no right of return to England. The third was the ticket-of-leave. —Robert Hughes

A couple was driving through the country one fall day when they came upon a large house with a sign hanging from the porch. The sign said: "Dr. E. Smith, Veterinarian and Taxidermist." This seemed like an odd combination, so the couple drove closer. Under the name, it said: "Either way, you get your dog back." —Anonymous

THE DEVELOPMENT OF PAROLE

The way prisoners are released has changed dramatically over the years (Pew, 2014). Some are released by a **parole board** (discretionary release, about 55 percent in 1980 and 47 percent in 2016), others finish their entire sentences and are released with no supervision (max out), and still others are given mandatory release with supervision (Kaeble, 2018). We also know that parole is implemented differently from state to state. So, what is parole, and how did we get to this point?

Parole is a correctional option that often evokes strong feelings. There are those who argue that it should be abolished entirely, whereas others believe that it provides men and women with an opportunity to demonstrate that they can re-enter society and lead law-abiding and productive lives. Regardless of one's position, parole is an important part of the American correctional system. Furthermore, because in 2016 more than 626,000 inmates were released to the community from prison, many of whom will be under some form of correctional supervision, it is important that we understand the roots of parole and how it is granted (Carson, 2018).

Although the percentage of prisoners released on discretionary parole has been growing since 2011, the rate is still low compared to the past, when the vast majority of inmates were released on parole. Of those released to parole in 2016, about 47 percent were released by a parole board. Thus, parole remains a commonly used mechanism by which offenders may be released from a correctional institution after completion of a portion of the sentence. Figure 5.1 shows the number percentage of adults entering parole by type of release between 2000 and 2016. Contemporary parole also includes the concepts of supervision, release on condition of good behavior while in the community, and return to prison for failing to abide by these conditions or for committing a new crime. As we shall see, earlier parole practices saw the development of these elements.

Box 5.1
Maxing Out

A recent study by Pew (2014) found that between 1990 and 2012, the number of inmates who maxed out of their sentences in prison grew 119 percent, from fewer than 50,000 to more than 100,000; and in 2012, the rate was about 22 percent of all inmates. They also found that the max-out rates varied widely from state to state, ranging from less than 10 percent in Arkansas, California, Louisiana, Michigan, Missouri, Oregon, New Hampshire, and Wisconsin, to more than 40 percent in Florida, Maine, Massachusetts, New Jersey, North Carolina, Ohio, Oklahoma, South Carolina, and Utah.

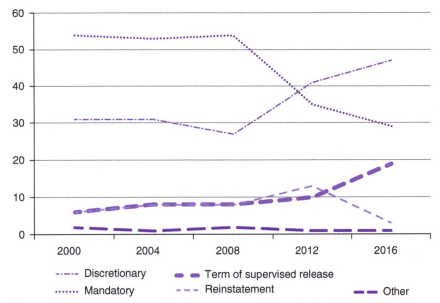

Figure 5.1 Adults Entering Parole by Type of Release, 2000–2016

Source: Kaeble, D. (2018). *Probation and parole in the United States, 2016*. Washington, DC: Bureau of Justice Statistics.

Box 5.2
Discretionary and Mandatory Release

Discretionary release is parole of an inmate from prison prior to expiration of the maximum sentence, according to the boundaries set by the legislature and sentence. Discretionary release is associated with the **indeterminate sentence** and implies that the offender is ready for release and continued treatment within the community.

Mandatory release is required release of the offender by the parole board because the statutes mandate release of any inmate who has served the equivalent of the maximum sentence. Mandatory release implies that the parole board refused to release an inmate prior to attainment of the maximum sentence imposed by the court. Mandatory release means that time served behind prison walls, when added to time credits for jail time, "good time," and earned time, totals the sentence imposed by the sentencing court. About one in five inmates leave prison under mandatory release (Pew, 2014).

THE ROOTS OF AMERICAN PAROLE

Although parole had its roots elsewhere, the widespread use of parole from prison, like the prison itself, is primarily an American innovation.[1] It emerged from a philosophical revolution and a resulting tradition of penal reform established in the late eighteenth century in the newly formed United States. As with many other new ideas that emerged in early America, parole had its roots in the practices of English and European penal systems.

In the late seventeenth and early eighteenth centuries, two massive social changes occurred that altered the direction of Western civilization and, consequently, had an impact on criminal law and penalties. The first was the Enlightenment, which gave rise to a conception of the human being as a rational and ultimately perfectible being and, along with this, a belief in basic human equality.[2] Second, urbanization and the earliest movements toward industrialism simultaneously changed the nature of social interactions and created a new social class, the urban working class.

The writing of such thinkers as Locke, Voltaire, Beccaria, and Montesquieu both created and reflected a changing conception of man and the social order. These writers believed that government or society existed because individuals allowed it to exist. In other words, a "social contract" governed society. In order to be secure in their persons and possessions, free and equal individuals banded together and surrendered certain of their freedoms to the government on condition that it protect them from their enemies.

Among those enemies were criminals. The State assumed the responsibility of controlling crime and, by administering justice, punishing offenders. Individuals surrendered their "rights" to seek revenge and to commit crimes or avenge themselves. The social contract was the product of rational, free individuals. Because rational and free people had control of their own fates, they could be held responsible for their actions.

A crime was considered a "breach of contract," an offense against all parties to the social contract, not just the injured party. This state of affairs enabled the establishment of a central body of law (such as the Common Law in England) and centralized control of enforcement. Finally, rational individuals, presumed to have prior knowledge of the law and its penalties, were expected to perceive that it was in their own interest not to violate the law and suffer the penalties. **Deterrence** was the rationale of the criminal law and its sanctions, which were severe so as to enhance the deterrent effect of the law (Beccaria, 1764/1963). In fact, more than 200 offenses carried the death penalty in England at one time. During the reign of Henry VIII, some 74,000 major and minor thieves were sent to the gallows. Under the reign of his daughter, Elizabeth I, 300 to 400 at a time were hanged, attracting large crowds where pickpockets flourished—even though pickpocketing was an offense punishable by death (Rennie, 1978).

Transportation

In England, orders of **transportation** were thought to be a severe punishment. In the eighteenth century, banishment, a common penalty for the aristocracy or nobility for centuries, was imposed on the common offender for the first time. The judge would order that the common offender should be transported to the colonies rather than go to the gallows or pillory. The criminal would be allowed to go at liberty in the new land, sometimes for a period of indenture (Pisciotta, 1982), on the condition of not returning to England for a specified time period (such as 10 years), if at all (Hawkins, 1971). The concept of transportation thus avoided the extreme harshness of existing criminal law, while at the same time serving to incapacitate the offender. The serious felony offender, of course, was still sentenced to death.

While transportation was a partial solution to England's crime problem and, for a time, helped to settle and develop new lands (the colonies, however, had no similar outlet for their offenders, with the exception of casting them into the wilderness, with usually the same results as the death penalty), it was only a temporary one. The colony of Georgia was one of England's early prison colonies, but after the American Revolution, England was forced to transport her convicts elsewhere (Campbell, 1994), and for a time they were sent to Australia; until, eventually, even Australia closed its doors to English convicts.[3] Criminologists commonly accept punishment by transportation as the principal forerunner of parole (Hawkins, 1971). They argue that transportation was an organized, uniform process by which thousands of convicts were punished in a manner short of execution or corporal punishment, as it was a system wherein offenders eventually obtained their freedom. In addition, transportation did not necessarily involve a period of incarceration.

THE RISE OF EARLY PRISON REFORM

The Treaty of Paris in 1783 acknowledged the creation of the first republic in Western civilization since the fall of the Roman Empire. The United States of America, free from the English monarchy and founded on the teachings of the Enlightenment, became fertile ground for the development of a new system of criminal justice. While the influence of English Common Law, with its harsh penalties, was strong in the new republic, even stronger were anti-British sentiment and the desire to abandon the oppressive regime of the English king. American reformers moved away from the archaic, tyrannical sanctions of colonial law and toward a more humane and rational penalty of incarceration.[4]

Chief among the reform groups were the Quakers (Offutt, 1995). The Judiciary Act of 1789 established imprisonment as the penalty for most crimes in Pennsylvania. In a nation that had newly acquired independence, what more fitting penalty could be found than the deprivation of liberty? When Patrick Henry uttered his now famous line, "Give me liberty or give me death," little did he know that he had identified the perfect penalty for crime. Prison replaced the penalty of death and yet denied liberty to its inmates. Much to the dismay of these first reformers, their efforts were not rewarded by a reduction in crime. Rather, the first penal institutions were dismal failures (Rothman, 1971, p. 62).

The search for the causes of crime continued. Reformers still believed that offenders were rational people who would strive to improve themselves, but the manner in which they could be convinced to obey the law was still unknown. In a time of rapid social change and movement from an agrarian to an industrial society, environmental factors came to be viewed as criminogenic: Cities, poverty, and idleness were believed to be the hotbeds of crime.

The proposed solution that emerged was to remove the offender from bad environments and teach them the benefits of industry and morality. Offenders needed to be shown the error of their ways. Criminal law was required to do more than punish and deter; it should change the prisoner into a productive citizen. Punishment should serve to allow the prisoner to repent, to be trained, and to be reformed into a good citizen. A place to repent was thus needed, and prisons were developed to fulfill that need.

The original basis of prison was the reformation of the offender, and the ideal of reformation placed high value on discipline and regimentation. In short, in the newly created free society, incarceration itself was punishment and, while the prisoner was incarcerated, the goal was to reform him or her. Offenders were expected to obey strict rules of conduct and to work hard at assigned tasks (Johnson, 1994). In this milieu, it was believed that the offender would learn the benefit of discipline and industry.

EARLY PRACTICES IN OTHER NATIONS

The first operational system of **conditional release** was started by the governor of a prison in Spain in 1835. Up to one-third of a prison sentence could be reduced by good behavior and a demonstrated desire to do better (Carter et al., 1975). A similar system was enacted in Bavaria in the 1830s, and many prison reformers in France in the 1840s advocated the adoption of similar conditional release systems. In fact, the term "parole" comes from the French *parole d'honneur*, or "word of honor," which characterized the French efforts to establish parole release. Prisoners would be released after showing good behavior and industry in the prison[5] and on their word of honor that they would obey the law.

Despite the fact that these efforts pre-date those of Alexander Maconochie, it is he who is usually given credit as being the father of parole. In 1840, Captain Maconochie was put in charge of the English **penal colony** in New South Wales at Norfolk Island, about 1,000 miles off the coast of Australia. To this colony were sent the criminals who were "twice condemned." They had been shipped from England to Australia, and then from Australia to Norfolk Island (Allen et al., 2019). Conditions were allegedly so bad at Norfolk Island that men reprieved from the death penalty wept and those who were to die thanked God (Barry, 1957, p. 5). The conditions on Norfolk Island were so unbearable that suicide became a means of escape and an act of solidarity. Hughes (1987) describes it in vivid terms:

A group of convicts would choose two men by drawing straws: one to die, the other to kill him. Others would stand by as witnesses. There being no judge to try capital offenses on Norfolk Island, the killer and witnesses would have to be sent to Sidney for trial—an inconvenience for the authorities but a boon to the prisoners, who yearned for the meager relief of getting away from the "ocean of hell," if only to a gallows on the mainland. And in Sidney there was some slight chance of escape. The victim could not choose himself; everyone in the group, apparently, had to be equally ready to die, and the benefits of his death had to be shared equally by all survivors.

(Hughes, 1987, p. 468)

It was under these conditions that Maconochie devised an elaborate method of granted conditional release. Maconochie's plan was based on five basic principles:

1. Release should not be based on the completion of a sentence for a set period of time, but on completion of a determined and specified quantity of labor. In brief, time sentences should be abolished, and task sentences substituted.
2. The quantity of labor a prisoner must perform should be expressed in a number of "marks" that he must earn, by improvement of conduct, frugality of living, and habits of industry, before he could be released.
3. While in prison he should earn everything he receives. All sustenance and indulgences should be added to his debt of marks.
4. When qualified by discipline to do so, he should work in association with a small number of other prisoners, forming a group of six or seven, and the whole group should be answerable for the conduct of labor of each member.
5. In the final stage, a prisoner, while still obliged to earn his daily tally of marks, should be given a proprietary interest in his own labor and be subject to a less rigorous discipline to prepare him for release into society.

(Barnes & Teeters, 1959, p. 419)

Under Maconochie's plan, referred to as the **mark system,** prisoners were awarded marks and moved through stages of custody until finally granted release. His system involved indeterminate sentencing, with release based on the number of marks earned by prisoners for good conduct, labor, and study. The five stages, based on the accumulation of marks, each carried increased responsibility and freedom, leading to a ticket of leave or parole resulting in a conditional pardon and, finally, full restoration of liberty.

Maconochie has been described as a zealot (Hughes, 1987); however, his reforms made life bearable at Norfolk Island and can be described as revolutionary in comparison to the horrible conditions that existed there before his arrival. While Maconochie's reforms transformed Norfolk Island from a place of despair to one of hope, it was short-lived. Petty bureaucrats and a general mistrust of Maconochie's ideas led to his recall as commandant in 1843.

Sir Walter Crofton, director of the Irish prison system in the 1850s, built upon the foundations laid by Maconochie. He decided that a transitional stage between prison and full release was needed and developed a classification scheme based on a system in which the prisoner progressed through three stages of treatment. The first was segregated confinement with work and training provided to the prisoner. This was followed by a transition period from confinement to freedom, during which the prisoner was set to work on public projects with little control being exercised over him. If he performed successfully in this phase, he was released on "license" (Clare & Kramer, 1976; Maguire et al., 1996).

Release on license was constrained by certain conditions, violations of which would result in reimprisonment. While on license, prisoners were required to submit monthly reports and were warned against idleness and associating with other criminals. Prisoners on license, then, had to report, could be reimprisoned for violating the conditions of release, and had not been pardoned. These distinctions from earlier systems of release were large steps toward modern parole.

EARLY AMERICAN PRACTICES

Convicts sentenced to prison in America in the early 1800s received definite terms; a sentence of 5 years meant the offender would serve 5 years in prison. This strict sentencing structure led to overcrowded prisons and widespread problems in the institutions. It was not uncommon for a governor to grant pardons to large numbers of inmates in order to control the size of prison populations. In some states, this pardoning power was even delegated to prison wardens (Sherrill, 1977).

This method of rewarding well-behaved prisoners with reductions in sentence was first formalized in 1817 by the New York State legislature. In that year, the first "good-time" law was passed. This law authorized a 25 percent reduction in length of term for those inmates serving 5 years or more who were well-behaved and demonstrated industry in their prison work. By 1869, 23 states had good-time laws, and prison administrators supported the concept as a method of keeping order and controlling the population size (Sherrill, 1977).

Liberal use of the pardoning power was continued in those states that did not have good-time laws, and the mass pardon was not uncommon even in those states that already allowed sentence reductions for good behavior. These developments are important because they represent the first large-scale exercise of sentencing power by the executive branch of government, the branch in which parole boards would eventually be located.

Another philosophical base for American parole was the indenture system established by the New York House of Refuge. Although not called parole, for all intents and purposes, a parole system was already operational for juveniles committed to the House of Refuge in New York. The House of Refuge had developed a system of indenture whereby youths were released from custody as indentured servants of private citizens. Unfortunately, this system permitted corruption.[6] There was no formal mechanism for releasing the youths from custody, but they

---

Box 5.3
Pardon

A **pardon** is an act of executive clemency that absolves the offender in part or in full from the legal consequences of the crime and conviction. Probably the most famous example is President Gerald Ford's pardon of former President Richard Nixon for his role in the Watergate crimes.

Executive clemency can include gubernatorial action that results in the release of an inmate from incarceration, as well as pardoning current and former inmates. The number of pardons granted by states is unknown, but for the most recent past presidents, the numbers were 396 by Bill Clinton, 189 by George W. Bush, and 212 by Barack Obama.

Source: www.thoughtco.com/number-of-pardons-by-president-3367600
(accessed May 25, 2018).

---

were able to work off their contracts and thus obtain their freedom. Their masters could break the contracts and return the youths to the House of Refuge at any time. In essence, a parole system was operating.

In addition to these forms of release from custody before expiration of the maximum term, the concept of supervising released offenders had also been operationalized. It is important to note, however, that supervision of released prisoners prior to the creation of parole in America only required providing assistance and not crime control duties.[7]

In 1845, the Massachusetts legislature appointed a state agent for discharged convicts and appropriated funds for him to use in assisting ex-prisoners in securing employment, tools, clothes, and transportation. Other states followed this example and appointed agents of their own. As early as 1776, however, charitable organizations, such as the Philadelphia Society for Alleviating the Miseries of Public Prisons, were already providing aid to released convicts (Sellin, 1970). By the late 1860s, dissatisfaction with prisons was widespread, and a concerted effort to establish a formal parole release and supervision system began. In 1870, the first meeting of the **American Prison Association** was held in Cincinnati, Ohio.[8] Reform was the battle cry of the day, and the meeting took on an almost evangelical fervor (Fogel, 1975). Both Sir Walter Crofton and American warden F.B. Sanborn advocated the Irish system (Lindsey, 1925).

Armed with the success of the meeting, prison reformers shifted their focus from incarceration as the answer to crime and, instead, concentrated on the return of offenders to society. Prisons remained central, but they were now seen almost as a necessary evil, not as an end in themselves. Prison reformers everywhere began to advocate adoption and expansion of good-time laws, assistance to released prisoners, adoption of the ticket-of-leave system, and parole. In 1869, the New York State legislature passed an act creating the Elmira Reformatory and an indeterminate sentence "until reformation, not exceeding 5 years" (Hawkins, 1971, p. 171).

This law created the reformatory as a separate institution for younger offenders, expressly designed to be an intermediate step between conviction and return to a law-abiding life. Administrators of the reformatory were empowered to release inmates upon demonstration of their reformation. Such release was conditional, and released offenders were to be supervised by a state agent (Lindsey, 1925).

With the passage of this law, parole in the United States became a reality. It soon spread to other jurisdictions, and by 1944, every jurisdiction in the nation had a parole authority (Hawkins, 1971). The spread of parole in the United States was rapid and between 1884 and 1900, parole was adopted in 20 states. The rapid growth of parole, however, was fraught with difficulties and criticism.

THE SPREAD OF PAROLE

Parole release was adopted by the various state jurisdictions much more rapidly than the indeterminate sentence. By 1900, some 20 states had adopted parole; by 1944, every jurisdiction had a parole system (see Table 5.1). The expansion of

Table 5.1 States with Parole Laws by 1900

State	Year enacted
Alabama	1897
California	1893
Colorado	1899
Connecticut	1897
Idaho	1897
Illinois	1891
Indiana	1897
Kansas	1895
Massachusetts	1884
Michigan	1895
Minnesota	1889
Nebraska	1893
New Jersey	1895
New York	1889
North Dakota	1891
Ohio	1896
Pennsylvania	1887
Utah	1898
Virginia	1898
Wisconsin	1889

Source: Adapted from Lindsey, E. (1925).
Historical origins of the sanction of imprisonment
for serious crime. *Journal of Criminal Law and
Criminology* 16, 9–126.

parole has been characterized as being a process of imitation (Lindsey, 1925), yet a great deal of variation in the structure and use of parole was observed.[9]

The growth and expansion of modern parole were assisted by a number of factors. One of the most important was the tremendous amount of support and publicity that prison reformers gave the concept. Its inclusion in the Congress's Declaration of Principles (1870), coupled with the publicity of Alexander Maconochie's work in New South Wales, provided the necessary endorsement of correctional experts.

In addition, it was quickly recognized that a discretionary release system solved many of the problems of prison administration. A major factor in favor of parole was that it supported prison discipline. A number of writers pointed out that by placing release in the inmate's own hands, the inmate would be motivated both to reform and comply with the rules and regulations of the prison.[10] Finally, parole provided a safety valve to reduce prison populations, which were generally over-crowded (Wilcox, 1929).

A third contributory factor was that the power to pardon was being exercised liberally in a number of states and was thought to be corrupt. The effect of liberal pardoning policies was to initiate parole even though it was not yet authorized by law.

These early parole systems were controlled by state legislators who, in general, rigidly defined which prisoners could be paroled. Most legislation authorizing parole release restricted it to first-time offenders convicted of less serious crimes.

Table 5.2 Significant Developments in Parole

Date	Development
1776	Colonies reject English Common Code and begin to draft their own codes.
1840	Maconochie devises mark system for release of prisoners in the Australian penal colony, a forerunner of parole.
1854	Crofton establishes ticket-of-leave program in Ireland.
1869	New York State legislature passes enabling legislation and establishes indeterminate sentencing.
1870	American Prison Association endorses expanded use of parole.
1876	Parole release adopted at Elmira Reformatory, New York.
1931	Wickersham Commission criticizes laxity in early parole practice.
1944	Last state passes enabling legislation for parole.
1976	Maine abolishes parole.
1979	Colorado abolishes parole release.
1984	Federal system abolishes parole as an early release mechanism.
1985	Colorado reinstates parole release.
1996	Ohio becomes 11th state to abolish parole.
2011	Kansas abolishes its parole board and establishes a three-member prisoner review board.
2016	626,000 inmates were released from prison, down from a high of 734,144 in 2008.

Source: Compiled by authors.

Through the passage of time and a gradual acceptance of the idea of discretionary early release, the privilege was eventually extended to serious offenders.

EARLY PUBLIC SENTIMENTS

The decade between 1925 and 1935 was a turbulent time, including both the economic boom (and the Prohibition Era) and the Great Depression. Crime, particularly as sensationalized in the mass media, appeared to be rampant. As crime rates increased, the public felt increasingly that crime was "public enemy number one."[11] This period also saw the rise of attempts by the federal government to stem interstate crimes, particularly kidnapping, bootlegging, bank robbery, and a host of newly enacted legislation that considerably widened the net of crime the government would seek to prevent and prosecute. Two significant events reflecting public concern about crime[12] were the establishment of the maximum-security federal prison on Alcatraz and a crusade headed by J. Edgar Hoover, chief of the Federal Bureau of Investigation, against interstate crime. Hoover's pronouncements assumed a political nature, as he strongly advocated neoclassical responses to crime: long-term prison sentences, abolition of parole, increased incarceration of offenders, use of the death penalty, and so on.[13]

Both the releasing and the supervising functions of parole were criticized sharply and roundly. The major concern of these criticisms was the failure of parole to protect the public safety. The Report of the Advisory Commission on Penal Institutions, Probation, and Parole to the Wickersham Commission in 1931 summarized the problems with parole, stating:

Parole is defective in three main respects:

1. in the chasm existing between parole and preceding institutional treatment;
2. in the manner in which persons are selected for parole;
3. in the quality of supervision given to persons on parole.

In short, parole was seen as failing to be effective in attaining the promised and lofty goals. Primary arguments were that convicted criminals were being set loose on society, supervised inadequately, and unreformed. The concept of parole and the general ideology of reform were not yet under attack; it was the means and not the ends that were being criticized.

Box 5.4
Parole

Parole is release of an inmate from confinement to expiration of sentence on condition of good behavior and supervision in the community. This is also referred to as post-incarceration supervision or, in the case of juveniles, aftercare.

Between the adoption of parole release in Elmira in 1876 and the enactment of enabling legislation for parole in Mississippi in 1944, the concept of parole faced two critical challenges. The first involved the issue of legality of executive control over sentencing and indeterminate sentences. The second centered on the administration of parole systems. Toward the end of the first quarter of the twentieth century, the rehabilitative ideal came into its own and grew to be a predominant goal of corrections and sentencing and gave new legitimacy to parole, endorsing discretion.

LEGAL CHALLENGES TO PAROLE

The basic legal challenge raised against parole was that the placing of control over sentence length and criminal penalties in the hands of a parole board was unconstitutional. The specific arguments varied across individual lawsuits, but they were basically of two types. First, questions of infringement of the principle of the separation of powers' clauses of the federal and state constitutions were raised in several states (Lindsey, 1925).

These suits claimed that parole release was an impairment of judicial sentencing power, an improper delegation of legislative authority to set penalties, and usurpation of the executive branch's power of clemency (Hawkins, 1971). For the most part, parole authorities emerged victorious from these court battles, and those constitutional questions of parole were laid to rest.

The second rationale behind challenges to the constitutionality of parole release was based on the Eighth Amendment prohibition against cruel and unusual punishment. Although the issue was weighty, most criminal penalties were limited by legislatively set maximum terms. The most common judicial response to these arguments was that indeterminate sentences could be interpreted as sentences that would not extend the maximum terms as set by the legislature or judge, thereby rendering moot the issue of cruelty by virtue of uncertainty (Hawkins, 1971).

Box 5.5
Parole Board

A **parole board** is any correctional person, authority, commission, or board that has legal authority to parole those adults (or juveniles) committed to confinement facilities, to set conditions for behavior, to revoke from parole, and to discharge from parole.

Parole boards can usually also recommend shortening a prisoner's sentence (commuting sentences), recommend pardons to a governor, set parole policies, and, in some jurisdictions, recommend reprieve from execution. An example of parole policy would be a "zero-tolerance" policy for parolees whose urine samples indicate recent use of illicit drugs, usually resulting in certain return to confinement.

ADMINISTRATIVE CHALLENGES

We have seen that in the late nineteenth and early twentieth centuries, parole practices were criticized for failing to protect the public. The basic arguments were that parole authorities were not following procedures that would lead to the release of only deserving inmates and that the lack of subsequent parole supervision placed the community in danger.

One salient argument, supported by ample evidence, was that parole had become a commonplace method of reducing prison populations. In several states, most inmates were released immediately upon expiration of their minimum terms. Only those inmates whose conduct records within prison showed a failure to conform were held longer. The problem was defined as inadequate or improper release decision making.

Blanket release policies were felt to be inappropriate for several reasons. First, because parole boards failed to consider that risk and parole supervision was inadequate, such wholesale release practices were felt to endanger public safety. Second, because most parole boards were dominated by prison officials, it was believed that too much weight was attached to prison conduct and the needs of the prison administration. Finally, failure to consider reformation efforts of the inmate, or the prison, worked to hamper the success of prisons in reforming criminals.

Proposed solutions were varied and involved beefing up parole supervision staffs and increasing post-release surveillance of parolees. It was believed that these actions could enhance public protection. Additionally, there were calls for professional parole boards composed of trained, salaried, full-time decision makers who would be removed from the pressures of day-to-day prison administration and its needs and who were skilled in identifying those inmates who were reformed.

These proposals arose at about the same time that behavioral sciences expanded into the world of public policy. Psychology and sociology were beginning to develop practical components in addition to their traditional theoretical bases. The new professions of clinical psychologist, social worker, and criminologist were developing. An ability to predict, change, and control undesirable human behavior was promised.[14] Corrections and parole seemed ideal places in which these professions could have their most positive impact. The dawn of the rehabilitative model was at hand, and this model caused radical changes in the practice and organization of the American parole system, as we shall see.

Box 5.6
Eighth Amendment

Excessive bail shall not be required, nor excessive fines imposed, nor cruel and unusual punishment inflicted.

GRANTING PAROLE

As noted earlier, parole was originally implemented as a method of releasing reformed inmates at the ideal time. The primary focus of parole was the rehabilitation and eventual reintegration of the offender to society, although it also functioned to incapacitate violent and dangerous offenders whose probability of reoffending was believed to be unacceptably high. Parole also serves as a decompression period that helps the offender make the adjustment between the institution and the outside world. As such, parole is an integral component of the re-entry process. Figure 5.2 shows that the number of offenders on parole has grown dramatically since 1985: from 300,000 to more than 870,000 in 2016. This dramatic increase is due to the incarceration binge that occurred in the 1980s and 1990s. Despite the large number of offenders on parole, the rate per 100,000 has remained relatively steady since 2000.

OVERVIEW OF THE PAROLE PROCESS

The parole process begins in the courtroom when the judge sentences an individual to a determinate or indeterminate prison sentence. The latter includes fixing a term by stating the minimum and maximum length of time the individual is to serve. At the expiration of a certain portion of that sentence, minus credit granted for good behavior and performance of duties, an individual becomes eligible for parole. The amount of the sentence that must be served and the amount of credit that can be given for good behavior and performance of duties vary from state to state. In Nebraska, someone sentenced to a 3- to 5-year term can become eligible for parole at the end of 2 years and 5 months if they have behaved "properly" within

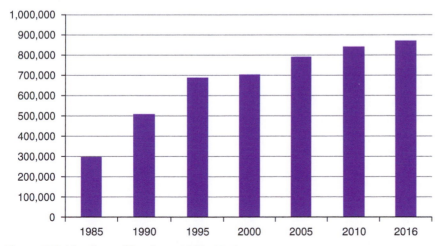

Figure 5.2 Number of Parolees: 1985–2016

Source: From the *Probation and parole in the United States* series. Washington, DC: U.S. Department of Justice, Bureau of Justice Statistics.

the institution.[15] This does not mean that a release will actually occur; it only means that the individual is eligible to be released. A number of states have mandatory parole release statutes which state that at the expiration of a certain portion of the sentence, inmates must be released on parole, unless the inmate chooses not to be released. A small number of inmates refuse to be released on parole because they do not want to be subject to a parole officer's supervision, and consequently, they choose to serve their entire prison sentence ("max out"). Table 5.3 shows the states where discretionary release by a parole board was 70 percent or higher, and those where more than 70 percent were mandatory release.

Regardless of whether these individuals wish to max out or receive parole, institutional officers compile information concerning their personal characteristics and backgrounds. Treatment progress is updated continually and, at some point in time, the staff begin working with the offender's friends, family, and employers to develop a release plan.

The information, along with the pre-sentence and institutional progress reports, is periodically brought to the attention of the releasing authority, usually a parole board. Some states review inmates' progress on a yearly basis, even though they are not eligible for release. In accordance with the eligibility guidelines and an interview with the offender, the parole board decides whether to release the offender

Table 5.3 Selected States by Type of Parole Release

States where over 70% were Discretionary Parole		States where over 70% were Mandatory Release	
State	**%**	**State**	**%**
Arkansas	84	Arizona	99
Georgia	100	Florida	88
Hawaii	100	Illinois	96
Iowa	100	Indiana	100
Massachusetts	100	Louisiana	94
Mississippi	72	Minnesota	93
Missouri	77	Ohio	97
Montana	100	Oregon	75
Nebraska	86	Washington	89
North Dakota	100		
Oklahoma	100		
Pennsylvania	94		
Rhode Island	100		
Tennessee	97		
Texas	96		
Utah	93		
West Virginia	98		

Source: Association of Paroling Authorities International (2005). *Paroling authorities survey.* Available at: www.apaintl.org

on parole. If the decision is to deny release, a future rehearing date is usually set. If a release is to be effected, the parole board then determines when and where the release is to be made. A contract, usually including very specific conditions of parole, is also established. Once a release has been achieved, inmates (now called parolees) come under the supervision of parole officers.

Box 5.7
Good-time Credits

Statutes in almost every state allow for the reduction of a prison term based on an offender's behavior in prison ("good time") or for participation in and completion of certain educational or treatment programs ("program time"). Reduction in time is awarded; such awards reduce the date to the parole board or minimum sentence, and the maximum time to be served.

Good-time credits are earned by a formula established within correctional settings, sometimes set into law but usually decided by institutional administrators in collaboration with the parole board. In California, the award is 4 months for each 8 months served (4 for 8, or 1:2). If an offender is serving a 3-year sentence (36 months) and earns maximum good time, that offender will be in prison for no more than 24 months.

Some jurisdictions award time for pretrial detention and post-conviction jail time while awaiting transport to prison. There are thousands of jail inmates who have been sentenced to prison, but are being held back pending availability of prison space and transport to prison. These inmates generally earn "jail credits" at a 1:1 ratio and will bring those credits to the parole board, further reducing the maximum time they will serve as prison inmates.

Finally, to encourage participation in institutional work and rehabilitation programs, credits may be awarded for participation in and completion of specific programs: welding, masonry, car repair, general educational development (GED), drug treatment, and so on. The awards across jurisdictions vary, but usually approximate the "good-time credit" ratio.

Thus, an inmate sentenced to 3 years in prison but detained for 4 months on a pretrial basis and held for 4 months in jail after sentencing before being transported to prison would bring 8 months of jail time credit and would generally receive an additional 4 months for good time, the equivalent of serving 1 year against the term of punishment. If the offender participates in and graduates from a drug treatment program within the first 12 months, that offender will usually serve less than 16 months before being released as having served the maximum sentence ("max out"): 36 months.

Current Operations

Parole is a complex procedure and has many functions and processes that differ from one jurisdiction to another. Traditionally, parole has five basic functions:

1. Selecting and placing prisoners on parole.
2. Establishing conditions of supervision (frequently case-specific).
3. Aiding, supervising, assisting, and controlling parolees in the community.
4. Returning parolees to prison if the conditions of parole are not met.
5. Discharging parolees when supervision is no longer necessary or when the sentence is completed.

Parole, unlike probation, is an administrative process located within the executive branch of every state, as well as the federal government. This may soon change, however, for a number of states have virtually eliminated the discretionary release power of these parole boards. Table 5.4 shows the jurisdictions that have abolished or limited parole board release. Connecticut abolished parole in 1981 but reinstated it 9 years later, after prison costs surged.[16] Similarly, Colorado abolished parole release in 1979 and reinstated it in 1985. Thirty other jurisdictions have developed various system-wide **parole guidelines** that have restricted the discretionary powers of the parole boards.[17] The operation of parole, obviously, is not all uniform.[18] State parole systems vary widely in terms of their organizational makeup and administrative process.[19] Most parole boards are independent state agencies that only administer parole. Depending on the state, there are anywhere from 3 to 19 members on a parole board (Camp & Camp, 2000). Only 22 states have any statutory requirements for specific qualifications for parole board members, and even those are usually stated in such broad terms as "possessing good character" or "judicious temperament." In 1967, the President's Commission on Law Enforcement and Administration of Justice recommended that parole board members be appointed solely on the basis of competence; however, in many states, appointment to the parole board appears to be based on political considerations. For example, in Wisconsin, with the exception of the chair, the members of the Parole Commission are hired in accordance with the state's civil service system. In Ohio, parole board members are appointed by the director of the Department of Rehabilitation and Correction and must be qualified by education or experience in correctional work, including law enforcement, prosecution of offenses, advocating for the rights of victims of crime, probation or parole, law, social work, or a combination of the three categories. The governor is directly responsible for parole board appointments in 45 states.

Parole Selection Process

In most jurisdictions, individual cases are assigned to individual members of the parole board, who review each case and make initial recommendations. These

Table 5.4 Jurisdictions That Have Abolished or Severely Limit Parole Board Release

State	Year
Arizona	1994
Arkansas	1994
California	1976
Delaware	1990
Florida	1983
Illinois	1978
Indiana	1977
Kansas	2011
Maine	1976
Minnesota	1980
Mississippi	1995
New Mexico	1979
North Carolina	1994
Ohio	1996
Oklahoma	2000
Oregon	1989
South Dakota	1996
Virginia	1995
Washington	1984
Wisconsin	2000
Federal Government	1986

Source: Association of Paroling Authorities International (2005). *Paroling authorities survey.* Available at: www.apaintl.org

---

Box 5.8
Parole Board Members

Governors appoint parole board members in 45 jurisdictions, usually with the advice and consent of the state legislature. The most frequent term is 4 years, and most states stagger the terms of office of members to achieve continuity of parole boards regardless of changes in the governor's mansion or philosophy. In Alabama, Arizona, and Georgia, 5-, 6-, and 7-year terms are found. In Utah, parole board members are appointed by the Board of Corrections and serve 6-year terms.

There are no statutory qualifications for parole board membership in 29 jurisdictions, but the other 22 jurisdictions have qualifications that speak to length of time and experience in corrections (or such related fields as welfare, religion, or law enforcement). Seven jurisdictions set the minimal educational level as at least a bachelor's degree.

recommendations are usually accepted, although occasionally the board as a whole may seek to obtain more details. While there are some jurisdictions that make the final release decision solely on the basis of written reports, most states conduct some type of a formal hearing. The hearing may be with one member of the parole board or the assembled board as a whole (en banc) or may be handled by a hearing examiner with no members of the board present. Occasionally, prison staff are also interviewed. Some states send the board members and/or hearing examiners to the institutions to conduct the hearings, whereas others bring those to be interviewed to the board/examiners. Video hearings are now commonplace in many states.

Parole selection guidelines differ widely from state to state. The U.S. Supreme Court has consistently held parole to be a privilege and, consequently, held that a full complement of due process rights does not need to be afforded at parole-granting hearings (*Greenholtz v. Inmates of the Nebraska Penal and Correctional Complex*, 442 U.S. 1 (1979). As a result, the states have been given the opportunity to establish whatever inmate privileges they feel are appropriate at parole-granting hearings.

Inmates are permitted the use of counsel in 21 states and are allowed to present witnesses in 19 states. The rationale for the parole decision must be formally articulated in 11 parole jurisdictions. Most states have established regulations as to the amount of time an inmate is required to serve prior to parole eligibility. In 16 states, eligibility is obtained upon completion of the minimum sentence. In ten states, eligibility is achieved upon completion of one-third of the maximum sentence. Other states use the number of prior felony convictions and length of prior sentences to calculate eligibility rules. Even in states that use the same eligibility guidelines, there is such a wide variation in the length of the minimum and maximum prison terms handed down for the same offense that, in reality, there are literally as many variations in eligibility as there are parole jurisdictions.[20] In addition to time factors, some states restrict the use of parole for those convicted of various serious personal offenses, such as first-degree murder, kidnapping, and aggravated rape.[21]

If an inmate does not meet parole standards, the sentence is continued and a date is set for the next parole review. If parole is approved, the individual is prepared for release to the parole field service authority. Just how long an inmate must

---

Box 5.9
States with Parole Boards for Juveniles

There is considerable variation among states on how decisions are made to release youth from state facilities. In some states, the decision is made by the agency, the court, or a combination of the two. In Colorado, California, Illinois, Ohio, New Hampshire, New Jersey, New York, South Carolina, and Utah, the decision is made by a parole board.

wait to hear the verdict varies greatly. In many jurisdictions, the inmate receives word immediately. In others, and in those jurisdictions where no hearings are held, inmates are notified by the prison staff or by mail. Receipt by the inmate of formal written notification varies from immediately in several states to as long as 3 to 4 weeks in New Jersey.

Civil Commitments

Release from prison does not always mean release from custody. According to the Association for the Treatment of Sexual Abusers (ATSA), 18 states, the District of Columbia, and the federal government have civil comment laws that provide a legal mechanism for the confinement of a limited number of adult sexual offenders in a secure treatment facility after release from incarceration and when a court determines they are likely to engage in future acts of sexual violence. To meet the criteria for commitment, the offender must suffer from a mental or personality disorder, such as antisocial personality, that predisposes the offender to commit future acts of sexual violence. Table 5.5 lists the states that have civil comment laws.

Table 5.5 Jurisdictions with Civil Incarceration Laws for Violent Sexual Predators

Jurisdiction
Arizona
California
Florida
Illinois
Iowa
Kansas
Massachusetts
Minnesota
Missouri
Nebraska
New Hampshire
New Jersey
New York
North Dakota
Pennsylvania
South Carolina
Texas, Virginia
Washington
District of Columbia
Federal government

Source: www.atsa.com/civil-commitment-sexually-violent-predators (accessed May 26, 2018).

Box 5.10
Sexually Violent Predators and Civil Commitment

California enacted a statute in 1996 that seeks to ensure that sexual predators in prison suffering from mental disorders and deemed likely to reoffend are treated in a secure facility through civil commitment and are not released prematurely into society to victimize others.

The Board of Prison Terms screens cases to determine if inmates meet criteria specified in the statute and then refers inmates to the California Department of Mental Health for clinical evaluations by two clinicians. If both clinicians concur that the inmate meets the criteria, a county district attorney may file a petition for civil commitment.

If the judge determines that probable cause exists, the prisoner is scheduled for a court trial. A jury hears the case and, based on the "beyond a reasonable doubt" test, may determine that the offender meets the statutory criteria. In such cases, the offender is civilly committed to a Department of Mental Health facility for 2 years of treatment. Annual examinations are conducted; the offender may petition the court for conditional release (parole). At the end of 2 years, the prisoner is re-evaluated and the court may enter an order for a new trial to seek a new commitment of the offender. Since 1996, more than 300 sex offenders have been found to be sexually violent predators and committed to the Department of Mental Health for treatment.

Parole Hearing

The parole-granting hearing is a very significant event for inmates. Regardless of the outcome, the result affects their lives greatly. They realize that a single inappropriate word or action could jeopardize their freedom for years to come. Historically, parole boards operated in relative secrecy, and were closed. Today, while parole hearings may be at least partially closed, many have become more open and transparent. In some states, victims are also allowed to attend hearings and offer testimony. Others, like Ohio, do not allow victims to participate in hearings, but there is a mechanism for them to provide input. If parole is recommended by a majority of the board, the case goes to a full-board, open hearing, which is open to interested parties.

FACTORS INFLUENCING PAROLE DECISIONS

In theory, parole decisions should be based on the factors outlined in state statutes. In practice, however, it appears that parole boards are influenced by a wide variety of criteria, not all of which are articulated by law. Furthermore, some states do not

> **Box 5.11**
> **Flopped**
>
> **"Flopped"** is inmate argot for being denied early release by the parole board for failing to meet parole board standards or expectations. When flopped, the inmate is usually given a "next review date" by the board, and his or her case will be heard again at that time. Frequently, the board suggests treatments, programs, or goals the offender is expected to complete or meet before the next review (learning to read and write, AA involvement, life skills, etc.).

have any legal guidelines. As suggested by Dawson (1966), there appear to be three major release criteria that influence parole boards:

1. factors for granting parole based on the probability of recidivism;
2. factors for granting parole other than probability of recidivism;
3. factors for denying parole other than probability of recidivism.

Figure 5.3 shows the percentage of parole exits in 2016 by type. As illustrated, the majority completed parole (56%), while 27% were returned to prison and 2% were absconders (whereabouts unknown).

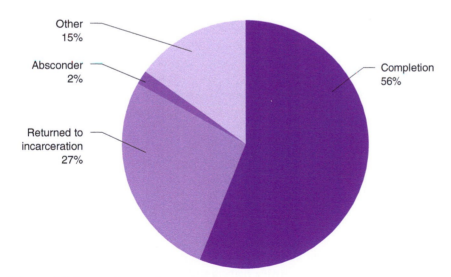

Figure 5.3 Parole Exits by Type, 2016

Source: Kaeble, D. (2018). *Probation and parole in the United States, 2016*. Washington, DC: U.S. Department of Justice, Bureau of Justice Statistics.

Probability of Recidivism

Perhaps the most basic aspect of the decision-making process is estimating the probability that an individual will violate the law if and when he or she is released on parole.[22] This is known as the recidivism factor. Parole boards, as quasi-political entities, are extremely sensitive to the public criticism that may arise when parolees violate parole, especially if they commit a serious offense. Just how parole boards determine the probability of recidivism is unclear. As early as 1923, Hart advocated the need to develop methodologically sound prediction tables for potential parolees that were based on data. Since this observation, many such scales and tables have been developed (Babst et al., 1970; Bromley & Gathercole, 1969; Burgess, 1928; Glaser, 1962; Gottfredson et al., 1958; Gottfredson & Gottfredson, 1993; Loza & Loza, 2000; Wilkins & MacNaughton-Smith, 1964). For more than 50 years, the value of prediction devices has been recognized as a means of standardizing parole release and assessing recidivism probability more accurately. At least one-half of all parole boards use formal risk assessment (Burke, 1997).[23]

Box 5.12
The Ohio Risk Assessment System Re-entry Tool

In 2009, researchers from the University of Cincinnati developed the Ohio Risk Assessment System (ORAS). One of the tools in this system is the Re-entry Tool. After examining the recidivism of inmates who had served at least 2 years in prison prior to release, 17 items were identified in three basic domains—Criminal History, Social Support, and Criminal Attitudes and Behavioral Patterns—that helped classify those exiting prison into three risk categories: low (with a 20 percent probability of failure), moderate (40 percent), and high (60 percent). Given the nature of the prison environment, many traditional risk factors are controlled, such as current employment and substance use, and were not found to be important in predicting risk at release.

Source: Latessa et al. (2010).

Factors for Granting Parole Other than Probability of Recidivism

There are occasions when inmates are granted parole despite the parole board's belief that they possess a relatively high probability of recidivism. In instances when offenders are believed to be unlikely to commit a crime of a serious nature, the parole board may vote to grant parole. This factor is often accompanied by a determination that the inmate will gain little additional benefit from further institutionalization. For example, although an inmate may be a drug user with a long record of drug-related arrests, the parole board may grant a release because it feels that the individual is relatively harmless and that continued institutionalization will very likely have little further impact upon the drug problem. Compassionate release of inmates dying of cancer and AIDS also falls under this category (Pagliaro & Pagliaro, 1992).[24]

Occasionally, situations arise in which inmates have only a short period of time to serve before the completion of their sentences. When such circumstances arise, parole boards frequently give these individuals parole, despite what may be a high perceived probability of recidivism, in order to provide even a brief period of supervisory control and, more importantly, to assist the parolee in the environmental decompression and social reintegration process.

An additional criterion that may swing a parole board, despite an apparent high recidivism probability, is the length of time served. If an inmate has failed to respond to institutional treatment but has served a relatively long sentence, the parole board may grant parole under the conviction that these individuals have paid their dues and that perhaps they will succeed on parole to avoid being sent back. Occasionally, the maturation process will play an important role. When lengthy sentences are mandated for young persons, the parole board may effect an early release, noting the general process of maturation that will enable these individuals to adopt more acceptable patterns of behavior once released.

Factors for Denying Parole Other than Probability of Recidivism

There are circumstances in which individuals may not be granted a release despite a relatively low recidivism probability. For example, when inmates have demonstrated occasional outbursts of violent and assaultive behavior, parole boards tend to be somewhat reluctant to grant release. As noted previously, parole boards are extremely sensitive to public criticism, and while the probability of a violent attack may be very small, the seriousness of the incident would likely attract considerable media attention. Consequently, release in such a situation will often be denied. Community attitudes and values often play major roles in overriding the recidivism probability factors. For example, murderers have traditionally been good parole risks in terms of likelihood of parole success. However, whether and how quickly they should be paroled is often a function of community attitudes. If a community attitude is unfavorable, parole is likely to be denied, for the release of such an inmate might expose the parole board to bitter public criticism, and most parole boards prefer to keep an inmate in prison rather than incur the public's anger.

There are also occasions when parole is used as a tool to support and maintain institutional discipline. Individuals may possess very high potential for success on parole, but violate institutional rules and regulations continually. In these situations, parole will frequently be denied. Occasionally, an inmate with a drug abuse problem may be counseled by the parole board to enroll in an existing drug-dependency program, sending a clear message to the inmate population that such rehabilitation programs are appropriate and functional for release. In this way, parole can be viewed as an incentive for good behavior and a sanction against inappropriate conduct. There are even situations in which parole may be denied so as to benefit the inmate. Circumstances occasionally arise when inmates are making rapid progress in academic pursuits or may be receiving and responding to necessary medical and/or psychological treatment. The parole board may temporarily postpone such a case for a few months to give these individuals the opportunity to complete their high school work, for example, or recover from medical treatment they are undergoing.

Box 5.13
Parole Board Functions

The most visible function of a parole board is the discretionary release of an inmate from confinement prior to the expiration of his or her sentence on condition of good behavior in the community. This is commonly known as the parole release decision. However, parole boards have extensive authority to undertake a variety of other functions seldom acknowledged in the justice area.

Setting policy. The parole board enunciates and refines broad policy governing specific areas of parole, such as directives to community supervision officers on offenders whose drug tests show illicit drug use. Some policies require the officer to hold a revocation hearing under *Morrissey v. Brewer*; other jurisdictions may only suggest that officers tighten up the conditions of parole ("motivational" jail time, house arrest, or Narcotics Anonymous). When parole boards establish a "zero-tolerance" policy, a large percentage of drug-abusing parolees may be returned to prison.

Modification of presumed release date. If an offender is given a presumed release date, it is usually based on conformity to institutional rules. When inmates persistently violate those, a decision may be made to delay release ("extend the time") based on institutional behavior. In effect, the parole board reinforces control of prison inmates and encourages participation in institutional programs.

Commutation of sentence. Inmates serving life sentences or double-life or life plus a day or minimum sentences of several hundred years have few hopes of ever leaving the facility alive. It is possible, however, to petition the executive branch for commutation, a reduction in sentence length. A parole board, whose recommendation for commutation is seriously considered by the governor, usually hears the initial plea. "Lifers" who receive commutations usually leave the penal institution shortly thereafter.

Revocation from parole. If a supervising officer requests a hearing for revocation of parole under *Morrissey* and the hearing officer finds reasonable cause, the case will be heard by the parole board (or its authorized

> designee) and the offender's grant of parole may be revoked. The offender is then returned to prison to serve additional time.
>
> *Pardon.* Only the executive branch may grant a pardon, absolving the offender in part or in full from the legal consequences of the crime and conviction. Governors usually receive such petitions after they have been considered by the parole board, generally authorized to advise the governor on these matters.
>
> *Reprieve.* A reprieve is a stay in imposition of sentence, typically associated with death row inmates nearing their execution date. Parole boards, sometimes in conjunction with the governor's cabinet, may recommend reprieve to a governor.
>
> *Incapacitation.* Some offenders have demonstrated a pattern of violent and dangerous criminal behavior that continues unabated in prison. By denying parole and thus forcing such inmates to serve longer prison sentences, parole boards protect the public through disabling future violent crime. This function is seldom recognized.

Finally, there are situations in which the parole board may feel that individuals are good risks but ineligible for release because they have not served the minimum terms as fixed by the sentencing judge. Some have expressed a concern over the fact that the courts occasionally err in handing down sanctions that are more severe than necessary. Correctional officials, after more careful observation and evaluation than the courts could originally consider, may clearly document greater progress than the court expected. Nevertheless, as noted previously, state parole statutes may mandate a minimum time to be served (calculated as a percentage of the minimum or maximum sentence) that even the parole board cannot ignore. Such inmates may be released, however, under work furlough programs.

PAROLE BOARD RELEASE DECISIONS

All persons eligible for parole are not automatically granted a release. Occasionally, parole boards will not release individuals who could be released safely. This is partially a desire by parole boards to minimize the number of persons who are classified as good risks and released, but whom the board feel are, in reality, bad risks and expected to fail on parole. Failed parole is a problem that the boards seek to minimize (Wiggins, 1984).

Our ability to predict future recidivism has improved over the years; however, it is not without its critics (Gottfredson & Gottfredson, 1994; Monahan, 1981; Smykla, 1984). Furthermore, our ability to predict future violent behavior is limited, and as a result, there is a general tendency to over-predict dangerousness, which results in more persons being classified as bad risks.[25] Although such tendencies have come under intense criticism, over-prediction of dangerousness continues (Morris, 1974; Smykla, 1984). This is probably due to the perception that over-prediction is viewed as having smaller short-term costs. In the short run, it may be less expensive to incarcerate larger numbers of offenders than to permit a few dangerous persons to roam the streets and commit crimes. Such an approach is quite costly in the long run, however, as more and more persons are housed and cared for within the prison system. Furthermore, indications show that after extended prison sentences are served, some former inmates will commit more serious crimes more frequently than they would have prior to their incarceration.

While the courts have ruled that parole cannot be denied on the basis of race, religion, or national origin,[26] they have really not become involved in parole board policies and practices. This is due in large part to the fact that the Supreme Court has defined parole as a privilege rather than a right (*Greenholtz*, 1979). Consequently, there is no constitutional mandate that there even be any formal parole release guidelines, no right to obtain access to institutional files, and no right to counsel at the hearing. Indeed, there is no constitutional requirement that there even be a formal hearing. The state is under no constitutional obligation to articulate the reason for denial of parole, and there is no right of appeal, except as given by an individual state.

Most states have adopted laws and/or administrative policies that outline parole procedures. Some allow inmates access to their files and permit the presence of legal counsel. As of 1977, the U.S. Parole Commission[27] and 23 states offered inmates the opportunity to internally appeal parole release hearing decisions (O'Leary & Hanrahan, 1977). Up to this point, however, courts have continued to refuse to become involved in any type of review of a negative parole board decision.

CONDITIONS OF PAROLE

Parole is, in essence, a contract between the state and the offender. If the offender is able to abide by the terms of the contract, or **parole conditions**, freedom is maintained. If a violation of these conditions occurs or if a parolee is charged with a new crime, the parole board may revoke parole and return the offender to prison. The offender must abide by the contract and stay under parole supervision for the period of time outlined by the parole board. While every state has its own policies and procedures, parole usually lasts more than 2 but less than 7 years. Table 5.6 is an example of parole conditions from Ohio. Some states in fact permit discharge from parole after a very short time, as long as the offender has diligently adhered to the pre-release contract.

PAROLE REVOCATION

In 1972, the U.S. Supreme Court established procedures for **parole revocation** with the case of *Morrissey v. Brewer*, 408 U.S. 471 (1972). In this case, the Supreme Court said that once parole is granted, it is no longer just a privilege but a right. Consequently, the court ruled that parolees should be granted certain due process

Table 5.6 Ohio Parole Conditions

STATE OF OHIO
Department of Rehabilitation and Correction
Adult Parole Authority
CONDITIONS OF SUPERVISION

In consideration of having been granted supervision on _____.

1. I will obey federal, state and local laws and ordinances, including those related to illegal drug use and registration with authorities. I will have no contact with the victim of my current offense(s).
2. I will follow all orders given to me by my supervising officer or other authorized representatives of the Court or the Department of Rehabilitation and Correction, including, but not limited to obtaining permission from my supervising officer before changing my residence and submitting to drug testing.
3. I will obtain a written travel permit from the Adult Parole Authority before leaving the State of Ohio.
4. I will not purchase, possess, own, use or have under my control, any firearms, ammunition, dangerous ordinance, devices used to immobilize or deadly weapons, or any device that fires or launches a projectile of any kind. I will obtain written permission from the Adult Parole Authority prior to residing in a residence where these items are securely located.
5. I will not enter the grounds of any correctional facility nor attempt to visit any prisoner without the prior written permission of my supervising officer. I will not communicate with any prisoner in any manner without first obtaining written permission from my supervising officer.
6. I will report any arrest, conviction, citation issued to me for violating any law, or any other contact with law enforcement to my supervising officer no later than the next business day following the day on which the contact occurred or, if I am taken into custody as a result of the law enforcement contact, no later than the next business day following my release from custody. I will not enter into any agreement or other arrangement with any law enforcement agency that might place me in the position of violating any law or condition of my supervision without first obtaining written permission to enter into the agreement or other arrangement from the Adult Parole Authority or a court of law.
7. I agree to the warrantless search of my person, motor vehicle, place of residence, personal property, or property that I have been given permission to use, by my supervising officer or other authorized personnel of the Ohio Department of Rehabilitation and Correction at any time.
8. I agree to fully participate in, and comply with, Special Conditions that will include programming/intervention to address high and moderate domains if indicated by a validated risk tool selected by DRC and any other special conditions imposed by the Parole Board, Court, or Interstate Compact.

Source: Special thanks to the Ohio Adult Parole Authority and Alicia Handwerk.

rights in any parole revocation proceeding. While the court did not grant a full array of due process rights in *Morrissey*, it did advance the mandate of fundamental fairness. The court required the following minimum due process rights in the event of a parole revocation proceeding:

- parolee given advanced written notification of the inquiry, its purpose, and alleged violation;
- a disclosure to the parolee of the evidence against him or her;
- the opportunity to be heard in person and present witnesses and documentary evidence;
- the right to confront and cross-examine adverse witnesses;
- a neutral and detached hearing body;
- a written statement by the hearing body as to the evidence relied upon and reasons for revoking parole.

The *Morrissey* case also established a dual state procedure, including a preliminary inquiry at the time of the alleged parole violations as well as a formal revocation hearing. Left unanswered, however, was the right to counsel, and whether the exclusionary rule should apply to revocation cases. One year later, in the case *Gagnon v. Scarpelli*, 411 U.S. 778 (1973), the court held that parolees do have a limited right to counsel in revocation proceedings and that the hearing body must determine, on a case-by-case basis, whether counsel should be afforded. While it need not be granted in all cases,

> Counsel should be provided where, after being informed of his right, the . . . parolee requests counsel, based on a timely and colorable claim that he had not committed the alleged violation or, if the violation is a matter of public record or uncontested, there are substantial reasons in justification or mitigation that make revocation inappropriate.
>
> (*Gagnon v. Scarpelli*, 411 U.S. 778, 1973)

The exclusionary rule issue remains unanswered. Although illegally seized evidence cannot be used in a criminal trial, many states do permit such evidence to be used in parole revocation cases, where the standard is "probable cause." To date, the courts have generally upheld this practice.

PROBLEMS WITH PAROLE BOARD DISCRETIONARY POWER

Beginning in the 1970s, dramatic shifts began in the field of corrections. Dissatisfied with high recidivism rates, many states opted to amend the traditional indeterminate sentencing model and adopt some of the aspects of a determinate or fixed sentencing model. Use of the indeterminate sentence in the United States represented a grand experiment in controlling, if not eliminating, criminal behavior. Indeterminate sentencing, in which the judge sets limits within legislatively determined minimum and maximum sentences (e.g., 1 to 7 years for burglary), would focus on the individual criminal and his or her needs rather than establishing a fixed penalty for certain types of crime. It sought to maximize the possibility of criminal rehabilitation through the use of various educational, vocational, and psychological treatment programs in the institution, and the use of a parole board that would release the inmate on parole at the optimum moment when change had occurred.

Through this "medical model of corrections," it was argued that such parole board decision making would offer several benefits:

- It would provide an incentive for rehabilitation by linking it to release from prison.
- This incentive would also apply as a mechanism to control the prison population, ensuring inmate discipline and safety.
- Another latent function of parole would be to provide a mechanism to control the size of the prison population.
- Similarly, the parole board would share the responsibility for societal protection with the judiciary through its control over prison release procedures. The board could also serve as a check and balance to judicial discretion by reducing sentencing disparities (such that inmates who committed the same crime would serve approximately the same amount of actual time in prison).

However, a number of factors combined to question the efficacy and fairness of this medical model. Penologists, such as Martinson (1974) and MacNamara (1977), reviewing the outcome of research reports on correctional rehabilitation programs, concluded that the medical model failed to cure criminals, reduce recidivism, or protect the public.[28] Others (Morris, 1974) argued that the medical model harmed inmates because the program participation was tied to and dependent on such participation. From the inmates' point of view, the decisions of the board were arbitrary, capricious, prejudicial, unpredictable, and not subject to external review by any other governmental body (Irwin, 1977). In fact, a number of studies (see Goodstein, 1980) have indicated that inmate frustration over failure to obtain release on parole is a factor that contributes to prison violence (Hassine, 2004).

PAROLE BOARD DECISION-MAKING GUIDELINES

Concerns over some of these issues led a number of jurisdictions to adopt parole release guidelines. The major complaint against parole board decision making has been, and remains, the great amount of discretionary power. The parole decision-making guidelines proposed to structure this discretionary power to promote equity and fairness[29] and also to reduce **sentencing disparity**. The task was to make the decisions of the parole board less arbitrary and more explicit.

These guidelines usually involve a consideration of the seriousness of the offense committed and a "risk" score that includes factors predictive of failure or success on parole. Recommended terms of incarceration are predetermined. For example, if the offender is rated at a "good" risk level and has committed a less serious offense, his or her recommended term of incarceration might fall between 6 and 9 months. Conversely, an offender rated as a "high risk" and convicted of a more serious offense might serve a much longer term prior to consideration for parole. In this fashion, the guidelines system attempts to structure the discretionary power of the parole board while at the same time maintaining equity and fairness (Hoffman, 1983).

Parole boards are also permitted to deviate from the guidelines. They can shorten or lengthen the amount of time specified by the guidelines when, in their judgment, the case at hand appears to merit such consideration. However, when such a step is taken, the examiner is usually required to state the specific factors present that led to such a judgment.

Research indicates that guidelines appear to have some effect in reducing sentencing disparity among inmates. Sentencing disparity is divergence in the types and lengths of sentences imposed for the same crimes, with no evident reason for the differences. The use of parole board decision-making guidelines attempts to deal with the traditional problems of the parole process. They do not represent a panacea, but they are an alternative to the typical method, outright abolition, or use of determinate sentencing. There is evidence of more widespread adoption and use of formal risk assessment, as well as a move toward structural revocation decision making (Runda et al., 1994; Samra et al., 2000).

Abolition of Parole

While some criminologists and practitioners have been content to alter various aspects and procedures of the parole process, others have called for its complete abolition. A number of states have, for all intents and purposes, abolished parole. Whatever the change, one should be aware of the argument by Bill Woodward, former Director of Criminal Justice in Colorado (Gainsborough, 1997, p. 3): "The problem with abolishing parole is you lose your ability to keep track of the inmates and the ability to keep them in treatment if they have alcohol and drug problems." As seen in Table 5.7, the attack on parole release has been ongoing for more than 40 years.

PAROLE EFFECTIVENESS

What is actually known about the effectiveness of parole and what should be future research priorities? The next section summarizes what is generally concluded about selected topic areas of interest in parole effectiveness. This discussion of topic areas is basically organized along the general flow of criminal justice decision points as they relate to parole.

Table 5.7 Some Significant Events in the Abolition of Parole Release

1976	Maine abolishes parole.
1978	California abolishes indeterminate sentences and discretionary parole release.
1980	Minnesota abolishes parole.
1983	Florida abolishes parole.
1984	Washington abolishes parole.
1985	Colorado re-establishes parole.
1986	Congress abolishes parole at the federal level.
1990	Delaware abolishes parole.
1994	Arizona and North Carolina abolish parole.
1995	Virginia abolishes parole.
1996	Ohio abolishes parole.
1998	New York passes *Jenna's Law*, which eliminates discretionary release for all violent felony offenders.
2011	Kansas abolishes the parole board and replaces it with a three-member prison review board under the Department of Corrections.

Source: Compiled by authors.

Institutional Factors

Several aspects of the institutional experience are thought to be related to parole and its effectiveness, such as length of time incarcerated, prison behavior, institutional programs, and parole conditions imposed as conditions of release.

Time Served

Early research that examined the effects of the amount of time served in prison on parole has generally concluded that the shorter the amount of time served, the greater the likelihood of successful parole (Eichman, 1965; Gottfredson et al., 1977).

Similarly, Smith et al. (2002) conducted a meta-analysis of the prison literature. Results included a total of 27 studies comparing community-based offenders (e.g., probationers) to inmates, as well as 23 studies comparing prisoners who served longer sentences with prisoners who served shorter sentences. Results indicated that offenders who were imprisoned had recidivism rates approximately 7 percent higher than community-based offenders, and inmates who served longer sentences had a recidivism rate that was 3 percent higher than inmates with shorter sentences.

Most researchers have concluded that longer prison terms have an adverse effect on a parolee's chances of success, implying that the negative aspects of prisonization seem to intensify with time. For example, in his study of **shock probationers,** Vito (1978) concluded that even a short period of incarceration has a negative impact.

Prison Programs

Does participation in prison programs have an effect on recidivism? Existing research on the effectiveness of institutional programs and prison behavior has been somewhat limited in its scope. Most such programs are analyzed in relation to institutional adjustment, disciplinary problems, and the impact of program participation on the parole-granting process. The few evaluations that included a parole period usually show few, if any, positive effects with regard to recidivism. A study by Smith and Gendreau (2007), however, examined the relationship between program participation and recidivism in a Canadian sample of 5,469 federal offenders. Results indicated that programs targeting criminogenic needs reduced post-release recidivism by 9 percent for moderate-risk offenders and by 11 percent for high-risk offenders. German correctional researchers evaluated the effectiveness of social therapy programs across eight prisons, and the results were remarkably similar (Egg et al., 2000). The overall average reduction in recidivism for what is generally described as moderate- to high-risk adult incarcerates was 12 percent.

In a recent large-scale study in Ohio, Lugo and her colleagues (2017) examined the effects of a prison-based re-entry program on both institutional behavior and recidivism. They found that most programs result in fewer misconducts (violence in particular) and returns to prison. Unfortunately, they did not look at the effects of parole supervision on recidivism.

Most research that has examined prison behavior has not found a relationship between prison behavior and success on parole (Morris, 1978; von Hirsch & Hanrahan, 1979). However, a study by Gottfredson et al. (1982) found that there was some relationship between institutional infractions and infractions while on parole, after controlling for prior record. French and Gendreau (2006) also examined the relationship between participation in prison-based programs and misconducts/post-release recidivism using meta-analytic techniques. Prison-based programs targeting criminogenic needs reduced misconducts by 26 percent and reduced post-release recidivism by 14 percent. Overall, however, there has not been a great deal of attention given to the relationship among institutional programs, prison behavior, and subsequent success or failure on parole.

Parole Conditions

Offenders who are granted parole are required to follow rules and conditions. Failure to do so can lead to re-incarceration. With regard to the imposition of parole conditions, in a nationwide survey of 52 parolee field supervision agencies, Allen and Latessa (1980) found that 49 had residency requirements as a condition of parole and 47 had an employment requirement. A survey by Travis and Latessa (1984) found similar results. In a 1996 review, Hartman and colleagues found that there was a discernible movement away from treatment requirements toward conditions aimed at strengthening surveillance and control. In the most recent survey, Travis and Stacey (2010) found a substantially greater number of conditions imposed than those reported by Hartman et al. (1996), with an average of 18.6 conditions for each jurisdiction ranging from a low of ten to a high of 24. Travis and Stacey concluded that

> current parole rules reflect current and emerging technologies (drug testing, bans of possession of police radio scanners, etc.), and changing views of crime and criminals including an increased emphasis on financial responsibility for offenders (payment of fees and restitution), and risk control (reporting and home visits).
>
> (Travis & Stacey, 2010, p. 607)

Despite the widespread requirement of parole conditions, the literature produced only three studies that were directly related to the imposition of these conditions and parole effectiveness. Although two studies (Beasley, 1978; Morgan, 1993) showed a relationship between stability of residency and parole success, the lack of research in this area makes generalization difficult.

One of the most important conditions of parole is the requirement to report regularly to a parole officer and not to leave a prescribed area, such as the county, without permission. Offenders who fail to report or whose whereabouts are unknown are called **absconders**. A study by Williams et al. (2000) found that 27 percent of parolees in California were listed as absconders, and another study conducted by Schwaner (1997) in Ohio found 11 percent. Absconders have problems with alcohol abuse, have been convicted of a property crime, and have a history of prior parole violation and absence of suitable housing (Bucholtz & Foos, 1996). Despite these high numbers of absconders, there has been little research on this subject.

Parole Supervision

Primarily in response to the supporters of determinate sentencing, researchers have increasingly turned their attention to evaluating the success of parole supervision.

Critics of parole supervision rely on two basic arguments to support their views. The first is that parole supervision is simply not effective in reducing recidivism (Citizens' Inquiry on Parole and Criminal Justice, 1975; Wilson, 1977). The second, more philosophical argument is that supervision is not "just" (von Hirsch & Hanrahan, 1979). A more plausible conclusion is that the evidence is mixed; that parole supervision is effective in reducing recidivism rates among parolees (Flanagan, 1985).

Several studies have compared parolees to mandatory releases, but they have failed to control for possible differences in the selection of the groups (Martinson & Wilks, 1977). Other studies that controlled for differences have reported favorable results (Gottfredson, 1975; Lerner, 1977), whereas other studies have reported less positive results (Jackson, 1983; Nuttal et al., 1977; Waller, 1974). In one study, Gottfredson, Mitchell-Herzfeld et al. (1982, p. 292) concluded that "much of our data does indicate an effect for parole supervision, an effect that varies by offender attributes, and an effect that appears not to be very large." In several more recent studies, Pew Charitable Trusts (2013) and Ostermann (2012, 2013) found that while the differences were not large, New Jersey parolees were less likely to be rearrested, reconvicted, and reincarcerated for new crimes than inmates who maxed out their full sentences and were released without supervision. Ostermann and his colleagues (2015) also found that parole supervision could be considered effective or ineffective depending on the definition of recidivism, particularly when technical violations are factored in.

Despite its widespread use, little is actually known about whether parole reduces recidivism. We do know that about one-half of parole discharges successfully complete parole. In a 2005 study of parole, the Urban Institute concluded that parole supervision has little effect on rearrest rates of released prisoners (Solomon et al., 2005). The existing evidence seems to be mixed concerning parole supervision, and there is no clear consensus as to its effectiveness.

Even the most outspoken critics of parole agree that the agencies responsible for the task of supervision are often understaffed and that their officers are undertrained, underpaid, and overworked. They are inundated with excessively large caseloads, workloads, and paperwork. Community services are either unavailable or unwilling to handle parolees; as a consequence, parole officers are expected to be all things to all people. As indicated in Chapter 7, they are also expected to perform the dual roles of surveillance agent–police officer and rehabilitator–treatment agent.

Some evidence suggests that by shortening the amount of time on parole, we could save a considerable amount of money and time while not seriously increasing the risk of failure. Most data seem to indicate that the majority of failures on parole occur during the first 2 years (Durose et al., 2014; Flanagan, 1982; Hoffman & Stone-Meierhoefer, 1980) and drop significantly thereafter. There is also some evidence that early release into the community and from parole incurs no higher risk to the community and, in fact, is justifiable on cost considerations (Holt, 1975), a conclusion echoed by MacKenzie and Piquero (1994). It is also important to note that easing the offender back into the community through community residential centers and furlough programs can facilitate the early release process. The definition and purpose of community residential centers and furloughs are found in Box 5.14.

Box 5.14
Community Residential Centers and Furloughs

Community residential centers (also known as halfway houses) are residential facilities where parolees may be placed as part of transitioning back into the community. The primary purpose of a halfway house is to limit a parolee's freedom while encouraging reintegration into society through employment, education, treatment, restitution, job training, and other activities designed to help rehabilitate and deter future crime.

Furloughs

Furlough is a phased re-entry program designed to ease the offender's transition from prison to the community. Furloughs include escorted or unescorted leaves from confinement, granted for designated purposes and time periods (funerals, dying relatives, etc.), before the formal sentence expires. Used primarily for employment, vocational training, or education, furlough in effect extends the limits of confinement to include temporary residence in the community during the last months of confinement. Furloughees are frequently required to reside in community residential centers. Furloughs allow parole boards to observe the offender's behavior in the community and may lead to faster release from parole supervision for those adjusting favorably. Because furloughees are closely screened and supervised in the community, failure rates appear to be low and many states have eliminated or severely limited furlough programs.

It is important to note that many of the failures on parole supervision are a result of technical violations (TVs); that is, failure to abide by the conditions imposed by the parole board. Technical violations can range from a positive drug test to failure to report as directed. Some states have implemented new policies to help reduce returns to prison for technical violations. For example, California's new realignment law requires non-violent parolees to be supervised by local probation departments and requires violators to be placed in jail rather than sent back to prison. Another example can be seen in South Carolina (Pelletier et al., 2017), which, in an attempt to reduce returns to prison for technical violations, authorized parole officers to use several types of responses including:

- verbal or written reprimands;
- public-service employment sanctions (requirement to work a certain number of hours in an unpaid position in a non-profit organization);
- public-service employment conversions (converting fees or other financial obligations to public-service employment hours);
- fee exemptions;
- fee restructures;
- home visits.

Types of Crime and Parole Risks

Studies of parole success by type of offense indicate repeatedly that those who commit murder are among the best parole risks. Reasons for this conclusion vary; the explanation offered most frequently is that most murderers tend to be first-time offenders who have committed crimes of passion. Another reason cited is age; because most convicted murderers spend a great amount of time incarcerated, they tend to be older (and more mature) when released, usually after the high-crime-risk years of 18 to 29.

In a study of murderers who had been given a death sentence and then had that sentence commuted when *G v. Georgia* was overturned, Vito et al. (1991) found that 43.5 percent of death-row inmates in Ohio were paroled and 25 percent were returned to prison (recidivated). These results were very similar to those found in Texas, where 19 percent of the paroled *Furman* cases recidivated (Marquart & Sorensen, 1988), and in Kentucky, which had a 29 percent failure rate (Vito & Wilson, 1988). Overall, studies examining murderers were found to generate consistent findings and conclusions over time.

Rearrest Rates

In the most recent study of recidivism of prisoners released in 30 states in 2005, and followed for 9 years to 2014 (Alper et al., 2018), the Bureau of Justice Statistics found very high rates of failure when measured by arrest. Especially concerning is that almost 68 percent were rearrested for new crimes within 3 years, 79 percent within 6 years, and 83 percent within 9 years. This study included both parolees and those released without post-release supervision. Unfortunately, the authors were not able to re-examine whether the rates varied for those under parole supervision. Table 5.8 lists some of the highlights from this study.

While rearrest is the broadest measure of failure (see Chapter 14), these figures do not present an encouraging picture of success for those who have been incarcerated. Clearly, there is more work to be done on this front.

Table 5.8 Highlights from a Recent Study of Arrest Rates

- Almost 47 percent of prisoners who did not have an arrest within 3 years of release were rearrested during years 4 to 9.
- More than 77 percent of drug offenders were rearrested for a non-drug related crime within 9 years.
- Forty-four percent were arrested within the first year of release; 82% were arrested within 3 years; while 24% were arrested during year 9.
- During each year released, property offenders were more likely to be arrested than violent offenders.
- Eight percent of those arrested during the first year were arrested outside the state that released them, compared to 14 percent arrested during year 9.

Source: Alper, M., Markman, J., Durose, M.R. (2018). *2018 update on prisoner recidivism: A 9-year follow-up period (2005–2014)*. Washington, DC: U.S. Department of Justice, Bureau of Justice Statistics.

SUMMARY

Although the early beginnings of parole can be traced to Europe and Australia, the process as it is known today is almost exclusively an American invention. Once embraced by early reformers, parole spread quickly and, by 1944, every state jurisdiction had a parole system. Despite growth, parole was not without its detractors. Early criticism of parole included a suspicion of the way in which prisoners were selected for release, concern over a lack of community supervision, and extensive abuse by prison authorities. Many of the criticisms leveled at parole continue today.

There is considerable contemporary discussion relative to the value of parole. Indeed, there are those who oppose the indeterminate sentencing mode in general and wish to see parole abolished in particular. Concerns over these issues, and the perceived ineffectiveness of the present parole system, have led jurisdictions to either abolish parole altogether or adjust the entire parole process dramatically. Of all community programs, parole faces perhaps the greatest challenge. There are new indications, however, that pragmatism in the form of simple economics may renew an interest in parole. As states look to reduce prison populations, criminal justice planners and politicians have begun to re-examine parole, as seen in California's realignment initiative. Parole emerges as a relatively inexpensive alternative model and, perhaps more importantly, one that is already in place. There is a need, though, to improve both the parole process and supervision so as to overcome the deficiencies detailed earlier.

As parole moves toward structuring release and revocation decisions, two facts remain. First, parole has always served as a "release valve" or mechanism to prevent (or reduce) prison overcrowding, a fact sadly ignored by policy makers and politicians. Second, discretionary parole has within it the authority to retain dangerous persons whose behavior would lead reasonable persons, citizens, and experienced correctional practitioners alike to protect society by not paroling them. If the nation is to avoid the even more extreme policy of hiking sentences by multiples of current statutory terms, parole authorities should have the ability to protect the public by selective incapacitation of those who have several convictions for crimes against a person (murder, rape, aggravated assault, robbery, etc.). Of course, it is important to remember that parole board members are human, and as such they cannot be expected to be infallible. Some inmates invariably are released who should not be, whereas others are kept far longer than necessary. Outcomes such as these require consideration of ways and means to intended objectives, as well as justice.

Review Questions

1. Contrast the punishment model with the reform model of corrections.
2. How did Maconochie contribute to the development of parole?
3. How did parole develop in the United States?
4. What were the early criticisms of parole in America?

5. What were three elements of corruption that emerged in American corrections between 1790 and 1930?
6. Contrast the view of criminals offered by Maconochie with that of J. Edgar Hoover.
7. How did the decade from 1925 to 1935 affect attitudes of the American public toward parole?
8. Debate the following resolution: Discretionary parole from prison should be abolished.
9. What functions do parole boards serve?
10. If parole boards could not release offenders into the community, would they be abolished? Why or why not?
11. How do sentencing guidelines work? Parole guidelines?
12. How can parole boards use and implement intermediate sanctions?

Notes

1   Various forms of conditional release from incarceration were developed in other countries before an American state adopted a parole system. However, the core elements of a parole system administrative board making release decisions and granting conditional, supervised release with the authority to revoke it were first created by legislation in New York State (1869).

2   For an excellent reading of the movement as it relates to the study of crime, see Rennie (1978).

3   For an excellent description of transportation to Australia, see Hughes (1987). Pre-transportation detention was usually in hulks, dilapidated and unseaworthy naval vessels. See Campbell (1994).

4   For a conflicting interpretation of the political purposes intended for prisons, see Durham (1990). It was argued that fair, simple laws, backed by certain and humane punishment, would eradicate crime.

5   See Chayet (1994).

6   It was not uncommon for juveniles to be indentured without a careful investigation of those who would hold the indenture contracts. Thus, juveniles were sometimes indentured to criminals, and the conditions of their indentureships were virtually uncontrolled.

7   The first legislatively authorized "parole officer" position was established in 1937 in Massachusetts. The officer was charged with assisting released convicts to obtain shelter, tools, and work. The legislation made no mention of any surveillance duties.

8   For a history of the American Correctional Association, see Travisono and Hawkes (1995).

9   See Lindsey (1925). Lindsey writes, "There has been considerable modification and variation in various phases of the system as it has spread from one state to another. Methods of administration are also widely different." For an update on parole practices, see Runda et al. (1994).

10 Perhaps chief among these were Wines and Dwight who, in 1867, published a report to the New York Prison Association entitled *Prisons and reformatories of the United States and Canada*. Other state committees echoed the call for a parole system. See *Report of the Massachusetts General Court Joint Special Committee on Contract Convict Labor* (1880). See also Roberts et al. (2000).

11 For a remarkably similar view of contemporary corrections and public fears, see Murphy and Dison (1990). See also Chiricos et al. (2000).

12 On media influence on citizen perception and fear of crime, see Barlow et al. (1995); Bennett and Flavin (1994); Chiricos et al. (1997); Wright et al. (1995).

13 But see DeLoach (1995).

14 Predicting post-release behavior is difficult. See Gottfredson and Gottfredson (1994); and Heilbrun et al. (2000).

15 The offender's mandatory release date in Nebraska is calculated as follows: For all odd-numbered maximum terms, $MR = (Max - 1)/2 + 11$ months. For all even-numbered minimum terms, $MR = Max/2 + 5$ months.

16 Editors (1995).

17 Runda et al. (1994).

18 Such interstate variations may also be true within states. For example, Sutton observed that the decision to place an individual in prison or not, and the length of the sentence *per se*, may be more a function of the county where the sentence was handed down than the nature of the offense. See Sutton (1981). See also Turner et al. (1997).

19 Rhine et al. (1992).

20 Florida Office of Program Policy Analysis and Government Accountability (1996).

21 English et al. (1996).

22 Oregon Intermediate Sanctions for Female Offenders Policy Group (1995). *Intermediate sanctions for females*. Salem, OR: Oregon Department of Corrections.

23 Sutton (1981).

24 Pagliaro and Pagliaro (1992). See also Hammett, Harrold and Epstein (1994), Hammett, Harrold and Gross (1994).

25 Monahan and Steadman (1994).

26 See *Block v. Potter*, 631 E2d 233 (3d Cir. 1980); *Candelaria v. Griffin*, 641 E2d 868 (10th Cir. 1980); *Farris v. U.S. Board of Parole*, 384 F.2d 948 (7th Cir. 1973).

27 Gottfredson and Gottfredson (1994).

28 The weight of evidence has shifted against the "nothing works in corrections" argument. Overwhelming evidence shows that programs designed specifically for offenders' needs and delivered in a coherent manner by trained intervention personnel, assisted by competent supervisors, work and are effective. See Cullen and Gendreau (2001).

29 As defined by Gottfredson et al. (1973, p. 34), equity and fairness mean that "similar persons are dealt with in similar ways in similar situations. Fairness thus implies the idea of similarity and of comparison."

Recommended Readings

Hughes, R. (1987). *The fatal shore*. New York: Alfred A. Knopf. [This is the definitive book on the history of Australia as a penal colony, and the roots of parole as developed by Captain Maconochie.]

Rothman, D.J. (1971). *The discovery of the asylum: Social order and disorder in the New Republic*. Boston, MA: Little, Brown. [This book presents an excellent history of the use of punishments and corrections in early colonial America.]

Rothman, D.J. (1980). *Conscience and convenience: The asylum and its alternatives in progressive America*. Boston, MA: Little, Brown. [A fastidious discussion of the modern effort to reform the programs that have dominated criminal justice in the twentieth century.]

References

Allen, H., Latessa, E. (1980). *Parole effectiveness in the United States: An assessment*. San Jose, CA: San Jose State University Research Foundation.

Allen, H.E., Latessa, E.J., Ponder, B. (2019). *Corrections in America*. 15th ed. New York: Pearson.

Alper, M., Markman, J., Durose, M.R. (2018). *2018 update on prisoner recidivism: A 9-year follow-up period (2005–2014)*. Washington, DC: U.S. Department of Justice, Bureau of Justice Statistics.

Babst, D.V., Inciardi, J.A., Jarman, D.R. (1970). *The uses of configural analysis in parole prediction research*. New York: Narcotics Control Commission.

Beasley, W. (1978). *Unraveling the process of parole: An analysis of the effects of parole residency on parole outcome*. Paper presented at the meeting of the American Society of Criminology, Atlanta, GA.

Barlow, M., Barlow, D., Chiricos, T. (1995). Economic conditions and ideologies of crime in the media: A content analysis of crime news. *Crime & Delinquency* 43, 3–19.

Barnes, H.E., Teeters, N.D. (1959). *New horizons in criminology*. Englewood Cliffs, NJ: Prentice Hall.

Barry, J.V. (1957). Captain Alexander Maconochie. *The Victorian Historical Magazine* 27, 1–18.

Beccaria, C. (1764). *On crimes and punishments*. Indianapolis, IN: Bobbs-Merrill (H. Paulucci, trans., 1963).

Bennett, R., Flavin, J. (1994). Determinants of the fear of crime: The effects of cultural setting. *Justice Quarterly* 11, 357–381.

Block v. Potter, 631 E2d 233 (3d Cir. 1980).

Bromley, E., Gathercole, C.E. (1969). Boolean predication analysis: A new method of prediction index construction. *British Journal of Criminology* 17, 287–292.

Bucholtz, G., Foos, R. (1996). *Profiling parole violators at large*. Columbus, OH: Department of Rehabilitation and Correction.

Burgess, E.W. (1928). Factors determining success or failure on parole. In: B. Harmo, E.W. Burgess, C.L. Landeson, Eds. *The workings of the indeterminate sentence law and the parole system in Illinois*. Springfield: Illinois State Board of Parole.

Burke, P. (1997). *Policy driven responses to probation and parole violators*. Washington, DC: U.S. National Institute of Justice.

Camp, C., Camp, G. (2000). *The 2000 corrections yearbook: Adult corrections*. Middletown, CT: Criminal Justice Institute.

Campbell, C. (1994). *The intolerable hulks: British shipboard confinement*. Bowie, MD: Heritage Books.

Candelaria v. Griffin, 641 F.2d 868 (10th Cir. 1980).

Carson, A.E. (2018). *Prisoners in 2016*. Washington, DC: U.S. Department of Justice, Bureau of Justice Statistics.

Carter, R.M., McGee, R.A., Nelson, K.E. (1975). *Corrections in America*. Philadelphia, PA: J.B. Lippincott.

Chayet, E. (1994). Correctional "good time" as a means of early release. *Criminal Justice Abstracts* 26, 521–538.

Chiricos, T., Escholz, S., Gertz, M. (1997). Crime, news and fear of crime. *Social Problems* 44(3), 342–357.

Chiricos, T., Padgett, K., Gerz, M. (2000). Fear, TV news and the reality of crime. *Criminology* 38(3), 755–785.

Citizens' Inquiry on Parole and Criminal Justice. (1975). *Prison without walls: Report on New York parole*. New York: Praeger.

Clare, P.K., Kramer, J.H. (1976). *Introduction to American corrections*. Boston, MA: Holbrook Press.

Cullen, F., Gendreau, P. (2001). From nothing works to what works: Changing professional ideology in the 21st century. *The Prison Journal* 81(3), 313–338.

Dawson, R.O. (1966). The decision to grant or deny parole: A study of parole criteria in law and practice. *Washington University Law Quarterly* June, 248–285.

DeLoach, C. (1995). *Hoover's FBI: The inside story by Hoover's trusted lieutenant*. Washington, DC: Regenery.

Durham, A.M. (1990). Social control and imprisonment during the American Revolution: Newgate of Connecticut. *Justice Quarterly* 7, 293–323.

Durose, M.R., Cooper, A.D., Snyder, H.H. (2014). *Recidivism of prisoners released in 30 states in 2005: Patterns from 2005 to 2010*. U.S. Department of Justice, Bureau of Justice Statistics.

Editors, (1995). APPA and APAI go on the offensive for parole. *American Probation and Parole Perspectives* 19(3), 12.

Egg, R., Pearson, F.S., Cleland, C.M., Lipton, D.S. (2000). Evaluations of correctional treatment programs in Germany: A review and meta-analysis. *Substance Use and Misuse* 35, 1967–2009.

Eichman, C. (1965). *The impact of the Gideon decision upon crime and sentencing in Florida: A study of recidivism and social-cultural change* (Unpublished master's thesis). Florida State University, Tallahassee.

English, K., Colling, C., Pullen, S. (1996). *How are adult felony sex offenders managed on probation and parole: A national assessment*. Denver: Colorado Department of Public Safety.

Farris v. U.S. Board of Parole, 384 F.2d 948 (7th Cir. 1973).

Flanagan, T. (1982). Risk and the timing of recidivism in three cohorts of prison releasees. *Criminal Justice Review* 7, 34–45.

Flanagan, T. (1985). Questioning the "other" parole: The effectiveness of community supervision of offenders. In: L. Travis (Ed.), *Probation, parole and community corrections* (pp. 167–184). Prospect Heights, IL: Waveland.

Florida Office of Program Policy Analysis and Government Accountability. (1996). *Information brief of control release workload of the Florida Parole Commission*. Tallahassee: FOPPAGA.

Fogel, D. (1975). *We are the living proof: The justice model for corrections*. Cincinnati, OH: Anderson.

French, S.A., Gendreau, P. (2006). Reducing prison misconducts. *Criminal Justice and Behavior* 33, 185–218.

Furman v. Georgia, 408 U.S. 238 (1972).

Gagnon v. Scarpelli, 411 U.S. 788 (1973).

Gainsborough, J. (1997). Eliminating parole is a dangerous and expensive proposition. *Corrections Today* 59(4), 23.

Glaser, D. (1962). Prediction tables as accounting devices for judges and parole boards. *Crime & Delinquency* 8, 239–258.

Goodstein, L. (1980). Psychological effects of the predictability of prison release: Implications for the sentencing debate. *Criminology* 18, 363–384.

Gottfredson, D. (1975). *Some positive changes in the parole process*. Paper presented at the meeting of the American Society of Criminology.

Gottfredson, D.M., Babst, D.V., Ballard, K.B. (1958). Comparison of multiple regression and configural analysis techniques for developing base expectancy tables. *Journal of Research in Crime and Delinquency* 5, 72–80.

Gottfredson, S., Gottfredson, D. (1993). The long-term predictive utility of the base expectancy score. *Howard Journal of Criminal Justice* 32, 276–290.

Gottfredson, S., Gottfredson, D. (1994). Behavioral prediction and the problem of incapacitation. *Criminology* 32, 441–474.

Gottfredson, D., Gottfredson, M., Garofalo, J. (1977). Time served in prison and parolee outcomes among parolee risk categories. *Journal of Criminal Justice* 5, 1–12.

Gottfredson, D., Hoffman, P.B., Sigler, M., Wilkins, L. (1975). Making parole policy explicit. *Crime & Delinquency* 21, 34–44.

Gottfredson, M., Mitchell-Herzfeld, S., Flanagan, T. (1982). Another look at the effectiveness of parole supervision. *Journal of Research in Crime and Delinquency* 18, 277–298.

Greenholtz v. Inmates of the Nebraska Penal and Correctional Complex, 442 U.S. 1 (1979).

Hammett, T., Harrold, L., Epstein, J. (1994). *Tuberculosis in correctional facilities*. Washington, DC: U.S. Department of Justice.

Hammett, T., Harrold, L., Gross, M. (1994b). *1992 update: HIV/AIDS in correctional facilities: Issues and options*. Washington, DC: U.S. Department of Justice.

Hart, H. (1923). Predicting parole success. *Journal of Criminal Law and Criminology* 14, 405–414.

Hartman, J., Travis, L., Latessa, E. (1996). *Thirty-nine years of parole rules*. Paper presented at the annual meeting of the Academy of Criminal Justice Sciences, Las Vegas, NV, March.

Hassine, V. (2004). *Life without parole: Living in prison today*. 3rd ed. Los Angeles: Roxbury.

Hawkins, K.O. (1971). *Parole selection: The American experience* (Unpublished doctoral dissertation). University of Cambridge, Cambridge, UK.

Heilbrun, K., Brock, W., Waite, D., Lanier, A., Schmid, M., Witte, G., . . . Shumater, M. (2000). Risk factors for juvenile criminal recidivism. *Criminal Justice and Behavior* 27(3), 275–291.

Hoffman, P. (1983). Screening for risk. *Journal of Criminal Justice* 11(6), 539–547.

Hoffman, P., Stone-Meierhoefer, B. (1980). Reporting recidivism rates: The criterion and follow-up issues. *Journal of Criminal Justice* 8, 53–60.

Holt, N. (1975). Rational risk taking: Some alternatives to traditional correctional programs. *Proceedings: Second National Workshop on Corrections and Parole Administration, Louisville, Kentucky*.

Hughes, R. (1987). *The fatal shore*. New York: Alfred A. Knopf.

Irwin, J. (1977). Adaptation to being corrected: Corrections from the convict's perspective. In: R.G. Legar, J.R. Stratton (Eds.), *The sociology of corrections* (pp. 276–300). New York: John Wiley and Sons.

Jackson, P. (1983). *The paradox of control: Parole supervision of youthful offenders*. New York: Praeger.

Johnson, E. (1994). Opposing outcomes of the industrial prison: Japan and the United States compared. *International Criminal Justice Review* 4(1), 52–71.

Kaeble, D. (2018). *Probation and parole in the United States, 2016*. Washington, DC: U.S. Department of Justice, Bureau of Justice Statistics.

Latessa, E., Smith, P., Lemke, R., Makarios, M., Lowenkamp, C. (2010). The creation and validation of the Ohio Risk Assessment System (ORAS). *Federal Probation* 74(1), 16–22.

Lerner, M. (1977). The effectiveness of a definite sentence parole program. *Criminology* 15, 32–40.

Lindsey, E. (1925). Historical origins of the sanction of imprisonment for serious crime. *Journal of Criminal Law and Criminology* 16, 9–126.

Loza, W., Loza, F. (2000). Predictive validity of the self-appraisal questionnaire (SAQ). *Journal of Interpersonal Violence* 15(11), 1183–1191.

Lugo, M., Wooldredge, J., Pompoco, A., Sullivan, C., Latessa, E.J. (2017). Reducing institutional misconduct and prison "returns" with Reentry Approved Unit management programs. *Justice Quarterly*.

MacKenzie, D., Piquero, A. (1994). The impact of shock incarceration programs on prison crowding. *Crime & Delinquency* 40, 222–249.

MacNamara, D.E. (1977). The medical model in corrections: Requiescat in Pax. *Criminology* 14, 435–438.

Maguire, M., Peroud, B., Dison, J. (Eds.). (1996). *Automatic conditional release: The first two years*. London: Her Majesty's Stationery House.

Marquart, J., Sorensen, J. (1988). Institutional and post-release behavior of Furman-commuted inmates in Texas. *Criminology* 26, 667–693.

Martinson, R. (1974). What works? Questions and answers about prison reform. *Public Interest* 25 (Spring), 22–25.

Martinson, R., Wilks, J. (1977). Save parole supervision. *Federal Probation* 42(3), 23–27.

Monahan, J. (1981). *Predicting violent behavior: An assessment of clinical techniques.* Beverly Hills, CA: Sage.

Monahan, J., Steadman, H. (1994). In: J. Monahan, H. Steadman (Eds.), *Violence and mental disorder: Developments in risk assessment.* Chicago: University of Chicago Press.

Morgan, K. (1993). Factors influencing probation outcome: A review of the literature. *Federal Probation* 57(2), 23–29.

Morris, N. (1974). *The future of imprisonment.* Chicago: University of Chicago Press.

Morris, N. (1978). *Conceptual overview and commentary on the movement toward determinacy. Determinate sentencing: Proceedings of the special conference on determinate sentencing.* Washington, DC: National Institute of Law Enforcement and Criminal Justice.

Morrissey v. Brewer, 408 U.S. 471 (1972).

Murphy, J.W., Dison, J. (1990). *Are prisons any better? Twenty years of correctional reform.* Newbury Park, CA: Sage.

Nuttal, C.P. and Associates. (1977). *Parole in England and Wales.* Home Office Research Studies No. 38. London: Her Majesty's Stationery Office.

Offutt, W. (1995). *Of "good laws" and "good men": Law and society in the Delaware Valley,* 1680–1710. Chicago: University of Chicago Press.

O'Leary, V., Hanrahan, K. (1977). *Parole systems in the United States: A detailed description of their structure and procedure.* 3rd ed. Hackensack, NJ National Council on Crime and Delinquency.

Oregon Intermediate Sanctions for Female Offenders Policy Group (1995). *Intermediate sanctions for females.* Salem, OR: Oregon Department of Corrections.

Ostermann, M. (2012). Recidivism and the propensity to forgo parole release. *Justice Quarterly* 29, 596–618.

Ostermann, M. (2013). Active supervision and its impact upon parolee recidivism rates. *Crime and Delinquency* 59, 487–509.

Ostermann, M., Salerno, L.M., Hyatt, J.M. (2015). How different operationalizations of recidivism impact conclusions of effectiveness of parole supervision. *Journal of Research in Crime and Delinquency* 52, 771–796.

Pagliaro, P., Pagliaro, A. (1992). Sentenced to death: HIV infections and AIDS in prison—current and future concerns. *Canadian Journal of Criminology* 34(2), 201–214.

Pelletier, E., Peterson, B., King, R. (2017). *Assessing the impact of South Carolina's parole and probation reform.* Washington, DC: Urban Institute.

Pew Charitable Trusts. (2013). *The impact of parole in New Jersey* Washington, DC: Pew.

Pew. (2014). *Max out: The rise in prison inmates released without supervision.* Available at: www.pewtrusts.org/en/research-and-analysis/reports/2014/06/04/max-out

Pisciotta, A. (1982). Saving the children: The promise and practice of Parens Patria, 1838–1898. *Crime & Delinquency* 28(3), 410–425.

President's Commission on Law Enforcement and Administration of Justice, (1967). *The challenge of crime in a free society.* Washington, DC: U.S. Government Printing Office.

Rennie, Y. (1978). *The search for criminal man.* Lexington, MA: D.C. Heath.

Report of the Massachusetts General Court Joint Special Committee on Contract Convict Labor. (1880). *Report of the Massachusetts General Court Joint Special Committee on Contract Convict Labor.* Boston, MA: State of Massachusetts.

Rhine, E., Smith, W., Jackson, R. (1992). *Paroling authorities: Recent history and current practices.* Laurel, MD: American Correctional Association.

Roberts, J., Nuffield, J., Hahn, R. (2000). Parole and the public. *Empirical and Applied Criminal Justice Research Journal* 1(1), 1–25.

Rothman D.J. (1971). *The discovery of the asylum: Social order and disorder in the new republic.* Boston, MA: Little, Brown.

Runda, J., Rhine, E., Wetter, R. (1994). *The practice of parole boards.* Lexington, KY: Council of State Governments.

Samra, G., Pfeifer, J., Ogloff J. (2000). Recommendations for conditional release suitability. *Canadian Journal of Criminology* 42(4), 421–447.

Schwaner, S. (1997). They can run, but can they hide? A profile of parole violators at large. *Journal of Crime and Justice* 20(2), 19–32.

Sellin, T. (1970). The origin of the Pennsylvania system of prison discipline. *The Prison Journal* 50(13), 13–15, 17.

Sherrill, M.S. (1977). Determinate sentencing: History, theory, debate. *Corrections Magazine* 3, 3–13.

Smith, P., Gendreau, P. (2007). The relationship between program participation, institutional misconduct and recidivism among federally sentenced adult male offenders. *Forum on Corrections Research* 19, 6–10.

Smith, P., Goggin, C., Gendreau, P. (2002). *The effects of prison sentences and intermediate sanctions on recidivism: General effects and individual differences.* A Report to the Corrections Research Branch. Ottawa, ON: Solicitor General of Canada.

Smykla, J.O. (1984). *Prediction in probation and parole: Its consequences and implications.* Paper presented at the annual meeting of the Academy of Criminal Justice Sciences, Chicago, IL.

Solomon, A.L., Kachnowski, V., Bhati, A. (2005). *Does parole work?* Washington, DC: Urban Institute.

Sutton, P.L. (1981). *Criminal sentencing in Nebraska: The feasibility of empirically based guidelines.* Williamsburg, VA: National Center for State Courts.

Travis, L., Latessa, E. (1984). "A summary of parole rules—thirteen years later": Revisited thirteen years later. *Journal of Criminal Justice* 12, 591–600.

Travis, L., Stacey, J. (2010). A half century of parole rules: Conditions of parole in the United States. *Journal of Criminal Justice* 38, 604–608.

Travisono, A., Hawkes, M. (1995). *Building a voice: The American Correctional Association, 125 years of history.* Lanham, MD: ACA. Available at: www.corrections.com/aca/history/html

Turner, M., Cullen, F., Sundt, J. (1997). Public tolerance for community-based sanctions. *Prison Journal* 77(1), 6–26.

Vito, G. (1978). *Shock probation in Ohio: A comparison of attributes and outcomes* (Unpublished doctoral dissertation) Ohio State University, Columbus.

Vito, G., Wilson, D. (1988). Back from the dead: Tracking the progress of Kentucky's Furman-commuted death row population. *Justice Quarterly* 5, 101–111.

Vito, G., Wilson, D., Latessa, E. (1991). Comparison of the dead: Attributes and outcomes of Furman-commuted death row inmates in Kentucky and Ohio. In: R.M. Bohm (Ed.), *The death penalty in America: Current research* (pp. 101–111). Cincinnati, OH: Anderson Publishing Co.

von Hirsch, A., Hanrahan, K. (1979). *The question of parole: Retention, reform, or abolition*. Cambridge, MA: Ballinger.

Waller, I. (1974). *Men released from prison*. Toronto, ON: University of Toronto Press.

Wiggins, M.E. (1984). *False positives/false negatives: A utility cost analysis of parole decision making*. Paper presented at the annual meeting of the Academy of Criminal Justice Sciences, Chicago, IL.

Wilcox, C. (1929). Parole: Principles and practice. *Journal of Criminal Law and Criminology* 20, 345–354.

Wilkins, L.E., MacNaughton-Smith, P. (1964). New prediction and classification methods in criminology. *The Journal of Research in Crime and Delinquency* 1, 19–32.

Williams, F., McShane, M., Dolny, H.M. (2000). Predicting parole absconders. *Prison Journal* 80, 24–39.

Wilson, R. (1977). Supervision (the other parole) also attacked. *Corrections Magazine* 3(3), 56–59.

Wines, E.C., Dwight, T.W. (1867). *Prisons and reformatories of the United States and Canada*. Albany: New York Prison Association.

Wright, J., Cullen, E., Blankenshin, M. (1995). The social construction of corporate violence: Media coverage of the Imperial Food Products fire. *Crime & Delinquency* 41(1), 20–36.

Chapter 6

OFFENDER ASSESSMENT

Key Terms

actuarial prediction
clinical prediction
dynamic risk predictors
false negatives
false positives
major risk factors
need
professional discretion

reassessment
reliability
responsivity
risk
risk management
risk reduction
static risk predictors
validity

> Assessment is the engine that drives effective interventions. —Edward Latessa

Over the years, the assessment of offenders has evolved from using a "gut feeling" to instruments that focused on past behavior (static indicators) to what are now called fourth-generation instruments. The latest instruments combine static and dynamic factors together to provide a more accurate prediction of risk, and they identify the crime-producing needs that should be targeted for change in correctional treatment programs. They also facilitate case planning as well as the identification of strengths and barriers that support or hinder the behavioral change of the offender.

IMPORTANCE OF ASSESSMENT AND CLASSIFICATION

There are a number of reasons why classification and assessment of offenders are important in community corrections. First, assessment and classification help guide and structure decision making and provide important information that correctional practitioners and officials can use as the basis for decisions such as parole release. Second, they can help reduce bias by eliminating extralegal factors, such as race and ethnicity, from consideration. Third, they enhance public safety by

---

Box 6.1
Static versus Dynamic Risk Predictors

Static risk predictors refer to those factors or characteristics of an offender that cannot change. An example would be criminal history. For example, the number of prior arrests, age at first arrest, number of times incarcerated, and so on, are good predictors of risk. However, once in place, they cannot change. Dynamic risk predictors are those factors or characteristics of an offender that contribute to their risk, but are changeable; for example, peer associations, substance abuse, criminal thinking, and lack of employment. These factors also help to predict reoffending and provide the probation or parole officer with areas to target. It should be noted that there are two types of dynamic factors: acute and stable. *Acute factors* can change quickly (such as employment), whereas *stable factors* are areas that take more time to change (such as attitudes and values).

---

allowing court and correctional agencies to identify higher-risk offenders. Fourth, they help in managing offenders in a more efficient manner. This allows agencies to develop caseloads and workloads around risk and needs, and to conserve scarce resources for those who need them most and prevent doing harm to low-risk offenders. Finally, the use of these instruments can aid in legal challenges. It is much easier to justify a decision based on a structured process that has been validated than one based on "gut feelings" (or so-called "expert opinion"). Perhaps the most important reason to conduct good assessments of offenders is that it improves the effectiveness of correctional programs. This is best illustrated by looking at the principles of effective intervention.

PRINCIPLES OF OFFENDER CLASSIFICATION

Through the work of a number of researchers, our understanding of classification and assessment and the important role they play in community corrections is becoming more apparent (Andrews, 1982, 1989; Bonta, 2002; Bonta & Motiuk, 1985; Gendreau et al., 1996; Jones, 1996; Kennedy & Serin, 1997; Latessa & Lovins, 2010).

The key findings of meta-analyses (or quantitative reviews) of the corrections literature have been summarized into a framework that is referred to as the "principles of effective intervention." Let us now review these principles in more detail.

- **Risk:** WHO we should target for intervention. Higher-risk offenders are characterized by greater criminogenic needs; use a valid and reliable measure to assess offender risk; target higher-risk offenders for treatment.
- **Need:** WHAT we should target for intervention. Match offenders to programs that address their criminogenic needs; target more criminogenic needs than

non-criminogenic needs (those needs that someone may have, but are not strongly correlated with criminal behavior).

- **Responsivity:** HOW we should target problem behaviors (including antisocial and criminal behaviors). Use potent behavior change strategies (i.e., social learning, cognitive-behavioral approaches); deliver intervention in a style and mode consistent with the ability and learning style of the offender and recognize that individuals may be more responsive to certain staff.
- **Professional discretion:** Having considered risk, need, and responsivity, decisions are made as appropriate under present conditions.

Risk

For our purposes, **risk** refers to the probability that an offender will reoffend. Thus, high-risk offenders have a greater probability of reoffending than low-risk offenders. It is important to remember that the seriousness of the offense usually trumps "risk." That is, someone who commits a violent offense may be incarcerated, even if they are at low risk to reoffend.

The risk principle involves predicting future criminal behavior *and* matching interventions and supervision to the risk level of the offender. This principle states that interventions should be focused primarily on higher-risk offenders. The reason is simple: They have the highest chances of reoffending. Besides, why should we devote resources to those offenders who have a low probability of coming back again? Here is another way to think about it. Suppose that half of all offenders who leave prison never return. Are we worried about this group? Well, not as much as about the half who will return. This is the group we are most concerned about and the one where we should place most of our efforts. Of course, in order to meet this principle, it is necessary to identify the higher-risk offender, a process that involves a valid and reliable assessment process. Not only is it a question of resources, but it is also an effectiveness question. A number of studies have shown that placing lower-risk offenders into intensive programs and higher levels of supervision can actually increase their failure rates.

Figure 6.1 shows the results from a study of intensive rehabilitation supervision in Canada. Data showed that higher-risk offenders placed in the intensive rehabilitation supervision program had a 32 percent recidivism rate after the 2-year follow-up. Higher-risk offenders not placed in the program had a 51

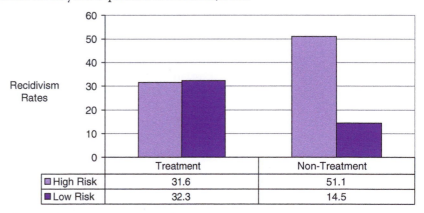

	Treatment	Non-Treatment
High Risk	31.6	51.1
Low Risk	32.3	14.5

Figure 6.1 Study of Intensive Rehabilitation Supervision in Canada

Source: Adapted from Bonta, J., Wallace-Capretta, S., Rooney, J. (2000). A quasi-experimental evaluation of an intensive rehabilitation supervision program. *Criminal Justice and Behavior* 27(3), 312–329.

percent recidivism rate. This is a 19 percent reduction in recidivism for higher-risk offenders. However, low-risk offenders placed in the treatment program reported the same recidivism rate as their high-risk counterparts. Conversely, lower-risk offenders not placed in the program reported a recidivism rate almost 20 percent lower. In a nutshell, the intensive rehabilitation supervision program worked for higher-risk offenders, but actually increased recidivism rates for lower-risk offenders.

The risk principle can also be seen in a study that Latessa, Lovins et al. (2010) conducted in Ohio. This study examined the effectiveness of 44 halfway houses and 20 community-based correctional facilities and involved more than 20,000 offenders. Figure 6.2 shows average changes in recidivism based on the risk level of the offender. Low-risk offenders actually showed an increase in recidivism, while there was a reduction in recidivism for high-risk offenders.

The question is: Why do programs that have such a positive effect on high-risk offenders have such a negative effect on low-risk offenders? There are a couple of explanations. First, placing low-risk and high-risk offenders together is never a good practice. For example, if you had a son or daughter who got into some trouble, would you want them placed in a group with high-risk kids? Of course not. Second, when we take lower-risk offenders, who, by definition, are fairly prosocial (if they weren't, they wouldn't be low risk), and place them in a highly structured, restrictive program, we actually disrupt the factors that make them low risk. For example, if you were sent to a correctional treatment program for 6 months, would you lose your job or have to drop out of school? Would you experience family disruption? Would your neighbors have a "welcome home from the correctional program" party when you got out? In other words, the criminal justice system would probably have inadvertently increased your risk by disrupting protective factors. Finally, increasing the conditions and surveillance of low-risk offenders can lead to more technical violations and higher rates of revocation. For example, if a low-risk offender is required to report two times a week, there is a greater chance that they will miss an appointment, possibly leading to a violation of their supervision. The risk principle, then, refers to WHO should be targeted for placement in more intense services and supervision.

Low risk	↑ recidivism by 3%
Moderate risk	↓ recidivism by 6%
High risk	↓ recidivism by 14%

Figure 6.2 Average Reduction in Recidivism by Risk Level for Halfway House Offenders

Source: Latessa, E., Lovins, L.B., Smith, P. (2010). *Follow-up evaluation of Ohio's community based correctional facility and halfway house programs— Outcome study.* Cincinnati, OH: School of Criminal Justice, University of Cincinnati.

Need

The second principle is known as the **need** principle and is the WHAT to target. The need principle states that interventions and programs should target criminogenic risk factors, those areas more strongly correlated with criminal behavior.

Box 6.2
Criminogenic Needs and Promising Targets

Criminogenic needs refer to those crime-producing factors associated with criminal behavior. The new generation of risk assessment tools measures these needs. Some of the promising need factors that should be identified by researchers include the following:

- Changing antisocial attitudes
- Changing antisocial feelings
- Reducing antisocial peer associations
- Promoting familial affection and communication
- Promoting familial monitoring and supervision
- Increasing self-control and problem-solving skills
- Reducing chemical dependencies.

Correlates of Criminal Conduct

What factors are correlated with criminal conduct? This is a critical question and one that criminologists have been wrestling with since criminology began. The first person to study criminals scientifically was Cesare Lombroso, who in 1876 wrote *Criminal Man.* Lombroso had personally studied more than 5,000 Italian criminals and, based on his studies, believed that about one-third of all offenders were "born" criminal, or what he called atavistic throwbacks. Lombroso believed that the born criminal could be identified through a number of factors: excessive hairiness, sloping foreheads, tattoos, solitary line in the palm of the hand, and other attributes. Despite the popularity at the time of this theory, Lombroso was incorrect and his work was flawed. The reason he is important, however, is that he was the first person to try to study criminals scientifically. Since Lombroso, there have been hundreds—if not thousands—of studies on this topic. Of course, this is part of the problem. If you start reading this literature, it will take years, and when you are done, you will be just as confused as when you started. For every study that says that something is a risk factor, there is another that says it isn't. So, what do we believe? Fortunately, through the use of meta-analysis, researchers have been able to review large numbers of studies and determine effect sizes (how strong factors are in predicting risk).

Over the years, research by scholars such as Gendreau (1996), Simourd and Andrews (1994), and Andrews and Bonta (1996) has provided an identification of the **major risk factors** associated with criminal conduct. Table 6.1 shows the eight major risk factors, or correlates of criminal conduct, starting with antisocial, pro-criminal attitudes, values, beliefs, and cognitive emotional states (such as anger and rage).

The risk factor of antisocial, pro-criminal attitudes, values, beliefs, and cognitive emotional states manifests itself in several important ways—negative expressions

Table 6.1 Major Set of Risk Factors

1. Antisocial/pro-criminal attitudes, values, beliefs, and cognitive emotional statesre
2. Pro-criminal associates and isolation from anti-criminal others
3. Temperamental and personality factors conducive to criminal activity, including:
   - psychopathy
   - weak socialization
   - impulsivity
   - restless/aggressive energy
   - egocentricism
   - below-average verbal intelligence
   - a taste for risk
   - weak problem-solving/self-regulation skills
4. A history of antisocial behavior
   - evident from a young age
   - in a variety of settings
   - involving a number and variety of different acts
5. Family factors that include criminality and a variety of psychological problems in the family of origin, including:
   - low levels of affection, caring, and cohesiveness
   - poor parental supervision and discipline practices
   - outright neglect and abuse
6. Low levels of personal educational, vocational, or financial achievement
   - lack of education and/or employment can lead to lower financial means, leading to high-crime neighborhoods or attempts to increase finances by illegal means
   - being in school or employed can be prosocial activities that occupy time
   - being in school or employed can expose a person to prosocial others
   - being in school or employed can provide reinforcement for prosocial activities
7. Low levels of involvement in prosocial leisure activities
   - allows for interaction with antisocial peers
   - allows for offenders to have idle time
   - offenders replace prosocial behavior with antisocial behavior
8. Abuse of alcohol and/or other drugs
   - it is illegal itself (drugs)
   - engages with antisocial others
   - impacts social skills

about the law, about conventional institutions, about self-management of behavior, and a lack of empathy and sensitivity toward others. In addition, offenders often minimize or neutralize their behavior. Neutralizations are a set of verbalizations which function to say in particular situations that it is okay to violate the law (see Sykes & Matza, 1957). Neutralization techniques include denial of responsibility—criminal acts are due to factors beyond the control of the individual ("I was drunk." "Some dude told me I could borrow his car."); denial of injury—the offender admits responsibility for the act, but minimizes the extent of harm or denies any harm was done ("Yeah, I beat him up, but he only went to the hospital so he could collect unemployment."); denial of the victim—reverses the role of the offender and victim and blames the victim ("She knows not to nag me." "I'm really the victim here."); system-bashing—those who disapprove of the offender's acts are defined as immoral, hypocritical, or criminal themselves ("Everyone uses drugs, I just got caught."); and appeal to higher loyalties—meaning that offenders live by a different code and the demands of larger society are sacrificed for the demands of more immediate loyalties ("You don't understand. Me and my friends have a different set of rules we live by.").

The second major risk factor is one that we are all familiar with—having pro-criminal friends and acquaintances *and* a lack of prosocial friends and acquaintances. As our mothers all knew, whom you hang around with is very important. Friends often act as role models, provide the context, and provide the reinforcement for criminal behavior.

The third major risk factor is one that is often ignored in assessment—temperament and personality factors. These include acting impulsively, weak socialization, being adventurous and a risk taker, and a lack of coping and problem-solving skills. Please note that egocentrism is correlated with risk. Many offenders are self-centered and have an inflated sense of self (as opposed to the commonly held perception that offenders suffer from low self-esteem). Studies are finding that criminals are more likely to be characterized as negative or hostile in interpersonal relationships, unempathetic, and lacking in self-control. However, personality is most likely working in tandem with other risk factors such as peers and attitudes. Just being egocentric will not make someone a high risk for criminal conduct. If that were the case, we would have to lock up most of the judges and professors in this country.

The fourth major risk factor is the one that is used most commonly: history. This includes criminal history and other antisocial behavior. Although history is a very strong predictor of future behavior, it has its limitations. The first limitation is that it is not very dynamic, and while it is useful for prediction, it does not provide much direction as to targets for change. The other limitation of history is that one has to have the history before it can be used in prediction. For example, it is not difficult to predict that someone who has four or five prior driving under the influence (DUI) offenses has a drinking problem and might drink and drive again. At one point, however, they had their first DUI. Undoubtedly, they probably had a number of other risk factors; however, because they had no history of DUI offenses, we would have had little on which to base prediction if we relied primarily on history. Again, this is not to say that history is not a very strong (if not the strongest) predictor of future behavior. Life course studies indicate that by age 12, up to 40 percent of later serious offenders have committed their first criminal act; and that by age 14, up to 85 percent have committed their first criminal act.

The fifth major risk factor involves family factors, including criminal behavior in the immediate family, and a number of other problems, such as low levels of affection, poor parental supervision, and outright neglect and abuse.

In at number six are low levels of personal educational, vocational, and financial achievement—essentially work and school performance are correlated with risk. Getting an offender a job or an education is important for several reasons (it structures time, gets them around prosocial people, helps them support family and self), but if a person thinks that working is for chumps, shows up late for work all the time, fights with the boss or co-workers, and so forth, how long will they last on the job? Can you see why attitudes and values are so important to identifying and reducing risk? It is a critical factor in determining how we behave.

Finally, factors seven and eight would include a lack of prosocial leisure activities and interests, and substance abuse. Of course, both of these allow for interaction with antisocial peers and, in the case of drugs, are usually illegal in and of themselves.

A minor set of risk factors includes lower-class origins as assessed by adverse neighborhood conditions as well as some personal distress factors, such as anxiety, depression, or being officially labeled as mentally disordered. Finally, some biological and neuropsychological indicators have also shown some correlation with criminal conduct. Again, however, these factors are relatively minor and should not be the major focus or targets for changing criminal behavior. For example, making an offender feel better about himself without reducing antisocial attitudes and values will only produce a happier offender. Many researchers believe that most of the secondary risk factors run through the first four: (1) attitudes, values, and beliefs, (2) peer associations, (3) personality, and (4) history. These are referred to as the "Big Four" by Andrews and Bonta (2010; also see Bonta & Andrews, 2017).

A study conducted by researchers at the Pennsylvania Department of Corrections looked at factors related to failure for parolees. As shown in Table 6.2, most factors were related directly to attitudes, peers and associates, and personality. These findings are consistent with the research on risk factors and the importance of targeting criminogenic areas of offenders. Not surprisingly, successes and failures did not differ in difficulty in finding a place to live after release, and were equally likely to report eventually obtaining a job.

Criminogenic risk factors should be the major target of programs and interventions, while non-criminogenic risk factors, such as lack of creative abilities, physical conditioning, medical needs, anxiety, and low self-esteem, may be barriers that get in the way of programming, but they are not highly correlated with criminal conduct and should not be the primary targets for programs.

Figure 6.3 shows results from a meta-analysis that compared effects from programs that target criminogenic versus non-criminogenic needs. As can be seen by this graph, programs that target at least four to six more criminogenic needs produced a 31 percent reduction in recidivism, while those programs that targeted one to three more non-criminogenic needs essentially showed no effect on recidivism. These data illustrate the importance of assessing and subsequently targeting dynamic risk factors that are highly correlated with criminal conduct. It also illustrates that the density of criminogenic needs targeted is also important. For

Table 6.2 Results from Pennsylvania Study of Parole Failures

Social Network and Living Arrangements

Violators were:

- More likely to hang around with individuals with criminal backgrounds
- Less likely to live with a spouse
- Less likely to be in a stable, supportive relationship
- Less likely to identify someone in their life who served in a mentoring capacity

Employment and Financial Situation

Violators were:

- Slightly more likely to report having difficulty getting a job
- Less likely to have job stability
- Less likely to be satisfied with employment
- Less likely to take low-end jobs and work up
- More likely to have negative attitudes toward employment and unrealistic job expectations
- Less likely to have a bank account
- More likely to report that they were "barely making it" (yet success group reported over double median debt)

Alcohol or Other Drug Use

Violators were:

- More likely to report use of alcohol or other drugs while on parole (but no difference in prior assessment of dependency problem)
- Poor management of stress was a primary contributing factor to relapse

Life on Parole

Violators had:

- Unrealistic expectations about what life would be like outside of prison
- Poor problem-solving or coping skills
- Did not anticipate long-term consequences of behavior
- Failed to utilize resources to help them
- Acted impulsively to immediate situations
- Felt they were not in control
- More likely to maintain antisocial attitudes
- Viewed violations as an acceptable option to situation
- Maintained general lack of empathy
- Shifted blame or denied responsibility

Successes and failures did not differ in difficulty in finding a place to live after release

Successes and failures equally likely to report eventually obtaining a job

Source: Bucklen, K.B., Zajac, G. (2009). But some of them don't come back (to prison!): Resource deprivation and thinking errors as determinants of parole success and failure. *Prison Journal* 89(3), 239–264.

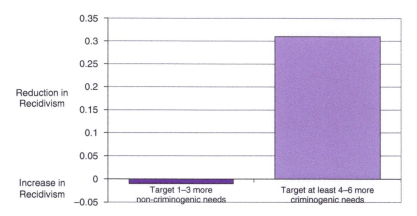

Figure 6.3 Targeting Criminogenic Need: Result from Meta-Analyses

Source: Gendreau, P., French, S.A., Taylor, A. (2002). *What works (what doesn't work) revised 2002.* Invited submission to the International Community Corrections Association Monograph Series Project.

example, most higher-risk offenders have multiple risk factors, not just one; as a result, programs that are limited to focusing on one or two targets for change may not produce much effect. Let's take, for example, employment. For many offenders on probation or parole, being unemployed is a risk factor, but is it a risk factor for you? If you were unemployed, would you start robbing people or selling drugs? Most of us wouldn't. What we would do if we lost our job is to go out and get another one. In other words, just being unemployed is not that big a risk factor unless, of course, you think things like, "I can make more money in a day selling drugs than most can in a month," or if you hang around others who don't work, and so forth. In this case, being unemployed is a risk factor because you have a number of other critical risk factors, plus you have a lot of time on your hands to do nothing but get into trouble. Just targeting employment without including other risk factors (such as attitudes) will not produce much effect.

Responsivity

The third principle is called the **responsivity** principle and has two parts: general and specific. General responsivity refers to the basic approaches to intervention that are most effective (i.e., yield the largest reductions in reoffending) for most offenders. Interventions that are based on cognitive theories, behavioral theories, and social learning theories have been found to be most effective. We will discuss these approaches in more detail in Chapter 8. Specific responsivity refers to matching offenders to programs and interventions based on learning styles and ability. Responsivity factors include those characteristics of an offender related to their learning ability and program engagement. Examples would include motivation or readiness to change, social support for change, intelligence, psychological development, maturity, and other factors that can affect an offender's engagement in a program. These factors are often ignored in the assessment process. For example, say you have identified the risk and need levels of an offender, but he or she is low functioning. Because that person will not do well in a program that requires normal functioning, this factor should be taken into consideration when matching him or her to a program, group, or caseworker. In a study of over 19,000 offenders, Cohen and Whetzel (2014) found that transportation, mental health, homelessness/unstable housing, and lack of motivation were the most common barriers, and not surprisingly, were more likely to be present for higher-risk offenders.

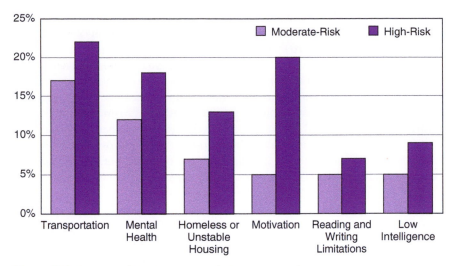

Figure 6.4 Percent of Participants with Responsivity Issues

Source: Adapted from Cohen, T., Whetzel, J. (2014). The neglected "R": Responsivity and the federal offender. *Federal Probation* 78, 11–18.

Box 6.3
Responsivity Factors

Recognizing differences in offenders that affect their engagement in treatment and their ability to learn is part of assessing responsivity. Developing a strategy to overcome these barriers is part of developing a good case plan. Some responsivity considerations include the following:

General population
- Anxiety
- Self-esteem
- Depression
- Mental illness
- Age
- Intelligence
- Gender
- Race/ethnicity
- Motivation

Factors more common with offenders
- Poor social skills
- Inadequate problem solving
- Concrete-oriented thinking
- Poor verbal skills
- Lack of social support for receiving services

Professional Discretion

The final principle is called professional discretion. Basically, this means that the person conducting the assessment, after considering risk, need, and responsivity factors, should include his or her professional judgment in making a final decision about the risk to reoffend. Remember that risk and need assessments are designed to help guide decisions, not to make them. At the same time, professional override of the results of risk assessment should be used cautiously and relatively infrequently (i.e., not more than approximately 10 percent of the time). When overrides are used, the vast majority are upward (from lower to higher risk). On average, the original risk levels were more strongly associated with recidivism. However, some researchers have concluded that inclusion of overrides "does no harm," but the data suggest that inclusion of professional discretion does not improve validity of the assessment tool (Cohen et al., 2016; Girard & Wormith, 2004; Wormith et al., 2012; see also McCafferty, 2015). So why allow professional discretion? There are several reasons:

- Staff may resist use of a tool that that totally supplants professional judgement and experience.
- Practical reasons, such as policies or political considerations that require certain offenses (serious felonies) to be treated as higher risk.
- Gaps in assessment information.

THE EVOLUTION OF CLASSIFICATION

How is offender risk determined? This is obviously a very important question because it can affect public protection and the manner in which an offender is supervised in the community (or whether they are even released).

The first generation of risk assessment in criminal justice refers to the use of "gut feelings" to make decisions about the risk of an offender. With this process, information is collected about the offender, usually through an interview or file review. The information is then reviewed, and a general assessment or global prediction is made: ("In my professional or expert opinion . . ."). The problems with this approach are considerable and have been delineated by Wong (1997) and Kennedy (1998):

- Predictions are subject to personal bias.
- Predictions are subjective and often unsubstantiated.
- Decision rules are not observed.
- It is difficult to distinguish levels of risk.
- Information is overlooked or overemphasized.

The second generation of formal classification instruments was pioneered by Bruce and colleagues (1928). Development of a standardized and objective instrument was brought about by the request of the Illinois Parole Board, which wanted to make more informed decisions about whom to release on parole. Bruce and colleagues reviewed the records of nearly 6,000 inmates. Table 6.3 illustrates factors found by Bruce et al. (1928) in their risk prediction instrument. While many of these categories seem out of date today, the Burgess scale was one of the first

Table 6.3　Factors in the Bruce, Harno, Burgess, and Landesco Scale

- General type of offense (e.g., fraud, robbery, sex, homicide)
- Parental and marital status (parents living, offender married)
- Criminal type (first timer, occasional, habitual, professional)
- Social type (e.g., farm boy, gangster, hobo, ne'er-do-well, drunkard)
- Community factor (where resided)
- Statement of trial judge and prosecutor (recommended or protests leniency)
- Previous record
- Work record (e.g., no work record, casual, regular work)
- Punishment record in prison
- Months served prior to parole
- Intelligence rating
- Age when paroled
- Psychiatric prognosis
- Psychiatric personality type (egocentric, socially inadequate, emotionally unstable)

Source: Bruce, A., Harno, A., Burgess, E., Landesco, J. (1928). *The workings of the intermediate-sentence law and the parole system in Illinois*. Evanston, IL: Northwestern University Press.

attempts to develop an actuarial instrument to predict offender risk. There are several pros and cons to this approach (Kennedy, 1998; Wong, 1997):

Pros
- It is objective and accountable.
- It covers important historic risk factors.
- It is easy to use and reliable.
- It distinguishes levels of risk of reoffending.

Cons
- It consists primarily of static predictors (i.e., factors that are immutable).
- It does not identify target behaviors.
- It is not capable of measuring change in the offender.

The second generation of risk prediction recognized that risk is more than simply static predictors. The best example can be seen in the Wisconsin Case Management Classification System. First developed and used in Wisconsin in 1975, the Case Management Classification (CMC) System is designed to help identify the level of surveillance for each case, as well as determine the needs of the offender and the resources necessary to meet them. With adequate classification, limited resources can be concentrated on the most critical cases—those of high risk (Wright et al., 1984). Following Wisconsin's development of the CMC, the National Institute of Justice (1983) adopted it as a model system and began advocating and supporting its use throughout the country.

The foundation of the system is a risk/needs assessment instrument completed on each probationer at regular intervals. Cases are classified groups, such as high, medium, or low risk/needs. In turn, these ratings are used to determine the level of supervision required for each case. When an offender is classified into a risk/needs level with the Wisconsin risk and needs assessment tools, a more detailed assessment of that case can be made with a profiling interview that helps determine the relationship between the officer and the offender. This element of the Wisconsin system is called the CMC system and is composed of four unique treatment modalities.

- **Selective Intervention:** This group is designed for offenders who enjoy relatively stable and prosocial lifestyles (e.g., they are employed, established in the community, and have minimal criminal records). Such offenders have typically experienced an isolated and stressful event or neurotic problem. With effective intervention, there is a higher chance of avoiding future difficulty. Goals of treatment for these individuals include the development of appropriate responses to temporary crises and problems and the re-establishment of prosocial patterns.
- **Environmental Structure:** The dominant characteristics of offenders in this group consist of deficiencies in social, vocational, and intellectual skills. Most of their problems stem from their inability to succeed in their employment or to be comfortable in most social settings—an overall lack of social skills and intellectual cultivation/ability. Goals for these persons include (a) developing basic employment and social skills; (b) selecting alternatives to association with criminally-oriented peers; and (c) improving social skills and impulse controls.
- **Casework/Control:** These offenders manifest instabilities in their lives as evidenced by failures in employment and domestic problems. A lack of goal directedness is present, typically associated with alcohol and drug problems. Offense patterns include numerous arrests, although marketable job skills are present. Unstable childhoods, family pressure, and financial difficulties are typically present. Goals appropriate for this group include promoting stability in their professional and domestic endeavors and achieving an improved utilization of the individual's potential, along with an elimination of self-defeating behavior and emotional/psychological problems.
- **Limit Setting:** Offenders in this group are commonly considered to be successful career criminals because of their long-term involvement in criminal activities. They generally enjoy "beating the system," they frequently act for material gain, and they show little remorse or guilt. Because of their value system, they adapt easily to prison environments and return to crime upon release. Goals for this group are problematic, but include changing the offender's basic attitudes and closely supervising his or her behavior within the community.

Information for the CMC is based on a structured interview with the offender. After a case has been classified, an individual treatment plan is developed. Results from the CMC have found that approximately 40 percent of probation caseloads are selective intervention, 15 percent are environmental structure, 30 percent are casework control, and 15 percent are limit setting.

> **Box 6.4**
> **Actuarial versus Clinical Prediction**
>
> **Actuarial prediction**, or statistical prediction, involves examining a group of offenders and identifying the factors associated with recidivism (or some other measure of outcome). With statistical prediction, offenders with a certain set of characteristics have a range of probabilities associated with success or failure. So, for example, if we have 100 high-risk offenders and our classification instrument indicated that the probability of failure for high-risk offenders is 75 percent, we are relatively confident that 75 out of 100 of those offenders will recidivate (assuming no intervention). Of course, we are predicting to the group and not the individual, so we do not know which 75 will fail. With **clinical prediction**, a trained professional gathers information and then uses his or her professional experience and judgment to render an opinion about the likelihood that an individual will fail or succeed. The evidence is very strong that actuarial or statistical prediction is more accurate than clinical prediction. In fact, several more articles have been published on the use of such measures for predicting risk with separate measures of dynamic needs in order to maximize the accuracy of risk classification (see Baird, 2009), but this idea has been rigorously debated.

Despite the advantages of the CMC, there are several shortcomings. One is the fact that risk and needs are assessed separately and not integrated fully. Another problem with this system is that the CMC component is time-consuming to administer and scoring is somewhat involved. In practice, many probation departments which use this instrument rely more heavily on the risk component, which is composed of mainly static predictors.

A later version of third-generation assessment instruments successfully combine risk and needs and are relatively easy to use. One example is the Level of Service Inventory–Revised (LSI-R), designed by Andrews and Bonta (1995). The LSI-R has been extensively tested and validated across North America. The LSI-R consists of 54 items in ten areas. Information is collected primarily through a structured interview process. The LSI-R has been found to be one of the most valid instruments in predicting recidivism.

More recently, the LSI-R was updated by reorganizing the original ten subcomponents into general and specific risk and need factors. This new instrument is considered fourth generation and is called the Level of Service/Case Management Inventory (LS/CMI) (Andrews et al., 2004). It represents an improvement over the previous version (and other third-generation classification instruments), as it emphasizes the link between assessment and case management. In addition to identifying risk and need factors, the LS/CMI acknowledges the role of personal strengths and specific responsivity factors in an offender's amenability to treatment. Figure 6.5 shows recidivism results from 561 probationers whose risk

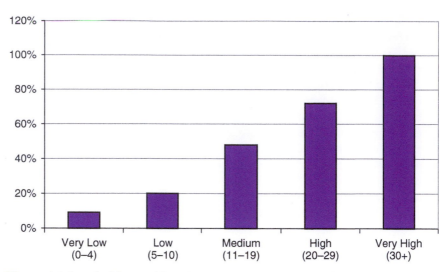

Figure 6.5 Level of Service/Case Management Inventory and Recidivism

Source: Adapted from Andrews, D.A., Bonta, J. (2006). *The psychology of criminal conduct.* 4th ed. Newark, NJ: LexisNexis Matthew Bender (Anderson Publishing), p. 69.

was assessed using the LS/CMI (see Andrews & Bonta, 2006). Recidivism rates increase directly with LS/CMI scores. A sample of some LS/CMI categories is shown in Table 6.4.

For federal probation, the Post Conviction Risk Assessment (PCRA) instrument was developed (Johnson et al., 2011) and has been found to be valid with a wide range of offenders including white-collar criminals (Harbinson, 2017), as well as across race, gender, and ethnicity (Lowenkamp et al., 2015). Recently, a new version, the PCRA 2.0 was released that includes a violence assessment component (Serin et al., 2016).

Another example of a fourth-generation assessment tool is the newly developed Ohio Risk Assessment System (ORAS) (Latessa, Lemke et al., 2010). Unlike previous tools, the ORAS was developed and validated by examining offenders at various decision points in the criminal justice system. The result is four assessment tools (pretrial, community supervision, prison intake, and re-entry), each designed to assess offenders based on where they are in the system. One of the primary advantages of this collection of instruments is that it establishes a common language for the purpose of case management across settings. Furthermore, several of the items are common across instruments (particularly the ones assessing static items) and can therefore reduce the time required to complete subsequent assessments in other settings. The ORAS is used in a number of jurisdictions; see Table 6.5.

The ORAS has been validated in a number of studies. Figure 6.6 and Figure 6.7 show the results from a study in Texas where the system is called the TRAS. The tool was valid for both males and females as well as different racial and ethnic groups. (Lovins et al., 2017).

Table 6.4 Areas of the Level of Service/Case Management Inventory

Section 1. General Risk/Need Factors
Criminal history
Education/employment
Family/marital
Leisure/recreation
Companions
Alcohol/drug problem
Procriminal attitude/orientation
Antisocial pattern

Section 2. Specific Risk/Need Factors
Personal problems with criminogenic potential
Diagnosis of "psychopathy"
Anger management deficits
Poor social skills
Underachievement

History of perpetration
Sexual assault, extrafamilial, child/adolescent/female victim
Physical assault (extrafamilial adult victim)
Gang participation

Section 3. Special Responsivity Considerations
Motivation as a barrier
Women, gender specific
Low intelligence
Antisocial personality/psychopathy

Section 4. Case Management Plan Program targets and intervention plan

Source: Adapted from Andrews, D.A., Bonta, J. (2006). *The psychology of criminal conduct.*
4th ed. Newark, NJ: LexisNexis Matthew Bender (Anderson Publishing).

Table 6.5 Jurisdictions That Use the ORAS*

Alabama
Arizona
California:
- Monterey County
- Ventura County
- Yolo County
- Calaveras County
Colorado
Connecticut
Florida:
- Alachua County
- Orange County

(Continued)

Table 6.5 (Continued)

- Osceola County
- Seminole County

Illinois

Indiana

Massachusetts

Missouri

- Kansas City

Montana

New Hampshire

Pennsylvania

- Dauphin County
- York County

Ohio

Oklahoma

Texas

Vermont

Note: *Some jurisdictions use selected tools from the ORAS.

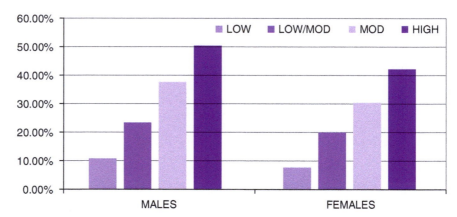

Figure 6.6 Texas Risk Assessment System (aka ORAS) Risk Levels by Gender

Source: Lovins, B., Latessa, E.J., May, T., Lux, J. (2017). Validating the Ohio Risk Assessment System Community Supervision Tool with a diverse sample from Texas. *Corrections: Policy, Practice and Research* 3, 1–16.

An example of a case management plan that could be used in conjunction with a fourth-generation assessment tool is provided in Figure 6.8. Note that the need domain (i.e., dynamic risk factor) is translated into a goal (long-term behavioral change) with associated objectives and strategies.

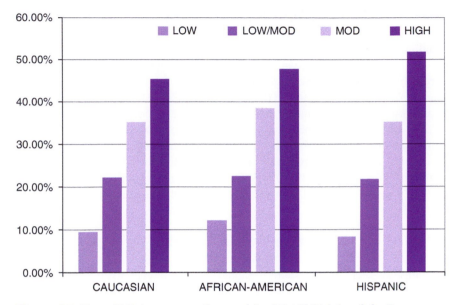

Figure 6.7 Texas Risk Assessment System (aka ORAS) Risk Levels by Race

Source: Lovins, B., Latessa, E.J., May, T., Lux, J. (2017). Validating the Ohio Risk Assessment System Community Supervision Tool with a diverse sample from Texas. *Corrections: Policy, Practice and Research* 3, 1–16.

Problem/need: Drug use	*Need area risk level:* Moderate		
Strengths: Prosocial family support	*Barriers:* Lack of motivation		
Goal: Eliminate use of marijuana			
Objectives:	*Strategies:*	Date Initiated:	Date Completed:
Participate in substance abuse assessment by October 1	Refer for substance-abuse assessment	9/10/18	9/29/18
By next meeting, list pros of participating in and cons for not complying with treatment	Cost–benefit analysis	10/1/18	10/15/18
Attend and participate in all substance-abuse treatment activities over next 2 months	Refer for services Monitor with drug screens Updates from treatment provider and offender	11/1/18	

Figure 6.8 Sample Case Management Plan

JUVENILE RISK/NEED ASSESSMENT TOOLS

Traditionally, there have been fewer actuarial instruments available for juvenile offenders. Recently, however, we have seen the development of a number of new instruments designed specifically for this population. The Ohio Youth Assessment System (OYAS), the Youth LS/CMI (Level of Service/Case Management Inventory), and the Youth Assessment and Screening Instrument (YASI), are examples of risk and need assessment tools that have been developed recently for use with the juvenile population. These instruments are very similar in nature to the latest generation of adult instruments. Figure 6.9 is an example of the report generated from the Dispositional Assessment of the OYAS. This tool includes seven domains and gives the judge a view of the overall risk of the youth as well as scores in each domain.

SPECIALIZED ASSESSMENT TOOLS

There are also classification systems designed for certain types of offenders or need areas, such as the mentally disordered, sex offenders, and substance abusers. Some of these tools help to classify and recommend levels of intervention. Figure 6.10 shows the use of specialized assessment tools across the United States.

One of the major advantages of actuarial risk and need assessment tools is that they are standardized and objective and help distinguish levels of risk or need (e.g., high, medium, low). Because they are based on statistical studies, they also reduce bias and false positive and false negative rates (Holsinger et al., 2001).

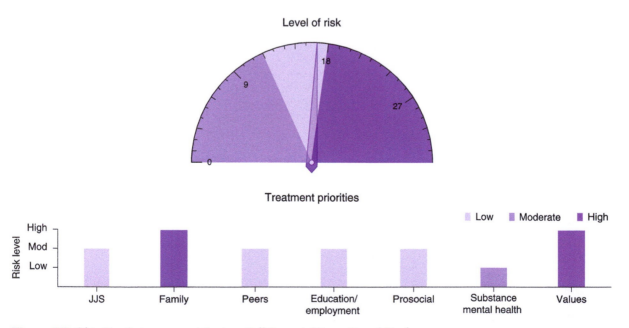

Figure 6.9 Ohio Youth Assessment System Full Report: Dispositional Tool

In a national survey of probation and parole agencies concerning the use and practices surrounding class classification, Hubbard et al. (2001) found that the vast majority of agencies reported using some actuarial instrument to assess and classify offenders. A summary of their findings is presented here.

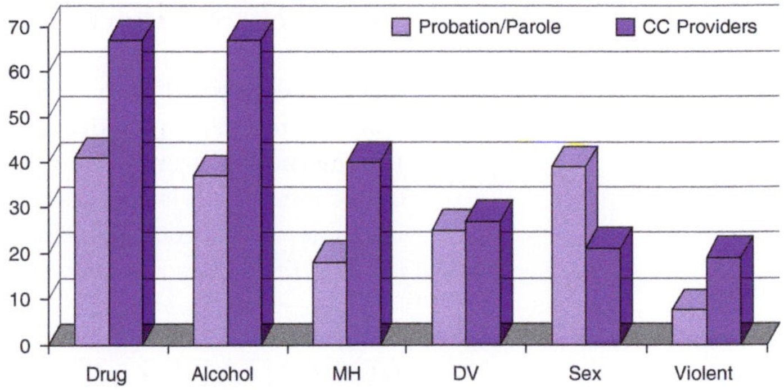

Almost 75 percent of the probation and parole agencies and about 56 percent of the community corrections service providers reported that they classify using standardized and objective instruments. Large agencies were more likely to classify clients than were smaller agencies. More than 83 percent of the respondents reported that it was "absolutely" or "very necessary" to classify on risk and 66 percent that it was "absolutely" or "very necessary" to classify on needs.

Nearly all respondents agreed that case classification makes their job easier, benefits the offender, creates a more professional environment, helps staff make better decisions, increases effectiveness of service delivery, and enhances fairness in decision making.

The most common uses of these tools were officer workloads (75 percent), staff deployment (54 percent), development of specialized caseloads (47 percent), and sentencing decisions (20 percent). Nearly 80 percent of the agencies reported using the various instruments to reassess offenders.

Figure 6.10 Use of Specialized Assessment Tools by Probation, Parole, and Community Corrections Service Providers (percent)

Note: DV = Domestic Violence; MH = Mental Health.

Source: Hubbard, D.J., Travis, L., Latessa, E. (2001). *Case classification in community corrections: A national survey of the state of the art.* Washington, DC: U.S. Department of Justice, National Institute of Justice; Cincinnati, OH: Center for Criminal Justice Research, University of Cincinnati.

CRITICISMS OF ASSESSMENT TOOLS

Offender classification is not without its critics. Some argue that the instruments are nothing more than "educated guesses" (Smykla, 1986, p. 127), whereas others are more concerned about their proper use and accuracy (Greenwood & Zimring, 1985; Wilbanks, 1985). Some critics, such as Baird (2009), argue that risk and need factors should not be combined because risk factors are distinct from need factors. However, others contend that most of what are called "needs" are, in fact, "risk" factors (i.e., substance use, peer associations, attitudes, and values) and should be integrated into the tools. Another issue that has been raised centers on the use of a risk instrument in one jurisdiction that has been developed and validated in another. The argument has been made that just because a risk instrument is accurate in one jurisdiction, it does not necessarily mean it will be effective in predicting outcomes in another (Collins, 1990; Kratcoski, 1985; Sigler & Williams, 1994; Wright et al., 1984). As Travis (1989, p. 17) stated, "ideally, a risk classification device should be constructed based on the population on which it is to be used." Most researchers, however, believe that while cut-off scores may vary across jurisdictions, risk factors are common across offender populations and jurisdictions, and most studies have confirmed this finding. Another important issue centers on the concern about bias—especially with regard to minority groups. The evidence, however, indicates that most tools are predictive across different groups (Skeem & Lowenkamp, 2016). Despite these concerns, risk assessment tools are commonly used in community corrections, and it is important to remember that the alternative is judgment and intuition—not a good substitute for science. As Skeem and Lowenkamp state (2016, p. 680), "data is more helpful than rhetoric if the goal is to improve practice."

ADVANTAGES OF ASSESSMENT TOOLS

Despite these concerns, most believe that the use of validated assessment instruments is a major advancement in offender management and treatment. For example, Clear (1988) maintains that the implementation of these prediction instruments has two main advantages:

> First, they improve the reliability of decisions made about offenders—in a sense they make correctional officials more predictable. Second, they provide a basis on which corrections personnel can publicly justify both individual decisions and decision-making policies. In both cases, the advantage is grounded in the powerful appearance of "scientific" decision-making.
>
> (Clear, 1988, p. 2)

In addition to the advantages just given, the use of assessment tools based on dynamic factors provides the ability to reassess the offender to determine whether there has been a reduction in risk score. This allows an agency to move beyond risk management to risk reduction, the ultimate goal of community corrections. Tools like the LSI-R and ORAS-CST (Community Supervision Tool) can be used to reassess offenders and there is a relationship between changes in scores and recidivism.

Figure 6.11 illustrates the percentage of offenders who changed scores from intake to reassessment. This study found that for every one point increased in the LSI-R score, there was a 5 percent increase in recidivism; and for every one point decreased, there was a 6.25 percent decrease in recidivism (Labrecque et al., 2014). As shown, these data can help a probation department better focus its resources and strategies.

Another example is demonstrated in Figure 6.12, which shows results from the **reassessment** of offenders sentenced to an Ohio community-based correctional facility. The purpose of these facilities is to provide up to 6 months of secure, structured treatment to felony offenders who would otherwise be incarcerated in a prison. Results from this study show that the greatest reductions in risk scores were for the highest-risk offenders, while low-risk offenders actually saw their risk scores increase. In general, treatment lowers offenders' risk of recidivism. These data demonstrate the risk principle, which states that intensive treatment services should be reserved for higher-risk offenders. As can be seen from these data, when lower-risk offenders are placed in an intensive intervention program, the outcome

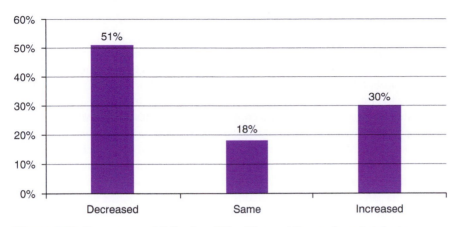

Figure 6.11 Percentage of Offenders Who Changed Scores from Intake to Reassessment

Source: Adapted from Labrecque, R., Smith, P., Lovins, B., Latessa, E. J. (2014). The importance of reassessment: How changes in the LSI-R risk score can improve the prediction of recidivism. *Journal of Offender Rehabilitation* 53, 116–128.

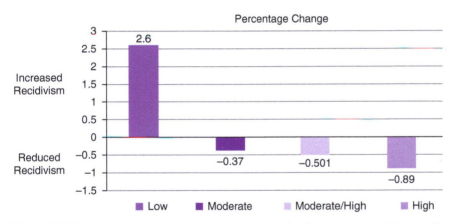

Figure 6.12 Changes in Recidivism Rates as a Result of Treatment as Measured by Changes in LSI-R Scores (by Risk Category)

Source: Latessa, E.J., Lowenkamp, C. (2001). *Testing the LSI-R in community-based correctional facilities.* Cincinnati, OH: Center for Criminal Justice Research, University of Cincinnati.

is often detrimental to the offender. There are two reasons why this effect occurs. The first may be due to the influence of higher-risk offenders on low-risk, more prosocial individuals. The second is probably due to the disruption of prosocial networks and other social support mechanisms that low-risk offenders usually possess (or they would not be low risk!). For example, placement in a program such as the one described earlier usually results in loss of employment and disruption to the family.

Reliability and Validity

A number of important considerations with any risk/need assessment process must be considered. How easy is the instrument to use and score? How long does it take to complete? How much training is involved? Is an interview involved; if so, how do you verify the information? How much does it cost? These and other questions are important considerations when selecting a risk/need assessment instrument. Of vital importance are the reliability and validity of the instrument. **Reliability** refers to the consistency of the instrument. For example, if two probation officers were to use the LSI to assess the same offender, how similarly would they score him or her? This is referred to as inter-rater reliability and can be a problem with more dynamic instruments. The second important consideration is **validity,** the accuracy of the instrument in predicting what we want it to predict. They are both important. It doesn't do any good to have an accurate tool if no one can agree on the score. Likewise, they might all agree on the score, but if it doesn't predict what we want it to, then that doesn't really matter. As a general rule, most good instruments are about 80 percent accurate. This is determined by validation studies in which we determine the correlation between the score and some outcome (usually some measure of recidivism)—the higher the correlation, the stronger the relationship. Two important factors have been found to increase the validation of assessment: training of staff on the tool and experience using the tool (Flores et al., 2006).

Box 6.5
False Positives and False Negatives

False positives occur when offenders predicted to fail actually succeed, whereas **false negatives** occur when predicted successes actually fail. False negatives are potentially very costly; hence most classification strategies err on the conservative side.

The goal of most assessment and classification processes is to minimize both false positives and false negatives. Some studies of clinical assessment have found that clinicians will over-predict violence in two out of three cases!

Points about "Good" Assessment

A number of points about classification and assessment should be considered. First, there is no one-size-fits-all approach. Each agency or jurisdiction has different needs. For example, if operating a pretrial release program, one of the considerations would be "failure to appear." This might not be important to a secure residential program. There is also no one instrument that will provide all the information needed for a comprehensive assessment. Assessment often has to be a flexible process that expands as warranted. Second, it is important to validate instruments to ensure accuracy and to determine the degree to which they can predict different outcome measures. For example, if an agency is interested in predicting sex-offending behavior, they need to make sure that the tools they are using can predict this outcome accurately. Third, classification and assessment are not one-time events. Risk can change over time. An offender who began supervision without a job, drinking, and hanging around with a bad crowd, but 6 months later is employed, sober, and attending to family responsibilities will be lower risk than when he or she began supervision. Fourth, statistical prediction is more accurate than clinical prediction. Instruments specifically designed and validated on offender populations will more accurately predict outcome than the best clinical assessment process. Classification based on standardized factors is also more reliable, less time-consuming, and less expensive than clinical assessment. Finally, as mentioned previously, decisions based on objective criteria are less vulnerable to legal challenges.

Other Problems with Assessment

Despite the obvious problems associated with developing, norming, and validating instruments designed to predict human behavior, there are also a number of other problems associated with offender assessment.

Many agencies assess offenders, but ignore important factors. An example would be an agency that relies on a static risk assessment instrument that focuses primarily on criminal history. An offender without a long criminal history might be classified as low risk even though they may have a number of other important risk factors. Another example would be an agency that focuses primarily on substance abuse and ignores antisocial attitudes, antisocial friends, and other criminogenic risk factors. Another problem common with offender assessment is that of processes that assess offenders but do not produce scores or distinguish levels. These processes are usually quasi-clinical in nature. The program or probation department will gather a great deal of information about the offender, write it up in narrative form, but when finished, will not be able to distinguish levels of risk or needs. A third problem is that of programs and agencies that assess offenders and then essentially don't use the information; everyone gets the same treatment or intervention regardless of the assessment results. A fourth problem is that some programs begin using an assessment tool without adequately training the staff in their use or interpretation. This affects the instrument's reliability and accuracy, and a host of other problems often emerge when this happens. Finally, many assessment instruments are adopted without being normed or validated on an offender population. Without this information, the accuracy of the instrument is essentially unknown.

Despite these concerns, the latest generation of classification instruments allows the probation or parole department an effective and fairly simple means of classifying and managing offenders. It is important to remember that instruments such as the ORAS or LSI-R can be important and useful tools in assisting the community correctional agency and the supervising officer in case management. They neither solve all the problems faced by probation and parole agencies nor fully replace the sound judgment and experience of well-trained probation and parole officers (Klein, 1989; Schumacher, 1985).

STANDARDS OF CLASSIFICATION

Travis and Latessa (1996) have identified ten elements of effective classification and assessment. They comprise:

1. **Purposeful:** Generally, the purpose of classification and assessment is to ensure that offenders are treated differentially within a system so as to ensure safety, adequate treatment, and understanding.
2. **Organizational fit:** Organizations and agencies have different characteristics, capabilities, and needs.
3. **Accuracy:** How well does the instrument correctly assess outcome? Is the offender correctly placed within the system? Basically, reliability and validity are the key elements to accuracy. Glick and colleagues (1998, p. 73) explain reliability and validity thus: "Reliability may be defined as hitting the same spot on a bull's eye all the time. If your system is reliable but not valid, you may be hitting the target consistently, but not the right spot."
4. **Parsimony:** This refers to the ease of use, the economy of composition, and achieving accuracy with the least number of factors. In other words, short and simple.
5. **Distribution:** How well does the system disperse cases across classification groups? If all offenders fall into the same group, there is little distribution.
6. **Dynamism:** Is the instrument measuring dynamic risk factors that are amenable to change? Dynamic factors also allow you to measure progress and change in the offender. It also facilitates reclassification.
7. **Utility:** To be effective, classification systems must be useful. This means that staff achieve the purposes of classification and the goals of the agency.
8. **Practicality:** Closely related to utility is the practical aspect of classification. The system must be practical and possible to implement. A process that is 100 percent accurate, but impossible to apply in an agency, does not help that agency. Similarly, a system that is easy to use, but does not lead to better decisions, is of no value.
9. **Justice:** An effective classification and assessment process should produce just outcomes. Offender placement and service provision should be based on offender differences that are real and measurable, and yield consistent outcomes, regardless of subjective impressions.
10. **Sensitivity:** This is really a goal of the classification process. If all elements are met, the most effective classification and assessment processes are sensitive to the differences of offenders. At the highest level, this would mean individualizing case planning.

CLASSIFICATION AND FEMALE OFFENDERS

Several scholars have questioned the notion that risk factors used to predict anti-social behavior for male offenders are similar to those needed for female offenders (Chesney-Lind, 1989, 1997; Funk, 1999; Mazerolle, 1998). The neglect of female offenders has been a consistent criticism in many areas of criminological and criminal justice research, from theory development to the development of correctional interventions (Belknap & Holsinger, 1998; Chesney-Lind & Sheldon, 1992; Funk, 1999). Furthermore, the lack of instruments that discriminate between males and females has been a common criticism of current risk/need assessment efforts (Funk, 1999). The basis for this criticism is twofold: (1) Different factors may be involved in risk assessment for females, and (2) the risk factors may be similar, but exposure to these factors may present different challenges for female and male offenders (Chesney-Lind, 1989; Funk, 1999; Gilligan & Wiggins, 1988).

There is no question that there has been considerably less research conducted on female offenders than on males; however, several studies that have examined risk factors and gender have found that instruments such as the LSI can be useful in assessing and classifying female offenders (Andrews, 1982; Bonta & Motiuk, 1985; Coulson et al., 1996; Hoge & Andrews, 1996; Motiuk, 1993; Shields & Simourd, 1991; Smith et al., 2009). In a study examining risk prediction for male and female offenders, Lowenkamp and colleagues (2001) added to this research by looking at 317 males and 125 females. They found that the LSI-R was a valid predictive instrument for female offenders. They also found that a history of prior abuse (sexual or physical), although more prevalent in female offenders, was not correlated with outcome. Smith and colleagues (2009) conducted a meta-analysis of studies involving the use of the LSI with females. With a sample of 14,737 offenders, they concluded that the LSI-R was a valid tool for use with women. Although the debate will likely continue, it appears that the evidence is mounting that instruments such as the LSI can indeed be used to assess and classify offenders, both male and female.

Box 6.6
Risk Management versus Risk Reduction

Risk Management: Involves determining the risk level of the offender and providing appropriate sanctions and supervision.
Risk Reduction: Involves determining the risk level and crime-producing needs and reducing risk factors through effective interventions and appropriate supervision.

SUMMARY

This chapter discussed an important aspect of community corrections: assessment of the offender. One of the most critical aspects of supervising the offender in the community is the determination of risk and need levels. Over the years, assessment and classification have advanced beyond guesswork about whether an offender might reoffend to more scientific approaches that examine both static and dynamic factors that can assist the community correctional professional in determining "who" and "what" to target in order to meet the goal of public protection. While offender assessment is not without its critics, the vast majority of community correctional agencies utilize assessment tools, which means that it is incumbent that these tools serve the purposes they were designed for: accurately sorting offenders into levels of risk *and* identifying those characteristics of the offender that are amenable to change.

Review Questions

1. How can risk/needs assessments be used in probation?
2. What are the major correlates of criminal conduct? What are the "Big Four"?
3. What was the first actuarial instrument developed for predicting risk? What is the major limitation of this tool?
4. What is the difference between the Wisconsin risk/need assessment tools and the LSI-R?
5. What are the ten standards of good classification?
6. What are the four principles of classification?
7. Give three examples of responsivity characteristics and discuss ways they can impede an offender.
8. What is the difference between a static and a dynamic predictor?
9. What are two ways to increase the validation of an assessment tool?
10. What are some of the criticisms of assessment tools?
11. Why do you think actuarial assessment tools have proven more reliable and valid than clinical assessment processes?

Recommended Reading

Singh, P., Kroner, D.G., Wormer, J.S., Desmarais, S., Hamilton, Z. (Eds.). (2018). *The handbook of recidivism risk/need assessment tools*. Hoboken, NJ: John Wiley.
Taxman, F. (Ed.). (2017). *Handbook on risk and need assessment: Theory and practice*. New York: Routledge.

References

Andrews, D. (1982). *The level of services inventory (LSI): The first follow-up*. Toronto: Ontario Ministry of Correctional Services.
Andrews, D. (1989). Recidivism is predictable and can be influenced: Using risk assessments to reduce recidivism. *Forum on Correctional Research* 1(2), 11–17.

Andrews, D., Bonta, J. (1995). *LSI-R: Level of Service Inventory–Revised*. Toronto, ON: Multi-Health Systems, Inc.

Andrews, D.A., Bonta, J. (1996). *The psychology of criminal conduct*. Cincinnati, OH: Anderson Publishing.

Andrews, D.A., Bonta, J. (2006). *The psychology of criminal conduct*. 4th ed. Newark, NJ: LexisNexis Matthew Bender (Anderson Publishing).

Andrews, D.A., Bonta, J. (2010). *The psychology of criminal conduct*. 5th ed. New Providence, NJ: LexisNexis Matthew Bender (Anderson Publishing).

Andrews, D.A., Bonta, J., Wormith, S.J. (2004). *The Level of Service/Case Management Inventory*. Toronto, ON: Multi-Health Systems, Inc.

Baird, C. (2009). *A question of evidence: A critique of risk assessment models used in the justice system*. Madison, WI: National Council on Crime and Delinquency.

Belknap, J., Holsinger, K. (1998). An overview of delinquent girls: How theory and practice have failed and the need for innovative changes. In: R.T. Zaplin (Ed.), *Female crime and delinquency: Critical perspectives and effective interventions* (pp. 31–64). Gaithersburg, MD: Aspen.

Bonta, J. (2002). Offender risk assessment: Guidelines for selection and use. *Criminal Justice and Behavior* 29(4), 355–379.

Bonta, J., Andrews, D.A. (2017). *The psychology of criminal conduct*. 6th ed. New York: Routledge.

Bonta, J., Motiuk, L. (1985). Utilization of an interview-based classification instrument: A study of correctional halfway houses. *Criminal Justice and Behavior* 12, 333–352.

Bonta, J., Wallace-Capretta, S., Rooney, J. (2000). A quasi-experimental evaluation of an intensive rehabilitation supervision program. *Criminal Justice and Behavior* 27(3), 312–329.

Bruce, A., Harno, A., Burgess, E., Landesco, J. (1928). *The workings of the intermediate-sentence law and the parole system in Illinois*. Evanston, IL: Northwestern University Press.

Bucklen, K.B., Zajac, G. (2009). But some of them don't come back (to prison!): Resource deprivation and thinking errors as determinants of parole success and failure. *Prison Journal* 89(3), 239–264.

Chesney-Lind, M. (1989). Girls' crime and women's place: Toward a feminist model of female delinquency. *Crime & Delinquency* 35, 5–29.

Chesney-Lind, M. (1997). *The female offender*. Thousand Oaks, CA: Sage.

Chesney-Lind, M., Sheldon, R. (1992). *Girls, delinquency, and juvenile justice*. Belmont, CA: Wadsworth.

Clear, T. (1988). Statistical prediction in corrections. *Research in Corrections* 1, 1–39.

Cohen, T., Pendergast, B., VanBenschoten, S.W. (2016). Examining overrides of risk classifications for offenders on federal supervision. *Federal Probation* 80(1), 12–21.

Cohen, T., Whetzel, J. (2014). The neglected "R": Responsivity and the federal offender. *Federal Probation* 78, 11–18.

Collins, P. (1990). *Risk classification and assessment in probation: A study of misdemeanants* (Unpublished master's thesis). University of Cincinnati, Cincinnati, OH.

Coulson, G., Ilacqua, G., Nutbrown, V., Giulekas, D., Cudjoe, F. (1996). Predictive utility of the LSI for incarcerated female offenders. *Criminal Justice and Behavior* 23, 427–439.

Flores, A., Lowenkamp, C.T., Holsinger, A., Latessa, E. (2006). Predicting outcome with the Level of Service Inventory-Revised: The importance of implementation integrity. *Journal of Criminal Justice* 34(4), 523–529.

Funk, S. (1999). Risk assessment for juveniles on probation. *Criminal Justice and Behavior* 26, 44–68.

Gendreau, P. (1996). The principles of effective intervention with offenders. In: A.T. Harland (Ed.), *Choosing correctional options that work: Defining the demand and evaluating the supply* (pp. 117–130). Thousand Oaks, CA: Sage.

Gendreau, P., French, S.A., Taylor, A. (2002). *What works (what doesn't work) revised 2002*. Invited submission to the International Community Corrections Association Monograph Series Project.

Gendreau, P., Goggin, C., Little, T. (1996). *Predicting adult offender recidivism: What works?* Ottawa, ON: Solicitor General Canada.

Gilligan, C., Wiggins, G. (1988). The origins of morality in early childhood relationships. In: C. Gilligan, J. Ward, J. Taylor (Eds.), *Mapping the moral domain: A contribution of women's thinking to psychological theory and education* (pp. 111–138). Cambridge, MA: Harvard University Press.

Girard, L., Wormith, J. (2004). The predictive validity of the Level of Service Inventory – Ontario Revision on general and violent recidivism among various offender groups. *Criminal Justice and Behavior* 31, 150–181.

Glick, B., Sturgeon, W., Venator-Santiago, C.V. (1998). *No time to play: Youthful offenders in the adult correctional system*. Lantham, MD: American Correctional Association.

Greenwood, P., Zimring, F. (1985). *One more chance: The pursuit of promising intervention strategies for chronic juvenile offenders*. Santa Monica, CA: The Rand Corporation.

Harbinson, E.E. (2017). *Is corrections "collar" blind? Examining the predictive validity of a risk/needs assessment tool on white-collar offenders* (Unpublished doctoral dissertation). University of Cincinnati, Cincinnati, OH.

Hoge, R., Andrews, D. (1996). *Assessing the youthful offender: Issues and techniques*. New York: Plenum Press.

Holsinger, A., Lurigio, A., Latessa, E. (2001). Practitioner's guide to understanding the basis of assessing offender risk. *Federal Probation* 64(2), 46–50.

Hubbard, D.J., Travis, L., Latessa, E. (2001). *Case classification in community corrections: A national survey of the state of the art*. Washington, DC: U.S. Department of Justice, National Institute of Justice; Cincinnati, OH: Center for Criminal Justice Research, University of Cincinnati.

Johnson, J., Lowenkamp, C.T., VanBenschoten, S.W., Robinson, C. (2011). The construction and validation of the federal Post Conviction Risk Assessment (PCRA). *Federal Probation* 75(2), 16–29.

Jones, P. (1996). Risk prediction in criminal justice. In: A.T. Harlan (Ed.), *Choosing correctional options that work: Defining the demand and evaluating the supply* (pp. 33–68). Thousand Oaks, CA: Sage.

Kennedy, S. (1998). *Effective interventions with higher risk offenders*. Longmont, CO: National Institute of Corrections.

Kennedy, S., Serin, R. (1997). Treatment responsivity: Contributing to effective correctional programming. *The ICCA Journal on Community Corrections* 7(4), 46–52.

Klein, A. (1989). The curse of caseload management. *Perspectives (Gerontological Nursing Association [Canada])* 13, 27–28.

Kratcoski, P. (1985). The functions of classification models in probation and parole: Control or treatment-rehabilitation? *Federal Probation* 49(4), 49–56.

Labrecque, R., Smith, P., Lovins, B., Latessa, E.J. (2014). The importance of reassessment: How changes in the LSI-R risk score can improve the prediction of recidivism. *Journal of Offender Rehabilitation* 53, 116–128.

Latessa, E.J., Lemke, R., Makarios, M., Smith, P., Lowenkamp, C.T. (2010). The creation and validation of the Ohio Risk Assessment System (ORAS). *Federal Probation* 74(1), 16–22.

Latessa, E.J., Lovins, B. (2010). The role of offender risk assessment: A policy maker guide. *Victims and offenders* 5(1), 203–219.

Latessa, E.J., Lovins, L.B., Smith, P. (2010). *Follow-up evaluation of Ohio's community based correctional facility and halfway house programs—Outcome study*. Cincinnati, OH: School of Criminal Justice, University of Cincinnati.

Latessa, E.J., Lowenkamp, C. (2001). *Testing the LSI-R in community-based correctional facilities*. Cincinnati, OH: Center for Criminal Justice Research, University of Cincinnati.

Lovins, B., Latessa, E.J., May, T., Lux, J. (2017). Validating the Ohio Risk Assessment System Community Supervision Tool with a diverse sample from Texas. *Corrections: Policy, Practice and Research* 3, 1–16.

Lowenkamp, C.T., Holsinger, A.M., Cohen, T.H. (2015). PCRA revisited: Testing the validity of the federal Post Conviction Risk Assessment (PRCA). *Psychological Services* 12(2), 149–157.

Lowenkamp, C.T., Holsinger, A.M., Latessa, E. (2001). Risk/need assessment, offender classification, and the role of childhood abuse. *Criminal Justice and Behavior* 28(5), 543–563.

McCafferty, J. (2015). Professional discretion and the predictive validity of a juvenile risk assessment instrument: Exploring the overlooked principle of effective correctional classification. *Youth Violence and Juvenile Justice* 15(2), 103–118.

Mazerolle, P. (1998). Gender, general strain, and delinquency: An empirical examination. *Justice Quarterly* 15(1), 65–91.

Motiuk, L. (1993). Where are we in our ability to assess risk? *Forum on Correctional Research* 5(1), 14–18.

National Institute of Justice. (1983). *Classification in probation and parole: A model systems approach*. Available at https://nicic.gov/library-list

Schumacher, M. (1985). Implementation of a client classification and case management system: A practitioner's view. *Crime & Delinquency* 31, 445–455.

Serin, R.C., Lowenkamp, C.T., Johnson, J.L., Trevino, P. (2016). Using a multi-level risk assessment to inform case planning and risk management: Implications for officers. *Federal Probation* 80(2), 10–15.

Shields, I., Simourd, D. (1991). Predicting predatory behavior in a population of incarcerated young offenders. *Criminal Justice and Behavior* 18, 180–194.

Sigler, R., Williams, J. (1994). A study of the outcomes of probation officers and risk-screening instrument classifications. *Journal of Criminal Justice* 22, 495–502.

Simourd, D.J., Andrews, D.A. (1994). Correlates of delinquency: A look at gender differences. *Forum on Corrections Research* 6(1), 26–31.

Skeem, J.L., Lowenkamp, C.T. (2016). Risk, race and recidivism: Predictive bias and disparate impact. *Criminology* 54, 680–712.

Smith, P., Cullen, F.T., Latessa, E.J. (2009). Can 14,737 women be wrong? A meta-analysis of the LSI-R and recidivism for female offenders. *Criminology and Public Policy* 8(1), 183–208.

Smykla, J. (1986). Critique concerning prediction in probation and parole: Some alternative suggestions. *International Journal of Offender Therapy and Comparative Criminology* 30(2), 125–139.

Sykes, G.M., Matza, D. (1957). Techniques of neutralization: A theory of delinquency. *American Sociological Review* 22(6), 664–670.

Travis, L. (1989). *Risk classification in probation and parole*. Cincinnati, OH: Risk Classification Project, University of Cincinnati.

Travis, L., Latessa, E. (1996). Classification and needs assessment module. *Managing violent youthful offenders in adult institutions curriculum*. Longmont, CO: National Institute of Corrections.

Wilbanks, W. (1985). Predicting failure on parole. In: D. Farrington, R. Tarling (Eds.), *Prediction in criminology* (pp. 78–94). Albany: State University of New York Press.

Wong, S. (1997). *Risk: Assessing the risk of violent recidivism*. Presentation at the American Probation and Parole Association, Boston, MA.

Wormith, S.J, Hogg, S., Guzzo, L. (2012). The predictive validity of a general risk/needs assessment inventory on sexual offender recidivism and an exploration of the professional override. *Criminal Justice and Behavior* 12, 1511–1538.

Wright, K., Clear, T., Dickson, P. (1984). Universal applicability of probation risk assessment instruments. *Criminology* 22, 113–134.

Chapter 7

ROLES OF PROBATION AND PAROLE OFFICERS

Key Terms

control
mission statement
passive officer
protective officer
punitive officer

referee or coach
synthetic officer
treatment
welfare officer

> We believe that these characteristics [warmth, accurate empathy, and genuineness] in themselves are necessary but not sufficient to produce an optimum therapeutic effect. —Beck, Rush, Shaw, Emery (1979)

While the role of the probation and parole officer (PO) has shifted over the past 100 years, most modern-day scholars describe it as a balance between law enforcement and social work activities (American Correctional Association, 1995). The role of the probation and parole officer is influenced by legislation, the agency's philosophy regarding offenders, the type of offenders the officer supervises, and the officer's beliefs about his or her job (Clear & Latessa, 1993; Klaus, 1998; Miller, 2015; Skeem & Manchak, 2008; Viglione, 2016; Viglione et al., 2015). Without clear direction, community supervision officers are often left to their own devices with regard to which role would be most appropriate in supervising their caseloads (Bonta et al., 2008; Reinventing Probation Council, 2000; Smith et al., 2012; Taxman & Byrne, 2001; Trotter, 1996). One thing is certain: The probation and parole officer's role is an important one in the administration of community supervision.

PROBATION AND PAROLE OFFICERS

While there is no such thing as a degree in probation or parole, according to the Bureau of Labor Statistics (2018), probation and parole officers must have a minimum of a Bachelor's degree (usually in a social service related field like criminal justice, social work, or behavioral science), be 21 years of age or older, and pass a criminal background check. The median pay for probation or parole officers in 2017 was $51,410. Most probation and parole officers either work for the county or state in some capacity. Some probation officers work under the judicial branch, while others work under the executive branch. In contrast, parole officers almost universally work under the executive branch of the government. Even though they fall under different branches of the government, O'Leary (1974) has argued that parole resembles probation in several ways. With both, information is gathered and presented to a decision-making authority (either a judge or a parole board). This authority has the power to release (parole) or suspend the sentence (probation) of the offender. In turn, the liberty that the offender enjoys is subject to certain conditions that are imposed by the decision-making authority. If these conditions are not obeyed, the offender may be sentenced, or returned, to prison.

The role of probation and parole officers varies across jurisdictions (and caseloads), but there are some consistencies across most agencies:

- conduct assessments including pre-sentence investigations;
- monitor conditions of probation or parole;
- conduct office and home visits;
- provide compliance reports to the court or parole board;
- develop a supervision (case) plan;
- provide referrals to social service and treatment agencies when appropriate;
- monitor drug use;
- collect fees.

In addition to these roles, some probation and parole agencies ask their officers to teach psycho-educational classes, while others require them to engage in more law enforcement activities (e.g., serve warrants). In the end, the probation and parole officer's primary role is to supervise the conditions of release. How officers choose to supervise justice-involved individuals is usually influenced by agency philosophy and societal pressures (e.g., legislature, public opinion) as well as their own personal views of the work.

AGENCY PHILOSOPHY AND SOCIETAL INFLUENCES

The agency's philosophy, or view on what they should focus on, is an important factor in how a PO goes about his or her day-to-day activities. The mission and values of an agency, the guiding principles, policies, and procedures all drive how a PO sees his or her role. The type of training that agencies select to provide has an impact on how the PO operates (Oleson et al., 2011; Taxman, 2014). There are also less formal ways in which agencies influence officer behavior, much coming from a daily exchange of information, shaping what is important by the type of feedback the officer receives (Mathews, 2015).

In corrections, there are generally two philosophies that drive probation and parole agencies: **control** or **treatment** (Clear & Latessa, 1993). These two orientations are often described as opposing forces—one focused primarily on public safety, surveillance, and monitoring; and the other focused on treatment, social service delivery, and rehabilitation. In practice, the relationship between control and treatment is more fluid, with agencies attempting to promote public safety while also providing intervention to justice-involved individuals. A perfect example of this mix of societal protection and rehabilitation is Oregon's Community Corrections Act of 2009. The act was written specifically to improve the effectiveness of community corrections, ultimately designed to reduce future recidivism rates while giving local jurisdictions flexibility to develop strategies that fit their community. The declared purpose of the act was to:

1. Provide appropriate sentencing and sanctioning options including incarceration, community supervision, and services;
2. Provide improved local services for persons charged with criminal offenses with the goal of reducing the occurrence of repeat criminal offenses;
3. Promote local control and management of community corrections programs;
4. Promote the use of the most effective criminal sanctions necessary to protect public safety, administer punishment to the offender, and rehabilitate the offender;
5. Enhance, increase, and support the state and county partnership in the management of offenders; and
6. Enhance, increase, and encourage a greater role for local government and the local criminal justice system in the planning and implementation of local public safety policies.

(Oregon Department of Corrections, 2011, p. 2)

As noted, Oregon's legislation introduces a mix of philosophies including control, punishment, and rehabilitation in an effort to implement effective interventions. What is clear from this legislation is that there is a strong desire for programs to be selected and administered at the local level. This gives an agency a significant amount of discretion in designing what probation and parole officers are to do in their day-to-day operations.

Agencies that are focused more on the control aspect of community corrections generally have a law enforcement feel to them. Officers are often seen as peace officers. They tend to carry guns, engage in surveillance and monitoring of offenders through electronic monitoring and GPS devices, serve warrants, conduct searches, and place individuals on probation in jail. In contrast, agencies that are focused more specifically on treatment or rehabilitation tend to be more office-based. Officers are trained in communication skills, case management concepts, and cognitive-behavioral techniques that are designed to influence behavioral change. The philosophical orientation of the agency often drives many decisions. Whom to hire, whom to promote, what officer behavior should be rewarded; these are all ways in which the philosophical orientation of an agency influences the behavior of staff. Even the **mission statement** can provide a clear understanding of what direction a probation or parole agency has adopted. Take, for example, Harris County Community Supervision and Corrections' (Houston, TX) mission statement: "Harris County CSCD is committed to using evidence-based strategies to help individuals on community supervision eliminate future criminal behavior and become productive citizens, which in turn, creates a safer community with fewer victims."

Notice that they talk about using strategies, or interventions, to help people under supervision change their lives with the final outcome of creating a safer community. Based on this mission statement, it is clear that Harris County CSCD has adopted a "treatment first" philosophy. They see their role as working with justice-involved individuals to help change their behavior. In contrast, look at the mission statement for the Probation Department of Fresno County, California:

> As a member of the criminal justice system, the Fresno County Probation Department's mission is to provide protection for the community, support victim advocacy, and deliver essential services to the courts. This mission is accomplished through collaboration and partnerships which encompass a continuum of sanctions including prevention/intervention programming, investigation, supervision, and incarceration.

As noted, Fresno County's primary mission is to provide protection for the community followed by supporting victims and delivering services to the courts. This is a perfect example of a department that is more oriented toward law enforcement strategies or control strategies and is not focused as much on the rehabilitative nature of probation. It is easy to understand, given the differing mission statements between these two departments, how agency structure and political atmosphere can impact an officer's work.

ROLE TYPOLOGIES

Regardless of the orientation of the agency, often probation and parole officers have flexibility in adopting their own personal approach. In one of the first studies of types of officers, Ohlin et al. (1956) describes the following typology of PO styles:

- The **punitive officer,** who perceives himself *[sic]* as the guardian of middle-class morality; he attempts to coerce the offender into conforming by means of threats and punishment and emphasizes control, the protection of the community against the offender, and the systematic suspicion of those under supervision.
- The **protective officer,** who vacillates literally between protecting the offender and protecting the community. His tools are direct assistance, lecturing, and, alternately, praise and blame. He is perceived as ambivalent in his emotional involvement with the offender and others in the community as he shifts back and forth in taking sides with one against the other.

■ The **welfare officer,** who has as his ultimate goal the improved welfare of the client, achieved by aiding him in his individual adjustment within limits imposed by the client's capacity. Such an officer believes that the only genuine guarantee of community protection lies in the client's personal adjustment, as external conformity will only be temporary and, in the long run, may make a successful adjustment more difficult. Emotional neutrality permeates his relationship. The diagnostic categories and treatment skills that he employs stem from an objective and theoretically based assessment of the client's needs and capacities.

(Ohlin et al., 1956, pp. 219–220)

Glaser (1969) later extended this typology to include, as a fourth category, the **passive officer**, who sees the job as non-engaging and inactive, requiring only minimum effort. For example, Erickson (1977) has satirically offered the following gambit to officers who wish to "fake it" and have an "ideal, trouble-free caseload":

"I'm just so busy—never seem to have enough time." A truly professional execution of this ploy does require some preparation. Make sure that your desktop is always inundated with a potpourri of case files, messages, memos, unopened mail, and professional literature. . . . Have your secretary hold all your calls for a few days and schedule several appointments for the same time. When, after a lengthy wait, the probationer is finally ushered into your presence, impress him (or her) with the volume of your business. . . . Always write while conversing with the subject, and continue to make and receive telephone calls. Interrupt your dialogue with him to attend to other important matters, such as obtaining the daily grocery list from your wife or arranging to have your car waxed. Apologize repeatedly and profusely for these necessary interruptions and appear to be distracted, weary, and slightly insane. Having experienced the full treatment, it is unlikely that the probationer will subsequently try to discuss with you any matters of overwhelming concern. He could even feel sorrier for you than he does for himself. You should henceforth be able to deal with him on an impersonal basis, if indeed he tries to report anymore at all.

(Erickson, 1977, p. 37)

The complete typology is presented in tabular form in Figure 7.1. The key distinction in this figure is the manner in which the supervising officer personally views the purpose of the job of supervision. Personal preference and motivations of the PO will often determine the style of supervision that is followed.

A similar typology was developed by Klockars (1972), based on the working philosophy of the officer. The first style that he presented is that of the "law enforcer." Such officers are motivated primarily by (1) the court order and obtaining offender compliance with it, (2) the authority and decision-making power of the PO, (3) officer responsibility for public safety, and (4) police work—the PO as police officer of the agency.

Emphasis on control

	High	Low
High	Protective officer	Welfare officer
Low	Punitive officer	Passive officer

Emphasis on assistance (vertical axis label)

Figure 7.1 Typology of Probation Officer Supervision Styles

Source: Jordan, F., Sasfy, J. (1974). *National impact program evaluation: A review of selected issues and research findings related to probation and parole.* Washington, DC: Mitre Corp.

The second category is that of the "time server." This person feels that the job has certain requirements to be fulfilled until retirement— "I don't make the rules; I just work here." The third type is the "therapeutic agent," a supervising officer who accepts the role of administrator of a form of treatment (usually casework-oriented) to help the offender.

Finally, the "**synthetic officer**" attempts to blend treatment and law enforcement components by combining the law enforcement and parental roles into a single approach. The synthetic officer attempts to reconcile what Miles (1965) terms criminal justice (offender is wrong, but responsible for own behavior) with treatment (casework, offender is sick) goals. In sum, Klockars' typology rounds out the original scheme developed by Ohlin et al. (1956) by providing an example through which the PO can integrate the best of each possible role.[1]

Czajkoski (1973) expanded on the law enforcement role of the officer's job by outlining the quasi-judicial role of the probation officer. He develops his thesis on five lines of functional analysis. The first line examines the plea bargaining; Czajkoski argues that the probation officer serves to "cool the mark" in the confidence game of plea bargaining by assuring the defendant of how wise it was to plead guilty. In this fusion, the PO certifies the plea-bargaining process—a task that can significantly undermine the helping/counseling role of the PO.

The second line of quasi-judicial functioning by the probation officer occurs at the intake level. For example, at the juvenile level, the officer is often asked which cases are appropriate for judicial processing. This function permits the probation officer, like the prosecutor, to have some control over the intake of the court.

The third quasi-judicial function of the probation officer concerns setting the conditions of probation, a power the judge often gives the probation officer. This often leads to discretionary abuses, as indefinite conditions (often moralistic or vague in terms of the offender's behavior) can become a vehicle for maintaining the moral status quo as interpreted by the probation officer. In addition, probation conditions can become substitutions for, or even usurp, certain formal judicial processes. For example, the monetary obligations[2] of the probationer (such as supporting dependents) can be enforced by the probation officer rather than by a court that is designed specifically to handle such matters (Schneider et al., 1982).

The fourth quasi-judicial role is concerned with probation violation procedures. Czajkoski (1973) contends that such procedures are highly discretionary, especially in view of the vague and all-encompassing nature of the probation conditions, which are usually not enforced until the officer has reason to believe that the probationer is engaged in criminal activity. Petersilia and Turner (1993) noted that increased surveillance increases the incidence of technical violations (Marciniak, 2000), jail terms, and incarceration rates, as well as program and court costs.

The final quasi-judicial role of the probation officer concerns the ability to administer punishment. Because the officer may restrict the liberty of his or her charge in several ways, this is tantamount to punishment. In this fashion, Czajkoski (1973) highlights some of the actions which officers take that relate to his or her function as a quasi-judicial official and illustrates more ways in which the PO uses discretionary power in judicial-like ways.

Tomaino (1975) also attempts to reveal some of the hidden functions of probation officers. Figure 7.2 summarizes the Tomaino typology. Once again, concern for control is contrasted with concern for rehabilitation. To Tomaino, the key probation officer role is the "Have It Make Sense" face. This role attempts to integrate the often-conflicting concerns of societal protection and offender rehabilitation. Accordingly, Tomaino recommends that the officer stress goals, not offender personality traits, to "organize legitimate choices through a collaborative relationship which induces the client to act in accord with prosocial expectations" (1975, p. 45). Perhaps, as Lindner (1975) suggests, the probation officer can create a learning situation for the offender and induce a desire for change.

In sum, these authors indicate that the supervising officer has a range of choices concerning the style of supervision to be followed and the ultimate goal of the entire probation/parole process. There is a strong emphasis here upon blending the need for control with the need for counseling. The officer must choose which style to adopt based on the individual client (severity of the offense, amenability to treatment) and the nature of the situation. Supervising officers clearly have the discretionary power to either enforce the law (i.e., conditions of supervision) or offer help and treatment. No doubt, the world view of the PO also plays a crucial role in this decision.

Box 7.1
All Things to All People

For larger probation departments, specialization has become more common. There are pre-sentence investigation units, assessment units, fugitive and warrant units, surveillance officers, and specialized caseload units. In rural departments, it is still common to have every probation officer perform all of these tasks.

9	**The 1/9 Face** **Help-Him-Understand**	**The 9/9 Face** **Have-It-Make-Sense**
8	Probationers will want to keep the rules once they get insight about themselves. The PO should be supportive, warm, and nonjudg-	Probationers will keep the rules when it is credible to do so because this better meets their needs. The PO should be open but
7	mental in his relations with them.	firm, and focus on the content of his relations with probationers.
6		
	The 5/5 Face **Let-Him-Identify**	
5	Probationers will keep the rules if they like their PO and identify with	
4	him and his values. The PO must work out solid compromises in his relations with the probationers.	
3		
	The 1/1 Face **It's-Up-To-Him**	**The 9/1 Face** **Make-Him-Do-It**
2		
1	Probationers should know exactly what they have to do, what happens if they don't do it, and it is up to them to perform.	Probationers will keep the rules only if you take a hard line, exert very close supervision, and stay completely objective in your relations with them.
1	2 3 4 5 6 7 8 9	

Figure 7.2 The Five Faces of Probation Supervision

Source: Tomaino, L. (1975). The five faces of probation. *Federal Probation* 39(4), 41–46.

SELF-IMAGE OF PROBATION AND PAROLE OFFICERS

To this point, most researchers (and practitioners) have defined probation and parole officers by their daily tasks—almost thinking about it as if the officer plays a different role depending on the task they are doing. If they are issuing a consequence, they are wearing a law enforcement hat; and if they are referring someone to treatment, they are wearing their social work hat, and so on. This view that they move in and out of different roles has caused significant confusion when trying to hire, train, and supervise staff. Even the concept of the synthetic officer described by Klockars shows the officer as vacillating between law enforcement and social work.

How a person sees themselves at work is important in how they do their job. One of the first articles to propose that the self-image of probation and parole officers influences their work was completed in 1969. Glaser (1969) believed that the officer's attitude toward the goals of supervision would affect how he or she responded to behavior.

In a study of job tasks, Colley and colleagues (1987) surveyed 70 juvenile probation officers in Illinois. Table 7.1 illustrates the tasks performed by at least 40 percent of the sample. While most studies of probation officers have been conducted in urban areas, it is important to note what appear to be differences in the roles and tasks performed by urban and by rural probation officers. Rural officers perform an even wider range of tasks than urban officers and are more generalists (Colley et al., 1986).

Today's probation and parole officers are asked to do even more. Where the role was relatively straightforward 20 years ago, probation and parole officer work has become more complicated. With the industry-wide adoption of risk assessment, officers are being asked to conduct face-to-face interviews to determine

Table 7.1 Tasks Performed by at Least 40 Percent of Respondents on a Weekly or Daily Basis

Skills	Percent
COURT	
Attends court hearings with client	58.6
Takes court notes on court proceedings of clients	47.2
Confers with State's Attorney about cases	64.2
SUPERVISION—CASELOAD MANAGEMENT	
Meets with minor in office, home, and at school	57.1
Listens to complaints and problems	72.9
Asks minors about any general problems and disturbances	56.5
Inquires about police contacts	44.3
Consults teachers, therapists, significant others, community services agencies	44.3
Intervenes in crisis situations	42.9
Counsels parents	47.8
Confers with dean of students or school counselors	47.8
CASE NOTING	
Accounts for the entire history of the case	65.7
MONTHLY STATISTICS	
Documents all intakes, transfers, terminations, etc.	44.9
STAFFINGS	
Confers with other staff on informal basis about cases	60.8

Source: Colley, L., Culbertson, R., Latessa, E. (1987). Juvenile probation officers: A job analysis. *Juvenile and Family Court Journal* 38(3), 1–12.

criminogenic needs, develop individualized case plans, provide graduated sanctions, and deliver cognitive-behavioral interventions while ensuring public safety. Viglione et al. (2015) found that officers have been able to conduct risk assessments with few problems, but when it comes to tying the results of the assessment to interventions, they fall short. They suggest that officers are not trained effectively and that agencies' policies and practices do not fully support rehabilitative efforts—that agencies often send mixed messages as to the role of rehabilitation over control.

Overall, the studies examined reveal that POs are aware of the surveillance/treatment dichotomy that exists with regard to style of supervision. A number of factors (age, education, years of job experience) are related to or influence the PO's style and method of supervision. Yet, in general, there is a distinct lack of consensus over which style of supervision should dominate.

REFEREE OR COACH?

As the rehabilitative orientation of community corrections has expanded, there has been a concerted effort to revisit the typologies of probation and parole officers to better understand the role of the rehabilitative probation officer. Lovins et al. (2018) suggest a different way of understanding probation and parole officers' work. Initially, probation and parole officers' roles were defined as either law enforcement or social work. Klockars (1972) provided an integrated role in which he coined the synthetic officer. While previous scholars suggested that two unique roles could not be executed by the same person under the same job title, Klockars suggested that officers can balance both philosophies at the same time—offering interventions that are therapeutic in nature while still applying external controls. Lovins and colleagues (2018) suggest that instead of looking at integrating the actions of officers, it is necessary to take a step back and look at the overarching role that the officer takes in his or her role—this role being one of either a referee or a coach.

A referee-type probation or parole officer is one who is interested primarily in procedural justice. Just like a referee in a sports game, they are not concerned about the outcome of the game, but more whether the rules are applied fairly and equally. Referees have a strong understanding of the rules, have a keen eye for spotting rule violations, and can exact the right penalty for the infraction. Imagine a "referee" probation officer and the approach they would take to working with offenders. They would understand the conditions ordered by the court (rules), they would watch offenders closely in order to spot any rule violations, and if a violation occurred, they would exact a predetermined penalty—ultimately reporting the behavior to the court if the offenders "foul out."

In contrast, a coach is a person who is invested in winning. They concentrate on training their players to be successful, challenging them when they are slacking, reinforcing them when they try hard with the ultimate goal of the players succeeding. Apply this to a probation "coach." A probation "coach" would be a person who cares about the justice-involved individual succeeding. They would foresee the skills that the individual would need to be successful and then train them to

---

Box 7.2
Motivating Offenders

Recently, many probation departments have begun training officers on motivational interviewing. First developed by Miller and Rollnick (1991) and based on Prochaska and DiClemente's (1983) stages of change, motivational interviewing is a technique designed to help prepare offenders to change their lifestyles. Officers are taught skills that can be used to overcome resistance to treatment and encourage offenders to think about the benefits of changing negative attitudes and behaviors.

---

develop and use those skills in real-life situations. Just like a sports coach, the probation coach would always be looking for ways to make sure that their "team" would be successful.

CHARACTERISTICS OF EFFECTIVE PROBATION COACHES

What are the characteristics of probation and parole officers that demonstrate the ability to reduce recidivism in the offenders they supervise? Research by Gendreau and Andrews (2001), as well as others, suggests that the most effective probation coaches possess several characteristics. First, they are able to develop a strong collaborative relationship with offenders. Warmth, genuineness, and flexibility characterize such relationships. Second, effective change agents are firm but fair, have a sense of humor, and believe that offenders can change. Third, they are able to model behavior in concrete and vivid ways. Fourth, they are a source of not simply punishment, but of reinforcement for positive behavior. Finally, an effective coach discourages negative attitudes and behaviors with strong, emphatic statements of disagreement, but also praises good behavior. Table 7.2 shows the core correctional practices that are fundamental to POs as agents of change.

Unfortunately, as Shichor (1978, p. 37) points out, such characteristics often stand in sharp contrast to current probation and parole practices that are more oriented toward "people processing" than "people changing." Research has also confirmed that the vast majority of officers do not target major criminogenic needs (such as antisocial attitudes and social supports for crime) and do not commonly use skills (such as prosocial modeling and effective reinforcement) to influence long-term behavioral change in offenders (Bonta et al., 2008; Viglione et al., 2015).

Most recently, training curricula designed to teach community supervision officers how to apply core correctional practices in their face-to-face interactions with offenders have been piloted in many jurisdictions (see Bonta et al., 2008; Latessa et al., 2013; Robinson et al., 2011; Smith et al., 2012; Trotter, 1996).

Table 7.2 Core Correctional Practices

1. Effective reinforcement
2. Effective disapproval
3. Effective use of authority
4. Quality interpersonal relationships
5. Cognitive restructuring
6. Anti-criminal modeling
7. Structured learning/Skill building
8. Problem-solving techniques

Source: Andrews, D.A., Kiessling, J.J. (1980). Program structure and effective correctional practices: A summary of the CaVIC research. In: R.R. Ross, P. Gendreau (Eds.), *Effective correctional treatment* (pp. 441–463). Toronto, ON: Butterworth.

Table 7.3 Traditional Officer–Offender Interactions

Traditional officer–offender interactions are often not effective because:

- They are too brief to have an impact
- Conversations focus almost exclusively on monitoring compliance conditions (and therefore emphasize external controls on behavior rather than developing an internal rationale for pro-social behavior)
- Relationship is often more confrontational and authoritarian in nature than helpful
- What is targeted is not always based on assessment
- More areas discussed = less effective

Source: Bonta, J., Rugge, T., Scott, T., Bourgon, G., Yessine, A.K. (2008). Exploring the black box of community supervision. *Journal of Offender Rehabilitation* 47, 248–270.

Research by Bonta and his colleagues (2008) has indicated that traditional officer–offender interactions are often not effective using traditional approaches. Table 7.3 summarizes their findings. Fortunately, results from several studies have demonstrated that trained officers achieve greater reductions in recidivism when compared to untrained officers (Bonta et al., 2010; Latessa et al., 2013; Robinson et al., 2011). Figures 7.3 and 7.4 show results from studies in Canada and Ohio.

With the coach/referee framework, it is easy to understand why researchers have found that it is difficult for some probation and parole officers to deliver effective practices in reducing recidivism (see Haas & DeTardo-Bora, 2009; Miller & Maloney, 2013; Oleson et al., 2012; Schwalbe, 2004; Taxman & Belenko, 2012; Viglione et al., 2015). They are "referee" officers and not coaches. Imagine giving a referee a playbook designed for a coach—they would not find it valuable and more than likely would not engage in the training associated with the new skills. A referee would be looking for training on identifying violations, supervising more effectively, and clarification on penalties.

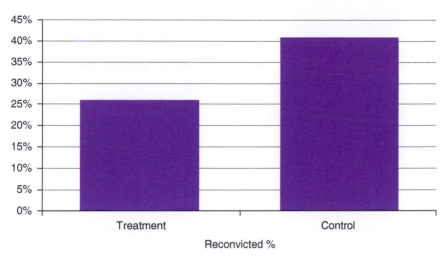

Figure 7.3 Two-Year Recidivism Results from Canadian Study: POs Utilize Core Correctional Practices

Source: Bonta, J., Bourgon, G., Rugge, T., Scott, T., Yessine, A.K., Gutierrez, L., Li, J. (2010). *The strategic training initiative in community supervision: Risk-need-responsivity in the real world.* Toronto, ON: Public Safety Canada.

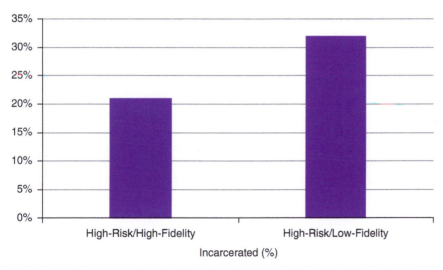

Figure 7.4 Recidivism Results from Ohio Study Looking at Fidelity and High-Risk-Offenders (Both Adult and Juvenile) Using Core Correctional Practices

Source: Latessa, E., Smith, P., Schweitzer, M., Labrecque, R. (2013). *Evaluation of the Effective Practices in Community Supervision model (EPICS) in Ohio.* Cincinnati, OH: School of Criminal Justice, University of Cincinnati.

SUMMARY

In summary, the conflict between counseling and surveillance is simply part of the job of the PO and a duality that makes his or her position in the criminal justice system vital, unique, and necessary. While some see role conflict as a reason for eviscerating some of the less salient tasks, others believe that the profession can find a way of integrating and balancing various role expectations.

The roles of probation and parole agencies are varied and range from investigating violations to assisting offenders in obtaining employment. Accordingly, the skills and education required of probation officers are often considerable. The need for college-educated staff has been advocated for many years and is becoming a reality. There has come to be a general acceptance of formal education as a prerequisite for a quality probation and parole service and of in-service development as a means of maintaining and improving that service. This need has been identified and encouraged by several national commissions and organizations, as well as by numerous individual writers and researchers. A decade from now, the entry-level educational requirement could be a Master's degree.

Finally, although in many ways, probation and parole officers perform the same basic duties that they did when the profession first began, there are many who argue that a change is in order. Current research has clearly demonstrated that when officers employ some core correctional practices, they can become more effective agents of change and can have a significant effect on reducing recidivism.

Review Questions

1. What are the four primary responsibilities of a probation or parole agency?
2. What are the quasi-judicial roles of probation officers?
3. How does a probation/parole officer serve a law enforcement role? A social work role?
4. List those tasks that a probation or parole officer can undertake to assist an offender and those to control an offender.
5. According to Andrews, what are the characteristics of effective agents of change?
6. What does the research show when POs utilize core correctional practices?

Notes

1   Nowhere is the dichotomy of rehabilitation-casework versus surveillance-control more evident than between juvenile and adult probation officers. Juvenile officers support the former by a wide margin, but felony probation officers, particularly males, are more likely to endorse law enforcement strategies. See Sluder and Reddington (1993); and Brown and Pratt (2000).
2   Most probationers satisfy financial obligations as ordered by the court (Allen & Treger, 1994).

Recommended Readings

Andrews, D.A., Carvell, C. (1998). *Core correctional treatment—core correctional supervision and counseling: Theory, research, assessment and practice.* Ottawa, ON: Carleton University.

Beck, A. (1991). Cognitive therapy as the integrative therapy. *Journal of Psychotherapy Integration* 1(3), 191–198.

Spiegler, M.D., Guevremont, D.C. (2003). *Contemporary behaviour therapy.* 4th ed. Pacific Grove, CA: Wadsworth.

Trotter, C. (1999). *Working with involuntary clients: A guide to practice.* Thousand Oaks, CA: Sage.

References

Allen, G., Treger, H. (1994). Fines and restitution orders: Probations' perceptions. *Federal Probation* 58(2), 34–40.

American Correctional Association. (1995). *Field officer resources guide.* Laurel, MD: ACA.

Andrews, D.A., Kiessling, J.J. (1980). Program structure and effective correctional practices: A summary of CaVIC research. In: R.R. Ross, P. Gendreau (Eds.), *Effective correctional treatment* (pp. 441–463). Toronto, ON: Butterworth.

Beck, A.T., Rush, A.J., Shaw, B.F., Emery, G. (1979). *Cognitive therapy of depression.* New York: Guilford Press.

Blumberg, A. (1974). *Criminal justice.* New York: New Viewpoints.

Bonta, J., Bourgon, G., Rugge, T., Scott, T., Yessine, A.K., Gutierrez, L., Li, J. (2010) *The strategic training initiative in community supervision: Risk-need-responsivity in the real world.* Toronto, ON: Public Safety Canada.

Bonta, J., Rugge, T., Scott, T., Bourgon, G., Yessine, A.K. (2008). Exploring the black box of community supervision. *Journal of Offender Rehabilitation* 47, 248–270.

Brown, M., Pratt, J. (Eds.). (2000). *Dangerous offenders: Punishment and social order.* New York & London: Routledge.

Bureau of Labor Statistics, U.S. Department of Labor. (2018). *Occupational outlook handbook. Probation Officers and Correctional Treatment Specialists.* Retrieved from www.bls.gov/ooh/community-and-social-service/probation-officers-and-correctional-treatment-specialists.htm (accessed June 28, 2018).

Clear, T.R., Latessa, E.J. (1993). Probation officers' roles in intensive supervision: Surveillance versus treatment. *Justice Quarterly*, 10, 441–462.

Colley, L., Culbertson, R., Latessa, E. (1986). Probation officer job analysis: Rural–urban differences. *Federal Probation* 50(4), 67–71.

Colley, L., Culbertson, R., Latessa, E. (1987). Juvenile probation officers: A job analysis. *Juvenile and Family Court Journal* 38(3), 1–12.

Czajkoski, E. (1973). Exposing the quasi-judicial role of the probation officer. *Federal Probation* 37(2), 9–13.

Erickson, C. (1977). Faking it: Principles of expediency as applied to probation. *Federal Probation* 41(3), 36–39.

Gendreau, P., Andrews, D.A. (2001). *The Correctional Program Assessment Inventory—2000 (CPAI 2000).* Saint John: University of New Brunswick.

Glaser, D. (1969). *The effectiveness of a prison and parole system.* Indianapolis, IN: Bobbs-Merrill.

Haas, S.M., DeTardo-Bora, K.A. (2009). Inmate reentry and the utility of the LSI-R in case planning. *Corrections Compendium* 34(1), 11–16.

Jordan, F., Sasfy, J. (1974). *National impact program evaluation: A review of selected issues and research findings related to probation and parole.* Washington, DC: Mitre Corp.

Klaus, H. (1998). *Handbook on probation services: Guidelines for probation practitioners and managers.* Rome: United Nations Interregional Crime and Justice Research Institute.

Klockars, C. (1972). A theory of probation supervision. *Journal of Criminal Law, Criminology and Police Science* 63, 550–557.

Latessa, E., Smith, P., Schweitzer, M., Labrecque, R. (2013). *Evaluation of the Effective Practices in Community Supervision model (EPICS) in Ohio.* Cincinnati, OH: School of Criminal Justice, University of Cincinnati.

Lindner, C. (1975). The juvenile offender's right to bail. *Probation and Parole* 7(3), 64–68.

Lovins, B., Cullen, F., Latessa, E., Jonson, C. (2018). Probation officer as a coach: Building a new professional identity. *Federal Probation* 82(1), 13–19.

Marciniak, L. (2000). The addition of day reporting to intensive supervision probation. *Federal Probation* 64(2), 34–39.

Mathews, B. (2015). Corrections, implementation, and organizational ecology: An introduction to the Purveyor Core-Skills Model. *Criminal Justice Studies* 28(4), 454–483.

Miles, A. (1965). The reality of the probation officer's dilemma. *Federal Probation* 29(1), 18–22.

Miller, J. (2015). Contemporary modes of probation officer supervision: The triumph of the "synthetic" officer? *Justice Quarterly* 32(2), 314–336.

Miller, J., Maloney, C. (2013). Practitioner compliance with risk/needs assessment tools: A theoretical and empirical assessment. *Criminal Justice and Behavior* 40, 716–736.

Miller, W., Rollnick, S. (1991). *Motivational interviewing: Preparing for change.* New York: Guilford Press.

Ohlin, L., Piven, H., Pappenfort, M. (1956). Major dilemmas of the social worker in probation and parole. *National Probation and Parole Association Journal* 2(3), 211–225.

O'Leary, V. (1974). Parole administration. In: D. Glaser (Ed.), *Handbook of criminology* (pp. 909–948). New York: Rand McNally.

Oleson, J., VanBenschoten, S., Robinson, C., Lowenkamp, C., Holsinger, A. (2011). Training to see risk: Measuring the accuracy of clinical and actuarial risk assessments among federal probation officers. *Federal Probation* 75(2), 52–56.

Oleson, J.C., VanBenschoten, S., Robinson, C., Lowenkamp, C.T., Holsinger, A.M. (2012). Actuarial and clinical assessment of criminogenic needs: Identifying supervision priorities among federal probation officers. *Journal of Crime & Justice* 35, 239–248.

Oregon Department of Corrections, Transitional Services Division. (2011). Evaluating Oregon's Community Corrections Act. Retrieved from www.oregon.gov/doc/CC/docs/pdf/evaluating_oregons_cc_act.pdf

Petersilia, J., Turner, S. (1993). Intensive probation and parole. *Crime and Justice: A Review of Research* 17, 281–336.

Prochaska, J., DiClemente, C. (1983). Stages and processes of self-change in smoking: Toward an integrative model of change. *Journal of Consulting and Clinical Psychology* 51(3), 390–395.

Reinventing Probation Council. (2000). *Transforming probation through leadership: The "Broken Windows" model*. Retrieved from https://www.manhattan-ins titute.org/html/transforming-probation-through-leadership-broken-windows-model-5814.html

Robinson, C.R., VanBenschoten, S.W., Alexander, M., Lowenkamp, C.T. (2011). A random (almost) study of staff training aimed at reducing re-arrest (STARR): Reducing recidivism through intentional design. *Federal Probation* 7(2): 57–63.

Schneider, P., Griffith, W., Schneider, A. (1982). Juvenile restitution as a sole sanction or condition of probation: An empirical analysis. *Journal of Research in Crime & Delinquency* 19, 47–65.

Schwalbe, C. (2004). Re-visioning risk assessment for human service decision making. *Children and Youth Services Review* 26, 561–576.

Shichor, D. (1978). The people changing versus people processing organizational perspective: The case of correctional institutions. *LAE–Journal of the American Criminal Justice Association* 4(3), 37–44.

Skeem, J., Manchak, S. (2008). Back to the future: From Klockar's model of effective supervision to evidence-based practice in probation. *Journal of Offender Rehabilitation* 47(3), 220–247.

Sluder, R.D., Reddington, F.P. (1993). An empirical examination of the work ideologies of juvenile and adult probation officers. *Journal of Offender Rehabilitation* 20(1–2), 115–137.

Smith, P., Schweitzer, M., Labrecque, R., Latessa, E.J. (2012). Improving probation officers' skills: An evaluation of the EPICS model. *Journal of Crime and Justice* 35(2), 189–199.

Taxman, F. (2014). Behavioral management in probation. In: G. Bruinsma, D. Weisburd (Eds.), *Encyclopedia of criminology and criminal justice* (pp. 134–145). New York: Springer-Verlag.

Taxman, F.S., Belenko, S. (2012). *Implementation of evidence-based community corrections and addiction treatment*. New York: Springer.

Taxman, F., Byrne, J. (2001). Fixing broken windows: Probation. *Perspectives* 25(2), 23–29.

Tomaino, L. (1975). The five faces of probation. *Federal Probation* 39(4), 41–46.

Trotter, C. (1996). The impact of different supervision practices in community corrections. *Australian and New Zealand Journal of Criminology* 29(1), 29–46.

Viglione, J. (2016). Acceptability, feasibility, and use of evidence-based practices in adult probation. *Criminal Justice and Behavior* 44(10), 163–193.

Viglione, J., Rudes, D., Taxman, F. (2015). Misalignment in supervision: Implementing risk/needs assessment instruments in probation. *Criminal Justice and Behavior* 42(3), 263–285.

Chapter 8

SUPERVISION STRATEGIES AND DELIVERING SERVICES TO OFFENDERS

Key Terms

ABC model
brokerage
casework
cognitive skills
contracting
EPICS
problem solving

single-factor, specialized caseload
    model
skills
supervision planning
thought–behavior link
vertical model
volunteers

INTRODUCTION

In terms of community safety, the most significant responsibility of a probation or parole agency is supervising offenders. Underlying this duty are the dual objectives of protecting the community and helping offenders change. As we have already learned, these objectives are not always compatible.

Depending on the jurisdiction in which the agency is located, offenders placed on probation and parole may have committed almost any type of criminal offense and may range from first-time offenders to career criminals. The number of offenders placed on probation or released on parole will also vary considerably over time, depending on political and fiscal climates in the jurisdiction, existing laws in the local jurisdiction, size of the prison overpopulation, and prevailing philosophy toward the use of probation and parole.

The bulk of probation and parole clients are under regular supervision, although about one in eight are under some other management program, such as intensive supervision, electronic monitoring, house arrest, or other special program (Camp & Camp, 2003). Two trends emerging over time are the increased number of clients under correctional control and the increasing use of alternatives

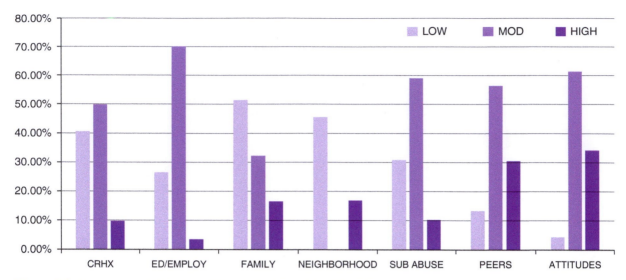

Figure 8.1 Percentage of Offenders Within Need Level for TRAS Domain

Note: CRHX = Criminal history.

Source: Harris County Community Supervision and Corrections Department (2017).

to regular supervision. The implications of these supervision strategies are explored here.

In addition, there is likely to be variation among probationers and parolees with respect to the type and extent of conditions imposed upon them by the court or the parole board. Finally, individuals being supervised will vary considerably in the types of problems they face (family difficulties, educational or employment needs, and alcohol or other drug abuse) (see Figure 8.1). As noted in Figure 8.1, the concentration of offender's needs are in employment/education, substance abuse, peers, and attitudes, with over 70 percent of the offenders falling within the moderate to high risk in each domain. As with other major responsibilities of a probation or parole agency, supervision necessitates an organizational structure that will enable the agency to protect the community efficiently and effectively and provide the necessary support to aid the offender.

Considering the complexity involved in complying with these duties, it is obvious that the agency will be faced with a number of critical management problems and alternatives from which to choose. Many of these, which are discussed separately, are, in reality, closely intertwined. They are not "either/or" alternatives. In fact, many strategies can easily be mixed into a variety of combinations.

This chapter addresses the broad area of service delivery and the ways in which probation and parole agencies handle offenders assigned for supervision. The philosophical models of treatment delivery are examined, as well as the planning process of supervision, different levels of caseload size, developments in the area of offender/officer interactions, and contracting for services and managing community resources.

> **Box 8.1**
> **Matching Offenders Using Big Data**
>
> With the increased access to software packages that can use big data sets, probation and parole departments are starting to explore ways in which offenders can be matched to appropriate officers as well as treatment facilities. With machine learning, it is possible to start developing algorithms that examine eight, nine, or even more characteristics of both the offender and officer and make the best match, similar to the technology used in online dating systems. Imagine a system that could pair up the offender with the most effective officer.

ASSIGNING OFFENDERS TO OFFICERS

As an offender is placed on supervision, he or she is assigned a primary officer. Some jurisdictions use teams to supervise offenders while others place the responsibility of supervision on a single person. So how do agencies actually select the staff person to whom the offender is assigned? In the best-case scenario, offenders are matched specifically to a probation or parole officer in an effort to make the most appropriate connection. In this scenario, an agency would need to collect enough information about the offender's needs, personality factors, demographics, type of offense, and motivation to change to be able to successfully connect them to an officer who has the skills to address the offender's needs (Box 8.1).

In reality, most agencies do not go to that extent to match offenders to officers—the process tends to be more pragmatic. Carter and Wilkins (1976) formally documented the process by which most departments used to assign officers to cases. They identified two primary means by which cases were distributed: horizontal and vertical models.

The horizontal model starts with the pool of offenders that needs to be distributed and then assigns them, officer by officer, until they are all assigned. This is the simplest and most straightforward method for case assignment. Basically, if 100 offenders need to be assigned and the agency has four probation officers, each officer would get 25 new cases regardless of how many they already have on their caseload, their current workload, or their style of supervision. Since the cases are randomly distributed, each officer's caseload should reflect the general pool of offenders. While this is the simplest form of distribution, there are significant problems. First, officers would need to be adept in dealing with a significant range of offenders, ranging from individuals who have committed property crimes to those who have committed violent crimes. Second, caseload sizes will fluctuate significantly over time. While the same number of offenders are placed on supervision, there is no uniform sentence length, nor are all offenders going to stay on supervision for the full term of the sentence (some will be revoked while others will successfully terminate early). With varied end points, some officers will have significantly larger caseloads than others, yet those officers will continue to get assigned the same number of offenders as the officer with a smaller caseload. Third, depending on the geographic size of the catchment area, officers could be supervising offenders across a large geographic space—creating a significant barrier to conducting field visits.

The second distribution model that Carter and Wilkins (1976) discovered being used by agencies was a horizontal model that grouped by geographic location. Solving the issue regarding field visits, officers were assigned to specific zip codes or geographic locations. Within that geographic catchment area, cases were then assigned the same way as in the conventional model—one to one until the cases within the geographic location are distributed across available officers. So, if there is one officer assigned to a set of zip codes and there are 45 offenders needing to be assigned, that officer gets 45 new intakes regardless of their existing caseload size. In contrast, if there are three officers assigned to a specific geographic space (generally an urban area where there is a higher population density) and there are 45 new intakes, these would be equally distributed across the three officers, resulting in 15 new intakes per officer. So, while this model fixes the issue with officers supervising offenders across a vast geographic space, it does not resolve any of the other issues with random assignment and still results in unequal caseload sizes.

In order to solve some of these issues, agencies used a method that controlled for current caseload size (Carter & Wilkins, 1976). While this variation still ignored differences in offenders and officers, it did ensure that officers' caseload sizes would remain relatively consistent. In this model, the agency calculates the average caseload size for the existing population (number of offenders divided by number of officers) and maintains the average across officers. So, the agency with the same 100 cases to assign across four officers, would first take into account the existing or starting caseload size of those officers before assigning the new cases (see Figure 8.2). The agency would assign cases to keep the average caseload similar across all four officers. As can be seen in Figure 8.2, 165 cases were balanced across all four officers. Again, there are several issues with this model. Similar to the previous model, offenders are randomly assigned without any consideration for geographic location, skills of the officer, or type of offenders. But this model also brings its own unique challenges. While each officer has the same number of cases in the end, their workload could be significantly unequal. Imagine getting 45 new offenders assigned at one time. Starting a new case is significantly more work than maintaining a case. Officers need to set up 45 intake appointments, review all the paperwork with the offender, complete an assessment, build

	Officer A	Officer B	Officer C	Officer D
Current Caseload	120	123	160	157
Need to assign 100 offenders	45	42	5	8
Final Caseload	165	165	165	165

Figure 8.2 Assigning Cases by Average Caseload Size

a case plan, and set future appointments—causing a significant workload issue between officers.

Agencies using these two previous methods began to recognize that some officers were not appropriate for specific types of offenders, while other officers worked well with some special populations. To address this issue, agencies began to create specialized caseloads. The **single-factor, specialized caseload model** is designed to address the barriers of previous models by identifying offenders with a single grouping characteristic (e.g., sex offenders) and assigning them to specially trained officers for supervision. This model allows for staff to be selected and trained to address specific issues associated with a population. For example, an agency may create a sex offender unit or identify a group of officers who are going to be assigned all offenders aged 18 to 21. The benefit—officers are trained to address the specific issue associated with the type of caseload. The con—while there is a single issue that groups the offenders together, there is still significant variation on other legal and extralegal characteristics.

Finally, the most complex but potentially most beneficial model is the **vertical model**. It takes into account multiple factors when assigning cases. Most agencies will use a risk assessment or other assessment process to determine the likelihood that those on supervision will be successful. Once all offenders in the agency are screened according to their probability of success, this classificatory scheme can then be used to create caseloads composed of offenders who have roughly the same chances of success or failure. This model is called vertical because it divides the range of offender characteristics into vertical slices in order to create caseloads.

Caseload size can be varied across both single-factor and multi-factor classifications. There can be specialized caseloads (e.g., sex offender) while separating other caseloads by risk level. In this case, an agency may have officers identified to specifically supervise mentally ill offenders, sex offenders, or younger offenders while also having officers who are assigned to supervise low-, moderate- and high-risk offenders. This type of assignment allows an agency to manage resources and focus their workforce on those individuals who need more intensive supervision. Low-risk offenders could be supervised on larger caseloads and fewer office visits while mentally ill offenders or higher-risk offenders may need to be seen more often by specifically trained officers.

Today, many departments employ workload formulas to determine caseload size. This technique takes into account the fact that not all offenders are the same and that some will require more attention than others. For example, higher-risk cases often have additional requirements for services and supervision (including the number of times per month that they must attend contact sessions with officers). Furthermore, higher-risk cases have higher failure rates, which means that additional time might reasonably be required in order to file paperwork for violations, etc. Here, cases are screened according to a number of factors, such as risk. Figure 8.3 shows an example of a monthly work unit ledger from the Montgomery County Adult Probation Department (Dayton, Ohio). In this particular department, a standard workload is 250 work units, based on 107.5 available hours per month. A high-risk case is equal to four work units, while a pre-sentence investigation (PSI) is equal to 14. Each type of case and activity is given a weight,

| (Team) | | | | | | | | | | | | (Month/Year) | |

SUPERVISION CLASSIFICATION			INVESTIGATIONS					WORK UNITS					
OFFICER	MAX	MED	MIN	NEW	ITS	UNS	CURT	TLC	INS	INC	PATH	PSI	SHCK	MISC

TOTALS

MAX—Maximum Supervision	4 work units
INS—Intercounty Transfer	1 work unit
MED—Medium Supervision	2 work units
PATH—Pay Thru	1 work unit
MIN—Minimum Supervision	1 work unit
PSI—Bond or Jail	14 work units
NEW—Not Yet Classified	5 work units
SHCK—Shock Report	2 work units
ITS—Intensive Treatment	8 work units
UNS—Unsupervised-Court	1/2 work units
MISC—Affidavit, Victim	1 work unit
CURT—Courtesy Supervision	1 work unit
TLC—Treatment in Lieu of Conviction	1 work unit

(Supervisor)

Figure 8.3 Work Units Monthly Ledger Summary

Source: Adapted from the Montgomery County Adult Probation Department.

based on a time study that was used as the basis for their formula. This is an excellent example of how work can be distributed equally across a department by taking into account differences between offenders and between certain activities.

Another creative example of how one probation department handles its caseloads can be seen in the Lucas County Adult Probation Department (Toledo, Ohio). Here, all cases are screened according to risk (high, medium, and low). In addition, screening devices are used to identify alcoholics, drug abusers, sex offenders, and offenders with high mental health needs. One probation officer, along with a team of volunteer probation officers, handles all of the low-risk offenders. High-risk offenders who do not require the assistance of a specialist are supervised in a "high-risk unit." Those special-needs offenders are placed in one of the four specialty units (e.g., alcohol, mental health). Caseloads for high-risk and specialty units are considerably smaller. Offenders without these needs who fall into the medium-risk category are supervised by regular treatment officers. In addition, this department has an intensive supervision unit that handles offenders of all types, provided they have been diverted from a state penal institution. Pre-sentence investigations are conducted by a separate unit. Using this scheme, Lucas County is able to divert a considerable number of low-risk, minimum supervision cases and to focus their attention on offenders who require more specialized treatment or increased surveillance.

When the general strategy for managing offenders is established, officers must deliver needed services to their clients. The remainder of this chapter discusses different strategies employed by probation and parole agencies to deliver those services to offenders under supervision. Although these strategies are discussed separately, they are not mutually exclusive, and "pure" types are seldom found in actual supervision practices.

SUPERVISION STRATEGIES

Once caseloads are established, agencies (and officers) need to determine the mode in which officers will deliver services—in other words, what they will do when they are face to face with offenders. Historically, there have been two major approaches toward an officer's in-person work: casework and brokerage. This chapter examines each approach, the assumption underlying its use, its advantages and disadvantages, and major operational concerns. We are discussing "pure" types as though the approaches were mutually exclusive, as if a department would adopt either a caseload or a brokerage approach, but could not combine any feature of the two. In reality, the two approaches are so mixed that it would be unusual if any two departments exhibited precisely the same approach as extreme positions. Most departments adopt positions somewhere along the continuum.

Brokerage Supervision

Agencies (and officers) that adopt the **brokerage** approach see the officer's role as connecting offenders to community resources, issuing referrals to external agencies, and monitoring the offender's compliance with these referrals. Ultimately, not charged with understanding or changing the behavior of the offender, a brokerage officer's role is to assess the concrete needs of the individual and send them to services that will address the identified needs. Because the officer is not seen as the primary agent of treatment or change, there is significantly less emphasis placed on the development of a close, one-on-one relationship between the officer and the offender. With the brokerage approach, the supervising officer functions primarily as a manager or broker of resources and social services already available from other agencies. It is the task of the probation or parole officer to assess the service needs of the offender, locate the social service agency that addresses those needs as its primary function, refer the offender to the appropriate agency, and follow up referrals to make sure the offender has actually received the services.

Under the brokerage approach, it may be said that the officer's relationship with community service agencies is more important than the relationship with an individual client.

The National Advisory Commission on Criminal Justice Standards and Goals (1973, p. 320) recommended that the probation system should "redefine the role of probation officer from caseworker to community resource manager." The Commission report (1973) characterized this approach in the following way:

> To carry out his responsibilities as a community resource manager, the probation officer must perform several functions. In helping a probationer obtain needed services, the probation officer will have to assess the situation, know available resources, contact the appropriate resource, assist the probationer to obtain the services, and follow up on the case. When the probationer encounters difficulty in obtaining a service he needs, the probation officer will have to explore the reason for the difficulty and take appropriate steps to see that the service is delivered. The probation officer will have to monitor and evaluate the services to which the probationer is referred.
>
> (National Advisory Commission on Criminal Justice
> Standards and Goals, 1973, pp. 322–323)

The Commission also addresses the problems of individual probation officers providing services that may be available elsewhere. It encouraged the reliance of probation departments on other social service agencies by suggesting that

> Probation systems should not attempt to duplicate services already created by law and supposedly available to all persons. The responsibility of the system and its staff should be to enable the probationer to cut through the barriers and receive assistance from social institutions that may be all too ready to exclude him.
>
> (National Advisory Commission on Criminal Justice
> Standards and Goals, 1973, p. 32)

With its emphasis on the management of community resources, the brokerage approach requires intimate knowledge of the services in the community and the conditions under which each service is available. It may not be feasible for each officer to accumulate and use this vast amount of information about all the possible community service sources. It has been suggested frequently, therefore, that the brokerage of community services might be handled more easily if individual probation or parole officers were to specialize in gaining knowledge about and familiarity with an agency or set of agencies that provide related services. For example, one officer might become extremely knowledgeable about all community agencies that offer services for individuals with drug-related problems, while another officer might specialize in all agencies that handle unemployed or underemployed individuals. Regardless of whether officers decide to specialize or would prefer to handle all types of community agencies, the essential requirements under the brokerage approach are for the supervising officer to develop a comprehensive knowledge of the resources already available in the community and to use those resources to the fullest extent for the benefit of clients.

Closely related to the brokerage approach is the role of advocate. Several authors have recently stressed the advocacy role for probation officers.[1] Recognizing the fact that some of the services the offenders need will not be available in the community, these authors suggest that instead of trying to supply those needed services themselves, probation and parole officers should concentrate on working with community agencies to develop the necessary service. This will ensure that these services will be available not only to probation or parole clients, but also to other individuals within the community who might require them.[2]

The essential tasks of the brokerage orientation to probation and parole are the management of available community resources and the use of those services to meet the needs of offenders. There is little emphasis on the quality of the relationship that develops between the officer and the offenders; rather, more emphasis is placed upon the close working relationship between the officer and the staff members of community social service agencies. Counseling and guidance are considered inappropriate activities for the probation and parole officer; no attempt is made to change the behavior of the offender. The primary function of the officer is to assess the concrete needs of each offender and make appropriate referral to existing community services. Should the needed service not be available in the community, it is the responsibility of the officer to encourage the development of that service.

Obviously, a pure brokerage approach has its drawbacks. In addition to the lack of a strong relationship between the probation or parole officer and the offender, community services may not be readily available. This is often the case in more rural communities, and even if these service agencies are available, they may not be designed to work with offender populations—making them resistant to accepting justice-involved individuals. As a rule, there appear to be more offenders in need of specialized treatment than there is program space available. Cutbacks in government funding have also resulted in fewer programs, which raises the question: How can a probation or parole officer be a broker if the services are not available?

CASEWORK SUPERVISION

In contrast to the brokerage model, a **casework** style of supervision asks the officer to be an agent of change—she or he is directly responsible for helping the offender change behavior. Casework is not synonymous with the term "social work"; rather, it is just one of the three major specialties of social work (the others are community organization and group work). Many definitions of casework and social casework have been offered. Bowers (1950) has provided this frequently cited definition:

Social casework is an area in which knowledge of the science of human relations and skills in relationships are used to mobilize capacities in the

Probation officer with an offender.
[Photo courtesy of Talbert House, Inc.]

individual and resources in the community appropriate for better adjustment between the client and all or any part of his total environment.

(Bowers, 1950, p. 127)

Meeker (1948) has elaborated further:

The modern emphasis in social casework is upon discovering the positive potential within the individual and helping him exploit his own capabilities, while at the same time revealing external resources in his social and economic environment which will contribute to his ability to assume the mature responsible obligations of a well-adjusted individual.

(Meeker, 1948, pp. 51–52)

It is apparent that the basic element in casework is the nature of the relationship between the caseworker and the individual in trouble. It is also obvious from these definitions that casework emphasizes changing the behavior of the offender through the development of a supportive one-to-one relationship. Because of the closeness, this approach views the caseworker as the sole, or at least the primary, agent of treatment for the client.

By following a casework approach, the supervising officer will also follow the basic assumptions of social work. Trecker (1955, pp. 8–9) divides these assumptions into four categories: people, behavior problems, the social worker (officer), and the relationship between society and the offender. One of the assumptions about offenders is that people are capable of changing under the right circumstances.[3] With respect to behavior problems, it is assumed that because problems are complex and intertwined with the total living situation, treatment of those problems must be individualized. The primary treatment agent is assumed to be the officer, and his or her most important tool is the quality of the relationship created with the client. Finally, it is assumed that the client must be motivated to participate in the treatment process; consequently, a key element of the working relationship between the officer and the client must be the development of the client's desire to change his or her behavior.

A common thread running through these assumptions is the idea that the offender must enter the casework relationship voluntarily, or at least willingly. The relationship involved in correctional supervision, however, does not usually rest on the offender's voluntary participation, but rather on the authority of the probation or parole officer. Under the casework approach, then, it is important to resolve the conflict between the voluntary self-determination of the offender and the authority inherent in the supervising officer's position.

Many authors characterize the authority of the probation or parole officer as an important tool that can be used in the treatment process. Mangrum (1975) refers to the use of "coercive casework" and states:

> While it is true that effective casework is not something done to or for the client, but with him, it is also true that sometimes it is a matter of some action which gets his attention or holds him still long enough for him to recognize that there is motivation from within.
>
> (Mangrum, 1975, p. 219)

Studt (1954, p. 24) notes that it is important for the offender to learn that "authority is power to help as well as power to limit." Hardman (1959) feels that authority, if used properly by the probation officer, can be an extremely powerful tool in the social service. He believes that all individuals, including probationers, entertain both positive and negative feelings toward authority and that a primary responsibility of the caseworker is to help the client understand and accept those conflicting feelings and learn new ways of controlling and expressing them.

Casework is used so extensively in probation and parole supervision that it is considered the "norm" as a service provision strategy. It basically follows the medical model of corrections in which the supervising officer, through a one-to-one relationship, diagnoses the offender, formulates a treatment strategy, implements that strategy, and finally, evaluates the offender in light of the treatment.

In reality, however, the supervising officer does not have the time or energy to devote to individual cases. Perhaps the most basic criticisms of the casework approach are that the probation and/or parole officer tries to be all things to all people, and therefore does not mobilize the community and its support systems adequately. In addition, large caseloads, staff shortages, and endless report writing leave supervising officers unable to perform all the tasks called for by casework. Coupled with the trend to move away from the medical model, probation and parole administrators have initiated both the brokerage approach and community resource management teams.

CASE PLANNING

Regardless of the approach used by an agency to deliver services, an essential ingredient to successful supervision is planning (Ellsworth, 1988). This **supervision plan** includes identifying the needs and problems of the offender, developing strategies to address these needs, and evaluating the effectiveness of those strategies. The probation and parole populations under supervision today are different from those supervised 20 years ago. Not only are there more high-risk offenders on probation, owing to prison and jail crowding, but the offender population is growing older (Burnett & Kitchen, 1989; McCarthy & Langworthy, 1987). With these changes comes a need to improve our planning of the actual supervision task. A solid supervision plan takes those risk, need, and responsivity factors identified in the assessment process and develops a plan or strategy to target or reduce those factors. Priorities are set, and criteria to gauge offender progress are developed to ensure that the focus remains on what the offender needs to do to improve. Historically, a case plan is one of those documents that are required by auditors, but are not used in the day-to-day practice (Haas & DeTardo-Bora, 2009).

The supervision plan, if used properly, can be a meeting-to-meeting guide that helps officers continue to target criminogenic needs before the offender gets into trouble. That is the key point that is often lost in community corrections—officers need to start working with the offender regarding his or her risk factors before they get into trouble. Too often, the officer is reactive to the needs of the offender and not **prescriptive** (Box 8.2). A prescriptive approach is one in which an officer works with an offender to identify the needs of the offender (generally through assessment) and starts working on those needs before they become an immediate threat. To develop a prescriptive plan, it is necessary to complete an assessment of the offender prior to creating the plan (Figure 8.4). In the plan here, the officer completes an assessment gauging the offender's risk factors as well as strengths and barriers. From there, the officer identifies individual needs the offender has and engages in interventions designed to address those needs. Finally, the officer is developing ways to track progress on each of the needs.

While there are all sorts of assessments, in corrections, a risk assessment is generally the tool used to gather this information. Designed to help officers identify the riskiest factors for an offender, the risk assessment flags the greatest areas of need. Once flagged, it is the officer's job to figure out how that area or **criminogenic domain** applies to the individual offender. For example, an offender might score as high risk on the employment domain. A brokerage-type officer will refer the offender to a job readiness program—not fully understanding why employment is a problem for this offender—but relying on the job readiness program to address the specific need. In contrast, a caseworker-type officer will first try and understand why the offender is struggling with

---

Box 8.2
Prescriptive Casework

Officers are trained to look for non-compliant behavior. If the offender is coming to his or her meetings, not getting in trouble with the law, not testing positive for drugs, and employed, the officer often determines that there is nothing to work on with the offender—regardless of the results of the assessment. This would be equivalent to someone going to the doctor for high blood pressure and high cholesterol. As long as the patient hasn't had a heart attack, there is nothing to work on. Of course, we know that is not how the medical field works and should not be how the corrections field works either. Instead, officers should be using the times in which the offender is compliant to focus on those areas that were flagged as risky by the risk assessment. So, if the offender was identified as having relationships with risky peers, the officer should be using interventions to help the offender identify who is risky, under what situations, and how to handle those situations effectively.

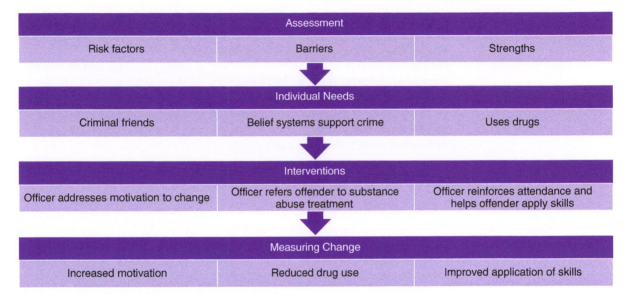

Figure 8.4 Supervision Plan for Casework Style

employment. From there, he or she will address the underlying issue associated with unemployment:

- Motivation to work?
- Childcare issues?
- Ability to read/write?
- Transportation?
- Lack of opportunity?
- Lack of skills?

As you can see, there are many reasons why a person may score as high risk on employment. The case plan helps officers tease out the issues and make a plan to address the offender's needs. After the needs are identified, the next step is to develop the interventions required to address the needs. A cost–benefit analysis may be used to address motivation to work or a problem-solving skill may be taught to the offender so that he or she can figure out the best way to address childcare issues. Some of these issues can be resolved relatively quickly, but others, like literacy, may be a longer-term target.

Once the needs and interventions are selected, the case plan is designed to track progress in addressing the offender's needs. Tracking the progress an offender has made on each need area is extremely important. Not only does it keep the officer on track, it is an opportunity to reinforce the amount of change the offender has made over time. This will keep the offender engaged in supervision and will help him or her keep moving forward, making incremental changes over time.

As we discussed in the previous section, officers oriented as caseworkers are designed to be part of the change process. In contrast, officers that identify as brokers are more likely to refer offenders to external resources to address the needs of the offender. Depending on the orientation of the officer, a case plan may look completely different. The next two sections will describe the different tools each type of officer uses to meet the needs of the offender. The first section will offer ways in which brokerage can be done in the most effective manner. The second section will examine some of the tools available for officers who see their role as changing offender behavior. Regardless of the officer's approach, it is important that the offender learn new ways to handle situations so that he or she can desist from crime when moving forward.

BROKERAGE OFFICERS: CONTRACTING FOR SERVICES

As indicated previously, recent events have called for a change in the role of the probation and parole officer. Instead of focusing on addressing the offender's individual needs, officers are expected to broker relevant services, acting as a sort of managed-care case manager who works with community providers to address the needs of the offender. In order for an officer to effectively broker services, he or she must understand the needs of the offender, but the officer must also be knowledgeable about the resources available in the community. Once the officer (or agency) identifies the appropriate resources, it is not uncommon to build both informal and formal relationships with those programs. Memoranda of Understanding (MOUs) are often formed between governmental and non-governmental agencies to define the relationship between the probation or parole office and the agency to which the offender is referred. In some cases, the probation and parole office will provide funding for these types of relationships, resulting in a more formal contract.

Contracts for a wide variety of client and administrative activities are particular to the unique responsibilities of community corrections (Jensen, 1987). These include the following:

- Residential programs (including halfway houses, house arrest, restitution centers, and facilities for juveniles, such as group or foster homes).
- Counseling and treatment programs for both general client groups and targeted offenders such as drug addicts and alcoholics.
- Administrative services for data processing, recordkeeping, evaluations, and so forth.
- Programs for victims of crime and crisis intervention. These would include traditional counseling services, as well as programs designed to aid victims as they struggle with the criminal justice system and to help them file for victim compensation.
- Programs that conduct private pre-sentence investigations and develop sentencing alternatives for offenders.
- Dispute resolution, mediation programs, and pretrial services.
- Testing, ranging from employment/educational to urinalysis for alcohol or other drug abuse.

Stricter punishment has brought offenders that are "new" to the criminal justice system, such as drunk drivers, domestic violence perpetrators, and persons who fail to pay child support. Crowded jail facilities often cannot handle these offender categories, and it is unlikely that they will find room for such offenders in the future. As a result, many jurisdictions have turned to private providers to handle these "specialized" groups.

Contracting can be an effective way to provide services. For example, many probation and parole agencies contract with local halfway houses for beds. It is much more cost-effective to "lease" the bed space than to build and operate a halfway house. Contracting also gives the agency the flexibility of being able to terminate the contract if the service fails to meet expectations or is no longer needed.

Many of these programs represent an attempt to treat some offenders in a non-traditional fashion and provide close ties between them and community programs. Such innovations can, when used with a particular type of client (such as mentally disordered offenders or drunk drivers), help offenders and relieve the burden of heavy caseloads upon a probation department. Their use could also permit a probation department to deploy its resources in a more efficient manner.

CASEWORKER SKILLS: ADDRESSING CRIMINOGENIC NEEDS

For caseworkers, the relationship between the offender and officer is very important. Yet, Spiegler and Guevremont (2003) warn us that while the relationship is necessary in the change process, it is not sufficient in changing others. The relationship builds trust; building on that trust, the interventions or tools that an officer uses can be introduced in such a way that the offender will be receptive to changing. These tools are usually designed to address three broad categories:

1. increase offender motivation to change;
2. restructure (change) offender thinking about crime;
3. increase the offender's skills.

Increasing Offender Motivation to Change

Increasing offender motivation to change is important. Without motivation, it is hard to get the offender to engage in the work needed to change his or her behavior. One such intervention, or approach really, to address offender motivation is **motivational interviewing**. Initially designed to address health issues, including reducing alcohol use, motivational interviewing (MI) has now been applied widely to correctional populations. Stephen Rollnick and William Miller (1995) describe MI as a counseling style that elicits behavioral change through strengthening motivation for change. Motivational interviewing uses collaboration, reflective statements, and scaling to help offenders explore their own support for change.

	Short-term	**Long-term**
Pros	Make money	Don't have to pay taxes
	Take care of family	Lots of money
	Nice car	Get respect from peers
	Feed family	
Cons	Go to jail	Get killed

Figure 8.5 Decisional Balance for Drug Dealing

	Short-term	**Long-term**
Pros	Make money	Be there for my family
	Free from jail	Don't have to go to prison
	Don't worry about being arrested	Safer than selling drugs
Cons	Less money than from selling drugs	Pay taxes
	Takes longer to get ahead	

Figure 8.6 Decisional Balance for Getting a Job

In addition to MI, officers will use a cost–benefit tool or a decisional balance to help offenders establish some motivation to change. The decisional balance tool is often used when the offender struggles with seeing the long-term consequences of his or her behavior—often focusing on the short-term benefits of criminal or maladaptive behavior. The decisional balance tool helps officers elicit both the positives and negatives of a behavior. Figure 8.5 provides an example of a decisional balance tool an officer used with an offender regarding selling drugs. As you see, the offender identifies more positives for selling drugs than negatives. In his head, he sees selling drugs as his only option to feed his family, not taking into account that if he is arrested and goes to prison, he will not be able to support his family. In Figure 8.6, the officer helps the offender to take an alternative option, obtaining employment, and list the pros/cons of getting a job. As you can see, the positives are not as powerful, but there are significantly fewer cons.

Restructuring Thinking

One of the primary needs of offenders is changing their belief systems that support crime. Referred to as thinking errors or criminal thinking, beliefs that support crime are identified as one of the core drivers for criminal behavior. Imagine an offender telling himself that it is okay to punch someone who has wronged them, or an offender telling herself, "I am not hurting anyone if I get high." These are examples of beliefs that justify or make it okay to engage in criminal behavior. These beliefs are usually organized in several categories (Sykes & Matza, 1957, 667–669):

- **Denial of Responsibility:** The criminal behavior is not the offender's fault—it is a consequence of external forces. An example is when an offender says, "The cops are out to get me."
- **Denial of Injury:** The offender takes responsibility for the behavior, but denies harming the victim. An example: "Yeah, I stole the shirt, but they have insurance."
- **Denial of the Victim:** The offender will blame the victim of the offense—"He shouldn't have got in my face, in fact, I was the real victim here."

These neutralizations allow offenders to convince themselves that the behavior is justified. In order for officers to help the offender see how these thinking patterns lead to criminal behavior, they incorporate tools that focus on the thought–behavior link (see Box 8.3). The thought–behavior link can be found in many different cognitive tools. One cognitive tool, the **ABC Model** (see Figure 8.7) demonstrates how it is a person's beliefs that lead to behavior and not the situation. Ultimately, the way we interpret or see a situation is why we have a negative response, be it negative feelings or dysfunctional behavior (Ellis, 1962). So, if thinking drives irrational behavior, changing one's thinking can change behavior. This why cognitive restructuring is an important tool for officers to use. In the situation described in Figure 8.7, imagine if the officer could help the offender "rethink" what it means to be cut off in traffic. Instead of the offender thinking that the other driver was out to get them, if the officer could get the offender to consider that the other driver might not have seen them, that it was an accident, or no harm/no foul occurred, the offender's response could be significantly different. Cognitive restructuring is not an easy tool to master, but once familiar, it is a powerful tool in the officer's tool kit.

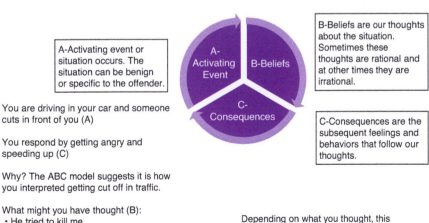

Figure 8.7 ABC Model

Box 8.3
The Thought–Behavior Link

This is the connection between what we think and how we behave. For example, we often drive over the speed limit (behavior) because of what we tell ourselves (thoughts).

- I'm a safe driver
- I am only going 8 miles over the speed limit
- I am late
- I am going with the flow of traffic
- There are no police

Increasing Offenders' Skills

The third tool that officers can use to change an offender's behavior is **cognitive skills.** Generally considered a core function of cognitive-behavioral interventions, cognitive skills are designed to teach offenders new ways of thinking or acting. Driven by a void in skills to navigate situations effectively, the offender formulates maladaptive ways of handling situations. The purpose of cognitive skills is to teach offenders a way to navigate situations that does not result in negative consequences. Cognitive skills that offenders might need include problem solving, learning to manage negative peers more effectively, or managing situations in which the offender feels disrespected (see Box 8.4)

Box 8.4
Problem Solving

A problem is a specific situation or set of related situations to which a person must respond in order to function effectively. A problematic situation is one in which no effective response alternative is immediately available to the person facing the situation. Teaching the steps to problem solving can be very helpful:

1. Stop and think—identify the problem
2. Clarify goals
3. Generate alternative solutions
4. Evaluation
5. Implement the plan
6. Evaluate the decision

Ultimately, the combination of increasing motivation, targeting criminal attitudes and beliefs, and teaching offenders new skills has resulted in significant reductions in recidivism (Pearson et al., 2002).

IMPROVING COMMUNITY SUPERVISION

Given the large caseload and varied responsibilities of probation and parole agencies, the question remains: Can probation and parole officers influence change in their offenders? Preliminary evidence from training initiatives in Canada (Bonta et al., 2008; Bourgon et al., 2010), the United States (Smith et al., 2012) as well as Australia (Trotter, 1996), has produced some promising results, but we need to continue to explore what officers are doing and how they are trained.

While it has been assumed that offenders will benefit from traditional community supervision much more than if they were incarcerated, recent empirical evidence on the effectiveness of community supervision challenges this assumption. For example, Bonta and colleagues (2010) have undertaken a review of the literature on the effectiveness of community supervision using meta-analytic techniques. The findings from 15 studies published between 1980 and 2006 yielded 26 effect size estimates. The average follow-up period was 17 months, and the mean effect size was *about zero*, indicating no statistically significant relationship between community supervision and recidivism.

While these studies show that supervision is ineffective at reducing recidivism, there is a move to combine community supervision and the "what works" literature. One pioneering study in this regard was conducted by Bonta and associates (2008, 2010). Audiotaped interviews between 62 probation officers and their offenders found relatively poor adherence to some of the basic principles of effective intervention. For the most part, probation officers spent too much time on the enforcement aspect of supervision (i.e., monitoring compliance with court conditions) and not enough time on the service delivery role of supervision. Major criminogenic needs, such as antisocial attitudes and social supports for crime, were largely ignored, and probation officers evidenced few of the **skills** (e.g., prosocial modeling, differential reinforcement) that could influence behavioral change in their offenders. This research led to the development of a strategic training initiative that has been implemented in several sites across Canada. At this point in time, it is evident that trained officers have higher caseload retention rates (i.e., fewer technical violations, new arrests, and AWOLs).

During the past decade, several attempts have been made to improve the effectiveness of community supervision by implementing RNR and other evidence-based research into community supervision practices (Bourgon et al., 2010; Robinson et al., 2012; Smith et al., 2012; Trotter, 1996, 2006). Research conducted by Trotter (1996) has also supported the use of core correctional practices in community supervision. He contends that establishing accurate roles, working with clients to define individualized goals, and reinforcing prosocial values are necessary components of an integrated practice model. His research has also underscored the importance of the client–worker relationship, case planning, use of community resources, and training families to support behavioral change (Trotter, 1996).

Research on the principles of effective intervention coupled with the most recent research on community supervision provided the impetus for the development of a new model by the University of Cincinnati: Effective Practices in Community Supervision (**EPICS**). This model represents a combination of the content included in both Canadian and Australian studies. The purpose of the EPICS model is to teach probation and parole officers how to apply the principles of effective intervention (and core correctional practices specifically, including relationship skills) to community supervision practices. The EPICS model has been piloted in Indiana and Ohio, and results have indicated that the trained officers are using the skills at a higher rate than untrained officers.

With the EPICS model, probation officers follow a structured approach to their interactions with their offenders. Specifically, each session includes four components: (1) *check-in*, in which the officer determines if the offender has any crises or acute needs, builds rapport, and discusses compliance issues; (2) *review*, which focuses on the skills discussed in the prior session, application of those skills, and troubleshooting of continued problems in the use of those skills; (3) *intervention*, where the probation officer identifies continued areas of need, as well as trends in problems the offender experiences, teaches relevant skills, and targets problematic thinking; and (4) *homework and rehearsal*, when the offender is given an opportunity to see the model the probation officer is talking about, is provided with opportunities to role play, assigned homework, and given instructions to follow before the next visit.

Box 8.5 illustrates the steps of the EPICS approach. The EPICS model is designed to use a combination of monitoring, referrals, and face-to-face interactions to provide the offender with a sufficient "dosage" of treatment interventions and make the best possible use of time to develop a collaborative working relationship. The EPICS model helps to translate the risk, need, and responsivity (RNR) principles into practice. Probation officers are taught to increase dosage to higher-risk offenders, stay focused on criminogenic needs, especially the thought–behavior link, and use a social learning, cognitive-behavioral approach to their interactions. The EPICs model is not intended to replace other programming and services, but rather is an attempt to more fully utilize probation officers as agents of change, thus combining the best elements of casework and brokerage. Results from the studies in Ohio and Indiana have indicated that implementation of the model was associated with reductions in recidivism, particularly for higher-risk offenders and in the case of officers who used the skills with higher fidelity (Smith et al., 2012). More recent versions of the model have further integrated EPICS with case management and motivational interviewing.

Box 8.5
Steps in EPICS

Step 1: Check in
Step 2: Review
Step 3: Intervention
Step 4: Rehearsal and homework

USE OF VOLUNTEERS

Community correctional programs operate under a basic philosophy of reintegration: connecting offenders with legitimate opportunity and reward structures, and generally uniting the offender with the community. It has become quite apparent that the correctional system cannot achieve this without assistance, regardless of the extent of resources available. Reintegration requires the assistance and support of the community. One important resource for the community correctional agency is the use of volunteers. If used properly, these individuals can serve as an important asset for a community correctional agency.

This concept is certainly not a new one. The John Howard Association, the Osborne Association, and other citizen prisoners' aid societies have provided voluntary correctional-type services for many years. The volunteer movement developed in this country in the early 1820s, when a group of citizens known as the Philadelphia Society for Alleviating the Miseries of Public Prisons began supervising the activities of inmates upon their release from penal institutions. This practice was later adopted by John Augustus, a Boston shoemaker, who worked with well over 2,000 misdemeanants in his lifetime (see Chapter 4).

Volunteerism is alive and well in corrections.[4] Judge Keith Leenhouts of the Royal Oak (Michigan) Municipal Court resurrected the concept some 30 years ago and continued through his passing to serve as a driving force behind this now relatively accepted, and still growing, movement. In addition to the many local programs in existence, there are several national and state-based programs supporting volunteerism, such as the Texas Division of Criminal Justice Volunteer Services Program, VIP (Volunteers in Probation), and the American Bar Association-sponsored VolunteerMatch. Although exact numbers are not known, it is safe to say that there are thousands of volunteers serving more than 3,000 jurisdictions nationwide.

Proponents of the volunteer concept consider it to be one of the most promising innovations in the field, claiming that it can help alleviate the problem of excessive probation and parole caseloads and contribute to rehabilitation and reintegration goals for the offender (Greenberg, 1988; Latessa et al., 1983). A good illustration of the effective use of volunteers can be seen in Lucas County (Toledo), Ohio. Here, probationers are screened according to risk. All "low-risk" probationers are assigned to one probation officer who, with the help of volunteers, supervises more than 1,000 clients.

Volunteers can range from student interns to older persons with time to devote. Some volunteers are persons who have a specific skill or talent to contribute, while others give their time and counsel.

Scope of Services

Volunteerism generally refers to situations in which individual citizens contribute their talents, wisdom, skills, time, and resources within the context of the justice system, without receiving financial remuneration. Volunteer projects operate on the premise that certain types of offenders can be helped by the services a volunteer can offer and that such services can be provided at a minimal tax dollar cost, resulting in significant cost savings.

By drawing upon the time, talents, and abilities of volunteers to assist in service delivery, community supervision officers can serve to broaden the nature of the services offered. Any community consists of persons who possess a diverse supply of skills and abilities that can be tapped effectively by volunteer programs. Scheier (1970) developed a list of more than 200 potential volunteer services, including the following:

addiction program volunteer	intake volunteer
case aide	newsletter editor
clerical courtroom assistance	presentence investigator
diagnostic home volunteer	recreation volunteer
educational aide	test administrator and scorer
foster parent	vocational service aide
fund-raiser	volunteer counselor.

In addition to the direct service offered, volunteers can supply a number of support services (Lucas, 1987). Volunteers often assist program operations in an administrative capacity. For example, a full-time volunteer for quite some time has supervised the well-known Royal Oak, Michigan program. One program in Los Angeles County (California) has likewise utilized volunteers to fill some of its clerical needs, such as handling supplies, photocopying, answering recruitment correspondence, and routine office contacts, as well as participating in research projects. In addition, many volunteers serve on advisory boards. Many non-profit community agencies, such as halfway houses, rely on volunteers to serve on their boards of directors. There can be little doubt that volunteers can serve as a means of amplifying the time, attention, and type of services given to clients by the system. However, it is also important that an agency not become over-reliant on volunteers to the extent that they do not hire enough professional officers and staff.

SUMMARY

This chapter discussed one of the most important aspects of probation and parole: supervision of the offender. We have noted that the assignment of offenders to a probation or parole officer for supervision can follow several models. Some offenders are assigned randomly to caseloads, others are assigned based on geography or special problems, while yet others are classified through the use of prediction devices.

Once assignment is complete, the approach or philosophy of supervision usually centers on casework and brokerage. Casework follows a belief that the supervising officer should be the primary agent of change and thus "all things to all people." The brokerage approach assumes that the best place for treatment is in the community and that the primary task of the probation or parole officer is to arrange for and manage community resources. While casework is the norm, in reality, most probation and parole officers and agencies use techniques from both approaches.

More recently, a new model of offender and probation officer interaction has arisen that attempts to restructure the way that POs work with offenders by focusing on criminogenic needs, skill deficits, and the thought–behavior link. By combining compliance with effective interventions, it is hoped that lower recidivism can be achieved. Finally, the use of volunteers is not a new concept. Volunteers play an important role in community corrections and, if used properly, can be a valuable asset to a community correctional agency.

Review Questions

1. List three ways that caseloads are assigned.
2. Describe the different supervision strategies used by officers.
3. Why are case plans important?
4. What are the four steps in the EPICS model and how is it different from traditional approaches?
5. How can volunteers be used in probation?

Notes

1 For a good example of advocacy in probation and parole, see Dell'Apa et al. (1976); and Mangrum (1975).
2 For discussions of advocacy, see Macallair (1994).
3 This point is argued eloquently by Cullen (1994). See also Scott and Wolfe (2000).
4 American Correctional Association (1993). See also American Correctional Association (1987); and Celinska (2000).

Recommended Readings

Ankersmit, E. (1976). Setting the contract in probation. *Federal Probation* 41(2), 28–33.

Harlow, C. (1999). *Prior abuse reported by inmates and probationers.* Washington, DC: Bureau of Justice Statistics.

Macallair, D. (1993). Reaffirming rehabilitation in juvenile justice. *Youth and Society* 25, 104–125.

Maruschak, L., Beck, A. (2001). *Medical problems of inmates, 1997.* Washington, DC: U.S. Department of Justice, Office of Justice Programs.

Mumola, C. (1999). *Substance abuse and treatment, states and federal prisoners, 1997.* Washington, DC: Bureau of Justice Statistics.

Sigler, R., Williams, J. (1994). A study of the outcomes of probation officers and risk-screening instrument classifications. *Journal of Criminal Justice* 22, 495–502.

Taxman, F.S. (2002). Supervision: Exploring the dimensions of effectiveness. *Federal Probation* 66(2), 14–27.

Taxman, F.S., Shepardson, E., Byrne, J. (2004). *Tools of the trade: A guide to incorporating science into practice.* Baltimore, MD: National Institute of Corrections, Maryland Division of Probation and Parole.

References

American Correctional Association. (1987). *Standards for administration of correctional agencies.* Laurel, MD: ACA.

American Correctional Association. (1993). *Community partnerships in action.* Laurel, MD: ACA.

Bonta, J., Bourgon, G., Rugge, T., Scott, T.Y., Yessine, A.K., Gutierrez, L., Li, J. (2010). *Corrections research report: User report on the strategic training initiative in community supervision: Risk-need-responsivity in the real world.* Toronto, ON: Public Safety Canada.

Bonta, J., Rugge, T., Scott, T.L., Bourgon, G., Yessine, A.K. (2008). Exploring the "black box" of supervision. *Journal of Offender Rehabilitation* 47(3), 248–270.

Bourgon, G., Bonta, J., Rugge, T., Scott, T.L., Yessine, A.K. (2010). Program design, implementation, and evaluation in "real world" community supervision. *Federal Probation* 74(1), 1–10.

Bowers, S. (1950). The nature and definition of social casework. In: C. Kasius (Ed.), *Principles and techniques in social casework* (pp. 126–139). New York: Family Services Association of America.

Burnett, C., Kitchen, A. (1989). More than a case number: Older offenders on probation. *Journal of Offender Counseling, Services and Rehabilitation* 13, 149–160.

Camp, C., Camp, G. (2003). *The corrections yearbook 2003.* South Salem, NY: The Criminal Justice Institute.

Carter, R., Wilkins, L. (1976). Caseloads: Some conceptual models. In: R.M. Carter, L.T. Wilkins (Eds.), *Probation, parole and community corrections* (pp. 391–401). New York: John Wiley and Sons.

Celinska, K. (2000). Volunteer involvement in ex-offenders' readjustment. *Journal of Offender Rehabilitation* 30(3/4), 99–116.

Cullen, F.T. (1994). Social support as an organizing concept for criminology. *Justice Quarterly* 11, 527–560.

Dell'Apa, F., Adams, W., Jorgensen, J., Sigurdson, H. (1976). Advocacy, brokerage, community: The ABCs of probation and parole. *Federal Probation* 40(4), 37–44.

Ellis, A. (1962). *Reason and emotion in psychotherapy.* New York: Stuart.

Ellsworth, T. (1988). Case supervision planning: The forgotten component of intensive probation supervision. *Federal Probation* 52(4), 28–32.

Greenberg, N. (1988). The discovery program: A way to use volunteers in the treatment process. *Federal Probation* 52(4), 39–45.

Haas, S.M., DeTardo-Bora, K.A. (2009). Inmate reentry and the utility of the LSI-R in case planning. *Corrections Compendium* 34(1), 11–16.

Hardman, D. (1959). Authority in casework: A bread-and-butter theory. *National Probation and Parole Association Journal* 5, 249–255.

Jensen, C. (1987). *Contracting for community corrections services.* Washington, DC: U.S. Department of Justice, National Institute of Corrections.

Latessa, E., Travis, L., Allen, H. (1983). Volunteers and paraprofessionals in parole: Current practices. *Journal of Offender Counseling Services and Rehabilitation* 8, 91–105.

Lucas, W. (1987). Perceptions of the volunteer role. *Journal of Offender Counseling, Services and Rehabilitation* 12, 141–146.

Macallair, D. (1994). Disposition case advocacy in San Francisco's juvenile justice system: A new approach to deinstitutionalization. *Crime & Delinquency* 40, 84–95.

Mangrum, C. (1975). *The professional practitioner in probation.* Springfield, IL: Charles C. Thomas.

McCarthy, B., Langworthy, R. (1987). Older offenders on probation and parole. *Journal of Offender Counseling, Services and Rehabilitation* 12, 7–25.

Meeker, B. (1948). Probation is casework. *Federal Probation* 12(2), 51–52.

National Advisory Commission on Criminal Justice Standards and Goals. (1973). *Corrections.* Washington, DC: U.S. Government Printing Office.

Pearson, F.S., Lipton, D.S., Cleland, C.M., Yee, D.S. (2002). The effects of behavioral/cognitive-behavioral programs on recidivism. *Crime & Delinquency* 48(3), 476–496.

Robinson, C.R., Lowenkamp, C.T., Holsinger, A.M., VanBenschoten, S.W., Alexander, M., Oleson, J.C. (2012). A random (almost) study of staff training aimed at reducing re-arrest (STARR): Using core correctional practices in probation interactions. *Journal of Crime and Justice* 35(2), 167–188.

Rollnick, S., Miller, W. (1995). What is motivational interviewing? *Behavioural and Cognitive Psychotherapy* 23(4), 325–334.

Scheier, I. (1970). The professional and the volunteer: An emerging relationship. *Federal Probation* 34(2), 8–12.

Scott, K., Wolfe, D. (2000). Change among batterers: Examining men's success stories. *Journal of Interpersonal Violence* 15(8), 827–842.

Smith, P., Schweitzer, M., Labrecque, R.M., Latessa, E.J. (2012). Improving probation officers' supervision skills: An evaluation of the EPICS model. *Journal of Crime and Justice* 35(2), 189–199.

Spiegler, M.D., Guevremont, D.C. (2003). *Contemporary behaviour therapy.* 4th ed. Pacific Grove, CA: Wadsworth.

Studt, E. (1954). Casework in the correctional field. *Federal Probation* 17(3), 17–24.

Sykes, G., Matza, D. (1957). Techniques of neutralization: A theory of delinquency. *American Sociological Review* 22(6), 664–670.

Trecker, H. (1955). Social work principles in probation. *Federal Probation* 19(1), 8–9.

Trotter, C. (1996). The impact of different supervision practices in community corrections: Cause for optimism. *Australian and New Zealand Journal of Criminology* 29, 1–18.

Trotter, C. (2006). *Working with involuntary clients: A guide to practice.* London: Sage.

Chapter 9

GRADUATED RESPONSES TO BEHAVIOR

Key Terms

boot camp
community service
day-reporting centers
diversion
electronic monitoring
enhancement
global positioning system (GPS)

graduated responses
home detention
intensive supervision
intermediate sanctions
negative reinforcement
positive reinforcement
shock incarceration

WHEN REGULAR PROBATION IS NOT ENOUGH

No discussion of contemporary probation would be complete without examining the development and application of **intermediate sanctions** and **graduated responses**. Faced with overcrowded prisons and jails, the American criminal justice system has been forced to search for alternative ways to sentence offenders on the front-end of the system and to respond to offenders' behavior on the back-end. A host of options designed to maintain the offender in the community have been developed and implemented over the past 30 years. Front-end alternatives to incarceration often include jail plus probation, intensive monitoring, or sentencing to local residential programs. Back-end responses include similar alternatives, with many probation and parole agencies developing robust response matrices that include graduated responses to non-compliant behavior as well as structured reinforcement systems to incentivize compliant behavior. While there is little uniformity across the United States in how alternatives to incarceration are used, there are two primary decision points at which they are issued:

1. at initial sentencing, usually referred to as intermediate sanctioning;
2. in response to non-compliant behavior, usually referred to as graduated response.

First, we will discuss the use of intermediate sanctions in the direct sentencing of offenders. Second, we will explore the use of graduated responses including the more recent use of swift, certain, and fair strategies as well as structured incentive programs. Third, we will examine the revocation process.

INTERMEDIATE SANCTIONS

The U.S. Department of Justice (1990, p. 3) defines *intermediate sanctioning* as "a punishment option that is considered on a continuum to fall between traditional probation and traditional incarceration." Intermediate sanctions were largely developed out of the need to relieve prison crowding[1] and satisfy the general public's desire for new correctional alternatives. Thus, policy makers began to experiment with programs to punish, control, and reform offenders in the community.

With prison and jail populations at a recent all-time high, most states have acknowledged that they cannot continue to build their way out of the crisis. The initial cost to build a prison is a high price tag. In 2018, Utah legislators passed a bill to build a new, 4,000-bed prison with a total price tag of $860 million (Harrie et al., 2018). That translates to $215,000 per bed to build and does not count the operating costs. The operating costs vary depending on the location of the prison, but the national per diem average to house a single prisoner for a year is more than $30,000 (Henrichson & Delaney, 2012). In addition to prisons, local jails carry a high price tag as well. In Maricopa County (Phoenix), it costs $325.65 for the first day a person stays in jail, called a booking rate, and then $101.72 per day after that. In 2016, there were 94,110 bookings and a total of 2,788,904 bed days, costing the county more than $310 million a year to operate the jail (Scharbach & Bohn, 2017). Beyond the cost to build and operate jails and prisons, research also suggests that there is a social cost to jails and prisons as well. Recent studies have found that people (especially lower-risk people) who spend time in jails and prisons are exposed to significant collateral consequences, potentially causing more harm than good or at least having no rehabilitative effect (see Chapter 2 for a full discussion).

Box 9.1
Intermediate Sanctions

Intermediate sanctions, ranging in severity from day fines to "boot camps," are interventions that are beginning to fill the sentencing gap between prison at one extreme and probation at the other. Lengthy prison terms may be inappropriate for some offenders; for others, probation may be too inconsequential and may not provide the degree of public supervision necessary to ensure public safety. By expanding sentencing options, intermediate sanctions enable the criminal justice system to tailor punishment more closely to the nature of the crime and the criminal. An appropriate range of punishments makes it possible for the system to hold offenders strictly accountable for their actions.

Source: Gowdy (1993).

To combat these costs, legislators and local officials have been working over the past 40 years to develop alternatives to incarceration programs. The following sections will discuss in detail these alternatives to incarceration.

INTENSIVE SUPERVISION

The most widely used community-based intermediate sanction that attempts to meet the aforementioned criteria is **intensive supervision**. Intensive supervision is most often viewed as an alternative to incarceration. Offenders who are sentenced to intensive probation supervision are supposed to be those offenders who, in the absence of intensive supervision, would have been sentenced to prison. However, intensive supervision is hardly a new idea. Previous programs of intensive supervision carried the common goal of maintaining public safety, but varied from the "new generation" of intensive supervision programs (ISPs) in very fundamental ways (Latessa, 1986).

Early versions of intensive supervision were based on the idea that increased client contact would enhance rehabilitation while allowing for greater client control. For example, California's Special Intensive Parole Unit experiments in the 1950s and the San Francisco Project in the 1960s were designed as intensive supervision, but they emphasized rehabilitation as the main goal. Later, with rehabilitation still as the main objective, experiments were "undertaken to determine the 'best' caseload size for the community supervision, despite the illogic of the proposition that a magical 'best' number could be found" (McCarthy, 1987, p. 33). Nevertheless, the failure of these experiments to produce results fueled two decades' worth of cynicism about the general utility of community-based methods.

Burkhart (1986) and Pearson (1987) contend that ISPs emphasize punishment of the offender, close accountability measures, and control of the offender in the community more than they do rehabilitation. It is easy to understand when we really consider the interventions. If we take a high-risk offender and watch them closely, we will find them breaking conditions, but do we deter criminal behavior in the process? Hyatt and Barnes (2017) say no. They found that offenders randomly assigned to ISPs reoffended at no higher a rate than those who were placed on regular probation, yet ISP probationers absconded from supervision at higher rates, were charged with technical violations more often, and ultimately were sentenced to prison at significantly higher rates. Even with juveniles, Hennigan et al. (2010) found that lower-risk youth who were placed in intensive supervision programs were incarcerated at three times the rate of those under regular supervision. Even the higher-risk youth showed no long-term benefit from being under intensive supervision.

Today, no two jurisdictions define intensive supervision in exactly the same way. However, one characteristic of all ISPs is that they provide for very strict terms of probation. As Jones (1991) points out:

> Their common feature is that more control is to be exerted over the offender than that described as probation in that jurisdiction and that often these extra

control mechanisms involve restrictions on liberty of movement, coercion into treatment programs, employment obligations, or all three.

(Jones, 1991, p. 1)

This increased level of control is usually achieved through reduced caseloads, an increased number of contacts, and a range of required activities for participating offenders that can include victim restitution, community service, employment, random testing for substance abuse, electronic monitoring, and payment of a probation supervision fee.

Intensive supervision programs vary in terms of the number and type of contacts per month, caseload size, type of surveillance conducted, and services offered. In addition, programs vary depending on whether they are staffed by specially trained officers or regular probation officers, and whether an officer "team" approach is used. A survey on the use of intensive supervision in the United States found that "the numbers of direct personal contacts required ranged from 2 per month to 7 per week. Some programs have specified no curfew checks, while others specified three curfew checks per week" (Pearson, 1987, p. 15). Ideally, supervising officers provide monitoring with a reduced caseload of about 15 offenders per officer. Yet most officers carry caseloads of nearly 25 offenders. Offender entry into an intensive supervision program may be the decision of the sentencing judge, a parole board, a prison release board, or probation agency. Table 9.1 shows some of the variations among selected ISPs. The types of clients served, the number of contacts

---

Box 9.2
Types of Intensive Supervision Programs

Intensive supervision programs (ISPs) are usually classified as prison diversion, enhanced probation, and enhanced parole. Each has a different goal.

Diversion is commonly referred to as a "front door" program because its goal is to limit the number of offenders entering prison. Prison diversion programs generally identify incoming, lower-risk inmates to participate in an ISP in the community as a substitute for a prison term.

Enhancement programs generally select already sentenced probationers and parolees and subject them to closer supervision in the community than regular probation or parole. People placed in ISP-enhanced probation or enhanced parole programs show evidence of failure under routine supervision or have committed serious offenses deemed too serious for supervision on routine caseloads.

Treatment and service components in the ISPs include drug and alcohol counseling, employment, community service, and payment of restitution. On many of these measures, ISP offenders participated more than control members; participation in such programs was found to be correlated with a reduction in recidivism.

Source: Petersilia and Turner (1993).

made each month, and the recidivism rates vary greatly from program to program. Many ISPs have revealed an increase in technical violations for ISP offenders as compared to offenders placed in other sentencing options, but no significant decreases in new offenses, suggesting that ISPs may not be effective in creating a safer community (Erwin, 1987; Hyatt & Barnes, 2017; Petersilia & Turner, 1993; Wagner & Baird, 1993).

As currently designed, many ISPs fail to produce significant reductions in recidivism or alleviate prison overcrowding. There does, however, appear to be a relationship between ISPs and offenders that encourages participation in treatment programs and lower failure rates (Jolin & Stipak, 1992; Pearson, 1987; Petersilia & Turner, 1993). This is one of the important issues facing intensive supervision. In an article summarizing the state of ISPs, Fulton et al. (1997, p. 72) drew the following conclusions:

- Intensive supervision programs have failed to alleviate prison crowding.
- Most ISP studies have found no significant differences between recidivism rates of ISP offenders and offenders with comparison groups.
- There appears to be a relationship between greater participation in treatment and employment programs and lower recidivism rates.
- Intensive supervision programs appear to be more effective than regular supervision or prison in meeting offenders' needs.
- Intensive supervision programs that reflect certain principles of effective intervention are associated with lower rates of recidivism.
- Intensive supervision programs provide intermediate punishment.
- Although ISPs are less expensive than prison, they are more expensive than originally thought.

Issues in Intensive Supervision

Intensive supervision, as a technique for increasing control over offenders in the community (and thereby reducing risk), gained wide popularity during the "get tough" era.[2] Since 1990, all states, plus the federal system, had some kind of intensive supervision program in place. This widespread acceptance has provided states with the needed continuum of sentencing options so that offenders are being held accountable for their crimes while, at the same time, public safety is being maintained. This popularity of intensive supervision has generated much research, thereby raising several issues.

Current issues largely revolve around the effectiveness of intensive supervision. However, measures of success vary depending on the stated goals and objectives each program set out to address.[3] For instance, goals of a treatment-oriented program differ from goals of a program that places emphasis on offender punishment and control. However, it is possible to isolate two overriding themes of recent ISPs that raise several issues. First, "intensive probation supervision is expected to divert offenders from incarceration in order to alleviate prison overcrowding,[4] avoid the exorbitant costs of building and sustaining prisons, and prevent the

Table 9.1 Intensive Supervision Probation/Parole

Author and year	Site	Sample	Control groups	Contacts	Recidivism
Jolin & Stipak (1992)	Oregon	N = 70 drug users	100 on EM 100 on work release. Stratified random sample matched on risk	5 counseling per week and 3 self-help per week, plus curfew and EM	47% ISP 32% EM 33% WR
Erwin (1987)	Georgia	N = 200 randomly selected from ISP	N = 200 probationers N = 97 prison releasees Matched samples	5 per week ISP	40% ISP 35.5% Probation 57.8% Prison
Georgiou (2014)	Washington State	51,867	*Very high risk = 7,902 High risk = 8,126 Moderate risk = 19,008 Low risk = 16,831*	Higher risk received significantly more supervision hours	No difference in recidivism rates for those who received more hours of supervision
Hyatt & Barnes (2017)	Pennsylvania	N = 447 ISP	N = 385 probation as usual	50 to 1 caseload 4 face-to-face contacts per month 2 UAs monthly Home visits	New offense: 40.5% rearrest rate ISP; 41.6% for comparison group (not statistically different) Revocation rates: 14.9% ISP; 8.3% Comparison
Pearson (1987)	New Jersey	N = 554 parolees	N = 510	20 per month	24.7% ISP 34.6% CG
Byrne & Kelly (1989)	Massachusetts	N = 227 high-risk probationers	N = 834 ISP Eligible offenders plus a 35% random sample of all offenders under supervision (N = 2,543)	10 per month ISP 2 per month probation	56.6% ISP 60.9% Probation

(*Continued*)

Table 9.1 (Continued)

Author and year	Site	Sample	Control groups	Contacts	Recidivism
Latessa (1993a)	Ohio	All offenders in specialized ISP Units Alcohol = 140 Drug = 121 Sex = 64 Mental = 76	N = 424 regular probationers randomly selected	6 per month alcohol and drug 4.5 per month sex and mental health 1 per month comparison	42% Alcohol 59% Drug 22% Sex 27% MH 46% Probation
Latessa (1992)	Ohio	N = 82 ISP randomly selected	N = 101 randomly selected from regular probation	7.5 per month ISP 2.2 per month probation	28% ISP 21% Probation
Latessa (1993b)	Ohio	N = 317 ISP N = 502 high-risk ISP	N = 424 randomly selected from regular probation	4 per month ISP 3 per month high risk 2 per month probation	35% ISP 43% High risk 34% Probation
Fallen et al. (1981)	Washington	N = 289 low-risk parolees	N = 102 matched parolees	4 per month	32.9% ISP 46.9% CG
Petersilia & Turner (1993)	Contra-Costra	N = 170	Randomly selected offenders placed in prison, probation, or parole	12 per month	29% ISP 27% CG
Petersilia & Turner (1993)	Los Angeles	N = 152	Randomly selected offenders placed in prison, probation, or parole	24 per month	32% ISP 30% CG
Petersilia & Turner (1993)	Seattle	N = 173	Randomly selected offenders placed in prison, probation, or parole	12 per month	46% ISP 36% CG
Petersilia & Turner (1993)	Ventura	N = 166	Randomly selected offenders placed in prison, probation, or parole	24 per month	32% ISP 53% CG

Study	Location	N	Description	Frequency	Results
Petersilia & Turner (1993)	Atlanta	N = 50	Randomly selected offenders placed in prison, probation, or parole	20 per month	12% ISP 4% CG
Petersilia & Turner (1993)	Macon	N = 50	Randomly selected offenders placed in prison, probation, or parole	20 per month	42% ISP 38% CG
Petersilia & Turner (1993)	Santa Fe	N = 58	Randomly selected offenders placed in prison, probation, or parole	20 per month	48% ISP 28% CG
Petersilia & Turner (1993)	Dallas	N = 221 parolees	Randomly selected offenders placed in prison, probation, or parole	16 per month	39% ISP 30% CG
Petersilia & Turner (1993)	Houston	N = 458 parolees	Randomly selected offenders placed in prison, probation, or parole	10 per month	44% ISP 40% CG
Latessa et al. (1998)	Iowa and Northeastern State	N = 401	Selected from urban probation department and rural probation and parole caseload	Varied	39% ISP 40% CG
Robertson et al. (2001)	Mississippi	N = 153	Juvenile offenders placed on intensive probation, monitoring on regular probation, or counseling with cognitive-behavioral (CB) therapy	12 months	Benefit–cost ratio of subjects receiving CB therapy was almost twice that of intensive supervision and monitoring

Note: EM = electronic monitoring; CG = control group; MH = mental health; UA = urinalysis; WR = work release.

Source: Compiled by authors.

stultifying and stigmatizing effects of imprisonment" (Byrne et al., 1989, p. 10). Second, ISPs are expected to promote public safety through surveillance strategies while promoting a sense of responsibility and accountability through probation fees, restitution, and community service activities (Byrne et al., 1989). These goals generate issues regarding the ability of ISP programs to reduce recidivism, divert offenders from prison, and ensure public safety.

In one study of ISPs, Lowenkamp and colleagues (2010) examined program philosophy and recidivism rates. They found that ISP programs that were "deterrence"- or control-oriented actually increased recidivism rates, whereas human service-oriented programs reduced recidivism. These results can be seen in Figure 9.1. The debate over control versus treatment has raged for many years. In recent years, there has been a revitalization of smarter punishment programs that look to punish more swiftly, use more certain consequences, and balance fairness.

SWIFT, CERTAIN, AND FAIR APPROACHES

In the mid-2000s, an intervention designed to embody swift, certain, and fair punishment, based on deterrence theory, was developed in Hawaii. Named Project HOPE (Hawaii's Opportunity with Probation Enforcement), Judge Steve Alm created the HOPE model to address low-level offending quickly so that offenders would learn that their behavior is not acceptable and therefore will refrain from future non-compliance. The HOPE model quickly spread to the Continental United States and even internationally (Alm, 2016; Bartels, 2016).

The core premise of the HOPE model is grounded in swift, certain, and fair strategies. The idea, again formed specifically from deterrence theory, is that when the offender engages in misconduct, the system emits a punishment as soon as the behavior is detected (swift), that the punishment is known to the offender prior to the behavior, and that the punishment must be balanced. In the original HOPE model, this meant that offenders who tested positive for drug use or missed a drug test were quickly taken into custody and served a short, but significant, jail sentence. Hawken and Kleiman (2009) found that offenders served through HOPE responded much better than those who received probation as usual within the first 12 months (26 percent lower recidivism rates and 8 percent lower revocation rates). In a follow-up study, Hawken et al. (2016) tracked offenders for up to 3 years and found that the effects had dissipated and that the HOPE participants did not reoffend at any significantly lower rate than probation as usual (42 percent to 47 percent).

Project HOPE was rolled out and implemented quickly across multiple states. The look and feel of HOPE were enticing to judges, correctional agencies, and even criminologists (Cullen et al., 2018). The idea that deterrence was finally solidified in a correctional program and that the delivery of a smarter punishment could change offender behavior was exciting. The HOPE model was relatively easy to implement and could be replicated quickly. The only problem was that as further evaluation was conducted, the HOPE model and the broader swift, certain, and

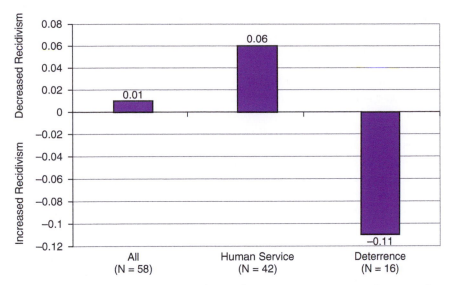

Figure 9.1 Average Change in Recidivism for Intensive Supervision Programs by Program Philosophy

Source: Lowenkamp, C., Flores, A., Holsinger, A., Makarios, M., Latessa, E. (2010). Intensive supervision programs: Does program philosophy and the principles of effective intervention matter? *Journal of Criminal Justice* 38, 368–375.

fair strategies did not produce the same effects. In a randomized controlled trial, Lattimore et al. (2018) replicated the HOPE model across four sites: 1,504 offenders were randomly assigned to HOPE or probation as usual. Agencies implemented HOPE with fidelity—ensuring that the evaluation was truly measuring the model. In the end, Lattimore and colleagues concluded that the HOPE model produced no better results across rearrests, revocations, or new convictions, and in fact, was significantly costlier in the long run.

DAY-REPORTING CENTERS

Unlike many other intermediate sanction alternatives, day reporting is of relatively recent vintage. While day reporting was used earlier in England, the first **day-reporting program** in the United States was opened in Massachusetts in 1986 (McDevitt, 1988). This inaugural program was designed as an early release from prison and jail placement for inmates approaching their parole or discharge date. Participants in the program were required to report to the center each day (hence the name, "day reporting"), prepare an itinerary for their next day's activities, and report by telephone to the center throughout the day (Larivee, 1990).

Parent (1990) reported that by the late 1980s, day-reporting programs were operational in six states, and many more states were considering the option. The characteristics of these programs and the clients they served varied considerably. As McDevitt and Miliano (1992) noted:

Box 9.3
Day-Reporting Centers

Certain persons on pretrial release, probation, or parole are required to appear at day-reporting centers on a frequent and regular basis in order to participate in services or activities provided by the center or other community agencies. Failure to report or participate is a violation that could cause revocation of conditional release or community supervision.

Reports indicate that offenders in these programs must not only physically report to their centers daily, but also provide a schedule of planned activities and participate in designated activities. In addition, offenders must call the center by phone throughout the day; they can also expect random phone checks by center staff both during the day and at home following curfew. In some programs, offenders must contact their respective centers an average of 60 times weekly and, in all but one, take random drug tests.

Source: Gowdy (1993).

Although all centers have similar program elements, such as frequent client contact, formalized scheduling, and drug testing, the operations of different DRCs (day-reporting centers) are quite varied. Therefore, it is difficult to define specifically what a day reporting center is; each center is unique.

(McDevitt & Miliano, 1992, p. 153)

In describing the development of day-reporting centers in Massachusetts, Larivee (1990) noted that these centers were created for the purpose of diverting offenders from confinement in local jails. Offenders live at home, but must report once each day to the center and are in telephone contact with the center four times each day. An evaluation of Massachusetts' day-reporting centers reported that more than two-thirds of day-reporting clients completed programs successfully and only 2 percent were returned to prison or jail for new crimes or escape (Curtin, 1990). An earlier evaluation of the Hampden County center (the first opened) reported more than 80 percent successful completion of the program and only 1 percent arrested for a new crime while in the program. Larivee (1990) concluded that the Massachusetts day-reporting centers provided an opportunity for individuals to remain out of jail or prison. The day-reporting center offers an alternative to incarceration that has demonstrated significantly lower recidivism rates.

Day-reporting programs offered a variety of services to program participants. Most centers offered job skills, drug abuse education, group and individual counseling, job placement, education, life-skills training, and drug treatment. While most services were provided in-house, it was common for drug treatment programs to be offered by providers not located at the day-reporting center. A trend noted in the survey was the tendency for newer, public programs to co-locate social service programs with the day-reporting program. The most common in-house programs

---

Box 9.4
Community Service

Community service requires that the offender complete some task that helps the community. It is considered a form of restitution, with labor rather than money being supplied. Common jobs include cleaning neighborhoods, working at nursing homes, painting schools, and doing assorted chores for the elderly. Community service can be a sentence in and of itself or can be included with other sanctions, such as probation.

(those offered at more than three-quarters of the centers) were job-seeking skills, group counseling, and life-skills training.

The costs of these services are usually paid by the day-reporting center. For some programs, other agencies pay the costs of services such as drug treatment, transitional housing, and education and job placement assistance. Seldom are offenders required to pay for services. The costs of operation ranged from about $10 per offender per day to more than $100 per offender per day, with the average daily cost per offender being slightly more than $35. Public centers were found to generally have lower daily operating costs, and costs increased with the stringency of surveillance/supervision requirements. Costs of day reporting were found to be more than intensive probation supervision, but less than residential treatment or incarceration.

Box 9.5
The Talbert House Day-Reporting Center

Talbert House, Inc., a private, non-profit organization, administers a day-reporting program in Cincinnati, Ohio. The program began in 1994. The objective of the program was to provide an alternative disposition for probationers facing revocation, which combines high levels of supervision and service delivery. The philosophy of the program emphasizes surveillance and compliance with probation supervision requirements. There are seven characteristics or components of the program:

1. Reporting 7 days each week.
2. Development and monitoring of daily itineraries.
3. Electronic monitoring.
4. Regular, random urinalysis.
5. Breath testing.
6. Close monitoring of income to ensure payments of court financial requirements.

7. Community service work through the Hamilton County Probation Department.

The program operates with a staff of three: two caseworkers and a manager. Day reporting is ordered as a condition of probation for all referrals. The program excludes those with a history of substance abuse, repeat violent crimes or assaultive behavior, sexual offenses against minors, a long-standing association with organized crime, or a conviction for arson. Additionally, clients are required to consent to treatment prior to acceptance to the program.

Cases referred to the center are given a risk/needs assessment. Offenders must report to the center 7 days each week, provide urine and breath tests as requested, and, if unemployed, must participate in employment-seeking activities. Offenders meet with center staff each afternoon to participate in program activities until 5 pm, when they leave to return home or go to other arranged treatment activities. Offenders stay in the program between 1 and 6 months, based on judicial stipulation. The program currently serves about ten offenders per day. The center provides in-house treatment, including individual and group counseling by appropriately licensed/registered staff. Other services include chemical dependency, case management, introduction to Alcoholics Anonymous and Narcotics Anonymous, life-skills education, HIV education, budgeting, and nutrition. Additional services available to offenders include education, parenting, financial management, community service, mental health services, and leisure. The goals of the programs are identified as follows:

1. Provide a community sanction option for probation violators.
2. Identify problems facing offenders that may lead to criminality.
3. Provide on-site or community referral to treat those problems.
4. Provide for public safety through intensive supervision, accountability, and retribution.

Unfortunately, there have not been many empirical studies of day-reporting centers in understanding the impact they have on future recidivism. Latessa and colleagues (1998) examined five pilot day-reporting programs in Ohio. Offenders from the day-reporting programs were compared with offenders supervised under regular probation, those on an intensive program, and those released from prison. Rates of rearrest for the day-reporting group were slightly higher than those reported for the other groups. The incarceration rates indicate that the day-reporting group performed slightly better than those offenders supervised under intensive supervision, worse than those on regular probation, and similar to those released from prison. It is noteworthy that the authors also found that the quality of the treatment provided by the five day-reporting centers in this study was judged to be poor.

While Latessa and colleagues (1998) found no effect, the results of more recent studies have been mixed. Craddock and Graham (2001) found that high-risk offenders who successfully completed the day-reporting center program were less likely to be rearrested. Another evaluation completed by Craddock (2004) found that participants in the day-reporting center were less likely to reoffend. Champion et al. (2011) also found overall benefits in reductions of recidivism for those that participated in a day-reporting center. Osterman (2009), studying the effects of reporting centers on parolees, found that the reporting centers had a positive effect on reductions of rearrests. In contrast, Boyle et al., (2013) found that day-reporting centers in New Jersey produced no positive long-term effects and that participants actually did worse initially.

Most recently, Hyatt and Ostermann (2017) evaluated community resource centers (CRC) in New Jersey. Using a quasi-experimental design, matching participants in the CRC with parolees using propensity scoring, Hyatt and Ostermann concluded that CRC participants reoffended at significantly higher rates, resulting in significantly more revocations than their matched counterparts. In the end, day-reporting centers do not appear to provide effective means to reduce reoffending. It may be that without them, more people would be revoked (as an intermediate intervention), but this has not been shown to be true in the extant research.

HOME CONFINEMENT, ELECTRONIC MONITORING, AND GPS TRACKING

Often used interchangeably, home confinement or detention, electronic monitoring, and GPS monitoring are all types of intermediate sanctions that are designed to improve surveillance of an offender in lieu of incarceration (Nellis, 2014). In fact, it is rare to have someone on home confinement who is not on some electronic or GPS monitoring; or vice versa, that there is someone on electronic monitoring or a GPS device who does not have restrictions as to where they are permitted to go (or not go).

In addition to being monitored, participants may be required to make victim compensation, perform community work service, pay probation fees, undergo alcohol or other drug testing, and, in some instances, wear electronic monitoring equipment to verify their presence in the residence. (In some jurisdictions, house arrest is used on a pretrial basis,[5] as an isolated sentence, in conjunction with probation or parole, or with a pre-release status such as education or work furlough.) House arrest only allows the offender to leave her or his residence for specific purposes and within hours approved by the court or supervising officer, and being absent without leave is a technical violation of conditions that may result in re-sentencing to jail or prison (General Accounting Office, 1990).

The National Council on Crime and Delinquency conducted an evaluation of the Florida Community Control Program (FCCP) and concluded that the impact on prison crowding, offender behavior, and state correctional costs has been positive. With an estimated prison diversion rate of 54 percent, community control is cost-effective, despite the combined effect of net widening and the punishments imposed on almost 10 percent of FCCP participants for technical violations. Furthermore, the new offense rate for community-control offenders is lower than for similar offenders sentenced to prison and released without supervision. For every 100 cases diverted from prison, Florida saved more than $250,000 (Wagner & Baird, 1993).

Home detention has a long history as a criminal penalty, but its new popularity with correctional authorities is due to the advent of **electronic monitoring,** and more recently, global positioning systems (GPS), a technological link thought to make the sanction both practical and affordable.

According to the Bureau of Justice Assistance (1989), the goals and objectives of electronic monitoring are to:

- Provide a cost-effective community supervision tool for offenders selected according to specific program criteria.
- Administer sanctions appropriate to the seriousness of the offense.
- Promote public safety by providing surveillance and risk control strategies indicated by the risk and needs of the offenders.
- Increase the confidence of legislative, judicial, and releasing authorities in ISP designs as a viable sentencing option.

(Bureau of Justice Assistance, 1989, p. 3)

In response to the continued interest in using tracking devices to monitor offender compliance, Bouchard and Wong (2018) conducted a meta-analysis to determine the effects of home confinement, electronic monitoring, and GPS devices on reducing recidivism. They found 11 studies (14 effect sizes) that examined the independent effects of electronic monitoring/home confinement. First, they found that the use of electronic monitoring for jail diversion resulted in significantly lower rearrest rates compared to those who remained in jail or prison and were eventually released. Second, those offenders who were released early from prison on electronic monitoring were no more likely to be re-incarcerated than those who were held in prison for their full sentence. Ultimately, home confinement, electronic monitoring, and GPS has shown some promise in being an effective intervention over incarceration.

Box 9.6
Global Positioning System Monitoring in Florida

The use of active **global positioning system (GPS)** technology was implemented in Florida in 1997 and utilizes global positioning satellites to track offenders' locations in "real time." Offenders monitored with active GPS are required to wear ankle bracelets that communicate with a larger device carried by offenders at all times, called a monitoring tracking device (MTD). The MTD communicates with a satellite and transmits a signal to a monitoring center through a cell phone. The MTD has an LCD screen to display messages to the offenders from supervising officers. Officers are able to track the exact location of offenders on a computer screen to determine if they have violated the conditions of supervision by entering prohibited areas. Currently, there are more than 14,300 offenders in Florida on electronic monitoring including those on probation, under community control, and post-prison. Of these, about 2,200 are on more advanced GPS.

Source: Bales et al. (2010).

SHOCK INCARCERATION PROGRAMS

Technically, **shock incarceration** programs, or **"boot camps,"** as they are commonly known, are institutional correctional programs, not community-based ones. However, they are considered intermediate sanctions and are a distant cousin to shock probation programs.[6] The first shock incarceration programs appeared in Georgia (1983) and Oklahoma (1984). The concept spread quickly, and by 2000, 54 boot camp programs had opened in 41 state correctional jurisdictions and handled more than 21,000 inmates that year (Camp & Camp, 2000), in addition to many programs developed and being considered in cities and counties, as well as programs for juveniles (Gover et al., 2000). Today, boot camps are almost non-existent.

The philosophy behind the prison boot camps was simple. Offenders who can be turned around before they commit a major crime can improve their own opportunities for living a successful life free of incarceration. Traditional prisons generally have not been viewed as successful in rehabilitating offenders. Boot camps focused on physical exercise, militaristic drills, and labor programs were the central themes of most boot camps. Favored in the late 1990s, they fell out of favor in the mid-2000s due to several well-documented studies which found that not only did boot camps not reduce crime, but in fact, people who were placed in boot camps often reoffended at higher rates than their counterparts.

Some programs have abandoned the military-style training and incorporated educational, wilderness, job corps, and industrial components (Gowdy, 1993). An outcome study conducted in Texas (Texas Department of Criminal Justice, 1999) compared the rearrest rates of four different types of community facilities for adult offenders: boot camps, treatment centers, intermediate sanction facilities (used for probation violators), and substance abuse treatment facilities. Results are presented in Figure 9.2.

The boot camp reported rearrest rates nearly double those of the other programs. It should also be noted that when risk and need scores from a standardized assessment tool were compared for offenders in all four programs, the only difference was in the need scores, with boot camp residents reporting *fewer* higher-need offenders than the other options. Finally, a meta-analysis conducted by researchers in Washington State (Aos et al., 1999) found that, on average, juvenile boot camps increased recidivism rates by about 11 percent.

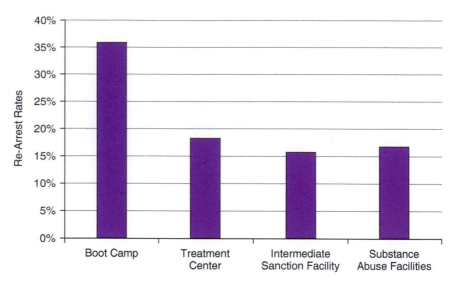

Figure 9.2 Rearrest Rates for Residents Discharged from Community Correctional Facilities in Texas: Two-Year Follow-Up (Percent)

Source: Texas Department of Criminal Justice (1999, January). Community corrections facilities outcome study.

REINFORCEMENT SYSTEMS

One aspect of graduated responses is the reinforcement of desired behavior. The idea of reinforcing wanted behavior is not new for community corrections, but it is still not universal. Some probation and parole officers feel that it is rewarding those individuals for engaging in crime, or that good behavior is just expected— we are often hearing from POs, "they don't deserve [to be] rewarded for stuff they are supposed to do." Reinforcement is bigger than just giving a reward or making someone feel good. It is actually a behavioral technique that is specifically designed to reinforce wanted behavior. As the behavior of an offender changes, it is important that the system—judge, officer, paroling authority— acknowledges the change in the offender to keep him or her moving forward. Often there are a lot of negative influences that impact an offender's behavior and the system should do what it can to reinforce the offender when change is occurring.

As stated earlier, stakeholders are beginning to understand the impact of reinforcements on behavior. There are two specific ways in which offenders can be reinforced: **positive reinforcement** and **negative reinforcement**. Positive reinforcement is the delivery of something pleasurable to the offender in response to a behavior. Examples of positive reinforcement are social praise (nice job), monetary praise (receive a gift card for having a negative drug test), and token rewards (e.g., points that can be spent in a store). A negative reinforcement is when something that is not desirable is removed. Examples of negative reinforcement would be if an inmate received a reduction in a sentence for good behavior or a probationer had 3 months removed from a probation term for completing substance abuse treatment.

There are many states that have incorporated reinforcement systems directly within the infrastructure of the criminal justice system. Texas is one of those states: HB 1205 provided probation departments with the ability to track completion of programs and submit this information to a judge to consider early release—and if the judge does not grant the early release, the defendant still gets the reduction on their probation term based on what they have completed. This would be considered a type of negative reinforcement—if the offender does well, the system will take away time on their sentence. The following credits were examples of some of those offered to offenders on probation in Texas through HB 1205:

- Obtain a high school diploma or GED: 90 days
- Obtain an associate's degree: 120 days
- Court costs paid: 15 days
- Fines paid: 30 days
- Restitution paid: 60 days
- Completion of substance abuse treatment: 90 days
- Completion of anger management: 30 days.

Another way in which offenders earn reinforcements is directly through the probation or parole agency. Agencies often offer positive reinforcement opportunities for offenders. These may take the form of earning travel passes, gift cards, bus passes, or certificates. A common practice for agencies is to create a response matrix that includes both reinforcement and punishment guidelines. These matrices guide officers' decisions, but allow for some discretion. See Figure 9.3 for an

---

Box 9.7
Reduction in Probation Sentence through Earned Time Credits

A probationer gets sentenced to 36 months on supervision and is ordered to complete substance abuse treatment, pay $500 in court costs and $1,000 fines. In addition, he was ordered to pay for the counseling of his victim at $100 an hour for 10 hours.

The offender is on supervision for 18 months at which time he has completed his substance abuse treatment (90 days), paid for counseling (60 days), and paid off his fees and fines (45 days). At this time, the probation officer would go to court and request early termination. If the judge agrees, the offender is considered an early termination. If the judge denies the early release, the offender has still earned 6 months and 15 days—so instead of serving 36 months, he will only have to complete 29 months, 15 days—in other words, he only has 11 months and 15 days to serve instead of 18 months.

	Behaviors			
Low	Compliance	Attendance	Report to UA	Payment
Moderate	Health/Prosocial	Employment	Progress in TX	Complete Tx LOC
		Progress towards TX Goals		
High	Specific Target Behaviors	Abstinence	Treatment Goals Completed	

	Potential Incentives			
Low	Verbal Praise	Raffle Ticket	</= $10 Gift Card	</= 1 Day Reduction of Curfew
	Bus Pass			
Moderate	Verbal Praise	Raffle Ticket	</= $20 Gift Card	Certificate
	Supervisor Praise	Written Praise	Positive Peer Board	Letter Home
	</= 3 Days Reduction of Curfew	Voucher for __ Hrs Community Service Hours (CSR)	Voucher for $__Probation Fee	Voucher for $__Court Fees/Fines
High	Verbal Praise	Raffle Ticket	</= $30 Gift Card	Certificate
	Supervisor Praise	Written Praise	Positive Peer Board	Voucher for $__Probation Fee
	Driving Privs	Letter Home	</= 5 Days Reduction of Curfew	Voucher for $__Court Fees/Fines
	Travel Pass	Reduction of Curfew	Raffle Ticket	Voucher for __ Hrs CSR

Figure 9.3 Reinforcement Schedule

Source: Harris County Community Supervision and Corrections Department.

example of Harris County's Community Supervision and Corrections response matrix. As noted, the observed behavior is rated as a low-, moderate-, or high-level behavior. Low-level behaviors are considered more compliance-based, while the moderate to higher levels of behaviors are more complex. With higher, complex behaviors, the "worth" of the reinforcement is increased—so an offender who achieves a high-level behavior could earn anything from a reduction in court costs/ fines up to permission to drive, a travel pass, or other freedoms. The next section will examine what happens if the offender does not do what is expected. Again, the same process happens—a behavior is observed, the officer would apply the response matrix and decide what to do next.

Response to Negative Behavior

Probation and parole officers have a significant amount of discretion as to what behavior they report to the judge or paroling authority. Many jurisdictions have created an administrative review process that is an internal review and response to some behavior in lieu of having the court or paroling authority respond. Even in these situations, there are some behaviors that are reported immediately to the governing authority (e.g., new law violation). Figure 9.4 provides an example of a response matrix that could be used by probation or parole agencies. Take note that the matrix is separated into three specific types of response: 1) Treatment, 2) Supervision, and 3) Judicial. The treatment response is often utilized when the behavior is linked to a criminogenic need of an offender. For example, an offender who has a serious drug problem tests positive for using drugs—one potential response could be to raise treatment from outpatient to inpatient treatment. The second, supervision response is one in which the officer would increase supervision requirements. This may include increased drug testing, addition of an external drug monitoring device or GPS, or increased contacts. The third,

Client being placed on SCRAM. *[Photo courtesy of Larry Vanderwood]*

judicial response could be jail time, additional community service, or even revocation. Using a response matrix ensures that there is consistency across staff and, ultimately, that the offender is treated justly. In those cases where revocation is on the table, a hearing must be held in order to find the offender guilty of the violations.

REVOCATION HEARING

While probation and parole are similar in many aspects, revocation hearings are often different depending on whether the offender is on probation or parole. For offenders on probation, a revocation hearing is a court process in which the probationer is facing the potential to have his or her probation revoked either due to a technical violation or a new law violation. While the revocation hearing is an administrative procedure (no jury), the offender still has a right to counsel and to present evidence on his or her own behalf that the violation did not occur or there were mitigating circumstances. Prior to the hearing, the probation officer compiles all of the information on the offender and reports any and all violations the offender has committed, based on the person's current conditions of supervision. The probation officer is often the person who will ultimately testify in the case—swearing to the authenticity of the record.

Once the officer compiles the information, it is sent to the district attorney's office in order to review and determine which conditions will be alleged at the hearing. Sometimes prosecutors will decide not to allege all violations, depending on the amount of evidence. Since it is an administrative hearing in most jurisdictions, the offender is not found guilty but the allegations are found to be true (a preponderance of guilt instead of the higher standard of "beyond a reasonable doubt"). At the hearing, the defendant has the ability to either plead true or not. If the offender pleads not true, the prosecutor presents the

Officer Review

Supervision	Sanctions	Treatment
Increase contacts	Admonishment	Assessment
Behavior chain	Supervisory admonishment	Referral to intervention
Increased UA frequency		

Administrative Review

Supervision	Sanctions	Treatment
Increase contacts	Admonishment	Referral to intervention
Behavior chain	Supervisory admonishment	Increase level of care
Increased UA frequency	Branch Director admonishment	
Behavior contract		

Court Reviews

Supervision	Sanctions
Jail	Community service
Move to residential	Judicial admonishment
Revocation	

Response Matrix

		Risk Level	
	Low	Moderate	High
Seriousness of Behavior			
Minor	Officer	Officer	Administrative
Major	Officer	Supervisor	Administrative
Serious	Administrative	Administrative	Administrative

Figure 9.4 Response to Negative Behavior Schedule

Source: Harris County Community Supervision and Corrections Department.

alleged violations to the judge. The defendant then will mount a defense and the judge will make a determination as to the final disposition. After the disposition is determined, the judge has a range of punishment anywhere from reinstating probation to revocation.

The process for parolees is different in that a hearing officer will hear the case instead of a judge or the parole board. The hearing officer operates in a very similar way to the judge in probation revocation hearings. The hearing officer will listen to the evidence—often presented by the parole officer. The defendant can offer a defense and has a right to counsel. Upon hearing the evidence, the hearing officer will collect the recommendations of the parole officer, generate all final notes, and supply the information along with a recommendation to the parole board. The parole board will then review the material and make a final determination as to the outcome of the hearing. In the same way as a judge, the parole board has the full range of punishment available to them.

SUMMARY

Intermediate sanctions and graduated responses have become a vital component of contemporary corrections. Front-end placements are necessary to reduce the prison population, but also provide judges (and juries) with an alternative to straight probation. Back-end responses are also an important component to address technical violations without resulting in a revocation to prison. In the end, a core function of probation and parole is to address behavior in ways that will help the offender change his or her behavior while limiting the number of offenders who end up in prison.

Review Questions

1. Describe the two purposes of intermediate sanctions.
2. What is one of the few intermediate sanctions that has been developed that has shown a positive effect?
3. Why would states and local jurisdictions build in "good time" policies that allow for offenders to reduce their sentence?
4. Describe the benefits of using a response matrix?
5. Should offenders be represented by legal counsel at probation and parole hearings?

Notes

1   Blumstein (1995) argues that the nation has not to date been able to meet the demand for additional prisons to build their way out of the crowding crisis. See also Garland (2001).
2   Byrne and Taxman (1994). See also Cullen et al. (1996).

3 Fulton et al. (1994). See also Cullen and Gendreau (2001).
4 For example, Whitehead et al. (1995) found that intensive probation in Tennessee resulted in both diversion and net widening. They argued that if diversion is the only objective of intensive probation, then the efforts might be misguided. See also Bonta et al. (2000).
5 A discussion of the issues can be found in Goldkamp (1993). See also Rosen (1993); and McCann and Weber (1993).
6 Shock probation originated in Ohio in 1965 and was designed to give first-time young adult offenders a "taste of the bars." Offenders were to be sentenced to prison and then, within 30 to 120 days, would be released on probation. It was assumed that the physical and psychological hardships of prison life would "shock" the offender straight.

Recommended Readings

Latessa, E.J., Listwan, S., Koetzle, D. (2015). *What works (and doesn't) in reducing recidivism*. New York: Routledge.

Marciniak, L. (2000). The addition of day reporting to intensive supervised probation. *Federal Probation* 64(2), 34–39.

Morris, N., Tonry, M. (1990). *Between prison and probation: Intermediate punishments in a rational sentencing system*. Oxford: Oxford University Press.

Sherman, L., Gottfredson, D., MacKenzie, D., Eck, J., Reuter, P., Bushway, S. (1998). *Preventing crime: What works, what doesn't, what's promising*. Research in Brief. Washington, DC: U.S. Department of Justice, National Institute of Justice.

References

Alm, S.S. (2016). HOPE probation: Fair sanctions, evidence-based principles, and therapeutic alliances. *Criminology & Public Policy* 15, 1195–1214.

Aos, S., Phipps, P., Barnoski, R., Lieb, R. (1999). *The comparative costs and benefits of programs to reduce crime: A review of the National Research findings with implications for Washington State*. Olympia, WA: Washington State Institute for Public Policy.

Bales, W., Mann, K., Bloomberg, T., McManus, B., Dhungana, K. (2010). Electronic monitoring in Florida. *The Journal of Electronic Monitoring* 22(2), 5–12.

Bartels, L. (2016). Looking at Hawaii's Opportunity with Probation Enforcement (HOPE) program through a therapeutic jurisprudence lens. *QUT Law Review* 16(3), 30–49.

Blumstein, A. (1995). Prisons. In: J. Wilson, J. Petersilia (Eds.), *Crime* (pp. 387–419). San Francisco, CA: Institute for Contemporary Studies.

Bonta, J., Wallace-Capretta, S., Rooney, J. (2000). A quasi-experimental evaluation of an intensive rehabilitation supervision program. *Criminal Justice and Behavior* 27, 312–329.

Bouchard, J., Wong, J. (2018) The new panopticon? Examining the effect of home confinement on criminal recidivism. *Victims & Offenders* 13(5), 589–608. doi: 10.1080/15564886.2017.1392387

Boyle, D.J., Ragusa-Salerno, L.M., Lanterman, J.L., Marcus, A.F. (2013). An evaluation of day reporting centers for parolees. *Criminology & Public Policy* 12, 119–143.

Bureau of Justice Assistance. (1989). *Electronic monitoring in intensive probation and parole programs.* Washington, DC: U.S. Department of Justice.

Burkhart, W. (1986). Intensive probation supervision: An agenda for research and evaluation. *Federal Probation* 50(2), 75–77.

Byrne, J., Kelly, L. (1989). *Restructuring probation as an intermediate sanction: An evaluation of the Massachusetts intensive probation supervision program.* Final Report to the National Institute of Justice. Washington, DC: U.S. Department of Justice.

Byrne, J., Lurigio, A., Baird, C. (1989). The effectiveness of the new intensive supervision programs. *Research in Corrections* 2, 64–75.

Byrne, J., Taxman, F. (1994). Crime control policy and community corrections practice. *Evaluation and Program Planning* 17, 227–233.

Camp, C., Camp, G. (2000). *The 2000 corrections yearbook: Adult corrections.* Middletown, CT: Criminal Justice Institute.

Champion, D.R., Harvey, P.J., Schanz, Y.Y. (2011). Day reporting center and recidivism: Comparing offender groups in a Western Pennsylvania County study. *Journal of Offender Rehabilitation* 50, 433–446.

Craddock, A. (2004). Estimating criminal justice system costs and cost-savings benefits of day reporting centers. *Journal of Offender Rehabilitation* 39(4), 69–98.

Craddock, A., Graham, L.A. (2001). Recidivism as a function of day reporting center participation. *Journal of Offender Rehabilitation* 34(1), 81–97.

Cullen, F., Gendreau, P. (2001). From nothing works to what works: Changing professional ideology in the 21st century. *Prison Journal* 81(3), 313–338.

Cullen, F., Pratt, T., Turanovic, J., Butler, L. (2018). When bad news arrives: Project HOPE in a post-factual world. *Journal of Contemporary Criminal Justice* 34(1), 13–34.

Cullen, F., Van Voorhis, P., Sundt, J. (1996). Prisons in crisis: The American experience. In: R. Matthews, P. Francis (Eds.), *Prisons 2000: An international perspective on the current state and future of imprisonment.* New York: Macmillan.

Curtin, E. (1990). Day reporting centers. In: A. Travisino (Ed.), *Intermediate punishment: Community-based sanctions* (pp. 72–73). Laurel, MD: American Correctional Association.

Erwin, B. (1987). *Final report: Evaluation of intensive probation supervision in Georgia.* Atlanta, GA: Georgia Department of Corrections.

Fallen, D., Apperson, C., Holt-Milligan, J., Roe, J. (1981). *Intensive parole supervision.* Olympia, WA: Department of Social and Health Services, Analysis and Information Service Division, Office of Research.

Fulton, B., Latessa, E., Stichman, A., Travis, L. (1997). The state of ISP: Research and policy implications. *Federal Probation* 61(4), 65–75.

Fulton, B., Stone, S., Gendreau, P. (1994). *Restructuring intensive supervision programs: Applying what works.* Lexington, KY: American Probation and Parole Association.

Garland, D. (2001). Special issue on mass imprisonment in the USA. *Punishment and Society* 3(1), 5–199.

General Accounting Office. (1990). *Intermediate sanctions*. Washington, DC: USGAO.

Georgiou, G. (2014). Does increased post-release supervision of criminal offenders reduce recidivism? Evidence from a statewide quasi-experiment. *International Review of Law and Economics* 37, 221–243.

Goldkamp, J. (1993). Judicial responsibility for pretrial release decisionmaking and the information role of pretrial services. *Federal Probation* 57(1), 28–34.

Gover, A., MacKenzie, D., Styve, G. (2000). Boot camps and traditional facilities for juveniles. *Journal of Criminal Justice* 28(1), 53–68.

Gowdy, V. (1993). *Intermediate sanctions*. Washington, DC: U.S. Department of Justice.

Harrie, D., Davidson, L., Baker, E. (2018, January 30). Utah leaders never disclosed an $860M estimate to build a new prison and now costs for the project are rising. *The Salt Lake Tribune*.

Hawken, A., Kleiman, M. (2009). *Managing drug involved probationers with swift and certain sanctions: Evaluating Hawaii's HOPE*. Washington, DC: U.S. Department of Justice, National Institute of Justice.

Hawken, A., Kulick, J., Smith, K., Mei, J., Zhang, Y., Jarman, S., . . . Vial, T. (2016). *HOPE II: A follow-up to Hawaii's HOPE evaluation* (Report # 2010-IJ-CX-0016). Washington, DC: U.S. Department of Justice, National Institute of Justice.

Hennigan, K., Kolnick, K., Tian, T., Maxson, C., Poplawski, J. (2010). *Five-year outcomes in a randomized trial of a community-based multiagency intensive supervision juvenile probation program*. Grant 2007-JF-FX-0066. U.S. Department of Justice, Office of Juvenile Justice and Delinquency Prevention.

Henrichson, C., Delaney, R. (2012). *The price of prisons: What incarceration costs taxpayers*. New York: Vera Institute of Justice.

Hyatt, J., Ostermann, M. (2017). Better to stay home: Evaluating the impact of day reporting centers on offending. *Crime & Delinquency*. doi: 10.1177/0011128717727739

Hyatt, J., Barnes, G. (2017). An experimental evaluation of the impact of intensive supervision on the recidivism of high-risk probationers. *Crime & Delinquency* 63(1), 3–38.

Jolin, A., Stipak, B. (1992). Drug treatment and electronically monitored home confinement: An evaluation of a community-based sentencing option. *Crime & Delinquency* 38, 158–170.

Jones, M. (1991). Intensive probation supervision in Georgia, Massachusetts, and New Jersey. *Criminal Justice Research Bulletin* 6(1), 1–9.

Larivee, J. (1990). Day reporting centers: Making their way from the U.K. to the U.S. *Corrections Today* (October), 86–89.

Latessa, E. (1986). Cost effectiveness of intensive supervision. *Federal Probation* 50(2), 70–74.

Latessa, E. (1992). *A preliminary evaluation of the Montgomery County Adult Probation Department's Intensive Supervision Program*. Cincinnati, OH: Department of Criminal Justice, University of Cincinnati.

Latessa, E. (1993a). *An evaluation of the Lucas County Adult Probation Department's IDU and high-risk groups.* Cincinnati, OH: Department of Criminal Justice, University of Cincinnati.

Latessa, E. (1993b). *Profile of the special units of the Lucas County Adult Probation Department.* Cincinnati, OH: Department of Criminal Justice, University of Cincinnati.

Latessa, E., Travis, L., Fulton, B., Stichman, A. (1998). *Evaluating the prototypical ISP: Results from Iowa and Connecticut.* Cincinnati, OH: Division of Criminal Justice, University of Cincinnati.

Lattimore, P., Dawes, D., MacKenzie, D., Zajac, G. (2018). *Evaluation of the Honest Opportunity Probation with Enforcement Demonstration Filed Experiment (HOPE DFE), final report.* RTI International. Retrieved from www.ncjrs.gov/pdffiles1/nij/grants/251758.pdf

Lowenkamp, C., Flores, A., Holsinger, A., Makarios, M., Latessa, E. (2010). Intensive supervision programs: Does program philosophy and the principles of effective intervention matter? *Journal of Criminal Justice* 38, 368–375.

McCann, E., Weber, D. (1993). Pretrial services: A prosecutor's view. *Federal Probation* 57(1), 18–22.

McCarthy, B. (1987). Intermediate punishment. In: B. McCarthy (Ed.), *Intermediate punishments: Intensive supervision, home confinement, and electronic surveillance* (pp. 181–187). Monsey, NY: Willow Tree Press.

McDevitt, J. (1988). *Evaluation of the Hampton County Day Reporting Center.* Boston, MA: Crime and Justice Foundation.

McDevitt, J., Miliano, R. (1992). Day reporting centers: An innovative concept in intermediate sanctions. In: J. Byrne (Ed.), *Smart sentencing* (pp. 153–165). Newbury Park, CA: Sage.

Nellis, M. (2014). Understanding the electronic monitoring of offenders in Europe: Expansion, regulation and prospects. *Crime, Law and Social Change* 62, 489–510. doi: 10.1007/s10611-014-9540-8

Ostermann, M. (2009). An analysis of New Jersey's day reporting center and halfway back programs: Embracing the rehabilitative ideal through evidence based practices. *Journal of Offender Rehabilitation* 48, 139–153.

Parent, D. (1990). *Day reporting centers for criminal offenders: A descriptive analysis of existing programs.* Washington, DC: National Institute of Justice.

Pearson, F. (1987). *Research on New Jersey's intensive supervision program.* New Brunswick, NJ: Administrative Office of the Courts.

Petersilia, J., Turner, A.S. (1993). *Evaluating intensive supervised probation/parole results of a nationwide experiment.* Washington, DC: U.S. Department of Justice.

Robertson, A.A., Grimes, P.W., Rogers, K.E. (2001). A short-run cost–benefit analysis of community-based interventions for juvenile offenders. *Crime & Delinquency* 47(2), 265–284.

Rosen, J. (1993). Pretrial services: A magistrate judge's perspective. *Federal Probation* 57(1), 15–17.

Scharbach, S., Bohn, L. (2017, February 1). Final jail per diem billing rates for FY 2017–18. Phoenix, AZ: Office of Assistant County Manager and Department of Finance. Retrieved from www.maricopa.gov/DocumentCenter/View/33649/Current-Jail-Per-Diem.

U.S. Department of Justice. (1990). *Survey of intermediate sanctions.* Washington, DC: U.S. Government Printing Office.

Wagner, D., Baird, C. (1993). *Evaluation of the Florida Community Control Program.* Washington, DC: U.S. Department of Justice.

Whitehead, J., Miller, L., Myers, L. (1995). The diversionary effectiveness of intensive supervision and community corrections programs. In: J. Smykla, W. Selke (Eds.), *Intermediate sanctions: Sentencing in the 1990s* (pp. 135–151). Cincinnati, OH: Anderson Publishing.

Chapter 10

COMMUNITY RESIDENTIAL CORRECTIONAL PROGRAMS

Key Terms

community-based correctional
   facilities
community residential centers
day-reporting centers
dual-diagnosed offenders
halfway house

humaneness
reintegration
residential community corrections
   programs
restitution centers
work release and furlough centers

> [Community residential centers] play a vital role in the criminal justice
> system. They provide additional sentencing options for the court, protect
> public safety, provide individualized and intensive service aimed at
> reducing recidivism, and are cost-effective. —Bobbie L. Huskey

Community residential programs for criminal offenders have a long history in the
United States (Hartmann et al., 1994; Latessa & Travis, 1992). Until recently, the
typical residential community correctional facility was known as a "halfway house,"
a transitional residence for criminal offenders (Wilson, 1985). While traditional
halfway houses still exist, today, community residential facilities have evolved to
include a wide range of programming and functions.

Box 10.1
Halfway House

A **halfway house** is a community-based residential facility for offenders
who are either about to be released from an institution or, immediately
after release, are in the initial stages of return to society. In the past three
decades, some halfway houses have been designed as alternatives to jail or
prison incarceration, primarily for probationers. "Halfway" could now mean
halfway into, or out of, prison.

This chapter discusses such programs within the larger context of corrections in the community, explaining the historical factors that contributed to the emergence of the halfway house movement; models of halfway houses; and their current operations and practices, effectiveness, costs, and futures. We will also discuss other forms of community residential programs and their role in the community correctional system. We begin with an explanation of the development of the halfway house over time.

HISTORICAL DEVELOPMENT OF THE HALFWAY HOUSE IN AMERICA

The halfway house concept first began in England and Ireland during the early 1800s, advocating transitional residences for criminal offenders. It spread quickly to the United States in 1817 when the Massachusetts Prison Commission recommended establishing a temporary residence to house destitute offenders after release from prison (Cohn, 1973.):

> The convicts who are discharged are often entirely destitute. The natural prejudice against them is so strong that they find great difficulty in obtaining employment. They are forced to seek shelter in the lowest receptacles; and if they wish to lead a new course of life, are easily persuaded out of it; and perhaps driven by necessity to the commission of fresh crimes. It is intended to afford a temporary shelter in this building, if they choose to accept it, to such discharged convicts as may have conducted themselves well in prison, subject to such regulations as the directors may see fit to provide. They will here have a lodging, rations from the prison at a cheap rate, and . . . a chance to occupy themselves in their trade, until some opportunity offers of placing themselves where they can gain an honest livelihood in society. A refuge of this kind, to this destitute class, would be found, perhaps, humane and political.
>
> (Cohn, 1973, p. 2)

The commission making this recommendation believed that ex-inmates needed an accepting transitional house immediately after release and a supportive environment to assist in the process of establishing a law-abiding and independent existence. It was also motivated by the intention to reduce the unacceptably high rate of recidivism among newly released inmates (Seiter & Carlson, 1977). Unfortunately, the Massachusetts legislature feared that ex-prisoners might "contaminate" each other if housed together, neutralizing their newly instilled crime resistance learned in prison.

The concept, however, found fertile ground in other locations and under private sponsorship. In 1845, the Isaac T. Hopper Home in New York City opened under the auspices of the Quakers and today operates as the Women's Prison Association and Hopper Home, serving female clients. Perhaps the most significant halfway house program in this earlier era was Hope Hall, established by Maud Booth and Ballington

Booth in 1896, in New York City. Supported both financially and morally by the Volunteers of America, other Hope Halls opened across the nation (Chicago, San Francisco, New Orleans, etc.). This earlier movement, and Hope Halls in particular, did not last. Parole was introduced and implemented widely in the early 1900s as a means for controlling and helping ex-inmates after release from prison. The belief in likely and malevolent contamination from association with other parolees continued. The Great Depression of the 1930s weakened financial support for these privately-operated homes, already underfunded. Phase I of the development of the halfway house ended shortly thereafter, not to revive until the 1950s.

The rebirth of the halfway house movement resulted, in part, from a growing awareness of the ineffectiveness of institutional corrections. High recidivism rates were interpreted as indications of the ineffectiveness of prison as a venue for rehabilitation. The growing dissatisfaction with prisons was buttressed by new evidence that parolees face problems in the transition from imprisonment to a free society, evidence of the need for supportive services in the transition to community life. In 1954, numerous halfway houses opened in America (such as Crenshaw House in Los Angeles and Dismas House in St. Louis, under the direction of Father Charles Dismas), England, and Canada. Private and religious groups pioneered both the historical and revival phases of development of the halfway house.

Earlier in the revival phase, most houses offered individualized treatment, counseling, employment referrals, and substance abuse counseling, reflecting the general correctional philosophy found within the prison: the medical model. Persons not yet committed to predatory criminal lifestyles, younger, and more malleable offenders were believed to be ideal clients for the medical model. Then Attorney General Robert Kennedy suggested in 1961 that federal funds be used to establish publicly-operated halfway houses for juvenile and youthful offenders, leading to the establishment of the Prisoner Rehabilitation Act of 1965. This legislation authorized the Bureau of Prisons (BOP) to establish community-based residences for adult and youthful pre-release offenders, as well as to transfer federal prisoners to privately-sponsored halfway houses. In 1968, the Law Enforcement Assistance Administration began to provide substantial funds for establishing non-federal houses, a thrust that continued until 1980.

Perhaps the most significant event in Phase II was the development of the International Halfway House Association (IHHA) in 1964.[1] This group, motivated by the absence of state and local support for halfway houses, established a voluntary professional organization of halfway house administrators and personnel (Wilson, 1985). The IHHA (now known as the International Community Corrections Association) conducted numerous training workshops, sponsored training programs and conferences, and affiliated with the American Correctional Association.[2] The organization grew from 40 programs in 1966 to more than 1,800 in 1989[3] and now holds annual conferences

Harris County YMAC. *[Photo courtesy of Jeff McShan]*

Box 10.2
Federal Prisoner Rehabilitation Act

The attorney general may extend the limits of the place of confinement of a prisoner as to whom there is reasonable cause to believe he will honor this trust, by authorizing him, under prescribed conditions, to:

1. Visit a specifically designated place for a period not to exceed 30 days and return to the same or another institution or facility. An extension of limits may be granted only to permit a visit to a dying relative, attendance at the funeral of a relative, the obtaining of medical services not otherwise available, the contacting of prospective employees, or for any other compelling reason consistent with the public interest; or
2. Work at paid employment or participate in a training program in the community on a voluntary basis while continuing as a prisoner of the institution or facility to which he is committed.

that deal with "what works" in correctional intervention. As a result of these and related efforts, few cities and counties run their own residential treatment centers, and state programs that operate halfway houses usually contract with private-sector, non-profit halfway houses to provide services. One other way in which halfway houses have changed is in terms of size. While smaller "Mom and Pop" halfway houses still exist, they are a dying breed. Today, many adult halfway houses and community residential facilities are large, some housing several hundred residents. This is hardly the image of the "home-like" environment of the past.

Box 10.3
Types of Community Centers

Day-Reporting Centers (DRC)
Although not "residential" in the true sense, in these community centers, adults and sometimes juvenile offenders are expected to report frequently in lieu of incarceration or as a condition of probation. A variety of community or in-house programs may also be offered, including individual and group counseling, job readiness training, educational services, substance abuse groups, and so on. Participants usually return to their individual homes at night. There is not much research on the effectiveness of day-reporting centers (discussed in Chapter 9), and the findings are mixed. In one study of DRCs in New Jersey, the results were promising (Ostermann, 2009); however, in other studies (Boyle et al, 2013; Hyatt & Ostermann (2017) participants in day-reporting centers had higher failure rates than comparison groups.

Restitution Centers

These community residential centers are for offenders ordered by the court to make financial payments to victims. Offenders may also be remanded as a condition of probation. The offender must seek and obtain employment, make restitution to victims, reimburse the center for room and board, and set aside any residual earnings for use after release. Center programs usually require curfews, strict alcohol and drug abstinence, and participation in community or in-house programs.

Work Release and Furlough Centers

This type of residential facility is for sentenced offenders released from a correctional institution for work during the day. Residents typically spend nights and weekends in the facility and must participate in available community or in-house programs. Participants are generally charged a per diem fee for services, room, and board.

USES OF HALFWAY HOUSES

Over the past 50 years, as suggested earlier, the numbers, roles, and uses of halfway houses have increased considerably. There has been considerable role expansion in residential placements of adult (and juvenile) offenders. For the most part, the increase has been in the services provided to new groups: probationers, the accused awaiting trial, and offenders directly sentenced for treatment, ordered by a judiciary eager to secure services and supervision for offenders. Some judges are usually reluctant to incarcerate clients likely to give up criminal behavior if a supportive and facilitating community environment can be provided in which the offenders remediate their needs and improve their functioning. These changes in roles, sentencing alternatives, clients, and use of halfway houses have rendered "halfway house" an obsolete term, one that has been replaced by the more accurate "community corrections residential facility." Rush (1992) defines such facilities as:

A halfway house. *[Photo courtesy of Connecticut Halfway Houses, Inc.]*

A correctional facility from which residents are regularly permitted to depart, unaccompanied by any official, for the purposes of using community resources, such as school or treatment programs, and seeking or holding employment. This definition not only deletes the term "halfway" but also defines a correctional mission for the facility. The definition does not require centers to provide direct services to clients. Halfway houses are thus subsumed under the larger umbrella term, further reflecting the more diverse populations served, as well as broader correctional mission and such newer programs as day, restitution, and work-release centers.

(Rush, 1992, p. 68)

Another major factor influencing the development and use of community residential centers in the United States was the shift in the ideology of corrections, from the medical model to "reintegration," a term introduced by the President's Commission on Law Enforcement and Administration of Justice in 1967.

This correctional philosophy places a priority on helping those who have been incarcerated adjust to the community and on keeping offenders in the community whenever possible rather than committing them to prison. It also stresses the role of the community in corrections. Thus, the new ideology, new developments stressing community placement in local correctional programs, and existing halfway houses contributed to an accelerating expansion of community correctional residential programs. This thrust was further expanded by three factors:[4] (1) widespread correctional acceptance of the reintegration mission; (2) success of the reintegration movement in the mental health field; and (3) the lower costs of halfway houses as compared to prisons.[5] Prison overcrowding in the 1980s and early 1990s, as a result of the war on drugs, further accelerated the shift (Allen et al., 2019).

From 1980 until just recently, the number of prison inmates has increased dramatically, with well over 2 million prisoners held in federal or state prisons and local jails (Kaeble & Cowhig, 2018), creating a lack of prison capacity and need for better re-entry services. The primary reason for the burgeoning prison and jail population was believed to be the "war on drugs," and "get tough" sentences. Three major results of this development have been: (1) larger numbers of offenders placed on probation and parole; (2) a greater number of higher-risk offenders being served in the community; and (3) a heightened demand for community residential treatment facilities to provide transitional placement for offenders and to respond to such special-needs populations as narcotics and drug abusers, offenders driving under the influence of alcohol or other drugs, and mental health clients. Thus, community residential facilities and programs expanded and changed to address these new demands,[6] required programs, and heightened supervision levels (Huskey, 1992).

Box 10.4
Reintegration

Reintegration is a broad correctional ideology stressing acquisition of legitimate skills and opportunities by criminal offenders, and the creation of supervised opportunities for testing, using, and refining those skills, particularly in community settings.

Box 10.5
Community Residential Centers

Community residential centers (CRCs) are often non-confining residential facilities serving adjudicated adults or juveniles or those subject to criminal or juvenile proceedings. They are intended as an alternative for persons not suited to probation or who need a period of readjustment to the community after imprisonment.

There are more CRCs providing transitional and extensive services for juveniles than for adults. Some CRCs specialize by client or treatment modality: for example, women, abused women, pre-release federal furloughees, substance abusers, the mentally ill, those identified by the court diagnostic program, or the developmentally disabled.

Before addressing programs for these clients, it is necessary to understand the models on which the programs operate. The exact number of halfway houses is unknown, and no government agencies routinely gather information on them, although it is believed that well over 40,000 adults a year are served in residential programs.

MODELS OF COMMUNITY RESIDENTIAL PROGRAMS

It should be remembered that Phase II of the development of community residential programs has been under way for more than 30 years. Thus, models under which halfway houses and related community programs operate have also undergone significant change. We start by examining an earlier model in a less complex environment.

In 1976, Allen and colleagues studied halfway houses and probation. These researchers developed three alternative models of halfway houses, based on referral

---

Box 10.6
Model

A model is a picture or representation showing the parts of a system. Models suggest the ways that segments of the criminal justice system (courts, probation, prisons, etc.) fit together and interrelate. One implication of a model is that change in one part of the system will have an impact on other parts of the system. A simplified demonstration of this is seen when law enforcement agencies increase arrests; judicial personnel, probation officers, and jail facilities face increased workloads.

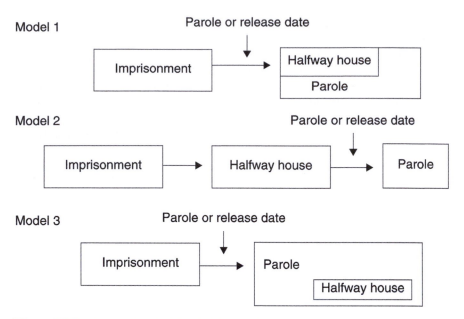

Figure 10.1 Alternative Models of Halfway Houses

Source: Latessa, E., Allen, H. (1982). Halfway houses and parole: A national assessment. *Journal of Criminal Justice* 10, 153–163.

service. This trichotomy is useful in depicting how halfway houses interface with the criminal justice system, as well as the advantages and services these programs offer to their clients. The trichotomy can be found in Figure 10.1 (Latessa & Allen, 1982).

Model 1 is the standard and most frequent pattern of referral to halfway house programs. In this model, an inmate granted a conditional release (such as parole, shock probation, or shock parole) enters a halfway house during the initial parole period. This model provides services to parolees who need support during their period of release. The length of residency in the halfway house may be specified before referral, but is usually a shared decision to be made collaboratively by the supervision officer, house staff, and client. Typically, this decision is based on such factors as the resident's readiness to leave the house, employment, savings, and alternative residential plan. After leaving the house, the offender generally continues on parole supervision.

Model 2 is similar to the first in that inmates' release plans call for placement in a halfway house as the initial phase of their release process. Unlike the first model, however, halfway house residency occurs prior to formal granting of parole and subsequent supervision as a parolee. Typically, these inmates have been scheduled for a definite release date before moving from the prison to the halfway house. These clients remain inmates, serving the remainder of their sentences in residency at a halfway house. Halfway house residency provides needed and significant services in the prison–community transition. Additional benefits include continuation of jurisdiction by the referring correctional agency, ability to return the inmate to incarceration without formal violation of parole, development of a more positive attitude toward the halfway house by the resident, and a less expensive aftercare service, that can be more legitimately compared to imprisonment, rather than the costs of parole.[7] The U.S. Bureau of Prisons was a leader in initiating this model for using halfway houses[8] and continues to use this model on a pre-release basis.[9]

The third model of halfway house use, also based on the reintegration model of corrections, differs by time of placement into the program. With Model 3, offenders on probation and inmates granted parole are assigned to the community without initially residing in a halfway house. If such clients revert to criminal behavior or encounter unanticipated problems that might be resolved by the program services of, or a period of residency in, a halfway house, the supervising agency may remand the offender to the residential setting for a short period. If and when conditions warrant, the client could then be returned to a lower level of supervision. It should be noted here that some residential correctional programs are large and can provide services and programs at many points in the supervision process, as explored later. Model 3 appears to best suggest the organization and practices of multiservice agencies in larger urban settings.

In addition to the models described earlier, halfway houses take on a wide range of functions and services depending on their size, mission, and resources. Figure 10.2 illustrates a continuum of types of programs based on the services they provide. Some halfway houses provide shelter, food, and minimal counseling and referral services. These programs are considered supportive halfway houses. Examples of these types of programs include shelters and drop-in centers. Halfway houses that offer a full range of services can be considered interventive programs. These are programs that offer a full range of treatment services. Most programs fall somewhere in the middle.

It should be obvious that the roles of halfway houses as residential probation and aftercare centers within the correctional process are varied in both operation and focus. Although all three models acknowledge the need for a residential setting at some point in the transition back to the community, there are various approaches and strategies for meeting these needs. To understand the range of alternatives, we examine a rural community residential treatment center, as well as a larger urban counterpart.

Box 10.7
Bureau of Prisons and Halfway Houses

The goal of BOP'S halfway house program is to provide federal prison inmates with a transition back to the communities where they will live upon release from federal custody. In addition to subsistence and housing, BOP guidelines state that halfway house operators are required to offer inmates job counseling, academic and vocational training, family reconciliation services, access to substance abuse programs, post-release housing referrals, and community adjustment services.

Source: U.S. Government Accountability Office (2001).

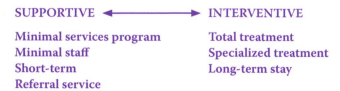

SUPPORTIVE ◄————————► INTERVENTIVE

Minimal services program	**Total treatment**
Minimal staff	**Specialized treatment**
Short-term	**Long-term stay**
Referral service	

Figure 10.2 Types of Halfway Houses Based on Services

RURAL COMMUNITY PROGRAMS

Rural correctional programs serve a wide range of offenders and are themselves diverse. Whereas the "Mom and Pop" stereotype possibly typical of the earliest developments of rural community corrections has surely died,[10] what has emerged is an increasingly diversified pattern of local programs that solidly reflect the concept of **"residential community corrections programs."**[11]

Community residential correctional programs in rural settings face differing challenges. They are generally smaller than urban programs and have fewer employment opportunities and treatment programs for offenders. Residents are drawn from a small pool of eligible offenders. These programs face and must overcome community suspicion that the center may attract recalcitrant offenders who will move their base of criminal activities to the local area—the "importation"

Box 10.8
Rural Community Corrections

Community corrections in its rural expression is the remnant of the grass-roots folk art of the original concept. Rural programs are generally not larger than 40 beds (a *large* rural program) and are concerned about the importation of offenders regularly into their community, the meeting of the next payroll, the expense of travel to training as opposed to the cost of training itself. The rural program is generally not faced with the challenge of adequately accessing and implementing brokerages to existing treatment in their community; we are worried about how to create, fund, and perpetuate treatment. Our "community" may be a town of 12,000 serving a catchment area of several hundred miles. Our worries are not typically of gang behavior between "Crips and Bloods." They may, however, include the American Indian in any of its numerous tribal groups, the rural Hispanic or black, all in the delicately interwoven and overwoven social fabric of the lineages of a rural community. Every individual job truly means the future of our programs. The failure of one client can affect the future political support of our program; a single incident cannot only destroy a program but also the potential efforts of any program to replace it.

Source: (Berry, 1990, pp. 6–7)

reaction. Decreased societal tolerance for certain offender types (such as rapists, child molesters, and drug pushers), coupled with concerns over public safety and demands for increased supervision, has great potential to restrict treatment, job and educational placement, access to existing treatment programs, and funding from community sources. Many facilities must work hard to interface with referral sources (probation and parole agencies, for example) and develop liaisons with other services offered by mental health, illegal drug, alcohol, family counseling, and court agencies.

These opportunities and challenges face Hilltop House,[12] a 28-bed private, non-profit agency providing residential services to male offenders and outpatient services to delinquents and victims referred from local, state, and federal sources. In its earliest days, this small program would close in the winter and reopen in the spring, housing not more than 12 clients referred from one judicial district. It now serves a much wider catchment area, working with six district court judges.

Hilltop House began to grow in this environment, even though it encountered the conservative political swing that demanded longer sentences, less diversion, and specialized programs to assist the higher-need clients the justice system was processing. This demand was met by:

- Developing liaisons with other court referral units and probation officers.
- Working with non-incarcerated populations (such as misdemeanant offenders, persons driving under the influence, self-referred persons with alcohol and other drug abuse problems, youths referred by their parents, and so on).
- Developing new service programs in the areas of incest treatment and domestic violence, and urinalysis collection and testing for a county youth home, private schools, social services, employers, individuals, and parents.
- Developing a sexual abuse treatment team, using workers from a number of agencies and providing a service to offenders, their non-offending spouses, victims, and adults who had been molested as children (AMACs). This multi-agency approach was expanded to include juvenile restitution, a program using many volunteers as mediators and providing subsidized employment and monitored restitution payments, as well as group therapy to reconcile victims and their offenders, and develop empathy among juvenile offenders.

Hilltop House appears to serve the specific needs of the community, to develop resources to plan and initiate specialized services, and to maximize therapeutic gains for clients, victims, and citizens. Individuals who resolve conflicts, personal problems, challenges, development problems, and the impacts of being victimized are more likely to become constructive citizens and lower the crime rate in their community.

METROPOLITAN RESIDENTIAL PROGRAMS

Residential community correctional programs for offenders located in urban areas are more numerous and diverse than those in rural areas. In addition, many of the largest programs make extensive use of existing community services, especially if these are needed adjuncts to a treatment plan for an individual client. Treatment generally falls into two categories—individual and group—and most halfway houses conduct detailed intake assessments to determine the needs of their clients. Figure 10.3 shows an example of a halfway house intake form.

Although halfway houses usually offer a range of programs and services, the most common include employment, substance abuse programs, and cognitive restructuring. Employment programming usually includes job readiness training, resumé writing and interviewing skills, job placement, and transportation assistance.

Programs for drug abusers might include methadone maintenance, weekly and unscheduled urinalysis, 12-step programming, cognitive-behavioral treatment groups, Alcoholics Anonymous and Narcotics Anonymous, and detoxification. It should be noted that, on average, more than 50 percent of all male arrestees tested positive for at least one drug (ADAM II, 2014), and while the use of crack and powder cocaine has declined in most cities, the use of opiates has increased dramatically. As the opiate epidemic has spread across the country, so has the need for residential treatment beds.

In recent years, there has been an increased focus on the effectiveness of cognitive-behavioral programs. These interventions involve targeting the antisocial attitudes, values, and beliefs that many offenders hold. Cognitive programming attempts to restructure the thinking of offenders and develop new skills that can be used to improve their problem-solving abilities. The goal with a cognitive-behavioral program is to use a very structured approach and to emphasize the importance of modeling and behavioral rehearsal techniques that engender

---

Box 10.9
Alcoholics and Treatment

Many community corrections center programs focus on Alcoholics Anonymous as part of the overall abstinence program. This may mean requiring residents to work the 12 steps of AA, demonstrate understanding of the program, design a post-release plan, chair an AA meeting, and participate in the affairs of the program. The latter might include house chores (vacuuming, cleaning restrooms, shoveling snow, cleaning ashtrays, etc.), attending house meetings, remaining sober and clean, working outside the program, and seeking specialized treatment. If the resident's family unit is not broken, reconciliation counseling may be required. If appropriate, the resident might be required to participate in meetings of Adult Children of Alcoholics (ACAS) or child sexual abuse and domestic violence programs.

GENERAL INFORMATION

1. ⬚⬚⬚⬚⬚⬚⬚⬚⬚⬚⬚ ⬚ ⬚⬚⬚⬚⬚⬚⬚⬚⬚⬚⬚

        (First)   (Middle)   (Last)   Client Name

2. ⬚⬚⬚⬚⬚⬚ Client T.H. ID #

3. ⬚⬚⬚-⬚⬚-⬚⬚⬚⬚ Client SS #

4. ⬚ Admission Status:
    (1) New Admission
    (2) Re-Admission (within fiscal year)
    (3) Re-Admittance after Escape/Absconding
       (within fiscal year)
    (4) Legal Status Altered

5. ⬚⬚ / ⬚⬚ / ⬚⬚ Date of Birth (mo/day/yr)

6. ⬚ Sex (1) Male   (2) Female

7. ⬚ Race
    (AI) American Indian   (OR) Oriental
    (BL) Black   (WH) White
    (HI) Hispanic   (Specify) Other _____

7a. ⬚ Appalachian   (1) Yes   (2) No

8. ⬚ Current Marital Status
    (1) Single   (4) Married
    (2) Divorced   (5) Separated
    (3) Widowed   (6) Common Law

9. ⬚⬚ Number of Dependents (financial responsibility other than self)

10. ⬚⬚ Number of Children

11. ⬚ Legal Responsibility for Children?   (1) Yes (2) No

12. ⬚⬚⬚⬚⬚ Zip Code of Last Community Address

13. ⬚ Homeless Before Arrest?   (1) Yes (2) No

14. ⬚ Place to Live When Discharged?   (1) Yes (2) No

15. ⬚ Primary Source of Income (at present)
    (1) Public Assistance   (5) Family
    (2) Investments   (6) No Income
    (3) Full-Time Employment   (7) Other _____
    (4) Part-Time Employment

15a. ⬚⬚⬚⬚⬚ Total Income Last Year (Nearest Dollar)

16. ⬚⬚⬚⬚⬚ Court Costs Owed (Nearest Dollar)

17. ⬚⬚⬚⬚⬚ Restitution Owed (Nearest Dollar)

CRIMINAL HISTORY

Note: When answering questions 19-30, if the information is not available from the referral source, use client-reported answers.

18. ⬚⬚⬚⬚.⬚⬚⬚ Ohio Revised Code for which convicted.

19. ⬚⬚ Number of prior felony convictions (adult/juvenile).

20. ⬚⬚ Number of prior adult felony commitments in a state or federal institution (when sentenced).

21. ⬚⬚ Age at admission to institution (or probation) for current offense.

22. ⬚⬚ Number of offenses (including current offense) committed while under parole/probation supervision.

23. ⬚⬚ Number of offenses (including current offense) involving drugs/alcohol.

24. ⬚⬚ Number of prior arrests during the past five years, prior to incarceration.

25. ⬚⬚ Number of offenses (including current offense) for auto theft.

26. ⬚⬚ Number of offenses (including current offense) involving serious injury to the victim.

27. ⬚⬚ Number of offenses (including current offense) involving the use of a weapon.

28. ⬚⬚ Has this individual been previously convicted for the same offense? (1) Yes   (2) No

29. ⬚⬚ Was the current conviction for multiple crimes? (1) Yes   (2) No

30. ⬚⬚ Was the offender employed at the time of arrest? (1) Yes   (2) No

Figure 10.3 Halfway House Intake Form (form A-2)

Source: Provided courtesy of Talbert House.

(Continued)

EDUCATION AND EMPLOYMENT HISTORY

31. ☐☐ Years of education attained (last grade completed).

32. ☐☐ Highest diploma/degree received and name major subject area where applicable.
    (1) None
    (2) G.E.D.
    (3) High School
    (4) College   Associate/Major   _____
                     Bachelor/Major   _____
                     Master's/Major   _____
                     Doctoral/Major   _____

33. ☐☐ Years of vocational training.

34. ☐☐ Certification of vocational training awarded
    (1) Yes _____ Trade
    (2) No

Enter 1 for YES   2 for NO for Questions 35-37

35. ☐☐ Physical/Health impairments (e.g., amputee, paraplegic, deaf, blind, serious illness, debilitating effect of age)

36. ☐☐ Mental capacity impairment (e.g., diagnosed mental retardation, diagnosed borderline MR)

37. ☐☐ Behavioral impairment (e.g., mental and/or emotional condition or disorders that require the treatment of a qualified mental health professional).

38. ☐☐ Number of jobs held in the last 2 years in the community prior to incarceration.

39. ☐☐ Longest stay on the job in the last 2 years in the community (number of months).

CLIENT/STAFF ASSISTANCE ASSESSMENT

Enter 1 for YES   2 for NO for Questions 40-55

40. ☐ Does client feel he/she needs assistance while in residency?
41. ☐ Does this individual need employment assistance?
42. ☐ Does this individual need assistance in academic or vocational training?
43. ☐ Does this individual need assistance in financial management?
44. ☐ Does individual need assistance in the area of domestic relations (e.g., marriage, family, etc.)?
45. ☐ Does this individual need assistance in the area of emotional or mental health?
46. ☐ Is this individual currently required to take medication for any psychological condition?
47. ☐ Does this individual need assistance for a substance abuse (alcohol/drug) problem?

48. ☐ Does this individual need assistance with securing suitable living arrangements?
49. ☐ Does this individual need assistance for a learning disability?
50. ☐ Has medication ever been prescribed for a psychological condition (e.g., nerves)?
51. ☐ Has client had prior psychiatric hospitalization?
52. ☐ Has client ever attempted suicide?
53. ☐ Was client ever a victim of child abuse?
54. ☐ Was client ever a victim of domestic violence?
55. ☐ Was client ever a victim of sexual abuse or incest?

DRUG/ALCOHOL HISTORY

56. ☐☐ # times client had prior drug/alcohol treatment.
57. ☐☐ # months prior outpatient treatment.
58. ☐☐ Successful?   (1) Yes   (2) No   (3) NA
59. ☐☐ # months prior inpatient treatment.
60. ☐☐ Successful?   (1) Yes   (2) No   (3) NA
61. ☐☐ # months prior Halfway House treatment.
62. ☐☐ Successful?   (1) Yes   (2) No   (3) NA

63. ☐ Has client participated in a halfway house **program** before this occasion?
    (1) Yes   (2) No

64. ☐☐ Longest period of drug/alcohol abstinence in community (months) **or** (99) No problem

Staff member completing form

_____

Date _____
Rev. 061992

Figure 10.3 Continued

self-efficacy, challenge cognitive distortions, and assist offenders in developing good problem-solving and self-control skills. For example, reductions in substance abuse are more likely if one's attitudes about substance use change, if there is a focus on the present factors that influence behavior, rather than the past, and if one develops the skills needed to resist peer pressure and other influences that contribute to use. These strategies have been demonstrated to be effective in reducing recidivism. Research is also showing that 12-step models, educating participants about the disease, admitting you're powerless over drugs and alcohol, self-actualization, and self-help approaches are not very effective with offenders (Lightfoot, 1999; Taxman, 2000). There is little empirical evidence that these approaches will lead to long-term reductions in recidivism. While the disease model is still widely used in many halfway houses and other residential programs, many today also offer groups to combat criminal thinking and other cognitive interventions aimed at substance abuse, anger and violence reduction, sexual behavior, negative peer associations, and improved problem-solving techniques.

Another group of problem offenders are those with both mental illness and substance abuse problems. These offenders are called "dual diagnosed" and pose a special problem for community corrections. Although research indicates that major predictors of recidivism are the same for mentally disordered offenders as for non-mentally disordered offenders (Bonta et al., 2014; Solicitor General of Canada, 1998), mental illness is often a barrier and contributing factor in substance abuse. The availability of treatment services in the community is often lacking for this special-needs group, and is best summarized by Peters and Hills (1999) who state:

> Offenders placed under community supervision who have co-occurring mental health and substance abuse disorders are quite diverse in symptom presentation, severity and chronicity of disorders. These individuals often have severe mental health disorders, and simultaneously use different types of drugs, presenting considerable challenges to treatment programs for this population. Many offenders with co-occurring disorders would benefit from specialized treatment services in the community.
>
> (Peters & Hills, 1999, p. 95)

Unfortunately, relatively few programs are designed specifically to deal with the **dual-diagnosed offender**. Most of these programs are located in large urban areas. One such program is the Substance Abuse–Mental Illness (SAMI) program operated by Talbert House in Cincinnati, Ohio. This specialized program has been in operation for more than 30 years and has served well over 600 offenders during that period of time.

Many urban communities across the nation face the problem of finding treatment opportunities that permit reintegration of high-need offenders, such as those described earlier. Increasingly, these jurisdictions are turning for assistance to the private sector, including for-profit and non-profit residential programs. Community residential correctional programs of these types exist across the nation and will increase in number and importance in the coming years. The private sector

Box 10.10
Residential Centers in Harris County (Houston, TX)

The Community Supervision and Corrections Department in Harris County (Houston, TX) is the third largest probation agency in the country. In addition to field supervision, the department also oversees three residential facilities. Below is a description of these facilities.

Harris County Residential Treatment Center

The Harris County Residential Treatment Center (HCRTC) is a 378-bed residential program designed to serve clients who are in need of intensive, out-of-home placement to address a broad range of criminogenic needs including substance abuse, criminal attitudes, criminal peers, criminal personality characteristics, employment/education issues, and family issues. The program is split into different tracks depending on gender, risk, and level of substance use. Males and females live in different units and low/moderate-risk clients are separated programmatically from high-risk clients. Those clients who are higher risk receive upwards of 300 hours of direct treatment, while moderate-risk clients receive about 200 hours, and low-to-moderate-risk clients will receive approximately 100 hours of treatment.

Young Men About Change

This is a 192-bed program serving males which has two unique tracks. The YMAC-Substance Abuse track (YMAC-SA) is for young men who have a significant substance abuse issue along with some criminality. The YMAC-SA is designed to help the participants focus on their substance abuse issues while addressing other criminogenic factors. The YMAC-Criminality track (YMAC-CR) is designed for young men who present with significant criminality issues and may have a low-level substance abuse issue as well. The YMAC-CR is designed to target primary criminogenic needs (peers, attitudes, and personality factors) in addition to employment, family, and substance abuse issues.

Dual Diagnosis Residential Program

This program is a 70-bed Community Corrections Facility (CCF) for male and female clients of all age groups who have been identified as having a significant mental health impairment. The program provides 6-month residential substance abuse treatment integrated with mental health treatment services to clients identified with co-occurring mental health/substance abuse issues. The clients participate in mental health counseling on an individual and group basis to address their co-occurring disorders. A Booster Track is available to clients who upon release struggle in the transition and need a short-term intervention. Aftercare services are also provided for all clients. Upon completion of the MH Residential Program, cases are placed in a specialized mental health caseload.

providing these programs, facilities, and centers will grow as cities and counties accept and introduce these programs in their local areas. Box 10.10 illustrates the type of residential programs in Harris County (Houston, TX). The county owns these facilities, but contracts out with private providers to operate them and offer programming. This is also an example of how the county has required the use of evidence-based approaches within its facilities.

JUVENILES IN RESIDENTIAL PLACEMENT

Although the population of juveniles in residential placement includes those in secure facilities, the use of group homes, halfway houses, and other forms of residential facilities is common in the juvenile justice system. Recent figures released by the Office of Juvenile Justice and Delinquency Prevention indicate a steady decline in the number of youths placed in such facilities between 1998 and 2015. It is also important to note that every state has significantly reduced the number of juveniles held in residential facilities, with most states cutting the rates by 50 percent or more between 2006 and 2016 (Hockenberry, 2018). Figure 10.4 shows that the number of juveniles in residential placement peaked in 2000 and has been declining ever since. Some states, such as Missouri, have moved from large juvenile institutions to smaller, residential facilities. Box 10.11 briefly describes community correctional facilities in Ohio and provides an example of some of the services offered in one of the facilities.

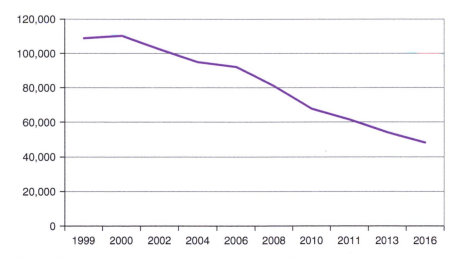

Figure 10.4 Number of Youth Held in Juvenile Residential Facilities 1999–2016

Source: Juveniles in Residential Placement series. U.S. Department of Justice, Office of Juvenile Justice and Delinquency Prevention.

Box 10.11
Community Correctional Facilities for Juveniles in Ohio

The Ohio Department of Youth Services (ODYS) funds 12 Community Correctional Facilities (CCFs) across the state. These facilities vary in size and are designed to provide an alternative to a state facility for youth adjudicated on felony charges. These facilities served 426 youth in 2017, and the average length of stay was 6.79 months. Below is a brief description of one of the facilities:

The mission of the Juvenile Residential Center of Northwest Ohio is to assist youth and their families in making positive changes that contribute to an improved functioning in the home environment while protecting the community. In collaboration with courts, families, and other outside service providers, the facility seeks to individualize each youth's treatment and enhance his prosocial development. The Juvenile Residential Center is a 42-bed facility, housing male felony offenders. Northwest offers:

- Individual Treatment Plans
- Cognitive-Behavioral Therapy
- Sexual Offender Specific Treatment
- Substance Abuse Specific Treatment
- Thinking for a Change/Role Play
- Problem Solving Group
- Social Skills
- Anger Management
- Thinking Error Education
- Academic Instruction
- Life Skills Education
- Physical Fitness
- Individual and Family Counseling
- Parent Education and Support Group
- Religious Service
- Community Service Work and Restitution Programs.

EFFECTIVENESS OF COMMUNITY RESIDENTIAL PROGRAMS

The question of the effectiveness of residential correctional programs, including halfway houses, is an important one, and one with no easy answer. The model obviously provides an opportunity to deliver programs and services to those in need; however, the quality and subsequent effectiveness of these facilities can vary greatly.

Evaluation of the effectiveness of halfway houses and, more recently, residential community correctional programs requires that they be considered across three dimensions: humaneness, recidivism, and cost studies (Latessa & Allen, 1982). There is little doubt that halfway houses are more humane than imprisonment. Halfway house programs were established in part to address the devastating economic and psychological effects of prisons and prisonization on most inmates. Prison crowding, the gross idleness of inmates, the absence of meaningful work and vocational training, unhealthy and unsafe physical plants, prison rape, and gang conflicts within prisons make them less than the pinnacle of humanitarianism (Donnelly & Forschner, 1987).

The weight of evidence to date demonstrates that halfway houses are cost-effective in terms of expenditure of public funds when compared to institutional placement. Further, their programs achieve some, if not all, stated objectives, including the maintenance of offenders' community ties and making community resources available to offender clients (Dowell et al., 1985). On average, halfway houses cost about $60 per day per offender, and one study concluded that halfway houses tend to be more cost-effective under private rather than public management (Pratt & Winston, 1999).

The issue of recidivism is much more complex, particularly with regard to halfway houses. The diversity of halfway houses, as well as the range of types of offenders they serve (parolees, probationers, pretrial detainees, work releasees, and furloughees, not to mention state, county, and federal offenders), makes it difficult to develop adequate comparison groups for follow-up studies.[13] Recidivism studies of CRC residents that exist indicate success with about 71 percent of the clients, and in-program rearrest rates of 2 to 17 percent (Huskey, 1992). Follow-up recidivism studies of alcohol-abusing clients show success rates ranging from 70 to 80 percent; driving under the influence (DUI) rates can be reduced significantly with residential treatment, significantly raising DUI survival rates (Langworthy & Latessa, 1993, 1996; Pratt et al., 2000). For clients who graduate from CRC programs, success rates can be as high as 92 percent (Friday & Wertkin, 1995). On the whole, follow-up recidivism studies indicate that halfway house residents perform no worse than offenders who receive other correctional sanctions. There is also some evidence that offenders placed in halfway houses have more needs than

---

Box 10.12
Humaneness of Halfway Houses

[B]ecause of the difficulty of assessing **humaneness** and behavioral changes, most researchers tend to ignore these variables to pursue more quantifiable data. However, anyone who has worked in or around halfway houses has seen positive changes of the lives of many who enter these programs.

Source: Wilson (1985, p. 161).

other offenders (Latessa & Travis, 1991). Latessa (1998) has examined a number of halfway houses across the country. He has several criticisms that are noteworthy:

- Many halfway houses fail to assess offenders adequately, and few distinctions are made between offenders based on risk.
- In general, qualifications of staff are low, and there is a great deal of staff turnover.
- Most halfway houses offer a wide range of "eclectic" treatment, with little if any theoretically-based treatment models in place.
- Despite some notable exceptions, most halfway houses can be classified as one step above "three hots and a cot."

Other researchers (Leon et al., 1999; Munden et al., 1999) have voiced similar concerns about poor offender assessment practices, frequent staff turnover, change in leadership, inadequate resources, and insufficient emphasis on treatment.

In a 2002 study of residential programs in Ohio, Lowenkamp and Latessa (2004) demonstrated the importance of assessing the risk level of offenders before assigning them to community-based correctional facilities (CBCFs) and halfway houses. Figure 10.5 and Figure 10.6 illustrate recidivism rates for individual CBCF and halfway house programs. Consistent with the risk principle, the programs generally increased the recidivism rates of low-risk offenders by 4 percent, but decreased the recidivism rates of higher-risk offenders by 8 percent. In a 2010 replication study, Latessa and colleagues (2010) examined 20 CBCFs and 40 halfway houses and a sample of more than 20,000 offenders. Results from this study were very similar

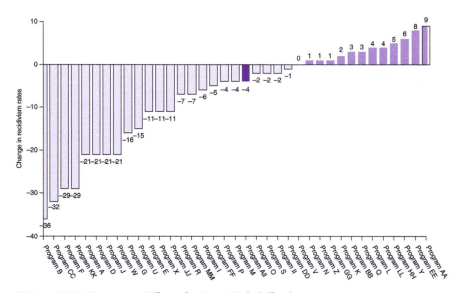

Figure 10.5 Treatment Effects for Low-Risk Offenders

Source: Lowenkamp, C.T., Latessa, E.J. (2004). Residential community corrections and the risk principle: Lessons learned in Ohio. In: *Ohio Corrections Research Compendium, Vol. II.* Columbus, OH: Ohio Department of Research and Corrections.

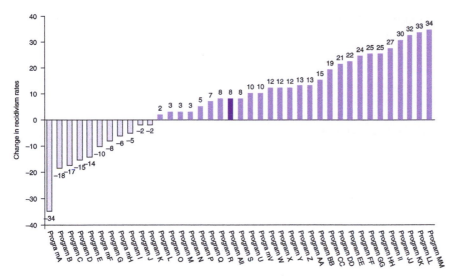

Figure 10.6 Treatment Effects for High-Risk Offenders

Source: Lowenkamp, C.T., Latessa, E.J. (2004). Residential community corrections and the risk principle: Lessons learned in Ohio. In: *Ohio Corrections Research Compendium, Vol. II.* Columbus, OH: Ohio Department of Research and Corrections.

Box 10.13
Community-Based Correctional Facilities

In one of the more unusual attempts to provide residential treatment programs, Ohio has developed a correctional alternative called **community-based correctional facilities** (CBCFs). Currently there are 19 operating CBCFs in Ohio. The size of the facilities ranges from 54 to 200 offenders, and several serve both males and females. Funding for the CBCFs is provided by the state; however, the operation and management of the CBCFs are left to a local judicial corrections board. In some instances, local courts operate the facilities, whereas private providers are retained in others. The CBCFs are secure facilities, but treatment is the primary focus. Ohio has also developed similar juvenile programs called community correctional facilities. Some other states, such as Indiana and Texas, have similar programs. Many of these programs have demonstrated that they can effectively deliver services to offenders and reduce recidivism.

---

to the earlier one: Overall recidivism *increased* by 3 percent for low-risk offenders and was *reduced* by 14 percent for high-risk offenders. As with the previous study, some programs were extremely effective, whereas others were not. The quality and implementation of the program were also major factors in determining the effectiveness of the program.

Others have also argued that while halfway houses can help meet the needs of offenders leaving prison, they also create additional avenues for failure and recidivism, especially through non-compliance violations (Hamilton & Campbell, 2013).

THE FUTURE OF RESIDENTIAL COMMUNITY CORRECTIONS

Predicting future correctional trends is difficult due to possible national policy changes, economic fluctuations, crime trends, and public sentiment. Currently, many states are trying to reduce their prison populations *and* reduce recidivism (Council of State Governments). Thus, it is reasonable to expect an increased need for community residential facilities and other community correctional programs.

Despite the increased use of punishment, the future of residential community correctional programs appears promising. Probation and parole populations are high, and approximately 95 percent of prison inmates will return to the community. Halfway houses and other community-based programs will be needed to assist in their reintegration. Early release programs, such as work and educational furlough and pre-parole release, will also increase, furthering the demand for the services of halfway houses and related programs.

It is also likely that local units of government will increasingly turn to private-sector providers for correctional programs, contracting with larger numbers of halfway houses to provide lower-cost and diverse services that the government cannot otherwise fund. To do less would decrease reintegration services and increase the possibility of offenders returning to prison for committing new crimes in local communities. Indeed, one of the issues facing community corrections is the increased privatization of services and programs. While non-profit providers have always been the mainstay of traditional halfway houses, the influx of for-profit providers will likely change the face of this industry. This has not been without its critics, however, and the onus on the government to evaluate the quality of programs and services will be even greater.

Halfway houses and related programs will also need to increase the quality and effectiveness[14] of programs to serve the demands of clients, communities, and corrections. To do this, they will need to maintain relationships with justice agencies, strengthen community ties and acceptance, adopt treatment models that have demonstrated effectiveness, and assist in ensuring the safety of the community in reintegrating offenders. Future research will also be needed to address the roles and effectiveness of community residential correctional programs. Fortunately, there is a movement under way to improve the effectiveness of community correctional programs. This movement is being supported by the National Institute of Corrections[15] and the International Community Corrections Association and is based on the work of scholars such as Paul Gendreau, Don Andrews, Francis Cullen, and others. Through their research we continue to learn about "what works" with offenders (Cullen & Gendreau, 2001).

SUMMARY

Halfway houses have been part of the correctional scene since the early 1800s. Originally designed to assist offenders who had been released from prison, today many halfway houses serve as both halfway "in" and halfway "out" facilities. Often called community residential correctional programs, these facilities include both privately- and publicly-operated programs and range from "three hots and a cot" to programs designed to meet all of an offender's treatment needs. Although halfway houses are often overlooked, they represent an important part of community corrections.

Community corrections centers serving high-risk clients have produced evidence of both lower recidivism and cost-effectiveness. Such centers are more humane, less expensive, and more effective in ensuring public safety. Community corrections centers will remain a major segment of community corrections and will be increasingly specialized to serve a wider variety of high-risk clients. This has been the case in a number of jurisdictions throughout the United States, especially as prisons are under increasing pressure to release inmates and reduce the incarcerated population and corresponding costs.

Review Questions

1. Why did Phase I of the halfway house movement die in the 1930s?
2. Explain the revival of the halfway house movement in the 1950s.
3. Define residential community correctional center.
4. What are some of the services offered by halfway houses?
5. What are the advantages of halfway houses?
6. What is "substance abuse"? Debate: Is it a disease or a learned behavior?
7. Define "reintegration" and discuss ways in which halfway houses can lower crime.
8. What are some of the criticisms of halfway houses?
9. Describe the CBCFs in Ohio.
10. Why does the demand for community residential facilities keep growing?

Notes

1. This organization is now known as the International Community Corrections Association; publishes the *ICCA Journal*; and sponsors local, state, regional, national, and international conferences and training programs concerned with halfway houses and community alternatives. Go to www.iccaweb.org/ for more information.
2. American Correctional Association, 206 N. Washington Street, Alexandria, VA 22314 (www.aca.org/).
3. The National Institute of Corrections lists more than 1,200 programs in its 1989 *Directory of Residential Community Corrections Facilities in the United States*. The

directory does not list all small programs, particularly in rural areas. For more information, go to www.nicic.gov.

4   Allen et al. (1976).

5   Halfway houses for juveniles tend to be more cost-effective than detention. Pratt and Winston (1999).

6   Chapple (2000, pp. 31–35).

7   This question is explored in more detail in Hicks (1987). See also Wilson (1985); Latessa and Travis (1992); Latessa and Allen (1982).

8   Federal Bureau of Prisons (2001). See also Thevenot (2001).

9   Valentine (1991). The Bureau of Prisons underutilizes their contracted bed space, further exacerbating their prison overcrowding problem.

10 This nostalgic view of warm-hearted, older rural Americans trying to help the less successful, downtrodden, and sodden of the Depression years by feeding any who asked, putting transients to work chopping wood or hauling water, and allowing the more needy to sleep in the barn has many adherents. No doubt this pattern of early philanthropic assistance was found in many sites and continues in isolated locales. These "Mom and Pop" programs, often unofficial, were undoubtedly major sources of humanitarian assistance to the needy in some, if not most, parts of the nation during the early twentieth century, providing "three hots and a cot." If they exist today, they are an endangered species.

11 See the *IARCA Journal* for a description of some more successful programs in rural America and urban England (Leeds Alternative to Care and Custody Scheme, and Roundabout Group). *IARCA Journal* 3 (July, 1990).

12 See Berry (1990).

13 It is important to note that studies which do not employ a control group make it very difficult to gauge the effectiveness of programs, at least in terms of recidivism.

14 There is some evidence that staff attributes within programs influence program effectiveness and recidivism. Staff selection and training, as well as program developments, could be improved by matching personality and attitudinal attributes. See Johnson and Bonta (1985).

15 For more information about this movement, write to NIC at 320 1st Street NW, Washington, DC 20534 (www.nicic.gov).

Recommended Readings

Lowenkamp, C.T., Latessa, E.J. (2005). Increasing the effectiveness of correctional programming through the risk principle: Identifying offenders for residential placement. *Criminology and Public Policy* 4(2), 263–290.

Lowenkamp, C., Makarios, M.D., Latessa, E.J., Lemke, R., Smith, P. (2010). Community corrections facilities for juvenile offenders in Ohio: An examination of treatment integrity and recidivism. *Criminal Justice and Behavior* 37(6), 695–708.

References

ADAM II. (2014). 2013 Annual Report Arrestee Drug Abuse Monitoring Program II. Washington, DC: Office of National Drug Control Policy, Executive Office of the President.

Allen, H., Bowman, E., Carlson, E., Parks, E., Seiter, R. (1976). *Halfway houses in the United States: An analysis of the state of the art. Paper presented at the International Halfway House Association*. Guilford, England.

Allen, H., Latessa, E.J., Ponder, B. (2019). *Corrections in America: An introduction*. 15th ed. New York: Pearson.

Berry, T. (1990). Rural community corrections and the challenge: Providing comprehensive services. *IARCA Journal* 3 (July), 6–7.

Bonta, J., Blais, J., Wilson, H.A. (2014). A theoretically informed meta-analysis of the risk for general and violent recidivism for mentally disordered offenders. *Aggression and Violent Behavior* 19, 278–287.

Boyle, D.J., Ragusa-Salerno, L.M., Lanterman, J.L., Marcus, A.F. (2013). An evaluation of day reporting centers for parolees. *Criminology & Public Policy* 12, 119–143.

Chapple, K. (2000). *Community residential programming for female offenders and their children. Responding to women offenders in the community*. Washington, DC: National Institute of Corrections.

Cohn, J. (1973). *A study of community-based correctional needs in Massachusetts*. Boston, MA: Massachusetts Department of Corrections.

Cullen, F., Gendreau, P. (2001). From nothing works to what works. *The Prison Journal* 81(3), 313–338.

Donnelly, P., Forschner, B.E. (1987). Predictors of success in a co-correctional halfway house: A discriminant analysis. *Journal of Crime and Justice* 10, 1–22.

Dowell, D., Klein, C., Krichmar, C. (1985). Evaluation of a halfway house for women. *Journal of Criminal Justice* 13, 217–226.

Federal Bureau of Prisons. (2001). *The Bureau in brief*. Available at www.bop.gov/resources/publications.jsp

Friday, P., Wertkin, R. (1995). Effects of programming and race on recidivism: Residential probation. In: J. Smykla, W. Selke (Eds.), *Intermediate sanctions: Sentencing in the 1990s* (pp. 209–217). Cincinnati, OH: Anderson.

Hamilton, Z.K., Campbell, C.M. (2013). The dark figure of corrections: Failure by way of participation. *Criminal Justice and Behavior* 40, 180–202.

Hartmann, D., Friday, P., Minor, K. (1994). Residential probation: A seven-year follow-up study of halfway house discharges. *Journal of Criminal Justice* 22(6), 503–515.

Hicks, N. (1987). Halfway houses and corrections. *Corrections Compendium* 12 (October), 1–7.

Hockenberry, S. (2018). *Juveniles in residential placement 2015*. Washington, DC: U.S. Department of Justice, Office of Juvenile Justice and Delinquency Prevention.

Huskey, B. (1992). The expanding use of CRCs. *Corrections Today* 54(8), 70–74.

Hyatt, J.M., Ostermann, M. (2017). Better to stay home: Evaluating the impact of day reporting centers on offending. *Crime and Delinquency*. doi: 10.1177/0011128717727739

Johnson, J., Bonta, J. (1985). Characteristics of staff and programs in correctional halfway houses. *Journal of Offender Counseling, Services and Rehabilitation* 9, 39–51.

Kaeble, D., Cowhig, M. (2018). *Correctional populations in the United States, 2016.* Washington, DC: U.S. Department of Justice, Bureau of Justice Programs.

Langworthy, R., Latessa, E. (1993). Treatment of chronic drunk drivers: The Turning Point project. *Journal of Criminal Justice* 21, 265–276.

Langworthy, R., Latessa, E. (1996). Treatment of chronic drunk drivers: A four-year follow-up of the Turning Point project. *Journal of Criminal Justice* 24, 273–281.

Latessa. E. (1998). *Public protection through offender risk reduction: Putting research into practice.* Washington, DC: National Institute of Corrections.

Latessa, E., Allen, H. (1982). Halfway houses and parole: A national assessment. *Journal of Criminal Justice* 10, 153–163.

Latessa, E., Brusman, L., Smith, P. (2010). *Follow-up evaluation of Ohio's community based correctional facility and halfway house programs—Outcome study.* Cincinnati, OH: School of Criminal Justice, University of Cincinnati. Available at www.uc.edu/criminaljustice.

Latessa, E., Travis, L. (1991). Halfway house or probation: A comparison of alternative dispositions. *Journal of Crime and Justice* 14(1), 53–76.

Latessa, E., Travis, L. (1992). Residential community correctional programs. In: J. Byrne, A. Lurigio (Eds.), *Smart sentencing? An examination of the emergence of intermediate sentencing* (pp. 166–181). Beverly Hills, CA: Sage.

Leon, A., Dziegielewski, S., Tubiak, C. (1999). A program evaluation of a juvenile halfway house: Considerations for strengthening program components. *Evaluation and Program Planning* 22, 141–153.

Lightfoot, L. (1999). Treating substance abuse and dependence in offenders: A review of methods and outcomes. In: E. Latessa (Ed.), *What works: Strategic solutions: The International Community Corrections Association examines substance abuse* (pp. 43–80). Lanham, MD: American Correctional Association.

Lowenkamp, C.T., Latessa, E.J. (2004). Residential community corrections and the risk principle: Lessons learned in Ohio. In: *Ohio Corrections Research Compendium, Vol. II.* Columbus, OH: Ohio Department of Research and Corrections.

Munden, D., Tewksbury, R., Grossi, E. (1999). Intermediate sanctions and the halfway back program in Kentucky. *Criminal Justice Policy Review* 9, 431–449.

National Institute of Corrections. (1989). *1989 directory of residential community corrections facilities in the United States.* Longmont, CO: National Institute of Corrections.

Ostermann, M. (2009). An analysis of New Jersey's day reporting center and halfway back programs: Embracing the rehabilitative ideal through evidence based practices. *Journal of Offender Rehabilitation* 48(2), 139–153.

Peters, R., Hills, H. (1999). Community treatment and supervision strategies for offenders with co-occurring disorders: What works? In: E. Latessa (Ed.), *What works: Strategic solutions: The International Community Corrections Association examines substance abuse* (pp. 81–136). Lanham, MD: American Correctional Association.

Pratt, T., Holsinger, A., Latessa, E. (2000). Treating the chronic DUI offender: "Turning Point" ten years later. *Journal of Criminal Justice* 28, 271–281.

Pratt, T., Winston, M. (1999). The search for the Frugal Grail. *Criminal Justice Policy Review* 10(3), 447–471.

President's Commission on Law Enforcement and Administration of Justice. (1967). *Corrections*. Washington, DC: U.S. Government Printing Office.

Rush, G. (1992). *The dictionary of criminal justice*. Guilford, CT: Duskin.

Seiter, R., Carlson, E. (1977). Residential inmate aftercare: The state of the art. *Offender Rehabilitation* 4, 78–94.

Solicitor General of Canada. (1998). Mentally disordered offenders. Available at www.publicsafety.gc.ca/cnt/rsrcs/pblctns/mtldrd-fndr/index-eng.aspx.

Taxman, F.S. (2000). Unraveling "what works" for offenders in substance abuse treatment services. *National Drug Court Institute Review* II(2), 93–134.

Thevenot, C. (2001). Halfway house: Training for freedom. *Las Vegas Review-Journal*.

U.S. Government Accountability Office. (2001). *Prisoner releases: Reintegration of offenders into communities*. Washington, DC: U.S. Government Accountability Office.

Valentine, H. (1991). *Prison alternatives: Crowded federal prisons can transfer more inmates to halfway houses*. Washington, DC: U.S. General Accounting Office.

Wilson, G. (1985). Halfway house programs for offenders. In: L. Travis (Ed.), *Probation, parole and community corrections* (pp. 151–164). Prospect Heights, IL: Waveland.

Chapter 11

SPECIAL POPULATIONS IN COMMUNITY CORRECTIONS

Key Terms

child abuse
child molestation
criminalization of the mentally ill
dangerous sex offenders
developmentally disabled offenders
exhibitionism
incest

Megan's Law
mentally disordered offenders
prostitution
psychopathy
rape
serial rapists
sex offenders

> Successful sex offender management requires more governmental funding. Unfortunately, public aversion to spending money on sex offenders undercuts their management. —R.J. Konopasky

As probation and parole agencies became more sophisticated with case assignment, the need for specialized officers quickly became apparent. From DUI drivers to sex offenders, from domestic violence offenders to mentally ill offenders, agencies began to realize that supervising these populations was not like supervising other offenders. Officers were in need of specialized training and agencies needed to select staff who were able to work with the specific population without taking things too personally. In this chapter, we review the research on special populations of offenders. We have chosen to focus on five specific types of offender: sex offenders, mentally disordered offenders, DUI offenders, domestic violence offenders, and youthful offenders. These categories do not exhaust the list of possible types of special category offenders.[1]

THE SEX OFFENDER

Each state has differing laws that regulate sexual conduct, and correctional systems typically deal with two special-needs groups of sexual offenders: rapists, and child molesters (pedophiles). Each of these categories has differing motivations, modes of operation, challenges, and dangers. Almost all are handled, either initially or later, by community corrections. We begin with a brief discussion of public opinion and fear, two factors that color both legal and treatment issues with sex offenders.

Box 11.1
Sex Offenders

Sex offenders are persons who have committed a sexual act prohibited by law, such as rape, **incest**, child molestation, or prostitution for sexual, economic, psychological, or situational reasons.

On a given day, there are approximately 234,000 offenders convicted of **rape** or sexual assault under the care, custody, or control of corrections agencies. Nearly 60 percent of these sex offenders are under conditional supervision in the community.

The median age of the victims of imprisoned sexual assaulters was less than 13 years; the median age of rape victims was about 22 years.

An estimated 24 percent of those serving time for rape and 19 percent of those serving time for sexual assault had been on probation or parole at the time of the offense.

Source: Bureau of Justice Statistics (2002).

Box 11.2
Exhibitionism

Exhibitionism is exposure of one's genitalia or other body parts to others in inappropriate circumstances or public places. An exhibitionist is the one who exposes those parts to others.

Public Opinion and Fear

With the possible exception of the violent offender, no type of correctional client evokes more concern from the public than the sex offender. Sex offenders, especially **child molesters**, are treated with both disdain and violence. Few offenders are as stigmatized or reviled as child molesters.

Many Americans fear sexual assaulters, gang rapists, **serial rapists**, stranger rapists, child abductors, and **child abusers**. Rape is one of the most feared events as well as a frightening and misunderstood crime. Others feel that treatment of sexual assaulters is undeserved and ineffective. Politicians tend to follow public opinion,[2] despite evidence that there is widespread support for treatment and rehabilitation of offenders ranging from the very young to geriatric prisoners. Opinion polls over-estimate the amount of support for punitive approaches to special-needs clients, particularly for juveniles (Cullen & Moon, 2002). There is no doubt that public sentiment works against the establishment and funding of treatment programs and options. However, substantial evidence shows that treatment works (Lipton et al., 1999; Sherman et al., 1997; Yates, 2002). Specifically, three meta-analyses on the topic have been conducted (Table 11.1), and results from each review indicate that treatment has an appreciable impact on recidivism. First, Gallagher and colleagues (1999) located a total of 25 studies and found a 21 percent reduction in sexual recidivism overall. Second, Hanson et al. (2002) reviewed 43 studies involving more

---

Box 11.3
Dangerous Sex Offenders

Washington State's 1990 Community Protection Act was the first law authorizing public notification when **dangerous sex offenders** are released into the community. It was thought that sex offender registration laws are necessary because:

- Ex-offenders pose a high risk of reoffending after release from custody.
- Protecting the public from sex offenders is a primary governmental interest, and the rights of sex offenders take a back seat to public interest.
- Releasing certain information about sex offenders to public agencies and the general public will contribute to public safety.

It took the brutal 1994 murder–rape of Megan Kanka (1994) to prompt public demand for broad-based community notification. President Clinton signed **Megan's Law** in 1996, which allows the states discretion to establish criteria for disclosure, but compels them to make personal and private information about registered sex offenders available to the public. It was believed that such notification:

- Assists law enforcement agencies during investigations.
- Establishes legal grounds to hold offenders.
- Deters sex offenders from committing new offenses.
- Offers citizens information useful in protecting their children from victimization.

Some states mandate registration and penalize non-registration with imprisonment. Sex offender registration has been criticized as a flawed strategy for controlling sex crime, reflecting a skewed view of sex offenders, and encouraging vigilantism. Probation and parole agents' responsibilities were impacted negatively.

Sources: Presser and Gunnison (1999); Zavitz and Farkas (2000).

Table 11.1 Meta-analyses Demonstrating that Treatment Reduces Sexual Recidivism

	Number of studies	Percent reduction
Gallagher et al. (1999)	25	21
Hanson et al. (2002)	43	12
Lösel and Schmucker (2005)	69	37

than 9,000 sex offenders and found a 12 percent reduction in sexual recidivism. More recently, Lösel and Schmucker (2005) quantitatively synthesized 69 studies and found a 37 percent reduction in sexual recidivism compared to controls.

Treatment for Sex Offenders

The risk factors emphasized for the prediction of sexual recidivism have historically been more static in nature. Examples of static risk factors include age, previous offense history, onset of sexually deviant interests, marital status, and specific offense characteristics such as stranger victim, male victim, and contact/non-contact offense (Hanson & Bussière, 1998; Harris, 2006). More recently, however, researchers have also underscored the importance of dynamic risk factors for sexual recidivism. Furthermore, these dynamic risk factors can be further subdivided into stable (or relatively enduring) and acute (or rapidly changing) risk factors (Hanson & Harris, 2000). Stable risk factors include social influences, sexual entitlement, attitudes, sexual self-regulation, and general self-regulation (Hanson & Harris, 2000; Hanson & Morton-Bourgon, 2004). On the other hand, acute dynamic factors include access to victims, non-cooperation with supervision, and anger (Hanson & Harris, 2000). Mann and colleagues (2010) have referred to these risk factors as *psychologically meaningful risk factors*.

Recall from Chapter 6 that the risk principle states that criminal behavior is predictable using actuarial assessments of both static and dynamic risk factors. The most commonly used static risk assessment tools for sexual recidivism include the Static-99 (Hanson & Thornton, 2000), Risk-Matrix-2000, and the Sex Offender Risk Appraisal Guide (Quinsey et al., 1998). In selecting risk assessment tools for sex offenders, it is important to consider both sexual and general recidivism as separate outcomes. This means that it is important for corrections professionals to assess all offenders with a composite measure of risk and need, but they should also use an additional measure to predict sexual recidivism. In fact, many sex offenders tend to score as low risk for general recidivism, but at the same time they can be high risk for sexual recidivism (McGrath et al., 2011). Failure to use a sex-offense-specific tool could result in the misclassification of sex offenders.

Similar to general populations of offenders, sex offenders identified as high risk for recidivism should receive more intensive services than those identified as low risk for recidivism. In the literature, the evidence supporting the application of the risk principle to sex offenders is beginning to emerge. For example, Hanson et al. (2009) found better treatment effects with higher-risk offenders compared to lower-risk offenders. Similarly, Lovins and colleagues (2009) found that higher-risk sex offenders had lower rates of general recidivism when they received more intensive services, such as residential placement, compared with less intensive services. Finally, Wakeling and colleagues (2012) recently reviewed the literature and concluded that lower-risk sex offenders should be kept separate from higher-risk sex offenders, and treatment services should not interfere with other activities that encourage a prosocial lifestyle.

In terms of treatment, there is considerable heterogeneity of sex crimes and specific acts of violence. As a result, treatment programs are as varied as crime type; some treatment programs fail to focus on those factors contributing to the commission of the crime and thus erroneously address objectives that would not lessen reoffending. A study of sex offender treatment in Vermont outlined the goals of an institutional treatment program:

- Get the offender to accept responsibility for his actions and the harm done to the victim and others.
- Deal with distorted thinking used to justify his actions.
- Teach the offender to understand the impact of his behavior on victims and show more empathic behavior with other people around him (recognize others' emotional distress, identify another's perspective, communicate empathy toward others, etc.).
- Address such competency issues as anger management, substance-abuse treatment issues, communicating with opposite gender adults, improving dating skills, and seeking therapy.
- Deal with sexual arousal to reduce inappropriate object arousal and enhance arousal with an appropriate adult partner.
- Plan relapse prevention that teaches the offender how and when to intervene in his own patterns of behavior that lead up to a sexual offense (drinking and remaining aloof, alone, and physically inactive can build up to fantasizing about a victim, and this requires such personal intervention as initiating counseling, attending Alcoholics Anonymous group meetings, and calling a designated crime prevention hotline). Relapse prevention includes teaching offenders how to recognize the chain of events leading up to their current offense and to practice strategies for breaking this chain.
- Plan for release into the community and set up a support team of people who know the offender's issues and can provide support and monitoring, including sex-offender-specific outpatient treatment.

Six years after release, 5 percent of the men who completed the Vermont treatment program had committed another sexual offense and were caught, in contrast to 30 percent of the men who got only partial treatment (left the program or were expelled from the program for rules violations). Thirty percent of the incarcerated men who refused to enter the program were arrested again for some form of sexual abuse (Cumming & Finch, 2001).

A study of adolescent sexual assaulters from a Wisconsin secure juvenile correctional institution (Nesbit et al., 2004) included perpetrators of sexual assault against children, rapists of same-age or older victims, and non-sex-offense-adjudicated adolescents. The rapists and child offender groups completed a mandatory, serious sex offender treatment program that included group psychotherapy, general education, sex education, behavior management programming, and individual and family therapy. Eight years later, adolescent sex offenders were found to less frequently offend sexually than the non-sex-offending adolescent delinquents, although all three groups were significantly more likely to be involved with sexual assaults than was the general male population in the nation.

Perhaps one of the most extensive reviews of treatment effectiveness on various types of sexual offenders was published by Yates (2002), who concluded that treatment can significantly reduce sexual reoffending for a variety of offenders, both juvenile and adult, if behavioral-specific treatments are based on an assessment of needs. Effective treatments also involve the development of a treatment plan, delivery of treatment in a coherent fashion by competent therapists, and the ability to adjust treatment if it is not working. For juveniles, treatment targets include:

- increasing responsibility and accountability for behavior;
- addressing cognitive, affective, and behavioral factors that support sexual offending;
- reducing deviant sexual arousal;
- improving relationships among family members;
- enhancing victim empathy;
- improving social skills;
- developing healthy attitudes toward relationships and sex;
- reducing the effects of personal trauma;
- targeting cognitive distortions.

Yates reported on treatment effectiveness for adolescents 6 years after a comprehensive, cognitive-behavioral, relapse prevention sexual offender program. Effectiveness was measured by recidivism, comparing a treatment group with a similar non-treatment group. Results are shown in Table 11.2. Treated sex

Table 11.2 Comparison of Recidivism of Treated and Untreated Adolescent Sex Offenders

Group	Recidivated sexually	Recidivated violently but not sexually	Recidivated non-violently
Treated	5.2%	18.9%	20.7%
Untreated	17.8%	32.2%	50.0%

Source: Yates, P. (2002). What works? Effective intervention with sex offenders. In: H. Allen (Ed.), *What works? Risk reduction: Interventions for special needs offenders* (pp. 115–164). Lanham, MD: American Correctional Association, p. 148.

offenders recidivated significantly less frequently and less violently. Sex offender criminal behavior is amenable to intervention, and the preponderance of evidence is that treatment works for most perpetrators (although there remain considerable challenges to develop effective treatment for the relatively rare **psychopathic** sex offender).

Box 11.4
Sex Offender Treatment: Does It Work?

The typical justice response to sex offenders involves punishment and incapacitation by eliminating offender access to victims, but does treatment work? Schmucker and Lösel completed a meta-analysis in 2015 examining the impact of sex offender treatment programs on future reoffending. They found that sex offenders who went to treatment had a 26.3 percent lower recidivism rate than those who did not attend treatment. In addition to reducing sex-offender-specific reoffending, they also found that sex offender treatment had a significant impact on general reoffending as well.

   In addition to finding an overall effect for treatment, Schmucker and Lösel found a strong linear effect with risk and effectiveness, suggesting that treatment had a stronger effect with higher-risk offenders. Their findings also suggested that programs that were cognitive-behaviorally based and delivered in the community were more effective.

Source: Schmucker and Lösel (2015).

MENTAL HEALTH DISORDERS

In 2012, the Bureau of Justice Statistics completed a survey, trying to understand the prevalence of mental health issues across jails and prisons. Based on the survey results, one in four jail inmates and one of seven state and federal inmates reported experiencing a serious psychological distress (SPD) event within 30 days of the survey (Bronson & Berzofsky, 2017). Moreover, 68 percent of jail inmates reported having a significant mental health issue, compared to 50 percent of those in state or federal custody. Most have co-occurring substance abuse problems, either alcohol or other drugs (or both).

   For constitutional and policy reasons, most general mental health facilities existing in the mid-twentieth century have closed; those remaining primarily service court-ordered forensic patients remanded by courts, including those not guilty by reason of insanity, or guilty but mentally ill; those who are a danger to self and others; and those transferred by probate court order due to mental illnesses associated with or as a result of imprisonment. A few are dangerous sex offenders who completed their sentences, but were ordered into mental health facilities due to the perceived probability of their repeating heinous crimes.

The Sentencing Project (2002, p. 2) argues that mental disorders among prisoners occur at five times the rate, at least, found in the general population and that this represents criminalization of the mentally ill: "the increased likelihood of people with mental illness being processed through the criminal justice system instead of through the mental health system." **Criminalization of the mentally ill** has occurred because:

- The deinstitutionalization movement that began in the 1960s was predicated on local communities providing sufficient mental health services, but funding was not forthcoming to underwrite treatment in the community.
- Reductions in treatment spending and availability, including fragmentation of treatment services.
- Barriers arising to involuntary commitment to a psychiatric hospital, and the difficulty of obtaining a court-ordered finding that the detained are either a clear and present danger to themselves or others, or are so markedly disabled by their conditions as not to be able to care for themselves. Involuntary hospitalization also requires legal representation and a full judicial hearing.

While there is a higher prevalence of mental health issues in jails and prisons, research has not found that these populations recidivate at any higher rate. In fact, most studies show that the presence of a mental illness is not predictive of future recidivism while controlling for general risk factors (Bonta et al., 2014; Eno Louden & Skeem, 2013). While mentally ill offenders do not engage in new crime any more than non-mentally ill offenders, there are several studies that have found that mentally ill offenders are significantly more likely to be returned for technical violations. Eno Louden and Skeem (2013) point out that mentally ill offenders often have a co-occurring substance abuse issue, have a higher level of criminal attitudes, have significantly more conditions (e.g., psychotropic compliance), and are generally supervised on more intensive caseloads. To these points, Eno Louden and Skeem found that officers were more likely to respond quickly with mentally ill offenders with technical violations. They viewed mentally ill offenders as higher risk (regardless of the risk assessment), and if they were non-compliant with medication—regardless of the person's risk to commit a new offense, harm him- or herself or someone else—they were more likely to file a violation with the court.

So, if mentally ill offenders are not riskier than non-mentally ill offenders, why do jails and prisons have higher proportions of mentally ill offenders than does the general public? There are several routes by which mentally ill offenders end up in jail or prison. First, a portion of homeless individuals have mental health issues. When the person is picked up for trespassing or other vagrancy laws, they have a difficult time being released on bond due to lack of a permanent address or ability to post bond. Once in jail, mentally ill offenders have a more difficult time managing behavior in jail and often struggle with compliance with the rules (Monahan and Steadman, 2012).

Box 11.5
Probation Supervision of the Mentally Disordered Offender

Despite claims by mental health advocates that people with mental illness pose no greater risk than those from the general public" (National Mental Health Association, 1987), strong evidence suggests that this is not the case. However, for the correctional system, the issue of whether the mentally ill are more "dangerous" than members of the general public is not a particularly relevant question. For mentally ill individuals who have been convicted of an offense, a more appropriate question is whether they pose more of a risk than other offender groups being supervised in the community.

Latessa (1996) compared arrest, conviction, and probation outcome data for several groups under probation supervision. The probation groups included sex offenders, drug offenders, high-risk offenders, regularly supervised offenders, and mentally disordered offenders. He found that mentally disordered offenders performed as well, and in some cases, better than other probation groups, and concluded that mentally ill offenders can and are being supervised in the community without increasing risk to public safety.

Source: Latessa (1996).

Box 11.6
Criminal Thinking and Mental Illness

Morgan and colleagues (2010) studied 414 adult offenders with mental illness (265 males, 149 females) and found:

- 66 percent had belief systems supportive of a criminal lifestyle (based on the Psychological Inventory of Criminal Thinking Scale).
- When compared to other offender samples, male offenders with mental illness scored similarly or higher than non-mentally disordered offenders.
- On the Criminal Sentiments Scale, 85 percent of men and 72 percent of women with mental illness had antisocial attitudes, values, and beliefs, which were higher than those of an incarcerated sample without mental illness.

They concluded:

- Criminal thinking styles differentiate people who commit crimes from those who do not, independent of mental illness.
- Incarcerated persons with mental illness are both mentally ill *and* criminal.
- Mental illness and criminality need to be treated as co-occurring problems.

Source: Morgan et al. (2010).

Box 11.7
Developmentally Disabled Prisoners

Few jails or prisons have sufficient facilities and programs to handle the special needs of **developmentally disabled offenders**, and hospitals and other health facilities are seldom capable of administering correctional programs with sufficient security to protect society's rights. Without alternatives, judges are left with no other choice than to sentence those individuals to prison.

- Some developmentally disabled offenders require incarceration because of the seriousness of their crimes or their records as repeat offenders, but most other developmentally disabled offenders could be diverted from prison to community treatment programs while still ensuring the safety of the community.
- There is a tremendous variation in estimates of the number of developmentally disabled persons incarcerated in prison: Earlier research indicates that the percentage of those offenders is higher than the percentage within the general population, while the most recent studies place the percentage at about the same level as that within the general population.
- Developmentally disabled offenders are often used by their peers, reflecting their great need for approval and acceptance. They have no long-term perspective and little ability to think in a causal way to understand the consequences of their actions.
- Developmentally disabled persons are often victimized or abused by other inmates.
- Identifying offenders who have special needs is essential for planning individualized programs. Due process, functional diagnosis, and evaluation performed by specially trained staff utilizing sophisticated assessment tools and procedures are essential.
- Because the developmentally challenged are usually undetected, violations of the legal rights of such persons are frequent.
- Criminal justice and corrections personnel are not presently trained to handle the special problems and needs of such offenders.
- Matters of competency relating to diminished mental capacity should be considered at the first point of contact with the criminal justice system and at each decision point in the continuum.
- Developmentally disabled offenders should be assigned to programs that meet their individual needs; some may be mixed in with the regular prison population; some need a segregated environment; some would benefit most from a community setting; and others might be placed in a regular developmentally disabled group home or guardianship arrangement.

■ A survey of local jurisdictions revealed the need for training about the developmentally challenged for criminal justice personnel who normally do not distinguish between the developmentally challenged and mental illness; the need for early identification of such persons once they come into contact with the criminal justice system; and the need for more community resources, particularly residential programs, to serve this category of offenders.

DRIVING UNDER THE INFLUENCE

One person across the United States was killed every 50 minutes in a drinking and driving accident in 2016. This translated to 10,497 people who lost their life in an accident that involved an impaired driver (United States Department of Transportation, 2017). Driving under the influence (DUI) is a nationwide problem. In all 50 states, the legal blood alcohol limit has been reduced for individuals 21 and over to .08, with zero tolerance for drivers under 21. At one point, driving drunk was a crime that was tolerated, maybe even ignored. Over the past 20 years, DUI has been targeted heavily from victim advocacy groups like Mothers Against Drunk Driving (MADD) due to increasing fatality rates. This public outcry along with legislative changes has resulted in the fatality rates for DUI declining by 40 percent over the past 20 years. But most recently, DUI fatalities are on the rise once again (see Figure 11.1). Researchers attribute this to an increased number of persons driving under the influence of drugs or a combination of drugs and alcohol.

Supervising DUI drivers is not easy. While national averages of recidivism are relatively low, there is research to show that people drink and drive between 80 and 200 times for every time they are caught—suggesting that detection of driving under the influence is very low. Many states have moved to the use of interlock devices or portable in-home devices to monitor the offender's alcohol consumption and limit their use of vehicles. Supervising offenders with these devices is quite tedious. Every time an offender gets behind the wheel, they must blow into the device. If a camera is installed, it takes a picture of the individual. In addition to the initial blow, interlock devices then prompt the driver to provide rolling retests to ensure that he or she did not start drinking alcohol after the car was started or have someone else provide the initial blow. Most interlock devices do not supply information in real time; instead, the results must be manually downloaded every 14 to 30 days. Upon downloading the results, the officer must sift through pictures and blow results to ensure that the offender did not drive with alcohol in his or her system and that they did not have someone else blow into the machine. Of course, interlock devices are only effective for alcohol, they do not currently detect drugs, rendering them useless for individuals who drive while under the influence of drugs.

If an offender does blow into the machine and it reads positive for alcohol, they must supply two more tests for the device to confirm positive for alcohol; that is

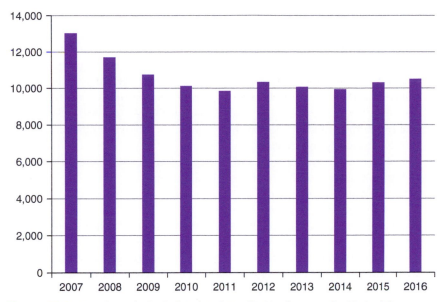

Figure 11.1 Number of Alcohol-Related Traffic Fatalities in the United States

Source: Built from data from the Fatality Analysis Reporting System: Annual Report File (2016). *FARS 2007–2015 final report.*

because there are a lot of false positives for alcohol. Mouthwash, untreated diabetes, spicy foods, chloraseptic, and donuts can all provide false positives. Generally, by the third attempt, if alcohol is not present, the readings will return to zero. If officers believe that the offender has been drinking, the officer can request that an offender undergo a urinalysis test and request that the lab run an ethyl glucuronide test (ETG). Alcohol can remain in your system for up to 24 to 72 hours and can be detected through an ETG test.

In addition to interlock devices and alcohol monitoring, DUI offenders can also be required to go to substance abuse treatment. While traditional substance abuse treatment will address the use of alcohol and drugs, it is also important to address the belief systems that support drinking and driving. Often, DUI offenders are in need of problem-solving skills, managing peers effectively, and restructuring criminal attitudes in addition to addressing substance use issues.

DOMESTIC VIOLENCE OFFENDERS

One of the more difficult types of offender to supervise are domestic violence (DV) offenders. Similar to sexual offenders, there is a negative public perception of domestic violence offenders. Until recently, it was assumed that all DV offenders are high risk and that the population is quite homogeneous (Fagan and Wexler, 1987; Johnson and Ferraro, 2000). Even community corrections has treated domestic violence offenders as a homogeneous group—assuming that

Box 11.8
The Duluth Model

The Duluth Treatment Model was designed in the early 1980s in Duluth, Minnesota. The Duluth Model is founded on a set of principles:

- a commitment to shift responsibility for victim safety from the victim to the community and state;
- a shared collective mission and strategy regarding intervention that is based on a number of core philosophical agreements;
- a shared understanding of how interventions are to be accountable to victim safety and offender accountability;
- a shared understanding of how an agency's actions either support or undermine the collective goals and strategy of intervention;
- shared definitions of safety, battering, danger and risk, and accountability;
- prioritizing the voices and experiences of women who experience battering in the creation of those policies and procedures.

Source: Domestic Abuse Intervention Programs, 2017. Retrieved from
www.theduluthmodel.org/what-is-the-duluth-model/

they are all high risk, they all engage in violence due to misogynistic attitudes and patriarchal structures, and their criminal behavior is limited to domestic violence only (Bouffard et al., 2008). For this reason, probation and parole supervision has been based on a containment model, and treatment has been mostly limited to the Duluth Model.

While the Duluth Model is the predominant model used across probation departments and domestic violence treatment, the research is not favorable. In a meta-analysis conducted by the Washington State Institute for Public Policy (Miller et al., 2013), they found only one study that had a reduction in recidivism, while all other studies either had no effect or increased recidivism, compared to non-Duluth models in which the overall treatment effect showed a 33 percent reduction in recidivism.

There are now studies which suggest that a majority of domestic violence offenders are generalists—that the DV is just one type of crime committed by the offender. Johnson (2008) developed a set of typologies to delineate the different types of DV offenders. The first typology, the intimate terrorist or coercive controller, is generally male and is violent to control his partner. The second typology is the violent resister. The violent resister is usually the responder to the initial violence—meeting violence with violence. Often female, this type of offender combats threats of violence and physical attacks by their partner with physical attacks.

Third, situational couple violence is the result of one or both partners engaging in threats and violence, but more from a lack of coping skills, ineffective communication, and poor conflict resolution (Kelly & Johnson, 2008). Situational couple violence is the most frequent type of domestic violence, resulting in a call to the police, but minimal physical injury to either partner (Klein, 2009).

Bouffard and Zedaker (2016) wanted to understand not only the types of DV offenders, but to examine the prevalence of the typologies. Are there more generalists than specialists? Are women different from men? What they found was that men who engaged in domestic violence were most often generalists. Specifically, 53.7 percent of the men in their sample engaged in a range of criminal behavior—DV being just one type of crime. Thirty-six percent of men were identified as DV specialists—their criminal behavior was limited to primarily domestic violence. The third type, the violent offender, made up 10 percent of the male population. These offenders tended to engage in violent behavior in relationships as well as outside the relationship.

For females, the story is significantly different. Just under 70 percent of the female DV offenders were coded as specialists, suggesting that women who commit domestic violence were significantly less likely to have been arrested for other types of offenses. Twenty-three percent of the females were identified as generalists and 8 percent were identified as violent offenders. Interestingly, most males who were flagged as a violent offender were more likely to engage in violence only; while females who were identified as a violent offender tended to have a broader range of offending (drugs, theft) than their male counterparts.

With this more nuanced view of domestic violence offenders, it is important to examine the ways in which community corrections handles specialized domestic violence caseloads. Domestic violence caseloads tend to be smaller than general offender caseloads and are often more concerned with containment and accountability than rehabilitation (Burrell, 2004). Klein and Crowe (2008) found four characteristics of successful DV caseloads:

1. specialized training of supervision officers
2. mandatory treatment
3. engaged with victim
4. increased contact.

Ultimately, community supervision of domestic violence offenders must be as nuanced as the offenders themselves. Identifying risk to reoffend, the individual needs of the offender, and developing strategies to help the offender change his or her behavior will have the greatest impact on future offense.

JUVENILE OFFENDERS

In the juvenile court, disposition decisions are based on individual and social factors, offense severity, and youths' offense history. The dispositional philosophy includes a significant rehabilitation emphasis as well as many dispositional options that cover a wider range of community-based and residential services. Dispositional orders can be and often are directed to people other than the offender (family members, in particular), and dispositions may be indeterminate, based on progress toward correctional goals and treatment objectives. In some cases, the authority of the juvenile court can extend to majority age (as defined by individual states).

Box 11.9
Detention

Juvenile courts sometimes hold youths in secure detention facilities during court processing. The court may decide detention is necessary to protect the community from the juvenile's behavior, ensure a juvenile's appearance at subsequent court hearings, or secure the juvenile's own safety. Detention may also be ordered for the purpose of evaluating the juvenile. About one in five of all delinquency cases are detained. Property offenders are least likely to involve detention.

Adolescent Development

When the juvenile court system separated from the adult system, intuitively people understood that juveniles were different from adults. Prior to the separation, juveniles were seen as "mini" adults. They worked at early ages. They got married at early ages. They died at early ages. With the industrial revolution, the shift began. By 1930, every state had separated juveniles from adults in the criminal justice system. Over the past 15 years, our understanding of adolescent development has evolved significantly thanks to developmental psychologists and their ability to understand the human brain.

The United States' criminal justice system is predicated on the fact that the individual being charged is competent to stand trial, meaning that they can understand the "character and consequences of the proceedings against him or her or is able properly to assist in his or her defense" (RI Gen L, 2012). In 2005, the Supreme Court heard the case of *Roper v. Simmons.* This is the first case in which the court was presented with the overwhelming data on brain development and the fact that adolescents' brains are significantly different from adult brains (Steinberg, 2017). From there, the Supreme Court has found the death penalty and life without the possibility of parole to violate the Eighth Amendment, or that these penalties applied to adolescents equate to cruel and unusual punishment. These findings, driven by the neuroscience research, have reshaped community corrections significantly. The ultimate scientific finding that tipped the scales—the adolescent's lack of ability to self-regulate during heightened periods of social and emotional stimuli. In other words, when adolescents are faced with highly charged situations, it is very difficult for them to self-regulate, "compromising adolescents' abilities to temper strong positive and negative emotions and inclining them toward sensation-seeking, risk-taking, and impulsive antisocial acts" (Steinberg, 2017, p. 10).

Diversion Programs

Diversion programs function to divert juveniles out of the juvenile justice system, and avoid formal contact with the juvenile court. These programs include remedial education programs,[3] foster homes, group homes, community drug treatment,[4] attendance centers,[5] and local counseling facilities and centers. The effectiveness of such programs is not yet definitively documented, but preliminary evaluation reports indicate high efficacy.

In 1995, Ohio began a program entitled RECLAIM Ohio (Reasoned and Equitable Community and Local Alternatives to Incarceration of Minors). This statewide initiative is designed to assist counties in providing community services to adjudicated juvenile offenders. Essentially, local juvenile courts are given an allocation of funds to use for community-based alternatives. In turn, they must pay for most youths who are incarcerated in a state institution from their allocation. Figure 11.2 provides a review of the effects of RECLAIM in addressing juvenile offender recidivism by program type.

In 2009, Targeted RECLAIM began, which focused on the counties with the largest commitment rates. In addition to reductions in commitments, each Targeted RECLAIM county was required to develop evidence-based programs.

Research results indicated that they are successfully reducing the commitment rate of juveniles to state facilities. Figure 11.3 shows the number of admissions to state facilities before and after the implementation of RECLAIM

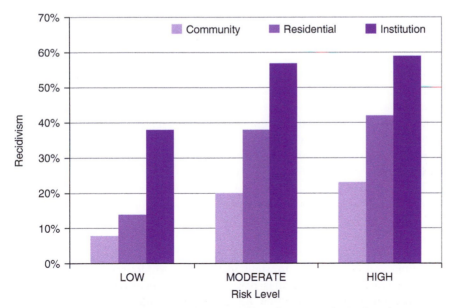

Figure 11.2 Results from Study of RECLAIM: Failure Rates by Risk and Placement Type

Source: Latessa, E., Lovins, B., Lux, J. (2014). *Evaluation of Ohio's RECLAIM programs.* Cincinnati, OH: Center for Criminal Justice Research, University of Cincinnati.

Box 11.10
Costs and Benefits of Early Childhood Intervention

A series of small-scale programs attempted to assess the costs and benefits of early childhood (prenatal through to age 4) intervention, asking if early interventions targeted at disadvantaged children benefit participating children and their families, and whether government funds invested early in the lives of children yield compensating decreases in later government expenditures.

Peter Greenwood examined five of the most rigorously designed programs for younger children; programs had a matched control group that was assigned randomly at program onset. In particular, he found:

- IQ differences between program participants and control group members approached or exceeded 10 points at the end of the program.
- The difference in rates of special education and grade retention at age 15 exceeded 20 percent (Abecedarian project).
- Participating children experienced 33 percent fewer emergency room visits through to age 4 than children in the control group (Elmira, NY Prenatal/Early Infancy Project).
- Mothers were on welfare 33 percent less time in the same Elmira Project.
- Earnings at age 27 were 60 percent higher among program participants (Perry Preschool Program).
- Benefits outweighed costs, and savings were $25,000 versus $12,000 for each family participating in the Perry program, and $24,000 versus $6,000 for each higher-risk family participating in the Elmira program.

In addition, other advantages to program participants (relative to those in the control group) were decreased criminal activity, improved educational outcomes, and improved health-related indicators such as decreased child abuse, improved maternal reproductive health, and reduced substance abuse.

Carefully targeted early childhood interventions can yield measurable benefits, and some of those benefits endure for some time after the program has ended.

Source: Greenwood (1999). See www.ncjrs.gov/pdffiles1/fs9994.pdf

---

and the later Targeted RECLAIM. As shown, there has been a significant reduction in commitments to state institutions within the Department of Youth Services. The costs savings have also been impressive, with more than $40 saved for every $1 spent on RECLAIM programs. RECLAIM has also strengthened local juvenile courts; private-sector service providers increased their participation; and cooperation across prosecutor, court, and court services increased. Failure rates were not unusually high, and the percentage of youths participating in RECLAIM who were eventually committed to state

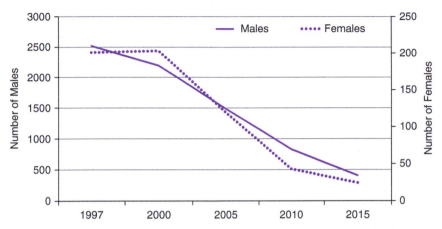

Figure 11.3 Ohio Department of Youth Services Admissions by Gender from 1997 to 2015

Source: Adapted from Ohio Department of Youth Services. (2018). Statewide felony adjudications and commitments 1997–2015. Retrieved from www.dys.ohio.gov/Portals/0/PDFs/Home/NewsAndFacts/Statistics/Msc_StatewideFelonyAdjCommit_97-15_20161103.pdf

institutions has remained low. RECLAIM is a constructive example of a strategic policy decision that included coordination and use of community corrections to avoid sending youths to secure institutions (Lowenkamp & Latessa, 2005; Latessa et al., 2014).

Aftercare and Community Corrections

The majority of juveniles committed to state-managed residential facilities and training schools are serious, chronic offenders. They will eventually be released to the community through parole and onto aftercare. Previous research has shown that recidivism rates among juvenile parolees are unacceptably high, ranging from 53 to 75 percent (Krisberg et al., 1991; Ohio Department of Youth Services, 2014). A large percentage of previously incarcerated juvenile offenders continue their criminal involvement into adulthood. A major part of the problem is that a juvenile corrections and aftercare system that fails to utilize evidence-based programs is likely to continue to face the kind of youths whom the system had either ignored or failed: serious, chronic offenders. What is needed with this population are effective interventions, intensive supervision and services, a focus on reintegration while incarcerated, and a gradual transition process that utilizes community resources and social networks. This includes aftercare planning, parole officer contact during the institutional phase, and community-based providers working within the residential setting. The latter would include working more closely with families, developing cognitive-behavioral treatment programs, supervised trips to the community, overnight or weekend home passes, substance abuse services, and mental health treatment. Virginia, Colorado, and

Nevada are implementing such efforts (Office of Juvenile Justice and Delinquency Prevention, 2000).

SUMMARY

While the front-end of the criminal justice system works from criminal records and levels of offenses, it is clear that not all offenders are the same. This chapter provides a brief overview of a few of the different populations that are served by probation and parole agencies. Ultimately, the future of community corrections depends on agencies tailoring services to these specific-need populations.

Review Questions

1. Explain "special needs" offenders.
2. What effects have public fears had on the treatment of sex offenders?
3. Does treatment for sex offenders work?
4. Describe the differences between types of domestic violence perpetrators.
5. Describe the supervision process of a DUI offender.
6. Do you think we need to have a separate system for juveniles, and if so, why?
7. Why are offenders with mental health disorders concentrated in correctional systems?
8. Explain why criminalization of the mentally ill has occurred.
9. How can corrections better respond to developmentally disabled offenders?

Notes

1   Other special needs offenders include geriatric offenders and clients with HIV. Gang members (security threat groups) are usually subsumed under institutional corrections.
2   Kerschener (1996).
3   An example of this is Project READ, San José State University.
4   Mauser et al. (1994); and Sarre (1999).
5   McDevitt et al. (1997).

Recommended Readings

Abt Associates. (1994). *Conditions of confinement: Juvenile detention and corrections facilities*. Washington, DC: Office of Juvenile Justice and Delinquency Prevention.

Bazemore, G., Umbreit, M. (1995). Rethinking the sentencing function in juvenile court: Retributive or restorative response to youth crime. *Crime & Delinquency* 41(3), 296–316.

Bouffard, L., Zedaker, S. (2016). Are domestic violence offenders specialists? Answers from multiple analytic approaches. *Journal of Research in Crime and Delinquency* 53(6), 788–813.

Eno Louden, J., Skeem, J. (2013). How do probation officers assess and manage recidivism and violence risk for probationers with mental disorder? An experimental investigation. *Law and Human Behavior* 37(1), 22–34.

Hanson, R.K., Bourgon, G., Helmus, L., Hodgson, L. (2009). The principles of effective correctional treatment also apply to sexual offenders: A meta-analysis. *Criminal Justice and Behavior* 36, 865–891. [Review of characteristics of effective treatment for sexual offenders.]

Lovins, B., Lowenkamp, C.T., Latessa, E.J. (2009). Applying the risk principle to sex offenders: Can treatment make some sex offenders worse? *Prison Journal* 89, 344–357.

Wuth, C., Cavaiola, A.A. (2016). *Assessment and treatment of the DWI offender.* Routledge.

References

Bonta, J., Blais, J., Wilson, H. (2014). A theoretically informed meta-analysis of the risk for general and violent recidivism for mentally disordered offenders. *Aggression and Violent Behavior* 19(3), 278–287.

Bouffard, L.A., Wright, K., Muftic, L., Bouffard, J. (2008). Gender differences in specialization in intimate partner violence: Comparing the gender symmetry and violent resistance perspectives. *Justice Quarterly* 25, 570–594.

Bouffard, L., Zedaker, S. (2016). Are domestic violence offenders specialists? Answers from multiple analytic approaches. *Journal of Research in Crime and Delinquency* 53(6), 788–813.

Bronson, J., Berzofsky, M. (2017). *Indicators of mental health problems reported by prisoners and jail inmates, 2011–12.* Washington, DC: U.S. Department of Justice, Bureau of Justice Statistics.

Bureau of Justice Statistics. (2002). *Criminal offenders statistics.* Washington, DC: BJS.

Burrell, W. (2004). Trends in probation and parole in the States. Retrieved from www.appa-net.org/eweb/docs/appa/pubs/TPP.pdf.

Cullen, F., Moon, M. (2002). Reaffirming rehabilitation: Public support for correctional treatment. In: H. Allen (Ed.), *What works? Risk reduction: Interventions for special needs offenders* (pp. 7–26). Lanham, MD: American Correctional Association.

Cumming, G., Finch, S. (2001). A primer on the understanding, use and calculation of confidence intervals based on central and noncentral distributions. *Educational and Psychological Measurement* 61, 530–572.

Eno Louden, J., Skeem, J. (2013). How do probation officers assess and manage recidivism and violence risk for probationers with mental disorder? An experimental investigation. *Law and Human Behavior* 37(1), 22–34.

Fagan, J., Wexler, S. (1987). Crime at home and in the streets: The relationship between family and stranger violence. *Violence and Victims* 2, 5–23.

Gallagher, C.A., Wilson, D.B., Hirschfield, P., Coggeshall, M., MacKenzie, D.L. (1999). A quantitative review of the effects of sex offender treatment on sexual reoffending. *Corrections Management Quarterly* 3, 19–29.

Greenwood, P. (1999). *Costs and benefits of early childhood intervention.* Factsheet 94. Washington, DC: Office of Juvenile Justice and Delinquency Prevention.

Hanson, R.K., Bourgon, G., Helmus, L., Hodgson, L. (2009). The principles of effective correctional treatment also apply to sexual offenders: A meta-analysis. *Criminal Justice and Behavior* 36, 865–891.

Hanson, R.K., Bussière, M.T. (1998). Predicting relapse: A meta-analysis of sexual offender recidivism studies. *Journal of Consulting and Clinical Psychology* 66, 348–362.

Hanson, R.K., Gordon, A., Harris, A.J.R., Marques, J.K., Murphy, W., Quinsey, V.L., Seto, M. (2002). First report of the collaborative outcome data project on the effectiveness of psychological treatment for sex offenders. *Sexual Abuse: A Journal of Research and Treatment* 14, 167–192.

Hanson, R.K., Harris, A.J. (2000). Where should we intervene? Dynamic predictors of sexual offender recidivism. *Criminal Justice and Behavior* 27(1), 6–35.

Hanson, R.K., Morton-Bourgon, K. (2004). *Predictors of sexual recidivism: An updated meta-analysis* (Corrections Research User Report No. 2004-02). Ottawa, ON: Public Safety Canada.

Hanson, R.K., Thornton, D. (2000). Improving risk assessment for sex offenders: A comparison of three actuarial scales. *Law and Human Behavior* 24(1), 119–136.

Harris, A.J. (2006). Risk assessment and sex offender community supervision: A context-specific framework. *Federal Probation* 70(2), 36–43.

Johnson, M., Ferraro, K. (2000). Research on domestic violence in the 1990s: Making distinctions. *Journal of Marriage and Family* 62, 948–963.

Johnson, M.P. (2008). *A typology of domestic violence: Intimate terrorism, violent resistance, and situational couple violence.* Boston, MA: Northeastern University Press.

Kelly, J., Johnson, M. (2008). Differentiation among types of intimate partner violence: Research update and implications for interventions. *Family Court Review* 46(3), 476–499.

Kerschener, R. (1996). Adolescent attitudes about rape. *Adolescence* 31(121), 29–33.

Klein, A.R. (2009). *Practical implications of current domestic violence research: For law enforcement, prosecutors and judges.* Washington, DC: U.S. Department of Justice, Office of Justice Programs.

Klein, A.R., Crowe, A. (2008). Findings from an outcome examination of Rhode Island's specialized domestic violence probation supervision program: Do specialized supervision programs of batterers reduce reabuse? *Violence Against Women* 14(2), 226–246.

Krisberg, B., Austin, J., Steele, P. (1991). *Unlocking juvenile corrections.* San Francisco, CA: National Council on Crime and Delinquency.

Latessa, E.J. (1996). Offenders with mental illness on probation. In: *Community corrections in America: New directions and sounder investments for persons with mental illness and co-disorders.* Washington, DC: National Institute of Corrections and the National Coalition for Mental and Substance Abuse Health Care in the Justice System.

Latessa, E., Lovins, B., Lux, J. (2014). *Evaluation of Ohio's RECLAIM programs*. Cincinnati, OH: Center for Criminal Justice Research, University of Cincinnati.

Lipton, D., Pearson, F., Wexler, H. (1999). *National evaluation of the Residential Substance Abuse Treatment for State Prisoners program*. New York: Development and Research Institutes.

Lösel, F., Schmucker, M. (2005). The effectiveness of treatment for sexual offenders: A comprehensive meta-analysis. *Journal of Experimental Criminology* 1, 117–146.

Lovins, B., Lowenkamp, C.T., Latessa, E.J. (2009). Applying the risk principle to sex offenders: Can treatment make some sex offenders worse? *Prison Journal* 89, 344–357.

Lovins, B., Lux, J. (2014). *Cost benefit analysis of Ohio's RECLAIM, CCF and DYS programs and facilities*. Cincinnati, OH: Center for Criminal Justice Research, University of Cincinnati.

Lowenkamp, C., Latessa, E. (2005). *Evaluation of Ohio's RECLAIM funded programs, community corrections facilities, and DYS facilities*. Cincinnati, OH: University of Cincinnati, Center for Criminal Justice Research.

Mann, R., Hanson, K., Thornton, D. (2010). Assessing risk for sexual recidivism: Some proposals on the nature of psychologically meaningful risk factors. *Sexual Abuse: A Journal of Research and Treatment* 22, 172–190.

Mauser, E., Van Stelle, K., Moberg, P. (1994). The economic impacts of diverting substance-abusing offenders into treatment. *Crime & Delinquency* 40(4), 568–588.

McDevitt, J., Domino, M., Brown, K. (1997). *Metropolitan day reporting center: An evaluation*. Boston, MA: Center for Criminal Justice Policy Research, Northeastern University.

McGrath, R.J., Lasher, M.P., Cumming, G.F. (2011). *A model of static and dynamic sex offender risk assessment*. Washington, DC: U.S. Department of Justice, National Institute of Corrections.

Miller, M., Drake, E., Nafziger, M. (2013). *What works to reduce recidivism by domestic violence offenders?* (Document No. 13-01-1201). Olympia: Washington State Institute for Public Policy.

Monahan, J., Steadman, H. (2012). Extending violence reduction principles to justice-involved persons with mental illness. In: J. Dvoskin, J. Skeem, R. Novaco, K. Douglas (Eds.), *Using social science to reduce violent offending* (pp. 245–261). Oxford University Press.

Morgan, R., Fisher, W., Wolff, N. (2010). *Center for Behavioral Health Services criminal justice research policy brief, April 2010*. New Brunswick, NJ: Rutgers University.

National Mental Health Association. (1987). *Stigma: A lack of awareness and understanding*. Alexandria, VA: National Mental Health Association.

Nesbit, I.A., Wilson, P.H., Smallbone, S.W. (2004). A prospective longitudinal study of sexual recidivism among adolescent sex offenders. *Sexual Abuse* 16(3), 223–234.

Ohio Department of Youth Services. (2018). Statewide felony adjudications and commitments 1997–2015. Retrieved from www.dys.ohio.gov/Portals/0/PDFs/Home/NewsAndFacts/Statistics/Msc_StatewideFelonyAdjCommit_97-15_20161103.pdf.

Office of Juvenile Justice and Delinquency Prevention. (2000). *Implementation of the intensive community-based aftercare program.* Washington, DC: OJJDP.

Ohio Department of Youth Services. (2014). *DYS admissions.* Columbus: Ohio Department of Youth Services.

Presser, L., Gunnison, E. (1999). Strange bedfellows. *Crime & Delinquency* 45(3), 299–315.

Quinsey, V.L., Harris, G.T., Rice, M.E., Cormier, C.A. (1998). *Violent offenders: Appraising and managing risk.* Washington, DC: American Psychological Association.

RI Gen L § 40.1-5.3-3 (2012). Competency to stand trial.

Roper v. Simmons, 543 U.S. 551 (2005).

Sarre, R. (1999). Destructuring and criminal justice reform. *Current Issues in Criminal Justice* 10(3), 259–272.

Schmucker, M., Lösel, F. (2015). The effects of sexual offender treatment on recidivism: An international analysis of sound quality evaluations. *Journal of Experimental Criminology* 11(4), 597–630.

Sentencing Project. (2002). *Mentally ill offenders in the criminal justice system: An analysis and prescription.* Washington, DC: TSP. www.sentencingproject.org/doc/publications/sl_mentallyilloffenders.pdf.

Sherman, L., Gottfredson, D., MacKenzie, D., Eck, J., Reuter, P., Bushway, S.D. (1997). *Preventing crime: What works? What doesn't? What's promising?* Washington, DC: Office of Justice Programs.

Steinberg, L. (2017). Adolescent brain science and juvenile justice policymaking. *Pyschology, Public Policy, and Law* 23(4), 410–420.

United States Department of Transportation, National Highway Traffic Safety Administration. (2017). Drunk driving. Retrieved from www.nhtsa.gov/risky-driving/drunk-driving.

Wakeling, H., Mann, R., Carter, A.J (2012). Do low-risk sexual offenders need treatment? *The Howard Journal* 51(3), 286–299.

Yates, P. (2002). What works? Effective intervention with sex offenders. In: H. Allen (Ed.), *What works? Risk reduction: Interventions for special needs offenders* (pp. 115–164). Lanham, MD: American Correctional Association.

Zavitz, R., Farkas, M. (2000). The impact of sex-offender notification on probation/parole in Wisconsin. *International Journal of Offender Therapy and Comparative Criminology* 44(1), 8–21.

Chapter 12

WOMEN AND COMMUNITY CORRECTIONS

Key Terms

dual-diagnosed	Pathways Program
GSS model	RNR model
incarceration rate	Women Helping Ourselves

Male offenders constitute the majority (more than 80 percent) of adults under correctional control. The much smaller female offender population is handled primarily within the community corrections system, although the number of imprisoned females in prison and jail is over 212,000 (Carson, 2018; Zeng, 2018). This chapter looks at the crimes that place females under correctional control, the special problems female offenders face, and what the research says about "what works".

FEMALE CORRECTIONS POPULATIONS

There are more than 1.25 million women under the care, custody, or control of adult criminal justice authorities, and about 7,200 juvenile females under secure and non-secure state-managed and contract institutions. About 85 percent of females in the correctional system are supervised in the community, and 15 percent are confined in jails and prisons (Kaeble, 2018). As seen in Figure 12.1, the percentage

	Men	Women
1990	3,746,300	601,700
2016	5,621,475	1,225,800
Percent Increase	51%	103%

Figure 12.1 A Growing Population Under Correctional Supervision: 1990–2016

Source: These figures were obtained from the Correctional Populations in the United States series. Washington, DC: Bureau of Justice Statistics.

of females in the correctional system has grown more than the male population over the past 26 years.

Women in Prison

Figure 12.2 shows the types of crime committed by females incarcerated in state prison compared to males. Females are less likely to be in prison for a violent offense, but more likely to be incarcerated for property or drug crimes. Public Order crimes are similar and include weapons and DUI offenses.

The states with the highest and lowest female **incarceration rates** per 100,000 are shown in Table 12.1. As seen in these numbers, there is a great deal of discrepancy between the states, with Massachusetts and Rhode Island showing the lowest rates at 13, and Oklahoma and Kentucky the highest at 149 and 130, respectively (Carson, 2018). So, what are some of the characteristics of these females?

Nearly seven out of ten women under correctional sanction have minor children under the age of 18. These females report an average of 2.1 minor children; these estimates translate into more than 1.3 million minor children as the offspring of women under correctional sanction. About two-thirds of state prison inmates had lived with their children prior to entering prison.

Female prisoners generally have more difficult economic circumstances than male prisoners prior to entering prison. About four in ten women in state prison reported that they had been employed full time prior to their arrest, but in terms of income, they were well below the poverty line, and nearly 30 percent of female inmates reported receiving welfare assistance.

Health issues were more problematic for female offenders than for male offenders. About 3.5 percent of the female inmate population is reported as HIV positive. About one-half of the confined female offenders reported that they had been using alcohol, other drugs, or both at the time of the offense for which they had been

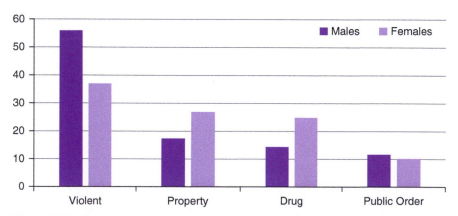

Figure 12.2 Percent of Sentenced State Prisoners by Most Serious Offense

Source: Carson, A.E. (2018). *Prisoners in 2016.* Washington, DC: Bureau of Justice Statistics.

Table 12.1 States with the Highest and Lowest Female Incarceration Rates per 100,000

HIGHEST		LOWEST	
State	**Rate**	**State**	**Rate**
Oklahoma	149	Massachusetts	13
Kentucky	130	Rhode Island	13
South Dakota	115	New Jersey	18
Idaho	113	Maine	23
Missouri	107	Maryland	26
Arizona	106	Utah	26
Wyoming	100	Vermont	26
West Virginia	95	Minnesota	28
Texas	92	Alaska	30
		California	30

Source: Carson, A.E. (2018). *Prisoners in 2016*. Washington, DC: Bureau of Justice Statistics.

incarcerated. Illicit drug use was reported more often than alcohol use. On every measure of illicit drug abuse (ever used, using regularly, using in the month before the offense, and using at the time of the offense), female offenders had higher rates of use than male offenders. Male offenders, however, had higher alcohol use on every measure of alcohol ingestion. An estimated 25 percent of women on probation, 30 percent of women in local jails and in state prisons, and 15 percent of women in federal prison had been consuming alcohol at the time of their offense. Nearly one in three women serving time in state prisons said that they had committed the offense that brought them to prison in order to obtain money to support their need for drugs.

Nearly 56 percent of women substance abusers in state prisons reported having received treatment for their alcohol and other drug abuse, and one in five said treatment had occurred since entry to prison. Another one-third said they had joined a voluntary program (such as Alcoholics Anonymous or Narcotics Anonymous) since entering prison. Forty-four percent of women under correctional authority reported that they were assaulted physically or sexually at some time during their lives. Forty-eight percent of women reporting an assault said that it had occurred before the age of 18.[1]

Women in Jail

The number of women in local jails increased from just over 98,000 in 2015 to just over 107,000 in 2016 (Zeng, 2018). Among convicted female inmates, nearly two-fifths reported that they had committed their first offense under the influence of drugs. Approximately four in ten used drugs daily. About one in four convicted female jail inmates reported that they committed their current offense to get money

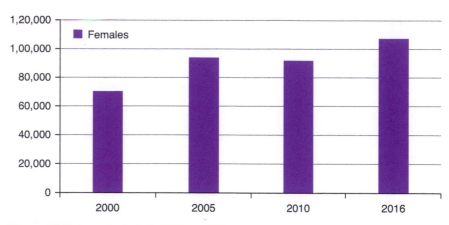

Figure 12.3 Females in Jail: 2000 to 2016

Source: Zeng, Z. (2018). *Jail inmates in 2016*. Washington, DC: Bureau of Justice Statistics.

to buy drugs. Some two-thirds of the jailed women had children under the age of 18, and most of these were with either a grandparent or father. Figure 12.3 shows how the population of females in jails has changed since 2000.

Mental illness among female jail inmates also appears to be high. Some studies have shown that nearly 80 percent of females in jail reported at least one lifetime psychiatric disorder, most commonly substance abuse or dependence, and post-traumatic stress disorder (PTSD). Rates for all psychiatric disorders (particularly depression) were significantly higher than those of the general population. Few female jail inmates appear to receive in-facility treatment, primarily because inmates' needs far exceeded current resources.[2]

Women who use drugs often have a host of other problems including health-related issues. In addition, minority women may face additional cultural and language barriers that can hinder or affect treatment and recovery. Many drug-using women do not seek treatment because they are afraid. They fear not being able to take care of or keep their children, reprisals from their spouses or boy-friends, and punishment from the authorities in the community. Many women report that their drug-using male partners initiated them into drug abuse. Finally, research indicates that drug-dependent women have great difficulty abstaining from drugs when the lifestyle of their male partner is one that supports drug use. Approximately 40 percent of female jail inmates grew up in a single-parent house-hold, and an additional 17 percent lived in a household without either parent. Close to one-third of all women in jail had a parent or guardian who abused alcohol or other drugs, and four in ten reported that another family member (usually brother or sister) had been incarcerated (Teplin et al., 1997).

This brief examination of jail inmates suggests a group of offenders with high needs who were victimized frequently as they were growing up. Broken homes, sexual and physical abuse, minority status, and parental/guardian abuse of alcohol or drugs characterize a large portion of the female jail population. This segment of offenders is not generally likely to receive effective treatment for the major, underlying problems. After an average stay of less than 6 months, most will be returned to the community to continue to break their drug dependences and, for the most part, their efforts will fail without intensive assistance (Teplin et al., 1997). It is, of course, possible for drug-dependent women, of any age, to overcome drug addiction, and those who have been most successful have had the help and support of significant others, family members, treatment providers, friends, and the community. We discuss specific issues later in this chapter.

Women on Parole

Despite the recent emphasis on studying female offenders, relatively little is known about females on parole. In 2016, females were an estimated 13 percent of all parolees, up from 8 percent in 1990. That translates into more than 113,000 female parolees (Kaeble, 2018). The growth in the number of female parolees reflects higher offending rates, more arrests per offense, increased commitments to prison per arrest, and parole recommitments. The lifetime likelihood of a female going to state or federal prison is now more than 1 percent, although Hispanic women have a 50 percent higher likelihood than white women. Black, non-Hispanic women have a likelihood of incarceration that is seven times that of white women.

Most women sent to prison have several factors that will work against successful reintegration following parole. Alcohol and other drug use, primary childcare responsibility, unemployment and few occupational skills, a history of sexual abuse, and incomplete education are difficult to overcome when treatment is a low priority to resource-strapped systems. A gap also exists between institutional treatment and transition to the community. Mental health is also an issue that faces many women during re-entry. In a recent study of re-entry and mental health, Bakken and Visher (2018) found that women with a mental health issue were significantly more likely to report experiencing poor health, hallucinations, suicidal thoughts, and trouble with violence. They were also three times more likely to report being hospitalized after release than men. Women with mental health issues were more likely to report substance abuse, criminal behavior, rearrest, and re-incarceration than men. Clearly, without meaningful treatment, one should not be surprised at high recidivism rates.

Female on street-cleaning work detail, San Francisco Jail, San Francisco Sheriff's Department/Sheriff's Work Alternative Program. *[Photo courtesy of Harry Allen]*

Women on Probation

Probation has the greatest number of offenders under correctional supervision and this is also true for females. About 25 percent of those on probation are females, which translates

---

Box 12.1
Talbert House Pathways Program

Pathways is a residential treatment program for adult female felony offenders on supervision. Services include curriculum to target criminal thinking, addiction treatment, medication-assisted treatment, trauma, life skills, vocational services, and electronic monitoring (GPS). Some of the benefits the program gives are help in finding and keeping a job; safe and temporary housing; help in reconnecting with family; learning how to stay out of prison, how to save money, how to communicate and solve problems, how to live independently; individualized treatment planning and case management; medical services.

---

into about 931,000 in 2016. This is up from 22 percent in 2000. Females on probation are usually subjected to the same conditions and supervision practice as males (see Chapter 4). The high percentage of females on probation compared to the percentage in prison or jail is probably due to several factors. First, females commit fewer violent and sex crimes than males, crimes which tend to draw harsher sentences. Second, some judges will also consider mitigating factors in sentencing, such as children, prior abuse, and harm to the victim. Finally, given the high percentage of women with substance abuse problems, many judges will seek community treatment options before prison. An example of a program specifically for women is described in Box 12.1. Pathways is a part of Talbert House, a large human services agency based in Cincinnati, Ohio, and is designed to serve women on probation or parole.

In order to examine some of the risk factors for women on probation, we examined some assessment data from Harris County (Houston, TX), based on the Texas Risk Assessment System. There are over 10,000 women on probation in Harris County, and the results in Figure 12.4 are based on a sample of over 2,600. These data indicate that over 50 percent of the women in this sample were high- or moderate-risk in a number of areas including criminal history, family and social support, substance use, peer associations, and attitudes and behavioral patterns.

Women in Residential Programs

If you recall, some of the first halfway houses in America were designed to assist women (see Chapter 10). While the number of such programs is unknown, many larger cities have residential facilities specifically for women. While some are non-secure halfway houses, others are used in lieu of jail and are designed to provide a host of programs and services. One example is Women Helping Ourselves (WHO). This facility is part of the community corrections system in Harris County, Texas, and is described in Box 12.2.

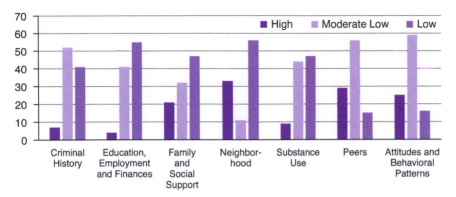

Figure 12.4 Risk Areas for a Sample of Women on Probation

Source: Data are based on a sample of over 2,600 women on probation in Harris County (Houston, TX) assessed with the Texas Risk Assessment System.

Women and Substance Abuse Treatment

Box 12.2
Women Helping Ourselves (WHO)

The WHO program is a women's 95-bed facility designed to better accommodate women's special needs and problems. The program comprises 6 to 12 months of residential services designed to assist female clients in addressing their substance abuse issues along with targeting antisocial attitudes, feelings, peer associations, and personality factors that are correlated with future criminal behavior. The treatment model is based on a cognitive-behavioral model and targets belief systems as well as teaching staff skills training in self-control and self-management. There is also a Residential Aftercare Program of intensive supervision after successful completion of the residential phases, designed to reinforce that which has been learned and to provide support for the women as they incorporate new ways of thinking into their lives.

Eligibility criteria:

- Females
- Low-moderate to high risk
- No significant physical health/mental health issues that would impede participating in group treatment
- At least one of the following criteria:
- high substance abuse or dependency issues
- unable to maintain sobriety/prosocial lifestyle in outpatient setting.

The recent opiate epidemic that has hit much of the country has not spared females and there is widespread need for effective treatment programs for substance abuse by female offenders. Research has shown that women receive the most benefit from drug treatment programs that provide comprehensive services for meeting their basic needs, including access to the following:

- food, clothing, and shelter
- transportation
- job counseling and training
- legal assistance
- literacy training and educational opportunities
- parenting training
- family therapy
- couples counseling
- medical care
- childcare
- social services
- social support
- psychological assessment and mental health care
- assertiveness training.

A comprehensive spectrum of services is needed for female offenders at every level of the criminal justice system. After all, even those incarcerated usually return to the community. Drug treatment programs are often in short supply, and since there are fewer female offenders, especially in jails, programs may not provide all of the services needed for this population. In addition, research also suggests that a continuing relationship with a treatment provider is an important factor throughout treatment for female offenders (TIP, 2009). Any individual may experience lapses and relapses during the treatment process. Learning how to identify and avoid circumstances that may lead to relapse is important. This is a treatment thrust for many community programs.

Jail-based projects include therapeutic communities (e.g., Sisters in Sober Treatment Empowered in Recovery [SISTERS], San Francisco, California; and Stepping Out, San Diego) that have a wide range of treatment programs (modalities). Aftercare (post-jail release) components provide intensive outpatient services and sober living, job development and placement assistance, referrals to supportive services, and a mutual-help group created for and by ex-offenders (Kassebaum, 1999). An example can be seen in Box 12.3.

Another example of the issues facing women can be seen in an example from Georgia. The state of Georgia faced a correctional population with 10 percent of males and 27 percent of females classified as mental health cases. The Georgia Board of Pardons and Parole reported on the Georgia Treatment and Aftercare for Probationers and Parolees (TAPP) program to boost post-prison support for Georgia's mentally ill and developmentally disabled offenders. A TAPP mental health professional in each service area acts as case manager to non-violent mental health offenders returned to the area, monitoring offenders'

Box 12.3
Sisters in Sobriety

Sisters in Sobriety is an organization dedicated to helping women in recovery with children; keeping mother and children together and cared for while they concentrate on getting better and conquering their addiction without fear of losing their children; offering a safe place where these women can come for the support and fellowship needed to succeed in their recovery.

Sober houses employ volunteers to assist in the seemingly unimportant and often forgotten daily chores, allowing these women to care for their children and learn or expand on the skill sets that will empower them to re-enter the workforce with the knowledge and confidence to secure jobs, obtain housing, and flourish so that they may be able to support their children and families on their own, pay taxes, and do the next right things that will eventually lead to a better life.

Source: Sisters in Sobriety (http://sistersinsobrietycleveland.com/index.html)

---

behavior and arranging ongoing community support and treatment. Such transitional programs are examples of the needed coordination between incarceration and gradual reintegration into the community for female offenders (Georgia Board of Pardons and Parole, 2005). Such coordination is needed throughout the corrections system.

Since substance abuse and mental illness are often co-occurring, there is a need for programs to work with what are called the **dual-diagnosed**. One example of a residential program that serves this population is illustrated in Box 12.4.

Box 12.4
Dual Diagnosis Residential Program (DDRP)

This program is a 100-bed Community Corrections Facility for male and female clients of all age groups who have been identified as having a significant mental health impairment. The DDRP program provides a 6-month residential substance abuse treatment integrated with mental health treatment services to clients identified with co-occurring mental health issues/substance abuse. The clients participate in mental health counseling on an individual and group basis to address their co-occurring disorders. A Booster Track is available to clients who upon release struggle in the transition and need a short-term intervention. Aftercare services will be provided for all clients. Upon completion of the MH Residential Program, cases are placed on probation in the Mental Health Initiative Specialized Caseloads.

Eligibility criteria

- Low-moderate to high risk on the TRAS
- Significant mental health issue (major depression, psychotic disorders, bipolar disorders)
- High substance abuse or dependency issues as identified on the TRAS
- Global Assessment Functioning (GAF) level of 50 or below
- Significant barriers to maintaining stability in the community.

WHAT WORKS FOR FEMALES

A number of scholars have studied the pathway to criminal behavior for females (Chesney-Lind, 2000; Daly, 1992) and have argued that females often follow different paths to criminal behavior from males. For example, Daly identified five paths. These comprise:

1. **street women** (those with more serious criminal histories who have often been abused and are substance addicts);
2. **harmed and harming women** (those who have experienced abuse or neglect as children and may be violent and have other psychological problems);
3. **battered women** who experienced abuse in romantic relationships;
4. **drug-connected women** (those who use or sell drugs as a result of relationships with men or family);
5. **"other"** (whose crimes are largely economically motivated).

While the pathways may indeed be different for some males and females, the question remains, "What works for females?" in reducing recidivism. Most agree that there are many fewer programs and services for females, and many of the programs on offer to women are male-oriented.

There are two competing schools of thought. Feminist scholars believe that trauma, mental health, parental stress, unsafe housing, anxiety/depression, family support, and self-esteem are risk factors. This approach is referred to as the **Gender Specific Strategy (GSS)**. Other scholars believe that the major risk factors are similar for males and females (see Chapter 6), and see these as barriers or responsivity factors that need to be addressed in order to improve treatment outcomes. This is the **risk, need, and responsivity model (RNR)**. Some of the differences between these two perspectives are illustrated in Table 12.2.

The GSS research is often criticized for using small samples, qualitative methods that lack generalizability, and failing to compare males and females in their studies. Critics of RNR contend that much of the research relies on male-oriented groups and assumes that the findings are true for both males and females.

Table 12.2 Differences between RNR and GSS

RNR	GSS
Risk assessment should be objective and standardized to determine risk and needs	Assessment should be qualitative, review of social history to better understand the pathways
Focus should be on criminogenic needs	Focus is often on non-criminogenic needs
Views mental illness, depression, self-esteem, housing, etc., as responsivity factors	Views mental illness, depression, self-esteem, housing, etc., as risk factors
Treatment approaches should use structured behavioral strategies, such as CBT, that focus on current risk factors and are action-oriented	Treatment approaches should be based on process-oriented groups that focus on relationships and empowerment

So, what does the research tell us? In terms of risk assessment, the evidence supports the use of actuarial instruments for both males and females. In a study of more than 14,000 females, Smith and her colleagues (2009) found that the Level of Service Inventory–Revised (LSI-R) predicted recidivism equally well for males and females. Since the LSI-R is based on the major criminogenic needs identified by Andrews and Bonta (1996), this study would indicate that risk factors for males and females are often similar. Similarly, in a study examining the risk principle with females, Brusman Lovins et al. (2007) found that the treatment effects were higher for high-risk females, confirming that the risk principle has wide application and is applicable for females as well as males.

In a meta-analysis of the RNR model for females, Dowden and Andrews (1999) found support for the RNR model for females. Figure 12.5 shows the results and indicates that when risk, need, and responsivity were taken into consideration, the effects on recidivism were greater for females. In a meta-analysis of cognitive-behavioral programs, Landenberger and Lipsey (2005) found that CBT was equally effective for males and females. In a 2016 meta-analysis, Gobeil et al. compared gender-neutral versus gender-informed approaches. Across all studies, gender-neutral and gender-informed approaches were equally effective; however, when limited to studies with higher methodological quality, gender-informed interventions showed slightly larger effect sizes.

Finally, the results from a 2018 follow-up of released prisoners found that 76.8 percent of females were rearrested within 9 years of release, compared to 84.2 percent for males (Alper et al., 2018). Figure 12.6 shows the rates of failure by year. While females did slightly better than males, the failure rates of both groups are exceedingly high, with between 35 and 22 percent of women arrested each year over a 9-year period.

Despite the debate, there is clearly a need for more research on justice-involved females, and failure rates remain too high. While females may have

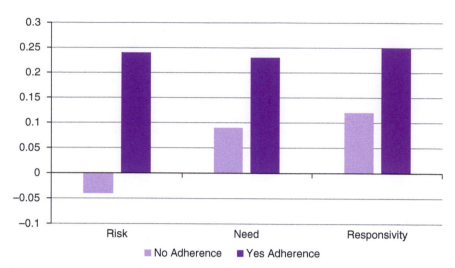

Figure 12.5 Average Effect Size on Recidivism for Adherence to the RNR Model for Studies that Only Included Females

Source: Dowden, C., Andrews, D.A. (1999). What works for female offenders: A meta-analytic review. *Crime and Delinquency* 45, 438–452.

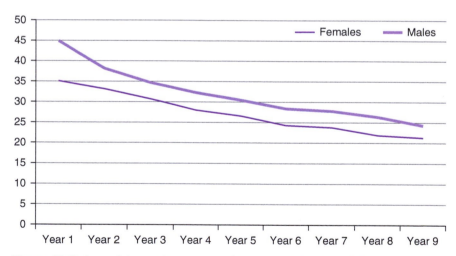

Figure 12.6 Annual Arrest Percentage of Prisoners: Nine Year Follow-Up for Males and Females

Source: Alper, M., Markman, J., Durose, M.R. (2018). *2018 update on prisoner recidivism: A 9-year follow-up period (2005–2014)*. Washington, DC: Bureau of Justice Statistics.

different pathways to criminal behavior than males and more barriers, the research is clear about one thing: Well-designed and properly implemented programs and services can reduce recidivism, and there is a growing need for more programs.

SUMMARY

Our discussion of females involved in the correctional system suggests that they are not a unitary group of similarly situated offenders, but a complex combination of individuals facing the problems of living, complicated by self-defeating behaviors that require change. Women often have certain distinct characteristics and problems that are related to offense situations and basic needs, almost all of which are not addressed effectively. While they are alike in that they have been convicted of criminal activities, underlying those events are unaddressed social, family, personal, and medical needs best handled through treatment. Future corrections will need to apply a range of classification systems to determine the most effective way to manage and treat females.

Review Questions

1. Why do you believe the female prison population has grown?
2. What are the differences between the RNR and GSS models?
3. What are the pathways for females involved in the justice system?
4. What are some of the special needs of female offenders?
5. Why is there a higher proportion of females on probation than in prison or jail?
6. What usually constitutes a dual-diagnosis?

Notes

1   Much of this was drawn from: Glaze and Maruschak (2008); Garza and Ritter (2012).
2   Much of this was drawn from: Teplin et al. (1997); James and Glaze (2006).

Recommended Readings

Belknap, J. (2007). *The invisible woman: Gender, crime and justice*. 3rd ed. Stamford, CT: Wadsworth.
Latessa, E.J., Listwan, S., Koetzle, D. (2015). *What works (and doesn't) in reducing recidivism*. New York: Routledge.
Matthews, B., Hubbard, D.J. (2008). Moving ahead: Five essential elements for working effectively with girls. *Journal of Criminal Justice* 36, 494–502.

References

Alper, M., Markman, J., Durose, M.R. (2018). *2018 update on prisoner recidivism: A 9-year follow-up period (2005–2014)*. Washington, DC: Bureau of Justice Statistics.

Andrew, D.A., Bonta, J. (1996). *The psychology of criminal conduct*. Cincinnati, OH: Anderson Publishing.

Bakken, N.W., Visher, C.A. (2018). Successful reintegration and mental health: An examination of gender differences among reentering offenders. *Criminal Justice and Behavior* 45, 1121–1135.

Brusman Lovins, L., Lowenkamp, C.T., Latessa, E.J., Smith, P. (2007). Application of the risk principle to female offenders. *Journal of Contemporary Criminal Justice* 23(4), 383–398.

Carson, A.E. (2018). *Prisoners in 2016*. Washington, DC: Bureau of Justice Statistics.

Chesney-Lind, M. (2000). Women and the criminal justice system: Gender matters. In: *Topics in community corrections: Responding to women offenders in the community* (pp. 7–10). Washington, DC: National Institute of Corrections.

Daly, K. (1992). Women's pathways to felony court: Feminist theories of lawbreaking and problems of representation. *Southern California Review of Law and Women's Studies* 2, 11–52.

Dowden, C., Andrews, D.A. (1999). What works for female offenders: A meta-analytic review. *Crime and Delinquency* 45, 438–452.

Garza, M., Ritter, N. (2012). *Improving access to services for female offenders returning to the community*. Washington, DC: National Institute of Justice.

Georgia Board of Pardons and Parole. (2005). *FY 2005 annual report*. Georgia: State Board of Pardons and Paroles. Available at https://pap.georgia.gov/.

Glaze, L., Maruschak, L. (2008). Parents in prison and their minor children. Bureau of Justice Statistics Special Report NCJ 222984. Washington, DC: Bureau of Justice Statistics. Retrieved from https://bjs.gov/content/pub/pdf/pptmc.pdf

Gobeil, R., Blanchette, K., Stewart, L. (2016). A meta-analytic review of correctional interventions for women offenders: Gender-neutral versus gender-informed approaches. *Criminal Justice and Behavior* 43, 301–322.

James, D.J., Glaze, L.E. (2006). Mental health problems of prison and jail inmates. Bureau of Justice Statistics Special Report NDJ 213600. Retrieved from www.bjs.gov/content/pub/pdf/mhppji.pdf.

Kaeble, D. (2018). *Probation and parole in the United States, 2016*. Washington, DC: Bureau of Justice Statistics.

Kassebaum, P. (1999). *Substance abuse treatment for women offenders: Guide to promising practices. Technical Assistance Publication Series 23* [DHHS Publication No. (SMA) 00-3454]. Rockville, MD: U.S. Department of Health and Human Services.

Landenberger, N., Lipsey, M. (2005). The positive effects of cognitive-behavioral programs for offenders: A meta-analysis of factors associated with effective treatment. *Journal of Experimental Criminology* 1, 451–476.

Smith, P., Cullen, F.T., Latessa, E.J. (2009). Can 14,737 women be wrong? A meta-analysis of the LSI-R and recidivism for female offenders. *Criminology and Public Policy* 8(1).

Teplin, L., Abrams, K., McClelland, G. (1997). Prevalence of psychiatric disorders among incarcerated women. *Archives of General Psychiatry* 53(2), 505–512.

TIP. (2009). Treatment Improvement Protocol (TIP) series, No. 51. Rockville (MD): Center for Substance Abuse Treatment, Substance Abuse and Mental Health Services Administration (U.S.).

Zeng, Z. (2018). *Jail inmates in 2016.* Washington, DC: Bureau of Justice Statistics.

Chapter 13

PROBLEM-SOLVING COURTS

Key Terms

drug courts

Harrison Act of 1914

mental health courts

net widening

problem-solving courts

re-entry court

truancy courts

veterans' courts

war on drugs

> Serving a jail sentence would've been a lot easier, but I don't know if I would've come out on the other end. —Joe M. (Drug Court Graduate)

THE DEVELOPMENT OF DRUG COURTS

Although some people might not consider **drug courts** to be an intermediate sanction, it appears that they fall into this category when you consider that they usually combine close probation supervision with substance abuse treatment in an attempt to keep the offender from being incarcerated. Indeed, the phenomenal growth and expansion of drug courts can be largely attributed to dissatisfaction with traditional methods of dealing with drug offenders, and the belief that drug courts will reduce substance abuse and criminal behavior through close judicial monitoring and community-based treatment services. According to Belenko (1998), drug courts differ from traditional courts in several important ways. First, drug courts attempt to manage cases quickly and make provisions for the treatment to start as soon as possible after arrest. Second, drug courts have adopted a collaborative rather than the adversarial approach found in most traditional courts. Third, judges in drug courts are actively involved in the cases, holding regular status hearings, meeting regularly with treatment providers and probation officers, and providing feedback to the offender. Finally, drug courts focus on providing treatment services rather than simply increasing sanctions.

The United States has been waging a **war on drugs** for more than 40 years and most of that effort has been spent on law enforcement and interdiction efforts. While stopping the flow of illegal drugs is important, it is the insatiable demand that keeps the drugs coming. Indeed, we cannot even keep drugs out of prisons, our most secure institutions, so what chance do we have to secure the borders?

Tired of the endless cycle of substance abusers coming through the court system and the failure of traditional approaches, many judges have begun to take the matter into their own hands by embracing drug courts as an alternative to jail or probation. Indeed, based on the drug courts model, a number of other "specialty" or therapeutic courts have emerged, including courts for mental health, veterans, driving under the influence (DUI), family, re-entry, domestic violence, guns, gambling, co-occurring disorders, and others. This chapter will examine the development and components of drug courts and some of their counterparts and look at the research concerning their effectiveness.

THE EMERGENCE OF THE DRUG COURT

There were three predominant conditions that set the stage for the emergence of the drug court. First, the war on drugs and "get tough" sentencing provided a continuous stream of non-violent drug offenders into the system. Second, the public's growing fear of drugs and violence, spurred on by the media focus and political agendas. Third, the ineffectiveness of the traditional system to treat drug-addicted offenders effectively. Separately, these conditions may not have had much of an effect, but together they created an opportunity for the drug court to take hold.

The War on Drugs

By 1989, the war on drugs was in full swing. Although many cite President Nixon as the initial commander in chief of the war on drugs, it actually can be traced to the **Harrison Act of 1914** (Belenko, 1998). The Harrison Act was designed to limit the access that drug users had to cocaine and opiates by making it illegal for medical professionals to supply addicts with drugs. By 1914, opiate and cocaine use had started to cause significant social problems including a spike in violence (Wisotsky, 1991). The Harrison Act was designed to reduce the use of cocaine and opiates by making the punishment severe enough that it would deter doctors from prescribing them to their patients. Although well intended, the Harrison Act was the first of many laws that the federal government has enacted through the war on drugs that led to the incarceration of many non-violent drug offenders. By 1928, one-third of the federal prison population was incarcerated owing to drug use, primarily as a consequence of the Harrison Act (Jones, 1995). Of course, the rise in the inmate population had a significant impact on the prison system's resources. Crowding, limited ability to supervise offenders, and lack of treatment were cited by wardens as primary problems associated with the rise in the prison population during this period (United States House of Representatives, 1928).

The next battle generally associated with the war on drugs was the Marihuana Tax Act of 1937. Initially focused on reducing the impact that hemp had on the textile and paper markets, the act leveraged a tax on all sales of hemp and any of its by-products. The maximum penalty for not paying the tax was a fine and up to 4 years' imprisonment for both the seller and the buyer. Although initially focused on the production of hemp, many local jurisdictions applied the law to individuals who possessed marijuana for personal use. Like the Harrison Act, the unforeseen consequence of this act was the significant spike in the number of offenders processed through the court and ultimately incarcerated (Wisotsky, 1991).

As the number of drug offenders processed through the courts increased, political responses to the war on drugs toughened. Near the middle of the twentieth century, drug users were again blamed for a significant portion of the country's violent crimes, leading to the third stage of the war on drugs (McBride & McCoy, 1997). During this time, the Boggs amendment to the Harrison Act set mandatory sentences for opiate possession, and the Narcotics Control Act increased the penalties for possession and distribution of narcotics (Sharp, 1994). By 1971, the war on drugs had reached the national spotlight. President Nixon, in a speech to the nation, identified drug abuse as a national epidemic and influenced Congress to pass the Comprehensive Drug Abuse Prevention and Control Act (Marion, 1994).

The effects of the Comprehensive Drug Abuse Prevention and Control Act of 1970 were felt immediately. The most important change was that Congress scheduled (or ranked) drugs based on their potential for harm against their medical utility. According to the new schedule, more dangerous drugs with no medical purpose, like LSD and marijuana, were reserved for Schedule I; while drugs with some medicinal purposes, like cocaine and methadone, were placed in Schedule II. Congress also provided some discretion to judges on sentencing, allowing probation to be given to drug offenders who were convicted of minor possession (Marion, 1994).

As the war on drugs progressed, the initial discretion provided to judges under the 1970 act was significantly limited. Under the original act, judges could sentence offenders to probation if the drugs were for personal use only. Under the Sentencing Reform Act of 1984 and the Anti-Drug Abuse Act of 1986, personal use was defined by the amount (or weight) of the drug, not the intent to sell, resulting in a significant spike in the number of offenders incarcerated for drug possession. By 1989, when the first drug court was implemented, almost 20 percent of the prison population was serving time for a drug crime (Snell, 1991).

Simultaneous to the war on drugs, the criminal justice system experienced a wave of "get tough" policies, which resulted in heavier reliance on prison as a primary intervention. The "get tough" era continued to impact drug offenders through the late 1970s and into the 1980s. The focus became less on probation and community services and more on incarceration. Mandatory minimum prison sentences were introduced across the nation. States adopted special punishments for offenders found guilty of having crack cocaine, in an effort to deter people from engaging in the violence associated with its use (Reinarman & Levine, 2004). Similar to the Harrison Act of 1914, these "get tough" laws had several unintended consequences. First and foremost, the cocaine laws were routinely applied unequally across social classes. Powder cocaine use rarely resulted in prison time, while drug offenders who were caught with crack cocaine faced mandatory prison sentences. Second, for those who remained in the community, high levels of supervision were provided regardless of the risk for recidivating. While these intensive services are needed for a select few, lower-risk offenders placed on intensive supervision can actually recidivate at higher rates (Lowenkamp & Latessa, 2004). Finally, in many states, three-strikes laws resulted in lifetime sentences for violation of minor drug laws, resulting in significant overcrowding of prison populations.

Public Fear of Drugs and Violence

At the same time that the first drug court was being implemented, the public concern about drug use was at a historic high (Levine & Reinarman, 1988). In August 1989, 64 percent of those polled by *The New York Times/CBS* (Oreskes, 1989) identified drugs as the number one problem facing the United States. This anti-drug sentiment was a complete reversal of the favorable attitudes of the 1970s. In fact, in 1978, nearly seven out of ten high school seniors reported that marijuana should be legalized for personal use. By 1980, 11 states had decriminalized small quantities of marijuana and several more had bills in front of their state legislatures to do the same (Johnson et al., 1989).

By 1980, however, the attitudes toward drugs had started to shift. National polls suggested that the public's tolerance of drug use had begun to decrease. States like Oregon and Alaska, which had legalized marijuana in the previous decade, reversed direction and passed laws that once again criminalized personal use of marijuana (Goode & Ben-Yehuda, 1994). As the country began to adopt anti-drug sentiments, crack cocaine hit the mainstream media. With drugs regarded as instantly addictive and tied directly to violent crimes, the war on drugs gained even more momentum. Media reports suggested that crack was widely available, was associated with high levels of violence, and caused significant birth defects in newborn babies (Reinarman & Levine, 2004). Television commercials depicting the effects of crack cocaine routinely aired (Oreskes, 1989). Even President George Herbert Bush, during a nationally televised primetime address, identified drugs as the most significant problem facing the nation and declared the United States at war (Kagay, 1990).

Ineffectiveness of the Criminal Justice System to Treat Drug Offenders

The third condition that set the stage for the implementation of the drug court was the lack of effective interventions for drug offenders. Since the Harrison Act was passed, the criminal justice system has struggled with managing the increased number of drug offenders. As early as 1928, wardens in the federal prisons complained that the drug offenders presented unique challenges to a prison system (United States House of Representatives, 1928). Since then, the number of drug offenders in the state and federal system has skyrocketed. To combat increasing prison populations, the federal prison system developed alternative placements for prison called Narcotic Farms. These minimum-security camps were designed as a diversion from prison for drug offenders. They were in operation for nearly 50 years, but in 1975, after widespread reports of inmate abuses and ineffective programming, they were closed (Campbell et al., 2008).

Beyond the Narcotic Farms, treatment programs were under fire. Martinson (1974) had just published an article where he and colleagues had found null effects for treatment. Although the criminal justice system had been focused on rehabilitation for the past 75 years, the goals of the system began to shift to deterrence and incapacitation. As stated earlier, the legislature began to control judges' discretion by placing mandatory minimums on specific types of drug offenses and limiting those where the offender could be sentenced to probation. At the same time that treatment was challenged, funding for criminal justice efforts (e.g., community surveillance, incarceration) had grown 62 percent (Lock et al., 2002). Clearly, treatment had taken a back seat to strategies of incapacitation and deterrence. During this time period, the prison population grew by nearly 300 percent (Lurigio, 2000).

By 2002, when drug courts were in full swing, there were nearly 200,000 drug offenders incarcerated. Processing speeds were slow, causing a log jam of offenders in the courts. Drug offenders were often arrested for new offenses before they even made it through court. Early attempts to provide pretrial services to drug offenders were fragmented and lacked continuity. There was some hope when federal funds created Treatment Alternatives to Street Crime (TASC), but there were still significant problems with integrating treatment services into the court when TASC was introduced (Falkin, 1993).

Even with rising concerns about drug use and the lack of treatment options, the nation was still highly supportive of providing prevention and treatment in lieu of incarceration. Lock et al. (2002) found that 83 percent of those surveyed believed that the nation should maintain or increase spending on treatment, while 92 percent supported spending as much, if not more, money on prevention services. The problem in the mid-1980s was finding treatment services that were effective for drug offenders.

The First Drug Court

The traditional criminal justice system clearly faced a number of barriers in addressing the needs of drug offenders. In 1989, Judge Klein of Dade County, Florida, formed a specialized docket for drug offenders in order to address the major gaps of the traditional system. The problem with the traditional system, as he saw it, was that it had become overburdened with the adversarial process. Drug offenders were sitting on dockets too long without treatment, and previous attempts to speed up the process resulted in just cycling the offenders through the system more quickly, but with no more success. To combat these gaps, he set forth to develop a collaborative process among the courtroom work group. Its focus was no longer on guilt and innocence, but what was the best course of action to help this defendant succeed in living a more prosocial life.

Freeing the prosecutor, defense attorney, judge, treatment provider, and defendant to work together to find the best option for the defendant addressed several deficiencies with the current system. First, the processing speed of the case increases significantly. Since there is limited friction between members of the courtroom work group, the system can process the defendant more quickly and ensure that the needs of the defendant are met in a timely fashion. Second, the defendant is available to enter treatment more quickly and therefore has less time at risk before receiving help. Historically, the waiting list for programming could be extremely long, and research suggests that the longer a person waits for treatment, the more likely he or she is to drop out (Belenko, 1998). Third, all parties are working together to help the defendant be successful; therefore, all interventions are geared toward behavioral change.

The second major area that the drug court addressed was the lack of oversight. In a traditional court, the probation officer takes the primary role of monitoring the defendant. In the drug court model, the judge or magistrate is the primary "case coordinator." The role of the judge is shifted to more of an agent of change than in a traditional court. The defendant is scheduled on a regular basis (usually weekly at the start) to attend a review hearing in which the his or her progress is discussed with all the key personnel. Hence, the participant is being monitored on a regular and consistent basis by the court.

Third, the drug court takes an active role in the treatment of the defendant. Community providers are part of the proceedings and provide ongoing updates to the team so as to remain up to date on the defendant's progress. If the defendant is progressing appropriately, the court is available to provide reinforcements, and if he or she is sliding, the court can provide timely interventions. Historically, treatment providers have not been active players in the court proceedings, if available at all. This model ensures that all relevant information is shared with the parties involved with the defendant. Furthermore, it promotes the integration of treatment with the court process.

Growth of Drug and Specialty Courts

Starting with the first drug court in Miami, the drug court has taken the criminal justice system by storm. Not since the separation of the adult and juvenile courts has there been such a significant change in how defendants are processed through the court system. After its initial development in 1989, the drug court concept quickly took root. Although adversaries of the drug court model predicted that the novelty would dissipate, it has grown exponentially each year (Huddleston et al., 2008). There were ten drug courts in 1992, and by 1998, there were 275 drug courts in operation, serving an estimated 90,000 offenders (Drug Court Programs Office, 1998). Figure 13.1 shows the rapid growth of drug court since their inception in 1989. As of 2015, there were 3,142 drug and other specialty courts operating in the United States. Table 13.1 shows the current number of drug and some related specialty courts operating in the United States as of 2015.

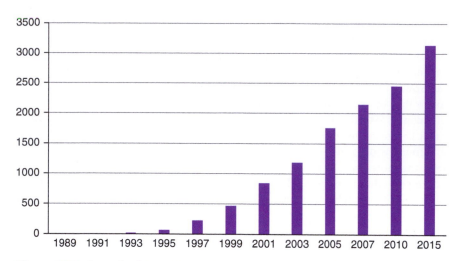

Figure 13.1 Growth of Drug Courts Programs in the United States

Sources: Huddleston, C.W., Marlowe, D., Casebolt, R. (2008). *Painting the current picture: A national report card on drug courts and other problem-solving court programs in the United States.* New York: Bureau of Justice Assistance; and www.nij.gov/topics/courts/drug-courts/Pages/welcome.aspx (accessed June 15, 2018).

Table 13.1 Number and Types of Drug and Other Specialty Courts

Types of Drug and Other Specialty Courts	Number
Adult drug courts	1,558
Juvenile drug courts	409
Family courts	312
Tribal courts	138
Designated DWI courts	284
Campus courts	3
Re-entry courts	29
Federal re-entry courts	27
Veterans' courts	312
Co-occurring disorder courts	70
TOTAL	**3,142**

Source: www.nij.gov/topics/courts/drug-courts/Pages/welcome.aspx (accessed June 15, 2018).

THE DRUG COURT MODEL

Based on the lessons learned from the early drug courts, the National Association of Drug Court Professionals (1997) set forth ten key components that should be incorporated in each adult drug court. Studies conducted since have refined these components and provided some clarification. First, the drug court should fully integrate court and treatment services. Previous attempts to target drug offenders were unsuccessful when the treatment services were not applied in conjunction with the court proceedings (Falkin, 1993). Second, the court work group should work collaboratively to ensure that the participant is prepared for long-term change; the adversarial approach of the traditional court should be avoided. Third, clear selection criteria should be established and participants should be referred to the drug court immediately. Fourth, the drug court should have access to an array of treatment services ranging from detox to residential care. The treatment should be responsive to the needs of the participant and involve family whenever possible. Fifth, the drug court should provide frequent and ongoing drug and alcohol urinalysis. Sixth, the court should monitor the progress of participants including results of the drug and alcohol tests. These should be shared with the court and be part of the reinforcement/punishment schedule. Although the court should recognize that relapse is typical, the expectation should always be abstinence. Seventh, the relationship between the judge and the participant is essential. Cooper and Bartlett (1996) found that 88 percent of the participants of the drug court felt that the judge (or magistrate) was key in their success in the program. Drug courts that are able to retain participants are more likely to be successful at long-term change (Goldkamp et al., 1998). Eighth, ongoing quality improvement is necessary to maintain the fidelity of the drug court model. Data should be collected to ensure that participants in the program are receiving effective services. Ninth, the professionalism and training of staff are extremely important. Staff should be trained in the drug court model, core correctional practices, and behavioral change. Tenth, the drug court staff must be active in the community, garnering support for the drug court and its participants. The drug court staff cannot operate in a vacuum; staff and participants must share the successes of the program to ensure long-term support. Table 13.2 summarizes the key components.

Guided by early attempts and the drug court principles, most drug courts have evolved into a unique blend between court procedures and treatment. Although there is not a single model for how drug courts have been implemented, there are some common themes. Most are structured like traditional courts, with the presence of a judge, prosecutor, and sometimes a defense attorney. The process takes more of a treatment team approach toward addressing the defendant than the traditional adversarial procedures. The judge operates as a hybrid case manager reviewing the defendant's progress, admonishing any negative behavior while praising prosocial alternatives. The prosecutor and defense attorney work together with the treatment provider to determine the best course of action.

Some courts serve as a pre-adjudication court while others are operated post-disposition. For the pre-adjudication courts, the defendant agrees to participate in the program, usually with the promise of either a dismissed charge or a heavily reduced charge (e.g., felony reduced to a misdemeanor). Post-dispositional programs are offered after the rendering of guilt (usually through plea) and are part of the supervision plan for the offender, offered to mitigate the sentence, or as a post-adjudication program that offers to reduce the conviction if specific indicators are met.

Most drug courts have set exclusionary criteria including a history of violence, and lack of motivation to participate. Once admitted, the defendant is expected to follow a set of strict rules designed to support a sober lifestyle. If these rules are

Table 13.2 Components for Drug Court Implementation

Key Component 1: Drug courts integrate alcohol and other drug treatment services with justice system case processing

Key Component 2: Using a non-adversarial approach, prosecution and defense counsel promote public safety while protecting participants' due process rights

Key Component 3: Eligible participants are identified early and promptly placed in the drug court program

Key Component 4: Drug courts provide access to a continuum of alcohol, drug, and other related treatment and rehabilitation services

Key Component 5: Abstinence is monitored by frequent alcohol and other drug testing

Key Component 6: A coordinated strategy governs drug court responses to participants' compliance

Key Component 7: Ongoing judicial interaction with each drug court participant is essential

Key Component 8: Monitoring and evaluation measure the achievement of program goals and gauge effectiveness

Key Component 9: Continuing interdisciplinary education promotes effective drug court planning, implementation, and operations

Key Component 10: Forging partnerships among drug courts, public agencies, and community-based organizations generates local support and enhances drug court program effectiveness

Source: The National Association of Drug Court Professionals, Drug Court Standards Committee. (1997, January). *Defining drug courts: The key components.* Washington, DC: Bureau of Justice Assistance. (Reprinted October 2004.)

violated, sanctions can be provided up to and including incarceration (Peyton & Gossweiler, 2001). Kassebaum and Okamoto (2001) suggest that oversight is key to the success of drug court programs. Unlike a traditional docket where there is very little oversight from the bench, the purpose of the drug court is for the judge to provide immediate feedback to the defendant, either to support the choices being made or to address them if they are leading the defendant down the wrong path (National Association of Drug Court Providers, 1997).

The length of the drug court varies specifically across site, but it is not uncommon to find drug courts that provide services for at least 12 months and sometimes up to 2 years. The types of interventions are quite mixed. Most rely heavily on Alcoholics Anonymous (AA) or Narcotics Anonymous (NA), while others have formal agreements with substance abuse providers to deliver treatment services. Treatment targets range from criminogenic to non-criminogenic needs. Usually separated by phases, successful completion is typically based on a combination of time, a period of documented sobriety, and other behavioral indicators (e.g., obtaining employment) (Peyton & Gossweiler, 2001).

Box 13.1
New Jersey Drug Court Program: Testimonials

I want to thank God, the court, my probation officer. I never really respected judges and probation officers before. But here they treat you like an adult, and you're made to feel part of a larger society. The judge has been very friendly and caring. He was there for me, as well as my probation officer. Life is beautiful, but I avoided life. You can't use mood- or mind-altering chemicals and be part of life. I'm grateful. —**Tommy**

This is truly, truly a blessed day. It feels so good being clean. Now, people come to me for help! —**George**

I never liked the program, but I love what it's done for me. —**Robert**

I want to thank all those who helped me believe that I can make a difference and a change in my life. —**Jo**

It was hard until I shared for the first time. They make you share. I didn't believe I had a problem at all until I shared, and then I started crying like a baby. —**Keith**

With drug court, I learned to be a man, not a kid. I'm studying music again. I don't know how to read or write, in English or Spanish, but God gave me the ability to have a band. When I go home, I kiss my instruments, because I can't believe I have this: my music, my apartment. I used to live in abandoned buildings and eat garbage. Now my eyes are open, my mind is clear. People respect me. —**Juan**

I thank God and family for giving me such a chance. Eighteen years of drug abuse. I was locked up in '99. I was scared of the real world. All I knew was selling and buying drugs. I thank drug court for helping me get this second chance at life. —**Susan**

Source: New Jersey Courts: www.judiciary.state.nj.us/index.html

The main purpose of drug court programs is to use the authority of the court to reduce crime by changing defendants' drug-using behavior. Under this concept, in exchange for the possibility of dismissed charges or reduced sentences, defendants are diverted to drug court programs in various ways and at various stages of the judicial process, depending on the circumstances. Judges preside over drug court proceedings; monitor the progress of defendants through frequent status hearings; and prescribe sanctions and rewards as appropriate in collaboration with prosecutors, defense attorneys, treatment providers, and others. Basic elements of a drug court include the following (Huddleston, 1998; Stageberg et al., 2001):

- A single drug court judge and staff who provide both focus and leadership.
- Expedited adjudication through early identification and referral of appropriate program participants, initiating treatment as soon as possible after arrest.
- Both intensive treatment and aftercare for drug-abusing defendants.

- Comprehensive, in-depth, and coordinated supervision of drug defendants in regular (sometimes daily) status hearings that monitor both treatment progress and offender compliance.
- Enhanced and increasing defendant accountability under a graduated series of rewards and punishments appropriate to conforming or violative behavior.
- Mandatory and frequent drug (and alcohol) testing.
- Supervised and individual case monitoring.

The Expansion of Drug and Problem-Solving Courts

Based on the success of the drug court model, jurisdictions were quick to broaden the scope of the drug court to meet the needs of other specialized populations that tend to get marginalized. Specifically, drug courts expanded to juveniles and DUI drivers, while the **problem-solving courts** began to target mentally ill offenders, families, re-entry, and veterans. Other problem-solving courts now include homeless, gun, community, prostitution, truancy, parole violator, sex offender, and child support courts (see Table 13.3). Although the problem-solving courts are fundamentally similar to the drug court, there are some distinct differences. The following section will briefly describe the models for the more widely used courts, including the juvenile drug court; the mental health court; courts for veterans, re-entry, and domestic violence; and the family drug court.

Box 13.2
Truancy Courts

According to the National Drug Court Resource Center, **truancy courts** are designed to assist school-aged youth to overcome the underlying causes of truancy by reinforcing and combining efforts from the school, courts, mental health providers, families, and the community. Many courts have reorganized to form special truancy court dockets within the juvenile or family court. Guidance counselors submit reports on the youth's weekly progress throughout the school year, which the court uses to enable special testing, counseling, or other necessary services. Truancy court is often held on the school grounds and results in the ultimate dismissal of truancy petitions if the youth can be helped to attend school regularly. Consolidation of truancy cases results in speedier court dates and more consistent dispositions and makes court personnel more attuned to the needs of truant youths and their families. Community programs bring together the schools, law enforcement, social service providers, mental and physical healthcare providers and others to help stabilize families and re-engage youth in their education.

Source: National Drug Court Resource Center: http://ndcrc.org/node/360

Table 13.3 Number and Types of Other
Specialty Courts

Types of Drug Courts	Number
Gun	5
Community	18
Prostitution	12
Parole violator	4
Sex offender	12
Homelessness	22
Truancy	199
Child support	50

Note: Numbers as at June 30, 2013.

Source: National Drug Court Resource Center.

The Juvenile Drug Court

The first juvenile drug court was established in 1995. As of June 2013, there
were 422 juvenile drug courts in operation across the United States. The juvenile drug court was initially adapted from the adult drug court model, but had
to be modified rather quickly to address several challenges that were unique to
juveniles (Drug Court Clearinghouse and Technical Assistance Project, 1998).
Typically, juvenile drug offenders have significant barriers, including lack of
family involvement, low motivation to change, and involvement with multiple
systems. These barriers, coupled with limited treatment options, made it even
more challenging to provide effective services to youth. The juvenile drug court
did have one advantage over the adult drug court: Juvenile courts operate more
collaboratively than adult courts and are usually focused primarily on rehabilitation. The juvenile court subscribes to the *parens patriae* doctrine, so the drug
court philosophy of therapeutic jurisprudence was not foreign to the juvenile
proceedings.

Specialty Courts for DUI Offenders

Offenders driving while intoxicated are increasingly being placed under the
jurisdiction of the drug court. Such courts are designed to reduce criminal reoffending by chemically-dependent adult drivers who are at high risk to recidivate
(see Chapter 11). The targeted group displays a repetitive pattern of driving under
the influence of alcohol or other drugs. Such drivers cause injuries and deaths on
highways, and are not deterred by usual DUI sanctions.

While DUI drug courts usually accept first-time DUI offenders, the typical court
focuses on multiple violators who are sent directly to the DUI court for arraignment and adjudication. The basic intentions are to aid such offenders, protect the

public by keeping offenders from reoffending, improve judicial efficiency, and reserve hard bed space for career and dangerous offenders. Georgia's DUI court is an accountability court authorized to process drug-using offenders through drug testing, intensive supervision, treatment services, and immediate incentives and sanctions. The DUI courts are designed to force the offender to deal with her or his substance-abuse problems through a blend of treatment and personal account-ability, as well as specialized case management. The DUI court is a treatment court with a specialized docket managed by a specially trained judge, working with pros-ecutors, public defenders, probation and law enforcement officers, treatment pro-viders, and other dedicated practitioners to compel the DUI offender to become clean and sober.

Tools used frequently in DUI courts include both early and long-term treatment intervention, frequent random drug testing, judicial supervision, intensive proba-tion coupled later with follow-up probation, assistance with school, education, and employment, bi-weekly court appearances, frequent 12-step AA or NA meeting attendance, and home visits by compliance officers. Failure to meet requirements will cause the DUI court judge to issue immediate sanctions, such as community service, jail time, or both. Interlock devices may be installed which prevent drug court offenders from driving a vehicle. Frequent failure may lead to revocation of probation and imposition of a sentence to incarceration.

The effectiveness of DUI courts has not yet been thoroughly investigated, but preliminary results from Georgia reveal that, 12 months post-graduation, DUI court clients are almost three times less likely to have a new DUI arrest; and 24 months post-graduation, drug court participants are 20 percent less likely to be arrested for a new felony. Hennepin County, Minnesota found that some 89 percent of program participants stayed crime-free. Keeping such offenders "off the bottle" results in one-quarter of the cost of sending a person to prison. In most drug courts, participant fees pay for treatment services (Eastern Judicial Circuit of Georgia, 2012).

Mental Health Courts

Mental health courts, like drug courts, were designed to address a growing pop-ulation of offenders who face significant barriers in the traditional court system. Lamb and colleagues (1999) found that mentally ill offenders have a difficult time engaging in the traditional criminal justice system and that the system is not responsive to the needs of the mentally ill offender. The goal of the mental health court is to reduce the barriers that exist in the system while assisting the offender in stabilizing his or her mental health symptoms.

To meet this goal, the mental health court works collaboratively with the judge, court workers, community supervision officer, treatment staff, and other consum-ers to engage the offender and ensure that he or she complies with the identified treatment plan (Miller & Perelman, 2009). Unlike the drug courts, the mental health court's focus is not directly on the criminal behavior. Instead, it focuses on reduc-ing the impact of the underlying mental illness, assuming that if the symptoms are

Table 13.4 The 16 Key Strategies for Juvenile Drug Courts Recommended by the National Drug Court Institute

- Strategy 1: Collaborative planning
- Strategy 2: Teamwork
- Strategy 3: Clearly defined target population and eligibility criteria
- Strategy 4: Judicial involvement and supervision
- Strategy 5: Monitoring and evaluation
- Strategy 6: Community partnerships
- Strategy 7: Comprehensive treatment planning
- Strategy 8: Developmentally appropriate services
- Strategy 9: Gender-appropriate services
- Strategy 10: Cultural competence
- Strategy 11: Focus on strengths
- Strategy 12: Family engagement
- Strategy 13: Educational linkages
- Strategy 14: Drug testing
- Strategy 15: Goal-oriented incentives and sanctions
- Strategy 16: Confidentiality

Source: National Drug Court Institute: www.ndci.org/

managed effectively, the offender will reduce his or her involvement in the criminal justice system.

The mental health court has gone through some recent modifications. Initially focused on offenders with low-level misdemeanors, mental health courts around the nation have begun to expand their services to higher-level misdemeanants and low-level felons. With the shift to more serious offenders, the mental health court has had to reconsider some of its earlier decisions. First, many courts have shifted from a pre-adjudication to a post-adjudication model. A post-adjudication model allows for the court to secure a guilty plea up front, so if the offender fails in treatment, it is easier to apply the underlying sentence. Second, supervision responsibilities have shifted from community mental health staff to probation officers. Third, the use of jail as an intermediate sanction has increased significantly (Miller & Perelman, 2009).

Common Elements in Mental Health Courts

- Participation in a mental health court is voluntary. The defendant must consent to participation before being placed in the program.
- Each jurisdiction accepts only persons with demonstrable mental illnesses to which their involvement in the criminal justice system can be attributed.
- The key objective of a mental health court is either to prevent the jailing of offenders with mental illness by diverting them to appropriate community services, or to significantly reduce the time spent incarcerated.

- Public safety is a high priority, and offenders with mental illness are carefully screened for appropriate inclusion in the program.
- Early intervention is essential, with screening and referral occurring as soon as possible after arrest.
- A multidisciplinary team approach is used, with the involvement of justice system representatives, mental health providers, and other support systems.
- Intensive case management includes supervision of participants, with a focus on accountability and monitoring of each participant's performance.

The judge oversees the treatment and supervision process and facilitates collaboration among mental health court team members (California Courts, n.d.).

Family Drug Courts

The family drug court is one of the most unique among the problem-solving courts. Developed in 1996, there are currently 331 family drug courts in operation. Although of similar structure to the other problem-solving courts, its primary target is not criminal behavior, but parental rights. The family drug court model is designed to reduce the impact that substance abuse has on families by working with them to increase retention of their children, reunite the children if removed, or assist in permanent custody where appropriate. Referrals are typically provided by the local Department of Human Services or prenatal/neonatal care workers. Many of the family drug courts handle both criminal and civil cases, but the court's sole interest is to manage the child protection cases (Wheeler & Siegerist, 2003).

Re-entry Courts

With more than 600,000 inmates leaving prison each year, there has been a growing concern about re-entry into the community. The **re-entry court**, designed to assist ex-offenders with reintegration issues, was first implemented in 2001. The goal of the re-entry court is to work with ex-offenders while they are still incarcerated, so that the barriers to successful integration can be removed prior to release (Hamilton, 2010). Re-entry courts were given a significant boost when President George W. Bush signed into law the Second Chance Act on April 9, 2008. This legislation was designed to improve outcomes for people returning to communities after incarceration. This first-of-its-kind legislation authorized federal grants to government agencies and non-profit organizations to provide support strategies and services designed to reduce recidivism by improving outcomes for people returning from prisons, jails, and juvenile facilities. With this influx of federal funding, many communities developed re-entry efforts that often include a re-entry court. The re-entry court was designed to increase collaboration between community supervision officers, court personnel, and community providers. In 2015, there were 29 re-entry courts at the local and federal levels.

Veterans' Courts

Veterans' courts are one of the newest versions of the problem-solving courts. According to the Office of National Drug Control Policy (2014), veterans' treatment courts use a hybrid integration of drug court and mental health court principles to serve military veterans, and sometimes active-duty personnel. Since veterans are often entitled to receive services through their veterans' benefits, these courts help to promote sobriety, recovery, and stability through a coordinated response that involves collaboration with the traditional partners found in drug courts and mental health courts, as well as the Department of Veterans Affairs healthcare networks, the Veterans Benefits Administration, state Departments of Veterans Affairs, volunteer veterans' mentors, and organizations that support veterans and veterans' families.

Domestic Violence Courts

The domestic violence court's primary purpose is to increase the accountability of the perpetrator. The domestic violence court started in 1998, and by 2013, there were 215 in operation. The court focuses on monitoring the offender through additional contacts, progress hearings, extended compliance monitoring of protection orders, and mandated batterer programming. Domestic violence courts are designed to address the traditional problems confronted in domestic violence cases (e.g., withdrawn charges by victims, threats to victims, lack of defendant accountability, and high recidivism). They apply intense judicial scrutiny of the defendant and there is close cooperation between the judiciary and social services. A designated judge works with the prosecution, assigned victim advocates, social services, and the defense to protect victims from all forms of intimidation by the defendant or his or her family or associates throughout the entirety of the judicial process; to provide victims with housing and job training, where needed; and to continuously monitor defendants in terms of compliance with protective orders, substance abuse treatment, and other services. Close collaboration with defense counsel ensures compliance with due process safeguards and protects defendants' rights. One variant of this model is the Integrated Domestic Violence and Other Problem-Solving Courts, in which a single judge handles multiple cases relating to one family, which might include criminal actions, protective orders, custody disputes, visitation issues, or divorce proceedings (Mazur & Aldrich, 2003). In a survey conducted by Labriola and colleagues (2009), 83 percent of the courts identified victim safety as the primary goal, while 79 percent cited offender accountability as extremely important. In contrast, only 27 percent of the courts stated that rehabilitation was a very important aspect of the domestic violence court.[1]

Sex Offender Courts

Sexual offender courts are one of the newest versions of the problem-solving courts. Working to increase communication between all parties involved in addressing sexual offenders' behavior, the sex offender court focuses on community management of the sexual offender. Herman (2006) suggests that sex offender courts provide a means to track the offender effectively through the use of specialized dockets, directed supervision plans, judicial monitoring of progress, and ongoing treatment team meetings. In addition, the sex offender court typically provides an avenue for the victim to get ongoing information about the offender. Unlike the typical drug court whose primary focus is rehabilitation, the sex offender courts are predominantly focused on offender management and community safety, the assumption being that if sexual offenders are monitored more effectively, they will not have an opportunity to offend (Herman, 2006).

PROBLEM-SOLVING COURT EFFECTIVENESS

The body of research on adult drug courts has grown substantially over the years, and the overall conclusion that can be reached is that they are effective in reducing recidivism. Because they differ substantially among jurisdictions, it has been a little more difficult to identify which components or combinations of features are contributing to success or failure.

There are enough studies of drug courts available for researchers to conduct meta-analysis (see Chapter 14 on evaluating community corrections). Overall, these reviews have found favorable results for adult drug courts. Table 13.5 lists some of these studies over the years.

In addition to reducing recidivism, adult drug courts have been found to be cost-effective. A study done by the Washington State Institute for Public Policy estimated that the average drug court participant produces $6,779 in benefits (WSIPP, 2003). In New York, researchers estimated that $254 million in incarceration costs were saved by diverting 18,000 offenders to drug courts. Finally, California researchers concluded that drug courts in that state save $18 million per year (NPC, 2002). Compared to jail and prison, adult drug courts appear to be cost-effective and to reduce criminal conduct.

Table 13.5 Average Reductions in Recidivism for Adult Drug Courts: Results from Meta-Analysis

Aos et al. (2001)	Average 8% reduction in recidivism
Barnoski & Aos (2003)	Average 13% reduction in recidivism
Lowenkamp et al. (2005)	Average 7% reduction in recidivism—stronger for higher-risk participants.
Latimer et al. (2006)	Average 14% reduction in recidivism
Wilson et al. (2006)	Average 26% reduction in recidivism
Shaffer (2011)	Average 9% reduction in recidivism
Mitchell et al. (2012)	Average 12% reduction in recidivism, similar results for DUI Courts
Drake (2012)	Average 25% reduction in recidivism

While the research has generally shown adult drug courts to be effective, studies of juvenile drug courts have not been as favorable. Most researchers have found considerably smaller effects for juvenile drug courts, and in a recent study of nine juvenile drug courts from across the country, researchers at the University of Cincinnati (Sullivan et al., 2014) found that youths in juvenile drug courts did worse than comparison cases. The researchers speculated that in general, most youths may not be particularly well suited to the treatment and monitoring process of a juvenile drug court.[2] Other explanations include the mixing of low-risk and higher-risk youths, the predominance of marijuana and alcohol users versus users of more serious substances, and the lack of motivation of many juveniles to abstain from experimenting with substances.

Although there is considerably less research on mental health courts, a body of research is emerging. For example, Cross's (2011) meta-analysis found a moderate, but significant, average reduction in recidivism; however, there was no effect on clinical outcomes. Other studies have found that mental health courts are having a positive effect on the quality of life for participants, and have a small to moderate effect on recidivism (Lee et al., 2012; Sarteschi et al., 2011; Utah Criminal Justice Center, 2012). Lee and colleagues (2012) also looked at the cost-effectiveness of mental health courts and found that for every $1.00 invested in mental health courts, there is a cost saving of $6.96. The total program benefits to taxpayers and others in society (such as potential victims) were estimated to be $20,424 per participant. Research on other types of problem-solving courts is just emerging, and it is too early to reach any conclusions on their effectiveness.

ISSUES FACING PROBLEM-SOLVING COURTS

Although generally supported across the nation, drug and problem-solving courts are not without their critics. Marlowe and colleagues (2003) acknowledge that research on the effectiveness of drug courts is not without its flaws. First, a majority of studies use no comparison group or do not overcome selection bias. Second, the methods used to collect data in some of the primary studies have been called into question. Third, most of the studies that show effects use successful graduates as the study population, not a sample of intent to treat. In fact, the Government Accountability Office (2005) found that only 27 of the 117 evaluations published on drug courts were acceptable methodologically.

In addition to some concerns regarding the evidence, Boldt (2002) argues that the non-adversarial nature of the drug courts can be problematic for vulnerable defendants. With judge, prosecutor, and defense attorney working together, Boldt posits that there is little protection in place for the drug offender. Similar arguments are made for mental health courts. Critics suggest that mentally ill offenders are often under-represented in court, are potentially forced to accept plea bargains that are not in their favor, and are coerced into maintaining compliance in taking psychotropic medications (O'Keefe, 2006).

Another concern centers on the challenge of funding problem-solving courts. For example, while many drug courts have been created with support from federal grants, as these funds have ended, many have struggled to continue the same level of programming and services. Finally, as is often the case with correctional alternatives, there is always the possibility that **net widening** can occur. This can happen when offenders who might otherwise be processed out of the system are brought into the problem-solving court simply because the court exists. This is a particular concern given the research which indicates that juvenile drug courts may be focusing their efforts on lower-risk youths.

Johnson and colleagues (2000) suggest that the drug courts, and presumably the problem-solving courts, have been adopted without considering the broader context of the research on effective correctional interventions. They argue that local jurisdictions should apply the broader principles of effective interventions to the drug courts in an effort to make them more effective. First, and foremost, the drug courts should adopt a method of classifying offenders into levels of risk. The drug court model is a relatively intensive intervention and should be reserved for moderate- to high-risk offenders (Bonta & Andrews, 2017; Lowenkamp & Latessa, 2004).

Second, the drug court should adopt a cognitive-behavioral model and insist that its community providers use a similar model to deliver treatment. Typically, drug courts rely on community providers to deliver the treatment services to the offenders. These providers should be monitored and the court should insist on the programs using models that have been shown to be effective for treatment. Latessa and Reitler (2015, pp. 787–788) identified some ways whereby drug courts can increase their effectiveness:

- **Duration:** Drug courts should rethink program length. Most drug courts are too long, and, as a result, completion rates are often low. While there is no magic number, it is clear that when interventions and treatment continue for too long, people give up and results begin to diminish.
- **Assessment:** Drug courts should do a better job of assessing needs by selecting instruments that cover *all* static and dynamic risk factors—not just substance abuse.
- **Target population:** The research is clear that we can do harm when we target low-risk offenders. Drug courts should focus on higher-risk offenders. By doing so, they will achieve the greatest effect on recidivism, and just as importantly, they will not have increased the failure rates for lower-risk offenders.
- **Match services:** Drug courts should provide, or match to participants, services that meet their major criminogenic needs—not just substance abuse.
- **Dosage:** Drug courts should increase intensity based on risk. Research indicates that moderate-risk offenders will require 100 to 150 hours of evidence-based treatment, while higher-risk offenders will require 200 or more hours.
- **Treatment:** Drug courts should move away from self-help, drug education, and unstructured groups, and instead they should use a curriculum-driven treatment based on cognitive-behavioral treatment and other behavioral approaches.
- **Family:** Whenever possible, family should be trained on how to assist their loved ones. The process for training family is similar to the training that should

be provided to the offender—that is, identifying and targeting criminogenic risk factors by modeling, practicing, and reinforcement.

- **Aftercare:** Most studies show that aftercare increases effectiveness of correctional programs. Drug courts should include structured care after completing the drug court as a *formal* part of the program, and not just as a voluntary option.

In addition to the concerns regarding the context of the programs, others have challenged the use of Alcoholics Anonymous and Narcotics Anonymous that often occurs in drug courts. Drug courts were found to rely heavily on 12-step models for either primary treatment or social support (Peyton & Gossweiler, 2001). Wells-Parker and Bangert-Drowns (1995) found that AA and NA were not effective for offender populations. Specific to drug courts, Shaffer (2011) found that drug courts which mandated attendance to AA/NA had lower effect sizes than those that did not mandate these services.

SUMMARY

Drug and other problem-solving courts will continue to play an important role in community corrections. In many ways, they represent the future and the hope that we will see the collaboration of close supervision practices and high-quality and effective treatment and services for offenders. In recent years, we have seen the original concept of the drug court expanded to include other special-needs populations who come into contact with the criminal justice system, such as the mentally ill, veterans, drunk drivers, sex offenders, and others. While the evidence indicates that drug courts for adults are effective in reducing recidivism, there is some indication that increased attention and involvement of the system with juveniles can be harmful, and only additional research will tell if some of the other problem-solving courts are effective. While the growth has been dramatic over the years, issues remain and it will be important for these efforts to apply what has been learned about designing effective programs from the larger body of research on correctional interventions.

Review Questions

1. Where was the first drug court, and why did the judge decide to create it?
2. What is the primary difference between drug courts and family courts?
3. Who is the target population for re-entry courts?
4. What are the issues facing drug and other problem-solving courts?
5. What are some of the steps that drug and other problem-solving courts can take to increase their effectiveness?
6. What are some of the reasons that juvenile drug courts have not been as effective as their adult counterparts?

Notes

1 This study examined nine juvenile drug courts from across the United States and was funded by the Office of Juvenile Justice and Delinquency Prevention (OJJDP). See Latessa et al. (2013).
2 Although 27 percent of the courts in the survey stated that rehabilitation was not very important, there was a clear distinction between New York State and the rest of the country. Only 19 percent of New York State's courts identified rehabilitation as very important, while 53 percent of the courts across the rest of the United States supported rehabilitation.

Recommended Readings

Johnson, S., Hubbard, D.J., Latessa E.J. (2000). Drug courts and treatment: Lessons to be learned from the "what works" literature. *Corrections Management Quarterly* 4(4), 70–77.

Miller, S., Perelman A. (2009). Mental health courts: An overview and redefinition of tasks and goals. *Law & Psychology Review* 33, 113–123.

Shaffer, D.K. (2011). Looking inside the black box of drug courts: A meta-analytic review. *Justice Quarterly* 28(3), 493–521.

Sullivan, C., Blair, L., Latessa, E.J., Sullivan, C.C. (2014). Juvenile drug courts and recidivism: Results from a multisite outcome study. *Justice Quarterly*. Online First: doi:10.1080/07418825.2014.908937

References

Aos, S., Phipps, P., Barnoski, R., Lieb, R. (2001). *The comparative costs and benefits of programs to reduce crime*. Olympia, WA: Washington State Institute for Public Policy.

Barnoski, R., Aos, S. (2003). *Washington State's drug courts for adult defendants: Outcome evaluation and cost-benefit analysis*. Olympia, WA: Washington State Institute for Public Policy.

Belenko, S. (1998). *Research on drug courts: A critical review*. New York: The National Center on Addiction and Substance Abuse at Columbia University.

Boldt, R. (2002). The adversary system and attorney role in the drug treatment court movement. In: J. Nolan (Ed.), *Drug courts: In theory and in practice* (pp. 115–143). New York: Aldine de Gruyter.

Bonta, J., Andrews, D.J. (2017). *The psychology of criminal conduct*. 6th ed. New York: Routledge.

California Courts, The Judicial Branch of California. (n.d.). Mental health courts. Retrieved from www.courts.ca.gov/5982.htm.

Campbell, N., Olsen, J.P., Walden, L. (2008). *The narcotic farm: The rise and fall of America's first prison for drug addicts*. New York: Abrams Publishing.

Cooper, C.S., Bartlett, S.R. (1996). *Drug courts: Participant perspectives*. Washington, DC: SJI National Symposium on the Implementation and Operation of Drug Courts, Justice Programs Office.

Cross, B. (2011). *Mental health courts effectiveness in reducing recidivism and improving clinical outcomes: A meta-analysis* (MA thesis). Graduate School Theses and Dissertations, University of South Florida. Retrieved from http://scholarcommons.usf.edu/cgi/viewcontent.cgi?article=4247&context=etd.

Drake, E. (2012). *Chemical dependency: A review of the evidence and benefit-cost findings*. Olympia, WA: Washington State Institute for Public Policy.

Drug Court Clearinghouse and Technical Assistance Project. (1998). *Juvenile and family drug courts: An overview*. Washington, DC: American University.

Drug Court Programs Office. (1998). *Looking at a decade of drug courts*. Washington DC: U.S. Department of Justice, Office of Justice Programs.

Eastern Judicial Circuit of Georgia. (2012) State Court DUI Court Program.

Falkin, G. (1993). *Coordinating drug treatment for offenders: A case study*. Report to the National Institute of Justice. New York: National Development and Research Institutes.

Goldkamp, J.S., White, M.D., Robinson, J. (1998). *An honest chance: Perspectives of drug court participants—findings from focus groups in Brooklyn, Miami, Seattle, Las Vegas, and San Bernardino*. Philadelphia, PA: Crime and Justice Research Institute.

Goode, E., Ben-Yehuda, N. (1994). *Moral panics: The social construction of deviance*. Oxford: Blackwell.

Government Accountability Office. (2005). *Adult drug courts: Evidence indicates recidivism reductions and mixed results for other outcomes*. Washington, DC: U.S. Government Accountability Office.

Hamilton, Z. (2010). *Do reentry courts reduce recidivism?* New York: Center for Court Innovation.

Herman, K. (2006). Sex offense courts: The next step in community management? *Sexual Assault Report* 9(5), 65–80. Kingston, NJ: Civic Institute.

Huddleston, C.W. (1998). Drug court and jail-based treatment. *Corrections Today* 60(6), 98–101.

Huddleston, C.W., Marlowe, D., Casebolt, R. (2008). *Painting the current picture: A national report card on drug courts and other problem-solving court programs in the United States*. New York: Bureau of Justice Assistance.

Johnson, L.D., Bachman, J.G., O'Malley, P.M. (1989, February 28). Teen drug use continues decline, according to U-M survey. Cocaine down for second straight year; crack begins to decline in 1988. *National press release*. Ann Arbor: University of Michigan News and Information Services.

Johnson, S., Hubbard, D.J., Latessa, E.J. (2000). Drug courts and treatment: Lessons to be learned from the "what works" literature. *Corrections Management Quarterly* 4(4), 70–77.

Jones, J. (1995). The rise of the modern addict. *American Journal of Public Health* 85(8), 1157–1162.

Kagay, M.R. (1990, July 25). Deficit raises as much alarm as illegal drugs, a poll finds. *The New York Times*, p. A9.

Kassebaum, G., Okamoto, D.K. (2001). The drug court as a sentencing model. *Journal of Contemporary Criminal Justice* 17(2), 89–104.

Labriola, M., Bradley, S., O'Sullivan, C., Rempel, M., Moore, S. (2009). *A national portrait of domestic violence courts*. New York: National Institute of Justice.

Lamb, H., Weinberger, L., Gross, B. (1999). Community treatment of severely mentally ill offenders under the jurisdiction of the criminal justice system: A review. *Psychiatric Services* 50, 907–913.

Latessa, E.J., Reitler, A.K. (2015). What works in reducing recidivism and how does it relate to drug courts? *Ohio Northern University Law Review* 41, 757–789.

Latessa, E., Sullivan, C.C., Blair, L., Sullivan, C.J., Smith, P. (2013). *Outcome and process evaluation of juvenile drug courts*. Cincinnati, OH: Center for Criminal Justice Research, University of Cincinnati.

Latimer, J., Morton-Bourgon, K., Chretien, J. (2006). *A meta-analytic examination of drug treatment courts: Do they reduce recidivism?* Ottawa, ON: Department of Justice Canada, Research and Statistics Division.

Lee, S., Aos, S., Drake, E., Pennucci, A., Miller, M., Anderson, L. (2012). *Return on investment: Evidence-based options to improve statewide outcomes*. Olympia, WA: Washington State Institute for Public Policy. Retrieved from www.wsipp.wa.gov/ReportFile/1102/Wsipp_Return-on-Investment-Evidence-Based-Options-to-Improve-Statewide-Outcomes-April-2012-Update_Full-Report.pdf.

Levine, H., Reinarman, C. (1988). The politics of America's latest drug scare. In: R. Curry (Ed.), *Freedom at risk: Secrecy, censorship and repression in the 1980s* (pp. 251–258). Philadelphia, PA: Temple University Press.

Lock, E.D., Timberlake, J.M., Rasinski, K.A. (2002). Battle fatigue: Is public support waning for "war"-centered drug control strategies? *Crime & Delinquency* 48(3), 380–398.

Lowenkamp, C.T., Holsinger, A., Latessa, E.J. (2005). Are drug courts effective? A meta-analytic review. *Journal of Community Corrections* XV(1), 5–10, 28.

Lowenkamp, C., Latessa, E. (2004). Increasing the effectiveness of correctional programming through the risk principle: Identifying offenders for residential placement. *Criminology and Public Policy* 4(1), 501–528.

Lurigio, A.J. (2000). Drug treatment availability and effectiveness: Studies of the general and criminal justice populations. *Criminal Justice and Behavior* 27(4), 495–528.

Marion, N. (1994). *A history of federal crime control initiatives, 1960–1993*. Westport, CT: Praeger.

Marlowe, D., Matteo, D., Festinger, D. (2003). A sober assessment of drug courts. *Federal Sentencing Reporter* 16, 153–157.

Martinson, R. (1974). What works? Questions and answers about prison reform. *Public Interest* 35, 22–54.

Mazur, R., Aldrich, L. (2003). What makes a domestic violence court work? Lessons from New York. *Judge's Journal* 42(2), 5–10.

McBride, D.C., McCoy, C.B. (1997). The drugs–crime relationship: An analytical framework. In: L.K. Gaines, P.B. Kraska (Eds.), *Drugs, crime, and justice*. Prospect Heights, IL: Waveland Press, Inc.

Miller, S., Perelman, A. (2009). Mental health courts: An overview and redefinition of tasks and goals. *Law & Psychology Review* 33, 113–123.

Mitchell, O., Wilson, D., Eggers, A., MacKenzie, D. (2012). Drug courts' effects on criminal offending for juveniles and adults. *Campbell Systematic Reviews* 4, 1–87.

National Association of Drug Court Professionals, Drug Court Standards Committee. (1997, January). *Defining drug courts: The key components*. Washington, DC: Bureau of Justice Assistance. (Reprinted October 2004).

NPC Research, Inc., and Administrative Office of the Courts, Judicial Council of California (2002). *California drug courts: A methodology for determining costs and avoided costs: Phase i: Building the methodology: Final report*. Portland, OR: NPC.

Office of National Drug Control Policy. (2014). Available at www.whitehouse.gov/ondcp/.

O'Keefe, K. (2006). *The Brooklyn mental health court evaluation: Planning, implementation, courtroom dynamics, and participant outcomes*. New York: New York State Office of Mental Health.

Oreskes, M. (1989, September 6). Drug war underlines fickleness of public. *The New York Times*, p. A22.

Peyton, E., Gossweiler, R. (2001). *Treatment services in adult drug courts: Report on the 1999 National Drug Court Treatment Survey*. Washington, DC: National Institute of Justice.

Reinarman, C., Levine, H.G. (2004). Crack in the rearview mirror: Deconstructing drug war mythology. *Social Justice* 31(1–2), 182–199.

Sarteschi, C.M., Vaughn, M.G., Kim, K. (2011). Assessing the effectiveness of mental health courts: A quantitative review. *Journal of Criminal Justice* 39, 12–20.

Shaffer, D.K. (2011). Looking inside the black box of drug courts: A meta-analytic review. *Justice Quarterly* 28(3), 493–521.

Sharp, E. (1994). *The dilemma of drug policy in the United States*. New York: HarperCollins.

Snell, T. (1991). *Corrections populations in the United States, 1989* (NCJ 130445). Washington, DC: Bureau of Justice Statistics.

Stageberg, P., Wilson, B., Moore, R. (2001). *Final report of the Polk County Adult Drug Court*. Des Moines, IA: Iowa Division of Criminal Justice Policy.

Sullivan, C., Blair, L., Latessa, E.J., Sullivan, C.C. (2014). Juvenile drug courts and recidivism: Results from a multisite outcome study. *Justice Quarterly*. Online First: doi:10.1080/07418825.2014.908937.

United States House of Representatives. (1928). *Establishment of two federal narcotic farms: Hearings before the Committee on the Judiciary, 70th Congress, 1st session, on Apr. 26–28, 1928*. Washington, DC: U.S. Government Publishing Office.

Utah Criminal Justice Center. (2012). *Mental Health Court for Adult Offenders: Technical report*. Salt Lake City: The University of Utah, Utah Criminal Justice Center. Retrieved from https://socialwork.utah.edu/reports/posts/statewide-mental-health-court-study/index.php.

Washington State Institute for Public Policy. (2003). *Drug courts for adult defendants: Outcome evaluation and cost benefit analysis*. Olympia, WA: WSIPP.

Wells-Parker, E., Bangert-Drowns, R. (1995). Final results from a meta-analysis of remedial interventions with drink/drive offenders. *Addiction* 90(7), 907–927.

Wheeler, M.M., Siegerist, J. (2003). *Family dependency treatment court planning initiative training curricula.* Alexandria, VA: National Drug Court Institute.

Wilson. D.B., Mitchell, O., MacKenzie, D.L. (2006). A systemic review of drug court effects on recidivism. *Journal of Experimental Criminology* 2, 459–487.

Wisotsky, S. (1991). Not thinking like a lawyer: The case of drugs in the courts. *Notre Dame Journal of Law, Ethics & Public Policy* 5(3), article 4. Retrieved from https://scholarship.law.nd.edu/ndjlepp/vol5/iss3/4.

Chapter 14

Evaluating Community Corrections

Key Terms

ballot counting	outcome measure
comparison group	performance measure
Correctional Program Checklist	program assessment
length of follow-up	program quality
literature review	recidivism
meta-analysis	

> With few and isolated exceptions, the rehabilitative efforts that have been reported so far have not had an appreciable effect on recidivism.
> —Robert Martinson

> The data have continued to accumulate, testifying to the potency of offender rehabilitation programs. —Paul Gendreau

After examining more than two decades of correctional research, Martinson's (1974) now famous conclusion had a tremendous impact on the field of corrections. Whatever the limitations of the Martinson study, and there were many, the conclusion drawn by a lot of people was that treatment or rehabilitation was not effective.[1] Thus, what became known as the "nothing works" doctrine led to renewed efforts to demonstrate the effectiveness of correctional programs.[2] As learned previously, there has been a great deal of research since Martinson that has added significantly to the body of knowledge about correctional effectiveness.

The effectiveness of community-based correctional programs has been debated and studied for many years. As more and more offenders have been diverted or released to the community, the question of effectiveness has become increasingly important. Many critics of both probation and parole point to discretionary abuses, high rates of technical violations, the arbitrary nature of the indeterminate sentence, the disparity in sentencing practices by judges, the failure of rehabilitation and supervision, and the inadequate delivery of services. In an attempt to offset some of these criticisms, mandatory and determinate sentencing systems have been imposed, sentencing tribunals have been formed, parole boards have adopted and implemented decision-making guidelines, probation and parole departments have tested new and innovative service delivery strategies, and intermediate sanctions have been developed. But these are also open to attack and are frequently criticized.

Much has been written about the effectiveness of probation and parole. We know that the use of discretionary parole release has declined dramatically over the past years, yet the number of offenders under supervision in the community is still the largest number under correctional control. The number of offenders placed on probation and parole has resulted in large caseloads and workloads for probation and parole departments.

There is also an acute shortage of residential programs and halfway houses. We continually experiment with service system components, such as brokerage, casework, house arrest, electronic monitoring, day reporting, drug testing, kiosks, intensive and specialized caseloads, and volunteers. In short, there have been nearly as many innovative programs and reported results as there are probation and parole agencies. The question of how we measure and determine effectiveness remains and, because it is so essential, it should be examined closely.

Perhaps the most limiting aspect of effectiveness studies has been the neglect of performance measures other than recidivism. By simply comparing recidivism rates, researchers have ignored some of the main effects that community correctional programs are designed to achieve. The quality of contacts and services provided to probationers and parolees needs to be defined and gauged adequately, as does the effect of officer style and attitude on outcome. There are also relatively few cost–benefit or cost-effectiveness studies. The importance of this type of information should not be overlooked. These types of studies can help community correctional agencies make more efficient selections in terms of the resources they will employ and the strategies used to deliver those resources. For example, Petersilia (1991) distinguishes between "passive" research designs and "active" ones. She argues that passive designs only look at the program in operation and ignore the selection of participants and levels of treatment. Without this kind of information, it is difficult to determine which attributes of a correctional program are effective.

Finally, a list of effectiveness indicators should include the degree of humaneness that community supervision affords offenders and their families, and the impact of these alternatives on reducing prison populations and overcrowded conditions in jails and prisons. We have come to understand that we cannot incarcerate everyone who breaks the law. Yet, probation and parole are often an afterthought, particularly when it comes to resource allocation.

There is little doubt that recidivism, no matter how it may be defined, should remain a main criterion; however, the need to measure additional outcome indicators appears obvious. Indeed, there has been a great deal of criticism directed at research conducted in the area of correctional programming. This chapter examines some of the ways in which community correctional programs are evaluated and how effectiveness is measured.

Box 14.1
Parole Violation

A parolee can be returned to prison for committing a new criminal act or failing to conform to the conditions of parole. The latter is frequently known as a technical parole violation: a rule violation that is not a criminal act, but is prohibited by the conditions of the parole agreement. The latter might include persistent consumption of alcohol, failure to observe curfew, refusal to make victim restitution, failure to file required reports, and so on. Drug use accounts for many of the violations, and often there are not enough treatment programs for probation and parole officers to use. Prison treatment programs for drug abuse are generally insufficient, and community resistance to implementing treatment centers can be considerable. Clearly, prisoner re-entry is a major issue facing corrections and policy makers.

THE IMPORTANCE OF EVALUATING COMMUNITY CORRECTIONAL PROGRAMS

The importance of evaluating correctional programs has never been more pronounced, especially given the scarcity of resources. With vast sums of money being spent on corrections, the public is demanding programs that work. What harm is done when we fail to develop and evaluate effective programs? One of the most important areas of contemporary concern for corrections officials is the design and operation of effective correctional intervention programs. This is particularly relevant, as there is consistent evidence that the public supports rehabilitation programs for offenders (Pew, 2012). Survey research also reveals strong support for public protection as an important goal of corrections (Applegate et al., 1997). As a result, disagreements are not uncommon about what the best methods are to achieve these goals. On one side are advocates for more punitive policies, such as an increased use of incarceration, "punishing smarter" strategies (e.g., zero tolerance), or simply increasing control and monitoring of offenders. The limits of these approaches have been outlined and debated by others (Bennett et al., 1996; Currie, 1985; Petersilia & Cullen, 2014). As Cullen and Applegate (1998) imply, the most disheartening aspect of these "get tough" policies is their dismissal of the importance of programming designed to rehabilitate offenders. Cullen and Applegate further question whether this rejection of rehabilitation is sound public policy. As many states have found, simply locking up offenders and "throwing away the key" has proven to be a very expensive approach to crime control. This approach is also very limited, as the vast majority of offenders will one day return to society. Many will return at best unchanged, and at worst, with many more problems and intensified needs for service.

Recently, there have been efforts to reduce the prison population through "Justice Reinvestment." Through the efforts of the Bureau of Justice Assistance, Pew, and the Council of State Governments, a number of states have begun to develop new policies and practices designed to reduce prison populations and to improve community supervision. At the heart of this movement is the need for data and the evaluation of programs and practices. Of course, evaluating correctional programs is not easy, and there are many limitations that researchers have to contend with.

LIMITATIONS OF EFFECTIVENESS STUDIES

Evaluating the effectiveness of community corrections is not easy even under the best of circumstances. First, political, ethical, and programmatic reasons may not permit random assignment of offenders to membership in the treatment or control group. Non-random assignment forces the evaluator to statistically make the groups comparable, an honored tradition in empirical research, but one which delivers results that are sometimes hard to communicate to policy makers and program directors (and sometimes to other researchers).

Even when random assignment is achieved, for the same reasons mentioned previously, treatment or program effects "bleed over" to the control group or the intended treatment is applied inappropriately or unevenly. This makes it difficult to determine whether the treatment group members received needed treatment, and whether the control group remained "treatment free." After all, no program, and no client, exists in a vacuum; historical accidents can impact both groups, one group more than another, or accidentally reinforce negative treatment effects in one group or another.

Another major problem in evaluating treatment effectiveness in community corrections is that it is rare to have only one treatment in operation at a time. For example, an offender ("Bob") may be sentenced initially to probation and restitution. The victim–offender interaction and mediation may have very positive effects on Bob's attitudes and behavior. His drinking problem, however, may lead the probation officer (PO) to recommend that the court tightens the conditions of probation to include mandatory participation in substance abuse treatment from which Bob derives much immediate and long-term benefit. Former antisocial friends may become reacquainted with Bob, and misdemeanor crime may occur. Alerted by Bob's subsequent arrest, the PO may have Bob (a failure?) assigned to group counseling that includes relapse prevention techniques to assist him in identifying high-risk situations and coping with them. After 3 years of probation, when the victim's losses have been compensated and with Bob securely employed in a job with a future and now voluntarily participating in substance abuse treatment, it is impossible to determine which of the treatment program elements will have been most effective in turning Bob around and aiding his reintegration. Was it probation supervision? The quality of PO supervision? Mediation and remorse associated with restitution? Substance abuse treatment? Relapse prevention techniques? Employment? Or some combination of treatment elements? Because "probation" is a generic term that can refer to a combination of treatment, supervision, and intermediate sanctions ("punishing smarter"), what element should be recognized as the "best intervention"?

Finally, we need to deal with the question of whether Bob should be labeled a "success" or a "failure" in corrections. Defining "failure" may mean using outcome indicators: arrest, reconviction or probation revocation, or incarceration (jail or prison). If the research design defines "success" as the absence of arrest, Bob failed: He was arrested. Yet the overall picture indicates that the arrest was just one critical incident in the long-range process of reintegration, one that Bob and his probation officer managed to overcome. However, that single arrest incident in the 3-year period would, from the perspective of reintegration, misclassify the probationer into the "failure" category. The bulk of evidence, however, clearly indicates that Bob was a success.

CORRECTIONAL EFFECTIVENESS

While the debate over correctional effectiveness will surely continue for some time, those attempting to evaluate and measure the worth of various strategies and programs found in corrections face a most difficult dilemma: defining "effectiveness."

Box 14.2
Cost–Benefit Analysis

One of the basic premises of cost–benefit analysis is that many decisions are often made on the basis of how resources can be optimally used, avoiding duplication, waste, and inefficiency. Cost–benefit analysis is a tool for decision makers who need to make choices among viable competing programs (including jail and prisons) to achieve certain goals. It is important to remember that cost–benefit analysis is not necessarily designed to favor the least expensive or the costliest programs, but rather optimal programs in terms of available resources and explicit goals (Latessa, 1986). Unfortunately, cost–benefit analysis is not a wholly satisfactory tool for evaluating social programs, as it is incapable of measuring social costs and benefits accurately (Vito & Latessa, 1979). However, when combined with other measures of program effectiveness and impact, cost–benefit information can provide policy makers with a valuable perspective. Comprehensive and meaningful cost–benefit analyses of criminal justice programs have been conducted. In these analyses, the amount of money saved for each dollar spent on the program is calculated (see Washington State Institute for Public Policy, n.d.).

Measuring Outcome and Recidivism

A large part of the problem lies in the desire on the part of researchers and practitioners alike to define failure or success in clear-cut, "either/or" terms. See Figure 14.1 for some of the ways in which offenders are classified at termination. Unfortunately, very few programs can be categorized in definitive terms. There is a strong need to view success or failure on a continuum rather than as a success-or-failure dichotomy. For example, an offender may complete a sentence of probation yet have erratic employment and numerous technical violations. This individual is certainly not as successful as one who finishes probation, gains upward mobility in a job, makes restitution, supports a family, and incurs no new charges of any type; still, both of these cases may be classified as successes. There is also a great deal of difference between the offender who is caught on a minor charge or a technical violation and one who commits a serious new felony. Some consider a new arrest a failure, whereas others count only those who are incarcerated.[3]

In addition to this problem, there is no consensus on the indicators of effectiveness. While most agree that recidivism should be a primary performance measure, there is no agreement on its definition or on the indicators used for its measurement. Indeed, one study of parole supervision found that the nature of outcome criteria had a significant effect on the interpretation of results (Ostermann et al., 2015). Researchers tend to define recidivism in terms that fit available data, yet we know that official sources are inadequate at best. Community follow-up and appropriate comparison groups are the exception rather than the rule when examining the recidivism of probationers and parolees. There is also some evidence that the amount of time given to the follow-up period may have a significant effect on the reported recidivism rates (Alper et al., 2018; Hoffman & Stone-Meierhoefer, 1980;

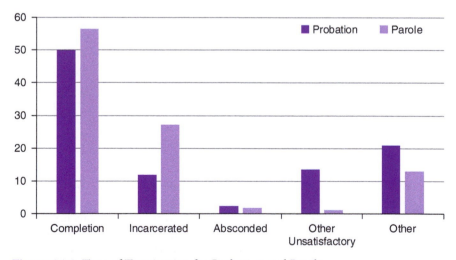

Figure 14.1 Type of Termination for Probation and Parole

Source: Kaeble, D. (2018). *Probation and parole in the United States, 2016.* Washington, DC: Bureau of Justice Statistics.

Nicholaichuk et al., 2000).[4] Some of the issues facing researchers when examining recidivism include:

- numerous definitions are applied
- length of follow-up is important
- rates will vary tremendously based on risk
- can be influenced by internal and external factors
- reliability of data
- when and whom to track
- outcomes rarely take into account the seriousness of a new crime—often treated as a dichotomous variable—all or nothing.

The correctional outcome, which is usually operationalized as recidivism, has inherent limitations. Indicators used to measure recidivism, length of follow-up, and external and internal factors affect recidivism rates. Indeed, the best way to ensure a low recidivism rate is to define it very conservatively (e.g., incarceration in a state penal institution) and to utilize a very short follow-up period.

Too often, arrest (and only arrest) is used as a primary indicator when measuring recidivism, and consequently, program success or failure. Certainly, arrest may serve as an indicator of post-program (or post-release) performance, but in and of itself arrest has many limitations. Some other factors overlooked when considering the impact of a correctional program or criminal sanction, even when arrest is being used, are: time until arrest; offense for which an offender was arrested (type of offense as well as severity level); whether or not the offender was convicted; and, if convicted, the resulting disposition.

Figure 14.2 shows how recidivism rates can vary based on the definition. With this sample of offenders, arrest, which is the broadest measure, has the highest rate of failure; whereas incarceration, which is a narrower measure, has the lowest rate. Another example of this can be seen from the results of a study of community corrections in Ohio. Figure 14.3 shows results from a 3-year follow-up of offenders supervised in the community. Four groups were used for this study: offenders supervised under regular probation; offenders under intensive supervised probation (ISP);

Box 14.3
Developing Comparison Groups

One of the greatest challenges in evaluating community correctional programs is identification and development of a **comparison group**. Because random assignment to correctional programs is rare, most researchers are forced to use quasi-experimental designs in which offenders in the treatment group are "matched" to those not participating in the program. Finding offenders who are similar and not receiving treatment can be one of the major issues facing researchers.

Box 14.4
Defining Recidivism

Defining recidivism can be a challenge and different measures are used by researchers. The most common include:

■ Arrests
■ Convictions
■ Incarceration

Can also include looking at:

■ Type of crime
■ Revocations/Technical violations
■ Severity of crime.

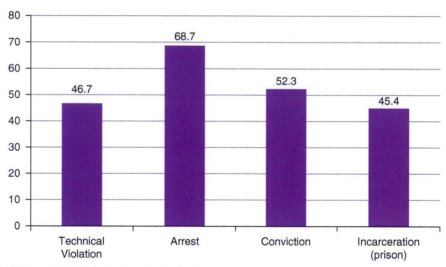

Figure 14.2 Failure Rate by Definition

Source: Latessa, E., Brusman-Lovins, L., Smith, P. (2010). *Follow-up evaluation of Ohio's community based correctional facility and halfway house programs—Outcome study.* Cincinnati, OH: School of Criminal Justice, University of Cincinnati.

those who were released from a community-based correctional facility (CBCF); and those released from prison. In this graph, the new arrest and new incarceration rates for each of the groups are presented. These data indicate that ISP and CBCF groups performed better than the prison groups (i.e., lower recidivism rates), at least when measured by a new arrest. However, when we examine incarceration rates, we see a somewhat different picture of recidivism. Here, we see that the ISP and CBCF groups had the highest failure rates (when defined as subsequent incarceration). Of course, what this figure does not show is that the majority of those ISP and CBCF

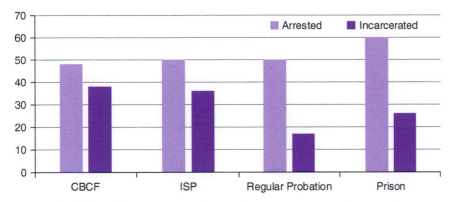

Figure 14.3 Offenders Supervised Under Community Corrections in Ohio: Percent Rearrested or Incarcerated During a 3-Year Follow-up

Source: Lowenkamp, C.T., Latessa, E.J. (2005a). *Evaluation of Ohio's CCA funded programs.* Unpublished Report, University of Cincinnati, Division of Criminal Justice.

offenders who were incarcerated were imprisoned as a result of a technical violation. Regular probationers who received a technical violation were often placed in ISP or a CBCF and, because the majority of offenders in the prison group were released without parole supervision, they were not subject to revocation.

Despite these limitations, recidivism remains the most important measure of public protection. When legislators and other public officials ask if a program works, recidivism is what they are generally referring to. Outcome studies provide much of our knowledge about the effectiveness of correctional programs in reducing recidivism. Unfortunately, outcome studies are usually focused on the results of intervention and provide little, if any, useful information about why a program is or is not effective. Besides the measurement of outcome, another factor that can influence recidivism rates is the quality of a program.

Reviews of Research

Given all the research that is conducted, and the sometimes contradictory findings, what do we believe? Looking at one study can be a mistake. For example, there are often limitations to research, especially evaluations conducted in the real world (limited sample size, lack of generalizability, lack of adequate control groups, program changes over time, etc.). One of the ways in which we attempt to address these problems is by looking at a body of knowledge. For example, most of us believe that cigarette smoking is bad for our health. How do we know this? "Research," you say, but don't you think that given the hundreds of studies that have been conducted, there aren't studies out there which say that cigarette smoking is not that bad? If you wanted to justify smoking based on some research, you can probably find these studies out there (even though the few studies may have been funded by the tobacco industry). The reason that most of us believe that smoking is harmful is because there is a body of knowledge concerning smoking and health which says that if you smoke, you increase your chances of cancer, heart disease, emphysema, and so forth. It turns out that we also have an extensive body of knowledge surrounding correctional interventions that can be summarized quantitatively. As noted in Box 14.5, there are three ways in which scholars summarize research: literature reviews, ballot counting, and meta-analysis. In a narrative literature review, all the studies are qualitatively summarized by the researcher. Although this is the most common approach, it has many limitations (e.g., studies chosen to review, bias of reviewer, no quantifiable summary statistics, etc.). Ballot counting involves identifying all of the studies published on a particular subject and then sorting the results; if more studies show negative results than positive, then the researcher would conclude that the preponderance of the evidence supported negative results. This approach is also problematic for a number of reasons, not the least of which is that it more or less ignores studies that do show a positive effect. The third approach is called meta-analysis, which is now the favored approach to reviewing large numbers of studies. Some of the advantages and disadvantages of this approach are listed in Table 14.1.

Table 14.1 Meta-analyses

Advantages
- Can summarize large bodies of literature
- Easy to replicate
- Easy to extend by gathering more studies in the future
- Can estimate range of treatment effects
- Can estimate changes in magnitude of the effect depending on type of offender, dosage, and quality of research design
- From a policy perspective, it provides more definitive conclusions than typical narrative reviews

Limitations
- Selection of studies—file draw problem
- Inadequacies of individual studies
- Choice of variables for coding
- Accuracy of coding is subjective

Box 14.5
Three Methods of Research Review

With all the studies conducted and published each year, it is often difficult to sort through all the research. There are three major techniques that researchers use to summarize and understand research findings:

Literature Review

The first and most common method for reviewing research is called a literature review. Using this approach, the researcher reads studies available on a topic and then summarizes what they think the major conclusions are from that body of research. Advantages to this approach are that most of us are familiar with the technique, it is easy to do, and it allows the reader to consider a wide range of issues. Disadvantages include the potential for bias of the reviewer, and the selection of studies to review.

Ballot Counting

The second approach is called ballot counting. With this technique, the researcher gathers research studies on a particular topic and then "counts" the number of studies that show or do not show some effect. This is the approach that Robert Martinson (1974) used to arrive at his now famous conclusion that "nothing works." He gathered 231 studies on correctional intervention, divided them into topics (e.g., education programs and work programs), and then determined that more studies showed no effect than those that did. Thus, his conclusion was based on a tallying of the number of studies that showed no effect (by the way, 48 percent of the studies he reviewed showed a positive effect). This approach is also relatively easy to do; however, because the majority wins, it tells us little about programs that do report positive effects.

Meta-analysis

The third approach which has become increasingly popular with researchers is called meta-analysis. This approach uses a quantitative synthesis of research findings in a body of literature. Meta-analysis computes the "effect size" between treatment and outcome variable—in our case, recidivism. The effect size can be negative (treatment increases recidivism), zero, or positive (treatment reduces recidivism). Meta-analysis also has some limitations. First, it is affected by "what goes into it"—what studies are included in the analysis. Second, how factors are coded can also be an important issue (e.g., into what treatment categories). There are major advantages, however, to meta-analysis. First, it is possible to control for factors that might influence the size of a treatment effect (e.g., size of sample, quality of research design, and length of treatment). Second, it provides a quantifiable result that can be replicated and tested by other researchers. Third, meta-analysis helps to build knowledge about a subject such as correctional treatment in a precise and parsimonious way.

All three approaches allow us to review a large body of knowledge; however, given the advantages of meta-analysis, it is becoming more popular with researchers. As we will see, the approach is not as important as what we can learn from the research.

Meta-analysis is very helpful in summarizing the research, and because it yields an "effect size," it can show the relative strength of the intervention or subject under study. Meta-analysis is a blunt instrument, however, because although it can point us in the right direction, it cannot correct deficiencies or limitations in original research.

Recidivism as an Outcome Measure

It is important to put recidivism as an **outcome measure** in perspective. **Recidivism** is and should be the primary outcome measure by which we assess correctional program effectiveness. However, recidivism is problematic for a number of reasons. First, numerous definitions are applied, such as arrests, incarceration, technical violations, convictions, and so forth. How we define recidivism can determine the rate. For example, using a new arrest as the definition will result in higher recidivism rates than using return to prison. Second, the **length of follow-up** can be critical. Figure 14.4 shows the 1-, 2-, and 3-year failure rates of a cohort of youth released from custody. As seen, the failure rates more than doubled between year 1 and year 3. For most offender groups, a 2- or 3-year follow-up is sufficient; however, for some offenders, such as sex offenders and drunk drivers, we need a much longer follow-up to gauge recidivism adequately. Many believe that this is because the odds of getting caught are much lower for these groups. Third, recidivism rates can be influenced by both

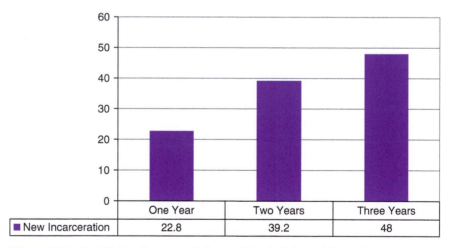

	One Year	Two Years	Three Years
■ New Incarceration	22.8	39.2	48

Figure 14.4 Recidivism Rates for Cohort of Youth Released from Ohio Department of Youth Services*

Note: *The number of youths returned to DYS or DRC within 1, 2, or 3 years of release from a DYS institution.

Source: Lowenkamp, C.T., Latessa, E.J. (2005b). *Evaluation of Ohio's RECLAIM funded programs, community corrections facilities, and DYS facilities*. Unpublished Report, University of Cincinnati, Center for Criminal Justice Research.

internal and external factors. For example, probation departments may change policies, such as increasing drug testing, which in turn can result in higher failure rates (internal), or police departments may focus on specific types of crimes, such as random stops for drunk drivers (external). Finally, recidivism is often treated as a dichotomous variable: an all-or-nothing measure, when in fact we know that variations in this outcome measure exist. That is, someone who is arrested for public intoxication is much less problematic than someone arrested for armed robbery, but we often simply count both instances as failures when examining program effectiveness. Nevertheless, recidivism is usually referenced when someone asks, "Does the program work?" This doesn't mean that we should not examine other "intermediate" measures. Let's now look at some ways this can be done.

Performance-Based Measures

In addition to long-term outcome measures, such as reductions in recidivism, we may also be interested in examining other intermediate measures. Unfortunately, in community corrections we often count activities that have little or no relationship to program or offender performance. An example would be counting the number of contacts between a probation officer and offenders. There is no empirical evidence that there is any relationship between the two factors, yet this is a common measuring stick in probation. The difference between counting an activity and a **performance measure** is illustrated in the following example:

- Activity: Counting the number of job referrals made.
- Performance: Number of unemployed offenders at the time of arrest and percentage employed within 6 months after being placed on probation.

Table 14.2 shows an example of the difference between counting activities and counting results for a juvenile court. One counts tasks, while the other counts outcomes.

Often, documenting performance in offenders will help you to determine treatment effects. Examples would be:

Table 14.2 Communicating What a Juvenile Court Does: Activities versus Results

Counting activities	Counting results
Number of contacts	Increase in number of school days attended
Number of drug tests	Percent drug-free
Number of youths on electronic monitoring	Reductions in runaways
Number of assessments completed	Average reduction in risk scores

- reductions in dynamic risk/need assessment scores;
- changes in pre/post measures, such as improvement in test scores, changes in attitudes, behaviors, etc.;
- changes in problem areas (e.g., drug test results);
- completion of behavioral objectives (meeting treatment plan);
- substance abuse: drug tests, attitude change, day's abstinence, etc.;
- education: improvement on standardized achievement tests;
- employment: days employed, earnings, savings, contributions to support, etc.;
- mental health: days hospitalized (pre/post-treatment).

By focusing on performance rather than activities, a community correctional program can develop intermediate goals, which, if achieved, can serve as a prelude to reductions in recidivism. Osborne and Gaebler (1993) have identified seven principles for results-oriented management:

1. What gets measured gets done.
2. If you don't measure results, you can't tell success from failure.
3. If you can't see success, you can't reward it.
4. If you can't reward success, you're probably rewarding failure.
5. If you can't see success, you can't learn from it.
6. If you can't recognize failure, you can't correct it.
7. If you can demonstrate results, you can win public support.

Measuring Program Quality

Few would argue that the quality of a correctional intervention program has no effect on outcome. Nonetheless, correctional researchers have largely ignored the measurement of **program quality** (Latessa & Holsinger, 1998). Traditionally, quality has been measured through process evaluations. This approach can provide useful information about a program's operations; however, these types of evaluations often lack the "quantifiability" of outcome studies. Previously, the primary issue for researchers has been the development of criteria or indicators by which a correctional program can be measured. While traditional audits and accreditation processes are one step in this direction, thus far they have proven to be inadequate. For example, audits can be an important means to ensure whether a program is meeting contractual obligations or a set of prescribed standards; however, these conditions may not have any relationship to effective intervention. It is also important to note that outcome studies and assessment of program quality are not necessarily mutually exclusive. Combining outcome indicators with assessments of program quality can provide a more complete assessment of an intervention's effectiveness. Fortunately, there has been considerable progress in identifying the hallmarks of effective programs (Andrews et al., 1990; Cullen & Applegate, 1998; Gendreau & Paparozzi, 1995; Gendreau & Ross, 1979, 1984; Lowenkamp et al., 2006; Palmer, 1995).

INTRODUCTION TO PROGRAM ASSESSMENT

The characteristics and quality of a community correctional program often help to determine its effectiveness. Let's now turn our attention to how we can measure the integrity of a community correctional program.

Examining the "input" of a program is usually referred to as *process evaluation*. Process evaluations usually involve a more qualitative methodology than an outcome evaluation. A process study helps determine whether the program is operating as it was designed to. The problem is that a program may in fact be operating efficiently, but not effectively. For example, a drug education program may be doing a great job of teaching offenders about the harm that drugs can do to them, without being effective in reducing drug usage.

The other problem with traditional process studies is that they do not provide a "quantitative" measure. One way to think of this would be the example from offender assessment. Some assessment processes gather a great deal of information about the offender (i.e., criminal history, employment, drug use, family, education). The problem is that when they are done, they don't really have a good way to pull it all together to measure risk quantifiably. Now compare that to using an actuarial risk assessment tool. The same information is gathered, but when you are finished, you produce a score that in turn helps to tell you the probability of recidivism, as well as whether the offender scores "high," "medium," or "low" in each domain.

The Correctional Program Checklist (CPC)

So how do we quantifiably measure program integrity, and what factors are examined? One tool used was developed by researchers at the University of Cincinnati Corrections Institute (UCCI); the Evidence-Based Correctional Program Checklist or CPC (Duriez et al., 2017).[5] This instrument is based in part on results from meta-analyses of correctional effectiveness studies as well as several large studies of correctional programs (Lowenkamp, 2004; Lowenkamp & Latessa, 2002, 2005a, 2005b). It is a tool for assessing correctional programs based on empirical criteria. However, unlike traditional process evaluations or audits of adherence to standards, this process looks at the degree to which a correctional program is meeting the principles of effective intervention. This tool has been used to evaluate programs all over the United States. For example, in 2005, Oregon's legislature passed Senate Bill 267, stipulating that 25 percent of state funding for correctional programs by the end of the year be allocated to programs that could show they were evidence-based. This percentage was increased to 50 percent by 2007 and 75 percent by 2009. To ensure that programs are meeting this requirement, the Oregon Department of Corrections uses the CPC to establish a baseline of CPC scores for future benchmarking (O'Connor et al., 2008). More than 1,100 programs have been assessed, and a number of states use the CPC to determine if programs are evidence-based.

The CPC (see Table 14.3) is divided into two basic areas: content and capacity. The capacity area is designed to measure whether a correctional program has the capability to deliver evidence-based interventions and services for offenders. There are three domains in the capacity area: Program Leadership and Development, Staff Characteristics, and Quality Assurance. The content area comprises the Offender Assessment and Treatment Characteristics domains, and focuses on the extent to which the program meets certain principles of effective intervention. There are 73 indicators in total, worth up to 79 total points that are scored during the assessment. Each domain, each area, and the overall score are tallied and rated as either Very High Adherence to EBP (65 to 100 percent); High Adherence to EBP (55 to 64 percent); Moderate Adherence to EBP (46 to 54 percent); or Low Adherence to EBP (45 percent or less).

As seen in Table 14.3, the first area looks at program leadership, as well as design and implementation of the program. The second area examined is staff. Effective programs have educated, experienced, supervised, and supportive staff who are well trained. The third area is evaluation and quality assurance. How does the program monitor the services it delivers? We also know that effective programs

Table 14.3 Correctional Program Checklist

Capacity

1. Program Leadership and Development
   - Influence and involvement of the program director
   - Leadership and qualifications
   - Development, design, and support for the program
2. Staff Characteristics
   - Type and education of the staff
   - Experience and involvement of the staff
   - Assessment and training of the staff
3. Quality Assurance
   - Types of feedback
   - Tracking of performance and evaluation
   - Quality assurance

Content

4. Participant Assessment
   - Selection of participants
   - Assessment of specific participant characteristics
   - Manner in which participants are assessed
5. Treatment Characteristics
   - Ability to target criminogenic behaviors
   - Use of assessment information
   - Types of treatment used
   - How treatments are used
   - Preparation of offenders to return to the community
   - Provision and quality of aftercare

Source: Latessa, E. J. (2005). *Correctional Program Checklist.* Center for Criminal Justice Research, University of Cincinnati.

routinely monitor recidivism and conduct outcome studies. The fourth area looks at the manner in which offenders are selected for the program and how they are assessed. As we have learned, good assessment involves the use of standardized and objective instruments that produce scores related to risk, need, and responsivity factors. The fifth area covered by the CPC is treatment delivered by the program. Does the program target criminogenic risk factors? What interventions does the program use? Does it try to "talk" the offender into changing or does it use approaches that have demonstrated effectiveness in reducing recidivism, such as cognitive-behavioral curricula?

Figure 14.5 shows average scores from nearly 400 program assessments conducted by University of Cincinnati researchers. As seen, Quality Assurance and Treatment remain areas of concern and score poorly. Figure 14.6 shows the percentage of programs in each category. Only about 30 percent of programs have scored as High or Very High Adherence to evidence-based practices.

Two recent studies have assessed the predictive validity of the CPC. Ostermann and Hyatt (2017) found that programs for parolees which scored higher on the CPC reduced recidivism at greater rates than less rigorous programs. Makarios and his colleagues (2017) found that sex offender programs with higher CPC scores were the most effective.

While these results indicate that the majority of correctional programs assessed are not fully meeting the principles of effective intervention, they also

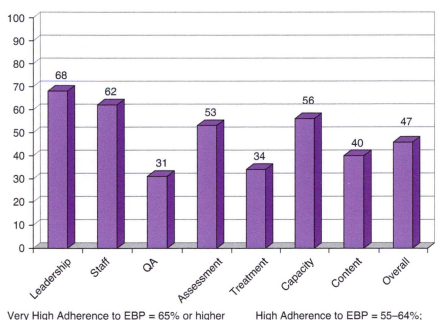

Very High Adherence to EBP = 65% or higher   High Adherence to EBP = 55–64%;
Moderate Adherence to EBP = 46–54%   Low Adherence to EBP = 45% or less.

Figure 14.5 Average CPC Scores

Note: *The average scores across a wide range of programs.

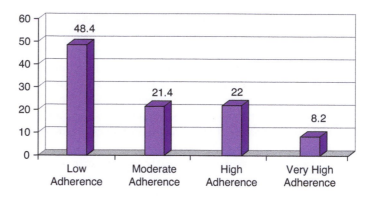

Figure 14.6 Percentage of Programs in Each Category

Note: *The average scores are based on results across a wide range of programs. Very High Adherence to EBP = 65 percent or higher; High Adherence to EBP = 55–64 percent; Moderate Adherence to EBP = 46–54 percent; Low Adherence to EBP = 45 percent or less.

provide some useful information on how to improve the quality of correctional interventions.

Latessa (2018) has identified several reasons why it is important to measure and study correctional program quality:

1. ***Poor quality programs undermine our confidence in treatment and can hurt high-quality programs.*** When a judge requires offenders to participate in a program and they fail, they are quick to assign blame—to the offender. The end result is that we often hear the refrain "treatment doesn't work" when some of the responsibility lies with the program. As Van Voorhis, Cullen, and Applegate (1995:20) stated, much of what reportedly "did not work" in actuality "did not happen."

2. ***Using tools to assess program integrity and quality allows us to become more prescriptive and to provide feedback that can be used for program development and improvement.*** Not only can we better identify the areas that a program needs to work on to improve outcomes, but also we can provide information about what the program is doing that is consistent with the research. In other words, we can provide useful feedback about what a program is doing well, and on how to improve practice, which in turn gives program designers and policy makers more concrete and specific information. For example, in a study of staff attributes, Makarios et al. (2016) provided direction to programs that suggests that correctional agencies should (a) attempt to hire and retain experienced and qualified staff, (b) provide both initial and ongoing training on a regular basis, and (c) provide clinical supervision that is focused on the development of skills involved in service delivery. These authors also indicated that other staff domains were important as well, which suggests

that not only is the quality of the staff that agencies hire important but also of importance is how agencies work to develop the personnel they hire through appropriate training and clinical supervision. This type of research can be used to facilitate the development of indicators as well as to find more refined ways to measure staff attributes that are associated with lower recidivism rates. It also gives program administrators and developers more clear direction on how to improve the services they offer.

3. *Using program assessment tools based on empirical evidence allows researchers to get inside the "black box" of a program.* This lets us move beyond traditional process evaluations or audits that are simply aimed at measuring whether a program is doing what it is designed to do. In some cases, however, if the model is flawed, then delivering it with fidelity may not matter. For example, with many programs, audits are passed because interventions are delivered or models are used as designed but recidivism is still not reduced—for example, talk therapy, drug education, and boot camps. In other words, with some interventions, no matter how well they are delivered, an appreciable effect on recidivism may not occur, or as Van Voorhis et al. (1995: 23) stated, "[B]efore asking whether a program does work, we must ask whether there is any reason why it should work."

4. *Using program assessment tools facilitates the improvement of programs and allows policy makers to allocate scarce resources better.* Demonstrating that high-quality programs are effective not only gives program administrators direction that helps them improve their practice but also provides policy makers with the tools to help them decide where to put their resources.

5. *Program assessment can provide a means of determining "evaluability" of a correctional program.* According to Van Voorhis and Brown (1996), one of the major impediments to conducting evaluations is poor program design and implementation. Another problem noted by Van Voorhis et al. (1995) is that we sometimes see outcome data with no indication of what the program did to achieve the results. Program assessments can thus serve as an evaluability study (Matthews, Jones-Hubbard, & Latessa, 2001; Prosavac & Carey, 1992; Rutman, 1980) to determine whether a program is ready to undergo a costly and time-consuming outcome study. In a correctional program that does not meet some minimal threshold of "quality," administrators should devote their program's resources to improving the services it provides—that way the evaluators will not be blamed when the outcomes do not show the results program administrators hoped for.

6. *Program assessment can "quantify" program integrity.* Tools such as the CPC enable researchers to "quantify" the quality of a program through a scoring process. This allows for comparisons across programs, as well as for benchmarking (i.e., reassessment allows for reevaluating a program's progress). It also provides researchers with a numeric value that can be more easily disaggregated and analyzed than a qualitative narrative.

7. ***Program assessment identifies program areas for improvement and gauges progress.*** In many ways, it is similar to risk assessment conducted on an offender. Researchers identify the factors correlated with reoffending, develop the indicators, assign weights, and then assign a score that allows sorting into groups (i.e., high, moderate, or low). Someone that scores high has a greater probability to reoffend than does someone that scores low, and the assessment can be used to help identify the factors in the offender's life that need to be targeted for change. With program assessment, the difference is that the program is the unit of analysis rather than the individual but the process is essentially the same. Through research, we identify those program characteristics that are correlated with positive outcomes (i.e., staff qualifications, dosage of treatment, and delivery of services), assess the program, and identify strengths and areas that need improvement, which then allows program administrators to target those areas of deficiency for improvement. We can also measure change. For example, the CPC has been used to conduct numerous reassessments. This provides the program with a quantitative measure of change in program quality and helps show the areas that have improved, stayed the same, or regressed.

8. ***Program assessment helps increase public safety and support for treatment.*** The evidence is strong that when we develop and implement evidence-based programs and practices that lower recidivism rates will follow. This can increase public safety as well as support for treatment. The end result is safer communities, fewer tax dollars spent on incarceration, and increased funding for treatment programs.

(Latessa, 2018, pp. 183–185)

SUMMARY

Evaluating community correctional programs is a challenge. Defining recidivism, measuring outcomes, and identifying comparison groups are some of the issues confronting researchers. Summarizing research has taken several forms, but the favored approach today is meta-analysis. Meta-analysis is a type of research method that examines other studies on a specific subject or topic and produces an "effect size" that helps policy makers and practitioners to determine the best approaches.

Even though there appear to be programs and interventions that are effective, research conducted to date has been hampered by many constraints and limitations and, as a result, is less than adequate. Part of this dilemma rests with the concept of effectiveness. While, as noted earlier, most would agree that recidivism should be a primary performance measure, there is no consensus on its definition or the indicators to be used for its measurement. Researchers often ignore other performance measures of effectiveness, especially those examining the management or supervisory aspects of parole and probation, and the quality of correctional programs.

Review Questions

1. What are some of the indicators of effectiveness used in correctional research?
2. List the three major ways that research studies are summarized.
3. List some of the factors related to outcomes.
4. What is the difference between an activity and a result. Give an example of each.
5. What are the five areas of the Correctional Program Checklist? Describe what is in each category.
6. According to the research presented in the text, approximately what percentage of correctional programs can be classified as "High Adherence" or "Very High Adherence" to evidence-based practices?

Notes

1   For a discussion of the limitations and criticism of the Martinson study, see Palmer (1975); and Cullen and Gendreau (2001).
2   Francis T. Cullen eloquently argues that rehabilitation reduces recidivism across programs by about 50 percent when interventions are based on principles of effective treatment (Cullen, 1994).
3   For a discussion of the various alternative definitions of recidivism, see Champion (1988, pp. 95–97); Palmer (1995); and National Policy Committee of American Society of Criminology (2001).
4   Length of follow-up can affect recidivism rates. For most types of offenders, most failures will occur within 3 years. Exceptions to this are sex offenders and drunk drivers who, because of the lower probability of being caught, require longer follow-up periods.
5   The CPC was based on the Correctional Program Assessment Inventory (CPAI) developed by Gendreau and Andrews (1989). The development of the tool included retaining items from the CPAI that were correlated with reductions in recidivism. Further, items that did not appear on the CPAI, but were found to be correlated with program success, were included in the CPC, while items not correlated with recidivism were excluded from the new instrument. Finally, select items found to be strongly correlated with recidivism were weighted (Lowenkamp & Latessa, 2002, 2005a, 2005b).

Recommended Readings

Gendreau, P. (1996). The principles of effective intervention with offenders. In: A. Harland (Ed.), *Choosing correctional options that work: Defining the demand and evaluating the supply* (pp. 117–130). Thousand Oaks, CA: Sage.

Latessa, E.J., Listwan, S., Koetzle, D. (2015). *What works (and doesn't) in reducing recidivism*. New York: Routledge.

Martinson, R. (1974). What works? Questions and answers about prison reform. *The Public Interest* 35, 22–54.

Washington State Institute for Public Policy. (n.d.). Benefit–cost results: Adult criminal justice. Retrieved from www.wsipp.wa.gov/BenefitCost/Pdf/2/WSIPP_BenefitCost_Adult-Criminal-Justice.

References

Alper, M., Markman, J., Durose, M.R. (2018). *2018 update on prisoner recidivism: A 9-year follow-up period (2005–2014).* Washington, DC: Bureau of Justice Statistics.

Andrews, D., Zinger, I., Hoge, R., Bonta, J., Gendreau, P., Cullen, F. (1990). Does correctional treatment work? A clinically relevant and psychologically informed meta-analysis. *Criminology* 28, 369–404.

Applegate, B., Cullen, F., Fisher, B. (1997). Public support for correctional treatment: The continuing appeal of the rehabilitative ideal. *Prison Journal* 77, 237–258.

Bennett, W., Dilulio, J. Jr., Walters, J. (1996). *Body count: Moral poverty and how to win America's war against crime and drugs.* New York: Simon & Schuster.

Champion, D. (1988). *Felony probation, problems and prospects.* New York: Praeger.

Cullen, F. (1994). Social support as an organizing concept for criminology. *Justice Quarterly* 11, 52–59.

Cullen, F., Applegate, B. (1998). *Offender rehabilitation.* Brookfield, MA: Ashgate Dartmouth.

Cullen, F., Gendreau, P. (2001). From nothing works to what works. *Prison Journal* 81(3), 313–338.

Currie, E. (1985). *Confronting crime: An American dilemma.* New York: Pantheon.

Duriez, S.A., Sullivan, C., Latessa, E.J., Brusman Lovins, L. (2017). The evolution of correctional program assessment in the age of evidence-based practices. *Corrections, Policy Practice and Research.* doi: 10.1080/23774657.2017.1343104.

Gendreau, P., Andrews, D. (1989). *Correctional Program Assessment Inventory (CPAI).* Saint John: University of New Brunswick Press.

Gendreau, P., Paparozzi, M. (1995). Examining what works in community corrections. *Corrections Today* (February), 28–30.

Gendreau, P., Ross, R. (1979). Effective correctional treatment: Bibliography for cynics. *Crime & Delinquency* 25, 463–489.

Gendreau, P., Ross, R.R. (1984). Correctional treatment: Some recommendations for successful intervention. *Juvenile and Family Court Journal* 34, 31–40.

Hoffman, P., Stone-Meierhoefer, B. (1980). Reporting recidivism rates: The criterion and follow-up issues. *Journal of Criminal Justice* 8, 53–60.

Kaeble, D. (2018). *Probation and parole in the United States, 2016.* Washington, DC: Bureau of Justice Statistics.

Latessa, E.J. (1986). The cost effectiveness of intensive supervision. *Federal Probation* 50(2), 70–74.

Latessa, E.J. (2005). *Correctional Program Checklist.* Center for Criminal Justice Research, University of Cincinnati.

Latessa, E.J. (2018). Does treatment quality matter? Of course it does, and there is growing evidence to support it. (Policy essay.) *Criminology and Public Policy* 17, 181–188.

Latessa, E.J., Holsinger, A. (1998). The importance of evaluating correctional programs: Assessing outcome and quality. *Corrections Management Quarterly* 2(4), 22–29.

Latessa, E., Brusman-Lovins, L., Smith, P. (2010). *Follow-up evaluation of Ohio's community based correctional facility and halfway house programs—Outcome study.* Cincinnati, OH: School of Criminal Justice, University of Cincinnati.

Lowenkamp, C.T. (2004). *Correctional program integrity and treatment effectiveness: A multi-site, program-level analysis* (Doctoral dissertation). The University of Cincinnati, Cincinnati, OH.

Lowenkamp, C.T., Latessa, E.J. (2002). *Evaluation of Ohio's community based correctional facilities and halfway house programs: Final report.* University of Cincinnati, Division of Criminal Justice, Center for Criminal Justice Research.

Lowenkamp, C.T., Latessa, E.J. (2005a). *Evaluation of Ohio's CCA funded programs.* Unpublished Report, *University of Cincinnati*, Division of Criminal Justice.

Lowenkamp, C.T., Latessa, E.J. (2005b). *Evaluation of Ohio's RECLAIM funded programs, community corrections facilities, and DYS facilities.* Unpublished Report, University of Cincinnati, Center for Criminal Justice Research.

Lowenkamp, C.T., Latessa, E.J., Smith, P. (2006). Does correctional program quality really matter? The impact of adhering to the principles of effective intervention. *Criminology and Public Policy* 5(3), 201–220.

Makarios, M., Brusman Lovins, L., Myers, A.J., Latessa, E.J. (2017). Treatment integrity and recidivism among sex offenders: The relationship between CPC scores and program effectiveness. *Corrections, Policy, Practice and Research.* doi: 10.1080/23774657.2017.1389318

Makarios, M., Lovins, L., Latessa, E., Smith, P. (2016). Staff quality and treatment effectiveness: An examination of the relationship between staff factors and the effectiveness of correctional programs. *Justice Quarterly* 33, 348–367.

Martinson, R. (1974). What works? Questions and answers about prison reform. *Public Interest* 35, 22–54.

Matthews, B., Jones-Hubbard, D., Latessa, E.J. (2001). Making the next step: Using evaluability assessment to improve correctional programming. *The Prison Journal* 8, 454–472.

National Policy Committee of American Society of Criminology. (2001). *The use of incarceration in the United States.* Retrieved from https://www.asc41.com/policies/policypapers.html

Nicholaichuk, T., Gordon, A., Gu, D., Wong, S. (2000). Outcome of an institutional sexual offender treatment program. *Sexual Abuse* 12, 139–153.

O'Connor, T., Sawyer, B., Duncan, J. (2008). A country-wide approach to increasing programme effectiveness is possible: Oregon's experience with the Correctional Program Checklist. *Irish Probation Journal* 5, 36–48.

Osborne, D., Gaebler, T. (1993). *Reinventing government: How the entrepreneurial spirit is transforming the public sector.* New York: Penguin.

Ostermann, M., Hyatt, J.M. (2017). When frontloading backfires: Exploring the impact of outsourcing correctional interventions on mechanisms of social control. *Law and Social Inquiry.* https://doi.org/10.1111/lsi.12300.

Ostermann, M., Salerno, L.M., Hyatt, J.M. (2015). How different operationalizations of recidivism impact conclusions of effectiveness of parole supervision. *Journal of Research in Crime and Delinquency* 52, 771–796.

Palmer, T. (1975). Martinson revisited. *Journal of Research in Crime and Delinquency* 12, 133–152.

Palmer, T. (1995). Programmatic and nonprogrammatic aspects of successful intervention: New directions for research. *Crime & Delinquency* 41(1), 101–131.

Petersilia, J. (1991). The value of corrections research: Learning what works. *Federal Probation* 55(2), 24–26.

Petersilia, J., Cullen, F.T. (2014). Liberal but not stupid: Meeting the promise of downsizing prisons. *Stanford Journal of Criminal Law and Policy* (Summer), 1–43.

Pew Charitable Trusts, Pew Center on the States. (2012). Public opinion on sentencing and corrections policy in America. Public Safety Performance Project (Washington, DC) (in collaboration with Public Opinion Strategies [Alexandria, VA]; Mellman Group [Washington, DC]). Washington, DC: Pew.

Prosavac, E.J., Carey, R.G. (1992). *Program evaluation: Methods and case studies.* 4th ed. Englewood Cliffs, NJ: Prentice Hall.

Rutman, L. (1980). *Planning useful evaluations: Evaluability assessment.* Beverly Hills, CA: Sage.

Van Voorhis, P., Brown, K. (1996). *Evaluability assessments: A tool for program development in corrections* (Unpublished monograph). Washington, DC: National Institute of Corrections.

Van Voorhis, P., Cullen, F.T., Applegate, B. (1995). Evaluating interventions with violent offenders. *Federal Probation* 50, 17–27.

Vito, G.F., Latessa, E.J. (1979). Cost analysis in probation research: An evaluation synthesis. *Journal of Contemporary Criminal Justice* 1(3), 3–16.

Washington State Institute for Public Policy. (n.d.). Benefit–cost results: Adult criminal justice. Retrieved from www.wsipp.wa.gov/BenefitCost/Pdf/2/WSIPP_BenefitCost_Adult-Criminal-Justice.

Chapter 15

THE FUTURE OF CORRECTIONS IN THE COMMUNITY

Key Terms

ban the box
 behavioral change
certificates of qualification for
    employment (CQE)
collateral consequences

community corrections footprint
data analytics
diversion
expunge

> It is now mainstream thought—endorsed by the field's leading
> practitioners—that an important aspect of improving community
> corrections, increasing public safety, and restoring legitimacy will be
> to substantially downsize the grasp of community corrections by at
> least half and reduce violations to incarceration so that it can retool
> itself to focus on helping those most in need of community supports
> to become the kinds of citizens we all want them to become.
> —Schiraldi, 2018, p. 9.

INTRODUCTION

Between 1970 and 2010, the footprint of corrections has grown exponentially. In 1980, 1.8 million adults were under some form of correctional supervision. By 2008, there were 7.3 million. The total population under criminal justice control has since decreased slightly, but still remains incredibly high compared to pre-1970s levels (Figure 15.1).

Whether this is a trend or simply a short-term phenomenon of the times is yet to be seen, but it is clear that this trend has continued over the past 4 years. As seen in Figure 15.2, however, not all states have experienced a decline. The number of Americans on probation or parole has declined slightly over the past few years, and currently totals approximately 4.8 million people, or approximately one in every 50 adult Americans. About 82 percent of those were on

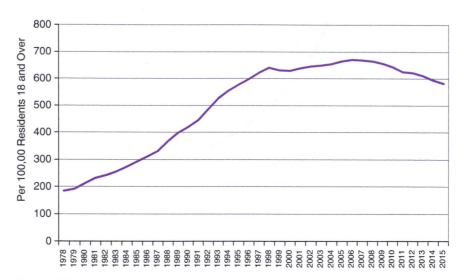

Figure 15.1 Imprisonment Rate Under State and Federal Jurisdictions, per 100,000 U.S. Residents 18 and Older

Source: Prisoners Series, Bureau of Justice Statistics.

probation and another 18 percent on parole. Taken together, we incarcerate more adult residents in this nation (690 per 100,000 residents) than any other major Western country. Similar rates are illustrated in Figure 15.3 (Pew Research Center, 2018). This high rate is due in large part to policies that encourage the use—and, some would say, overuse—of incarceration for property and drug offenders (Fish, 2000).

The use of imprisonment, of course, varies greatly by group. Although African Americans make up about 14 percent of the total population, they represent one-half of the jail and prison group. This turns out to be about one in 12 adult African-American men aged between 14 and 54. Disproportionate minority confinement is widespread throughout the criminal justice system.

While this higher rate reflects the differential rate of involvement of African Americans in violent crimes, it also reflects the impact of the war on drugs (Cullen et al., 1996).[1] Despite our efforts, the war on drugs has not had any major effect on the sale, distribution, or use of illicit controlled substances (General Accounting Office, 2007), but the war continues. At the present time, the correctional population in the United States totals more than 7 million offenders. The bulk of offenders are on probation or under parole supervision. Whether these numbers will continue to decline is yet to be seen. To truly address the footprint of community corrections, there are five areas that need to be explored. We provide a brief review of each of these five areas and discuss what community corrections might look like in 10 years if these areas were to be reformed.

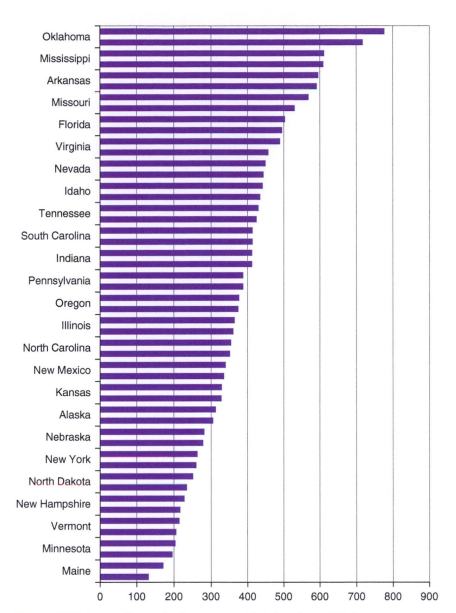

Figure 15.2 Prison Counts by State per 100,000 Residents, 2016

Source: Carson, E.A. (2018). *Prisoners in 2016*. Washington, DC: U.S. Department of Justice, Bureau of Justice Statistics.

MONEY BAIL

The first of the five areas that need to be addressed, if community corrections is to right size itself, is money bail. Discussed in Chapter 2, it is clear to see the impact

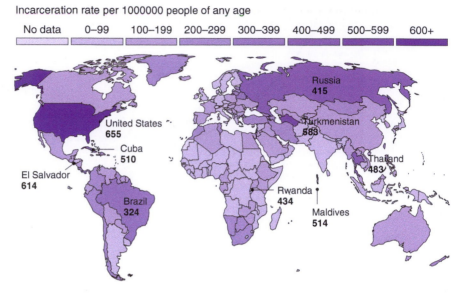

Figure 15.3 U.S. Incarcerates a Larger Share of Its Population than Any Other Country

Source: Pew Research Center (2018). Retrieved from www.pewresearch.org/fact-tank/2018/05/02/americas-incarceration-rate-is-at-a-two-decade-low/ft_18-04-27_incarcerationrate_map/

that money bail has on an individual's ability to be released under pretrial supervision. The money bond system makes it significantly easier for people with money to escape the potential iatrogenic effects of jail, leaving poor people to either sit in jail on pretrial status or plead guilty quickly.

Research tells us that those who sit in jail pretrial, controlling for legal variables, are convicted at higher rates, are incarcerated more often, and serve longer sentences than their matched counterparts who are released pretrial. Moreover, those who are released through commercial bond are charged significant fees for the bonding service—even if the charges are dropped or the final outcome is "not guilty." The collateral consequences of being held pretrial are also high. The biggest consequence is the potential loss of employment. For those who are employed at the time of arrest, sitting in jail for more than a day has a significant impact on the likelihood that the person will be able to maintain employment. If they lose employment, they run the risk to lose their car (which was impounded at arrest if they were in it), their apartment or house, and ultimately their freedom. Of course, releasing people from jail prior to their disposition is also risky. They may continue to engage in criminal behavior and risk the safety of the general public. They may fail to appear for court, resulting in lost court time, use of police and pretrial resources to find the defendant, and ultimately, inability to move forward with the case.

For these reasons, there is a national trend to develop more extensive ways for people to be released safely pretrial, and continue to ensure that they return to court, but without the use of money bonds or commercial bonds. Over the next 10 years, we can foresee five strategies that will reduce the number of defendants held pretrial while keeping the community safe.

1. **Improvement of risk assessment:** Pretrial tools are relatively rudimentary, often ranging from three to seven items, and are designed for those whom local jurisdictions are already comfortable with releasing. Over the next 10 years, jurisdictions will become more comfortable with releasing individuals with higher-level offenses based on risk. Currently, most jurisdictions that use some risk assessment at pretrial also use some calculation of seriousness. Lower-risk, lower-level offenses can receive a personal recognizance (PR) bond, but lower-risk, higher-level offenses generally cannot receive a PR bond. We could imagine in 10 years that risk assessment will become more advanced, will include some concept of machine learning, and will be used to drive decisions to a greater extent.

2. **Improved technology:** Technology is improving exponentially. Just in the last 3 years, companies are developing smaller, more efficient ways to check people in, monitor their movements, and track their whereabouts if needed. Watch-like GPS systems, car tracking systems, house arrest, and cell phone connections are all strategies that could expand the use of pretrial release. We could imagine in 10 years that the pretrial release process becomes automated, individuals will register their cell phones or some biometric data, and will be able to engage in pretrial services remotely while allowing pretrial officers greater access to monitor the defendant's whereabouts.

3. **Court bonds instead of commercial bonds:** To avoid the surcharges and commercial bond fees, courts will start to offer court bonds. Similar to commercial bonds, the court will set a bail amount and the amount will be financed by the court—the difference is that if the defendant shows up to court, the money is immediately returned with no fee. This could be a short-term bond that is released after the defendant's first appearance, or it could remain in place throughout the court hearing. A slight modification could allow the court to use other collateral instead of cash; this could include property or a car title or even personal possessions.

4. **Probation-eligible offenses:** If we actually consider the potential outcome of the case, deciding to release someone pretrial might just be easier. We foresee that eventually any defendant who is probation-eligible would be released on a PR bond. If the defendant is safe to go to probation in the community, they should be allowed to start "probation" early. There is no evidence that sitting in jail reduces the likelihood that a person will do better once placed on probation, and there is a growing body of literature that actually suggests that if the person is placed in jail prior to probation, the individual's recidivism rates are significantly higher (Caudy et al., 2017).

5. **Law enforcement diversion:** As jails continue to push their physical limits and data become clearer that jail stays, even short stays, have an iatrogenic effect, law enforcement agencies and communities are working together to develop **diversion** programs that provide law enforcement officers with options to

divert low-level, non-violent individuals from jail and sometimes even arrest. Examples include Seattle, with the development of LEAD (Law Enforcement Assisted Diversion), and Miami-Dade County's Mental Health Diversion Facility; diversion programs are starting to take hold across the country. In 10 years, we could imagine that very few low-level defendants will actually be booked into jail, but will be diverted at the scene or diverted into a program offering social service interventions.

CONVICTIONS AND COLLATERAL CONSEQUENCES

If there is one thing that has become abundantly clear over the past 10 years, it is that the motto "once an offender always an offender" does not work. Study after study finds that the **collateral consequences** of a criminal record reach well beyond the intended punishment. A 19-year-old college student who gets arrested for having less than a gram of cocaine, a 25-year-old nurse arrested for using opioids, a professional baseball player adjudicated at age 13 for a sexual offense—all of these are real-world examples of everyday people whose future path has been altered by a really bad decision, but more so by a system that continues to have grave effects after the punishment is over. This could include never voting again, losing a license to work in a current career, not having access to your own children, inability to obtain future employment, inability to hold public office (Olivares et al., 1996). Society is starting to recognize that labeling someone as an offender makes it significantly difficult for the individual to be accepted back into society, and with this realization comes reform. We provide four specific reforms that we believe will transform how the criminal justice system, and society in general, will address the issue of collateral consequences.

1. **Ban the box:** This is already under way; there are 31 states and hundreds of local jurisdictions which have passed laws that do not allow public agencies to ask about a person's criminal record at the initial application stage. Even further, 11 states have made companies which contract with the state **ban the box** as well. Generally, ban the box legislation has not made criminal history irrelevant, but pushes it to later in the process, giving the justice-involved individual the opportunity to get a foot in the door before having to explain his or her criminal record. In some jurisdictions, the record check comes after the conditional offer, forcing companies to balance the value of the incoming employee against the job-relatedness of the conviction, how much time has passed since the conviction, and the rehabilitative efforts of the future employee. We imagine that in 10 years, criminal history will be a near-protected class, with employers having to justify why they did not hire an equally qualified candidate who had a criminal record.

2. **Expunctions and expungements:** Almost every state has the ability for some offenders under some conditions to **expunge** or erase their criminal record. At times, this process is lengthy, costly, and in the end not always successful.

Very few criminal justice systems allow you to expunge violent crimes or sex offenses. Other states allow you to seal a record but not expunge it—meaning that the record is hidden to the general public but available to law enforcement agencies. Moving forward, we envision that states will begin to make the expungement process significantly easier, cheaper, and more efficient. One means to do this is to automate the process. Once a person is convicted and the penalty is served (be it a fine, probation, jail or prison/parole), the clock starts and after a specific waiting period, the paperwork is filed automatically with the jurisdiction and the record is expunged/sealed—truly allowing offenders to re-enter into society.

3. **Pretrial diversion programs:** The use of pretrial diversion programs has been shown to have a great impact on justice-involved individuals. Upfront diversion programs can reduce the number of people booking into jail, thus avoiding a conviction, and ultimately receiving necessary treatment services without the long-term collateral consequences of being in the justice system. To solve the collateral consequence issue, we can imagine a criminal justice system that offers first-, second- and even third-time offenders a pretrial diversion intervention program in lieu of conviction. Places like Harris County (Houston, TX) have already started offering individuals charged with prostitution multiple chances at pretrial diversion—understanding that a prostitution conviction just makes it harder for men and women to eventually move into a productive lifestyle and that the misdemeanor (or eventual felony) conviction is not a deterrent.

4. **Certificates of qualification for employment (CQE)** have been developed in several states (e.g., Ohio and New York). A CQE is a certificate issued by the court that allows ex-offenders to work in a field that was blocked due to the collateral consequence of being convicted of a felony (or misdemeanor). For example, in Ohio, a felon was not permitted to get a barber license. The CQE would allow the felon to get licensed as a barber as long as his or her offense was not directly related to the field. The certificate does not impact the direct consequences of a conviction (e.g., a bank robber cannot work in a bank), only those restrictions created by collateral consequences.

RACIAL, ETHNIC, AND GENDER DISPARITIES

Throughout the United States, people of color are over-represented at all stages of the criminal justice system. Moreover, women are one of the largest growing corrections populations. From arrest to parole, each decision point is a place for potential disparate responses. The claim that justice is color- and gender-blind is just not true. In an effort to address this, many states and local jurisdictions have developed strategies to ensure that racial, ethnic, and gender disparity cannot be attributed to non-legal factors.

1. **Biased penalties/laws:** The explicit and implicit impacts of laws on communities of color, females, and low-income families are clear—a half-century

of laws designed to be discriminatory toward people of color has created an incredibly unbalanced criminal justice system (Lutze et al., 2012). To move forward, we need legislators and public policy advocates to review every law and associated penalty to determine if it results in oppressive outcomes and revise/remove the law.

2. **Data analytics:** While the relative rate index provides a way to observe the disparate response between different racial and ethnic groups, it does not provide an understanding as to why disparity exists. Data analytics is starting to be incorporated in the field to understand the impact of decisions at each justice point, controlling for legal variables. Moving forward, we can imagine individual jurisdictions having racial, ethnic, and gender data coordinators who monitor decision points and provide real-time feedback to the criminal justice stakeholders on potential issues regarding disparity. These coordinators would work at the system and individual level, informing stakeholders, but also "unsticking" those justice-involved individuals who are held up for extralegal variables.

3. **Implicit bias:** As the system begins to solve racial and ethnic disparities, one strategy is to train probation and parole officers on implicit bias. Participation in training and exposure to implicit bias data have been found to modify the impacts. Training generally includes providing counter-stereotypical imagery, creating cross-racial and cross-ethnic interactions, and improving outcomes.

4. **Tying freedom to income:** Similar to the money bail discussion, many criminal justice interventions are tied to ability to pay. Bonds, treatment, supervision fees, external monitoring (interlock), and fines are all driven by ability to pay. Alternative interventions should be available at no cost to offenders who are unable to pay. In 10 years, we can imagine the ability to pay will be completely separated from the system and that pretrial release, probation, and parole will be financially neutral for those under its supervision.

COMMUNITY CORRECTIONS FOOTPRINT

Over the past 5 years, there has been a significant push to decrease the footprint (size) of community corrections. Columbia University's Justice Lab (Schiraldi, 2018) put out a paper that challenges the size of the corrections population, suggesting that too many low-level offenders are placed on supervision and monitored closely on a large set of conditions while agencies' resources have been downsized. Furthermore, a consensus paper published by the Executive Session on Community Corrections (2017) suggested that the fundamental paradigm on which community corrections has operated for the past hundred years is flawed and significant reform is needed to right the system. Moreover, Phelps and Curry (2017) have suggested that the criminal justice system represents the new version of the Jim Crow laws, and that it is designed to disrupt communities of color specifically. Whether intentional or not, the criminal justice footprint is significantly larger than it was (controlling for population increase) just 40 years ago. There are numerous strategies across the country to minimize the community corrections footprint and to reduce the number of people who fail on technical violations. Lutze et al. (2012) suggest that reform needs to be multileveled—reforming laws, agencies, and direct service.

1. **Mass incarceration:** The use of prison exploded after the 1970s. Prior to that period, prisons were reserved for violent offenders and those who needed rehabilitation. Prison populations were stable for 50 years. During the mid-1970s, legislative changes made it possible to sentence non-violent offenders to prison. Lutze et al. (2012) suggest that four steps should be taken to address the issue of mass incarceration:

   1. Re-examine how corrections policy is formulated by reserving prison for high-risk violent offenders
   2. Eliminate mandatory minimums, especially for nonviolent crimes
   3. Eliminate prison as a sanction for technical violations
   4. Eliminate most civil penalties attached to criminal convictions.

   (Lutze et al., 2012, p. 44)

2. **Pre-charge and pretrial intervention:** One of the more recent strategies to address the expanding criminal justice system is the increased opportunities for individuals to be diverted out of the system on a pre-charge or pretrial intervention. As discussed in an earlier strategy, pre-charge/pretrial diversion interventions or programs allow individuals who have interacted with law enforcement a way whereby their charges can be informally disposed of—limiting their exposure to the criminal justice system.

3. **Limiting mandated services to non-low-risk offenders:** One of the consequences of the "war on drugs" and other "get tough" strategies was the net widening of those individuals who historically had a) been diverted from the criminal justice system at police contact; b) served a short jail term and been released with no supervision; or c) been placed on non-reporting or administrative supervision. The explosion of community corrections has definitely come at the expense of low-risk offenders. Lowenkamp and Latessa (2004) were the first to really articulate the negative effects of placing low-risk offenders in more intensive services. From there, community corrections has toyed with the idea of limiting services to low-risk offenders, but there has been no holistic approach to remove them from the system. Ahlman and Kurtz's (2008) study randomly assigned non-violent, lower-risk offenders to probation as usual (seen monthly, drug tests, etc.) or 6 months' reporting with a phone call in the third month. They found that the "probation as usual" group failed at a 22 percent rate, while the experimental group failed at a 20 percent rate.

   There are two primary problems with placing low-risk offenders under supervision. First, community supervision can easily disrupt what makes the offender low risk. If you go back to Chapter 6 on risk assessment, those characteristics that make a person low risk (being employed, having prosocial friends, and limited antisocial beliefs) are easily disrupted when a person is placed on supervision or incarcerated. The second problem is the ease with which someone on supervision can face revocation. Probation and revocation hearings are based on the preponderance of evidence and the district attorney or parole officer needs only to find one allegation of a failed condition true to revoke the offender. So, for low-risk offenders, if they engage in no criminal behavior but receive several violations for technical reasons, their supervision can be revoked.

Systems across the country are starting to put limits on how deeply lower-risk, non-violent offenders can penetrate the system, minimizing the number of conditions and length of supervision, and providing alternative options to the criminal justice system. For example, California recently passed Proposition 47 which reclassified a significant number of felonies as misdemeanors. Coupled with Public Safety Realignment, lower-risk, non-violent offenders were not eligible to be sentenced to prison—capping the possibility of revocation to short, local jail sentences.

Moving forward, the criminal justice system needs to address the net widening of lower-risk offenders into the criminal justice system. In the next 10 years, we believe that there will be several initiatives to address this issue. First, community corrections will continue to expand the use of risk assessment and front-end diversion programs by law enforcement agencies. Communities will expand diversion options for lower-risk individuals pre-booking, and limit criminal justice exposure to the more serious, higher-risk individuals. Second, if a low-risk person does get processed through jail and ends up in court, prosecutors will have greater levels of discretion to divert the individual from the criminal justice system. Third, judges will limit the number of conditions placed on individuals—ensuring that they are assessment-driven and directly related to the rehabilitation efforts of the offender. Fourth, revocations of lower-risk individuals will be capped to new law violations only.

4. **Alternatives to fines, jails, probation, and prison:** Currently, there are only a few options that courts have at sentencing. They can issue a fine, or sentence a person to jail, probation, or prison. Each of these options is necessary, but may be more detrimental to some offenders. Low-income individuals might have difficulty paying the fine or a jail sentence might disrupt employment, while a probation sentence comes with many strings. Developing a larger number of alternative sentences could offer judges the ability to sentence an offender without the iatrogenic effects that the system bears. We could see a range of sentences including:

   ■ small day fines
   ■ community service
   ■ victim/offender restoration projects
   ■ judicial admonishments.

ESTABLISHING A NEW COMMUNITY CORRECTIONS SYSTEM

Prisons will continue to play a vital role in corrections in future years. The question is whether the United States can begin to undo the population explosion from the past 40 years, and to what degree. This will require an agenda for change, and the most effective way would be to encourage local communities to address better ways to manage crime and criminals in their own communities. This in turn would require leadership at the state governmental level to sentence "smarter," not just tougher. Is there a politician existing in today's political environment who believes that taking a "soft" approach to crime will help in winning an election? The problem to be addressed is not "softer" or "harsher," but a recognition that what is needed is a philosophy for organizing corrections and the use of evidence-based practices.

When the "nothing works in corrections" argument arose, many scholars and practitioners who should have known better abandoned the rehabilitation model. Corrections lost its organizing theme or premise. Now that the abandonment of rehabilitation has been recognized as both premature and erroneous,[2] the stage is set for a considerable and acrimonious battle over the purpose of handling offenders. Unfortunately, that will not likely occur until we are well into the twenty-first century and will probably be triggered by fiscal crisis, as states and local jurisdictions are unable to sustain the heavy cost of correctional systems, particularly prisons and jails.

Over the past decade, we have seen both internal stakeholders and external critics of the criminal justice system call for massive reform. Recent studies have shown that over 20 percent of individuals in prison were on probation at the time they were sentenced to prison (Phelps, 2017). Regardless of legislative changes, probation and parole agencies must also reform themselves to meet this growing crisis. Instead of a mismatch of competing goals, what if community corrections was truly focused on changing offender behavior? What would it look like? What services would be available? We explore these questions below.

DESIGNED FOR BEHAVIORAL CHANGE

The first question we must ask ourselves is if the system was truly designed to change, "What would it look like?" We suspect something very different from the current system.

First, and foremost, the criminal justice system would have to move away from monitoring compliance to promoting change. We know from the field of psychology and social work that change is incremental and needs to be reinforced. The current assumption of probation and parole is that the offender, once placed on supervision, must come under compliance immediately. With conditions like, use no drugs or alcohol, be employed, and pay fees/fines starting the first month, offenders often find themselves facing violations within the first 3 months. In fact, Gray et al. (2001) found that the largest proportion of offenders failed due to technical violations within 100 days of being placed on supervision.

To address this, we would set up probation completely differently. Probation departments would be set up similar to a university setting—incoming "students" would not have to have the skills necessary to graduate on the first day of classes, but would be working toward those skills throughout their term. Could you imagine a university in which you had to take comprehensive exams prior to taking any courses? The current probation structure is exactly like this—before an offender receives any intervention, he or she is expected to show up, have a job, pay fees, avoid criminal others, and stop using drugs. Probation as a university concept would allow for offenders who are first placed on supervision to grow over time, with the expectation that to "graduate," the offender will have to have changed his or her criminogenic risk factors.

Second, the system would have to do a significantly better job assessing the needs of offenders and creating individual plans for change. This assessment process would have to include a fourth-generation risk assessment, but would also include a battery of assessments that can assess the individual needs of the offender. For example, composite risk assessments can flag or identify broad areas of needs (e.g., peers), but do not tell the officer or the offender what are the specific issues with peers. Is the issue the influence that their best friend has over them, the lack of prosocial peers, or their general peer network? The successful system would help the offender identify how the broader criminogenic risk factors apply to them and develop specific interventions designed to help the offender change.

Third, the successful system would be operated by staff who see their role as being a coach and not a referee (Lovins et al., 2018). Under the current system, probation officers are asked to operate more like referees than coaches. Referees know the rule book. They are concerned primarily about procedural justice. They monitor for violations and when these are observed, blow the whistle and enact a penalty. The "probation as a university" model would employ coaches, not referees. The coach's role would be to produce a successful person. From there a successful coach would:

- assess the skills of the individual;
- identify what motivates the person to change;
- employ strategies to teach the offender the skills needed to be successful;
- reinforce small, incremental changes;
- admonish unwanted behavior;
- be focused on the individual's growth.

In the end, the coach's success would reflect the offender's success. Just like a sports coach, players are ultimately responsible for the individual success, but coaches are held accountable for the collective success. The same should apply to probation and parole. Community corrections coaches should know their win/loss record, should be actively looking for ways to improve it, and ultimately should be held accountable to it.

Third, treatment needs to be focused on criminogenic targets, but be based on the needs of the offender at the individual level. Currently, almost all correctional treatment services are delivered in a group format, using a generic curriculum, and facilitators often fail to individualize the interventions to the specific needs of the offender. Consider the recent developments of cancer treatment to understand the individualization of treatment services. At one time, cancer treatment was the same regardless of the type of cancer or the patient—chemotherapy, surgery, and then radiation. Now, cancer treatments are quite varied including immunotherapy, controlled drug delivery using nanotechnology, hyperthermia, and directed target therapies. Along with the primary therapies, doctors are exploring the use of gene therapy in combination with other components (e.g., folic acid) (Arruebo et al., 2011). The university model of probation would follow the same lines. Instead of having 16-week curricula that focus on the overall need (e.g., substance abuse treatment), the university would offer individual electives that focus on specific skills development tailored to the individual offender. Through the assessment process, an offender might be identified as needing problem solving, peer management, and emotional regulation skills. The offender's coach would work with the offender to enroll him or her in the necessary classes, avoiding the need to attend programming that is not specific to the offender's needs. This would allow for a higher dose of treatment concentrated specifically on the needs of the offender.

Fourth, completion of probation should be tied to the acquisition of skills, not a predetermined length of time. Similar to acquiring a degree, once the offender is done with "learning," he or she should be released. Under the current model, offenders are required to remain on probation for long periods of time—well beyond the amount of time needed to change behavior. In the "probation as a university" model, offenders would only remain in the university for as long as they needed to acquire the skills to be successful.

Fifth, like modern university settings, probation would be delivered with the benefit of technology. Current probation services are tethered to offices, cars, or classrooms. Officers are required to document their work in secondary case-management systems and memorize interventions designed to target change. The "probation as a university" model would incorporate up-to-date technology, allowing coaches and offenders to communicate in real time, receiving immediate feedback regarding skill acquisition and use, having access to treatment material instantaneously, and the ability to document conversations in real time.

Sixth, probation and parole agencies should be poised to understand the effectiveness of programming for offender populations. If funding for offender services and treatment programs were funneled directly through probation and parole agencies, this would allow funding decisions to be streamlined and reviewed by agencies that understand evidence-based practices. With this, probation and parole agencies could design models in which performance-based standards can be set and monitored. Agencies could even design pay-for-success programs or a voucher system that opens avenues for offenders to receive the best services available.

While this could be considered a radical approach to corrections, today's probation and parole systems are not that far away from many of these concepts. Agencies have begun training their officers in core correctional practices, focusing their efforts on reducing reoffending, and developing administrative ways to address non-compliance.

Ultimately, whatever form probation and parole take in the future, there are several specific areas that improve outcomes, as research has shown:

- Use of assessments: Agencies should adopt a validated risk assessment to help guide upfront decisions.

- Staff acquisition and retention: Agencies should develop strategies that recruit and retain staff who believe offenders can change and believe that their role is to impact that change.
- Training and coaching: The type of work that probation and parole officers are being asked to conduct has shifted significantly. Agencies should explore ways to better train and coach staff in the delivery of effective practices.
- Family and social connections: Agencies should continue to explore ways to engage families and social support networks.
- Quality assurance: Agencies would benefit from developing real-time strategies for shaping staff skills in delivering effective interventions and relying less on counting activities.

SUMMARY

The nation cannot build itself out of current prison and management crises, but states and local jurisdictions can manage and control not only the prison and jail populations, but also the costs and integrity of the justice system that deals with post-offense corrections. By developing a logical set of sentencing policies with clear goals and a wide range of sentencing options and sanctions, the nation would begin to address public safety on a sounder foundation. In addition, an aggressive public education and information initiative is necessary for public acceptance. In the long run, corrections must hold offenders accountable to the public and the legal system for their criminal behaviors, and politicians must be held accountable to the public for their actions.

Many issues face community corrections: risk management and handling of special-needs populations, officer safety and work conditions, and the appropriate use of technology. We have confidence that the field will rise to the challenge. We base this faith on our knowledge of the professionals who work in and will come to the field. Because of these dedicated individuals, the future of corrections in the community is bright, and the achievement of a logical, coherent, and safe system for handling criminal offenders is attainable. In doing this, we must remember that corrections is, above all else, a human issue, that change is not easy, and that partners in change are necessary. Community corrections has a bright future.

Review Questions

1. Why do you believe that the United States leads the world in incarceration?
2. How do you see community corrections changing in the next 5 years? 10 years?
3. How do we balance changing offender behavior with keeping the community safe? Are they opposite concepts?

Notes

1 This statement is not meant to imply that non-whites are not concerned about drugs and crime. Surveys indicate that both white and non-white Americans are concerned about drug abuse and the effects of drugs on communities.
2 Allen (2002).

Recommended Readings

Castle, M. (1989). *Alternative sentencing: Selling it to the public*. Washington, DC: U.S. Department of Justice.

Cullen, F., Moon, M. (2002). Reaffirming rehabilitation: Public support for correctional treatment. In: H. Allen (Ed.), *Risk reduction: Interventions for special needs offenders* (pp. 7–26). Lanham, MD: American Correctional Association.

Zhang, J. (1997). The effect of welfare programs on criminal behavior: A theoretical and empirical analysis. *Economic Inquiry* 35(1), 120–137.

References

Ahlman, L. C., Kurtz, E.M. (2008). *The APPD randomized controlled trial in low risk supervision: The effects on low risk supervision on rearrest*. Philadelphia Adult Probation and Parole Department. Retrieved from www.courts.phila.gov/pdf/report/APPD-Low_Risk_Internal_Evaluation.pdf.

Allen, H. (2002). Introductory remarks. In: H. Allen (Ed.), *Risk reduction: Interventions for special needs offenders* (pp. 1–6). Lanham, MD: American Correctional Association.

Arruebo, M., Vilaboa, N., Saez-Gutierrez, B., Lambea, J., Tres, A., Valladares, M., Gonzalez-Fernandez, A. (2011). Assessment of the evolution of cancer treatment therapies. *Cancers* 3(3), 3279–3330.

Carson, E.A. (2018). *Prisoners in 2016*. Washington, DC: U.S. Department of Justice, Bureau of Justice Statistics.

Caudy, M., Tillyer, M., Tillyer, R. (2017). Jail versus probation: A gender-specific test of differential effectiveness and moderators of sanction effects. *Criminal Justice and Behavior*. doi: https://doi.org/10.1177/0093854818766375.

Cullen, F., Van Voorhis, P., Sundt, J. (1996). Prisons in crisis: The American experience. In: R. Matthews, F. Francis (Eds.), *Prisons 2000: An international perspective on the current state and future of imprisonment* (pp. 21–52). New York: Macmillan.

Executive Session on Community Corrections. (2017). *Toward an approach to community corrections for the 21st century: Consensus document of the Executive Session on Community Corrections*. Cambridge, MA: Harvard Kennedy School Program in Criminal Justice Policy and Management. Retrieved from www.hks.harvard.edu/sites/default/files/centers/wiener/programs/pcj/files/Consensus_Final2.pdf.

Fish, J. (2000). Rethinking our drug policy. *Fordham Urban Law Journal* 28(9), 3–361.

General Accounting Office. (2007). *Drug control: U.S. assistance has helped Mexican counternarcotics efforts, but tons of illicit drugs continue to flow into the United States*. Washington, DC: GAO.

Gray, M.K., Fields, M., Maxwell, S.R. (2001). Examining probation violations: Who, what, and when. *Crime & Delinquency* 47(4), 537–557.

Lovins, B.K., Cullen, F.T., Latessa, E.J., Jonson, C.L. (2018). Probation officer as a coach: Building a new professional identity. *Federal Probation* 82(1), 13.

Lowenkamp, C., Latessa, E. (2004). Understanding the risk principle: How and why correctional interventions can harm low-risk offenders. *Topics in Community Corrections*. Retrieved from www.correctiveservices.justice.nsw.gov.au/Documents/Risk-principal--accessible-442577.pdf.

Lutze, F.E., Johnson, W.W., Clear, T.R., Latessa, E.J., Slate, R.N. (2012). The future of community corrections is now: Stop dreaming and take action. *Journal of Contemporary Criminal Justice* 28(1), 42–59.

Olivares, K., Burton, V., Cullen, F. (1996). The collateral consequences of a felony conviction: A national study of state legal codes 10 years later. *Federal Probation* 60, 10–17.

Pew Center on the States. (2010). *Prison count 2010*. Retrieved from www.pewtrusts.org/en/research-and-analysis/reports/2010/03/16/prison-count-2010-state-population-declines-for-the-first-time-in-38-years.

Pew Research Center. (2018). U.S. incarcerates a larger share of its population than any other country. Retrieved from www.pewresearch.org/fact-tank/2018/05/02/americas-incarceration-rate-is-at-a-two-decade-low/ft_18-04-27_incarcerationrate_map/.

Phelps, M. (2017). Mass probation and inequality: Race, class, and gender disparities in supervision and revocation. In J. Ulmer, M. Bradley (Eds.), *Handbook on punishment decisions: Locations of disparity* (pp. 61–84). New York: Routledge.

Phelps, M., Curry, C. (2017). Supervision in the community: Probation and parole. In: *Oxford Research Encyclopedia of Criminology*. Oxford: Oxford University Press.

Schiraldi, V.N. (2018). *Too big to succeed: The impact of the growth of community corrections and what should be done about it*. Columbia University, Justice Lab. Retrieved from http://justicelab.iserp.columbia.edu/img/Too_Big_to_Succeed_Report_FINAL.pdf.

Glossary/Index

Note: Entries in bold type and their corresponding emboldened page numbers refer to glossary terms.

For all other index entries, page numbers in bold type refer to tables and those in italic type refer to figures. Page numbers followed by 'n' refer to notes

Using this approach, the researcher reads studies available on a topic and then summarizes what they think the major conclusions are from that body of research. **345**

Lock, E.D., *et al.* 314

Locke, J. 98

Lombroso, C. 147

Lösel, F., and Schmucker, M. 275, 278

Lovins, B., *et al.* 184, 276

Lowenkamp, C.T.: *et al.* 84–85, 226; and Latessa, E.L. 264; and Skeem, J.L. 164

LSD 312

Lucas County Adult Probation Department (Ohio) 198–199, 213

Lugo, M., *et al.* 128

Lutze, F.E., *et al.* 367

Macallair, D. 66

McDevitt, J., and Miliano, R. 227–228

MacKenzie, D., and Piquero, A. 130

MacNamara, D.E. 125

Maconochie, Capt. A. 37–38, 100–104

Major risk factors There are eight major risk factors, or correlates, of criminal conduct: antisocial, pro-criminal attitudes, values, beliefs, and cognitive emotional states (such as anger and rage); pro-criminal associates and isolation from anti-criminal others; temperamental and personality factors conducive to criminal activity; history of antisocial behavior; family factors, including criminality and a variety of psychological problems in the family of origin; low levels of personal educational, vocational, or financial achievement; low levels of involvement in prosocial leisure activities; abuse of alcohol and/or other drugs. **147–152**; neutralizations **148–149**

Makarios, M., *et al.* 352

mandated service limitations 367–368

mandatory minimum sentences 44, 67, 336

Mandatory release means that the offender had to be released because the maximum sentence (or its equivalent) had been attained. Mandatory release implies that the parole board refused to release an inmate prior to attainment of the maximum sentence imposed by the court. Mandatory release means that time served behind prison walls, when added to time credits for jail time, "good time," and earned time, totals the sentence imposed by the sentencing court. About one in five inmates leave prison under mandatory release. **32–52**, **109–110**, **135n15**

Mangrum, C. 202–203

Manhattan Bail Project In 1961, with the implementation of the Manhattan Bail Project, an alternative to money bail became available With the Vera Institute of Justice's help, Manhattan was the first jurisdiction that explored the opportunity for defendants to be released with just a promise, or on their own recognizance, to return to court. **19–21**

marijuana 311–313

Marijuana Tax Act (1937) 311

Mark system In 1840, Captain Maconochie was put in charge of the English penal colony in New South Wales at Norfolk Island, off the coast of Australia, whose criminals were "twice condemned." They had been shipped from England to Australia, and then to Norfolk Island. Maconochie's "mark system" awarded prisoners marks and moved through stages of custody until finally granted release. His system involved indeterminate sentencing, with release based on the number of marks earned by prisoners for good conduct, labor, and study. The five stages, based on the accumulation of marks, each carried increased responsibility and freedom, leading to a ticket of leave or parole resulting in a conditional pardon and, finally, full restoration of liberty. Maconochie's reforms made life bearable at Norfolk Island and can be described as revolutionary in comparison to conditions before his arrival. Maconochie's reforms transformed Norfolk Island from a place of despair to one of hope, but

important consideration is validity, and refers to the accuracy of the instrument in predicting what we want it to predict. **166**

Van Voorhis, P.: and Brown, K. 353; Cullen, F.T. and Applegate, B. 352

Vera Institute of Justice 19–21

Vertical model Takes into account multiple factors when assigning cases. This model is called vertical because it divides the range of offender characteristics into vertical slices in order to create caseloads. **195–197**

Veterans Benefits Administration (VBA) 325

Veterans' courts One of the newest versions of the problem-solving courts, veterans' treatment courts use a hybrid integration of drug court and mental health court principles to serve military veterans, and sometimes active-duty personnel. Since veterans are often entitled to receive services through their veterans' benefits, these courts help to promote sobriety, recovery, and stability through a coordinated response that involves collaboration with traditional partners. **325**

victim denial 209

Victim Impact Statement Many probation departments now include a section pertaining to the victim as part of their Pre-Sentence Investigation report. **69**, *72*

vigilantism 274

Viglione, J., *et al.* 184

Visher, C.A., and Bakken, N.W. 299

Vito, G. 127

Volstead Act (1919) 61, 90n1

Voltaire 98

VolunteerMatch 213

Volunteers One of the important resources for the community correctional agency is the use of volunteers, which, used properly, can serve as an important asset for a community correctional agency. The volunteer movement developed in the United States in the early 1820s, when the Philadelphia Society for Alleviating the Miseries of Public Prisons began supervising the activities of inmates upon their release from penal institutions. Judge Keith Leenhouts of the Royal Oak (Michigan) Municipal Court resurrected the concept 30 years ago. Although exact numbers are not known, thousands of volunteers serve more than 3,000 jurisdictions nationwide. **213–215**, **255**, **303**, **336**; services scope **213–214**; veterans' mentors **325**

Volunteers of America 247

Volunteers in Probation (VIP) 213

Wakeling, H., *et al.* 276

Walsh, A. 67

War on drugs Although many cite President Nixon as the initial commander in chief of the war on drugs, it actually can be traced to the Harrison Act of 1914. The effects of the Comprehensive Drug Abuse Prevention and Control Act of 1970 were felt immediately. The "get tough" era continued to impact drug offenders through the late 1970s and into the 1980s. **250**, **310–313**, **360**, **367**, **373n1**

Washington State Institute for Public Policy 88, 284, 326

Watergate 103

Weber, K. 46

weekend confinement 35, 49

Welch, S., and Spohn, C. 73

Welfare officer has as his ultimate goal the improved welfare of the client, achieved by aiding him in his individual adjustment within limits imposed by the client's capacity. Such an officer believes that the only genuine guarantee of community protection lies in the client's personal adjustment, as external conformity will only be temporary and, in the long run, may make a successful adjustment more difficult. Emotional neutrality permeates his relationship. The diagnostic categories and treatment skills that he employs stem from an

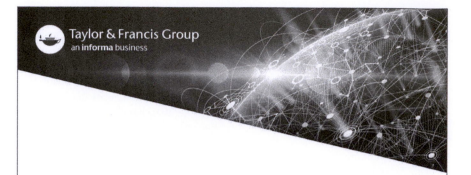